Indians of the Southeast

Series Editors

Theda Perdue, University of Kentucky
Michael D. Green, Dartmouth College

Advisory Editors

Leland Ferguson, University of South Carolina
Charles Hudson, University of Georgia
Mary Young, University of Rochester

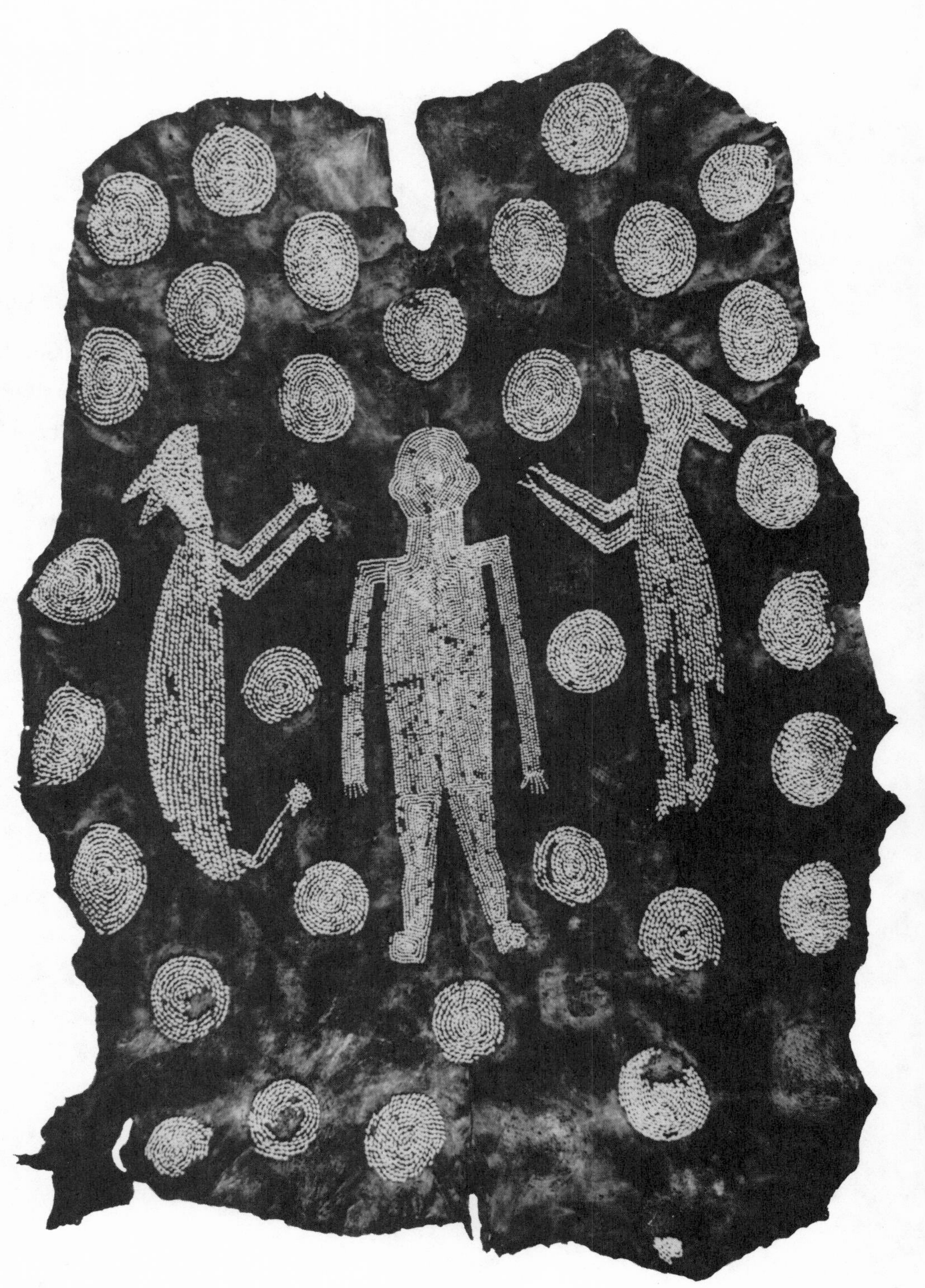

Powhatan's Mantle

Indians in the Colonial Southeast

Edited by Peter H. Wood, Gregory A. Waselkov, and M. Thomas Hatley

University of Nebraska Press Lincoln and London

Manufactured in the United States of America

Frontispiece: Powhatan's mantle, circa 1608 (courtesy of the Ashmolean Museum).

The paper in this book meets the minimum requirements of American National Standard for Information Sciences—Permanence of Paper for Printed Library Materials, ANSI Z39.48–1984.

Library of Congress Cataloging-in-Publication Data
Powhatan's mantle.
(Indians of the Southeast)
Includes index.
1. Indians of North America—Southern States—History—Colonial period, ca. 1600–1775. 2. Indians of North America—Southern States—Social life and customs. I. Wood, Peter H., 1943– . II. Waselkov, Gregory A., 1952– . III. Hatley, M. Thomas, 1951– .
IV. Series.
E78.S65P69 1989 975′.00497 88-20630
ISBN 0-8032-4745-1 (alk. paper)

This book is dedicated to the memory of two persons who, through their research and teaching, encouraged others to study Southeastern Indians in the colonial era: Roy S. Dickens, Jr., *and* J. Leitch Wright, Jr.

Contents

Part Three
Symbols and Society

Series Editors' Introduction

When Europeans invaded the southeastern region of North America, they had difficulty conceiving of a world radically different from the one they had left. Seeking some sort of common ground, they equated many aspects of native culture to their own institutions, customs, and beliefs, and usually they found these presumed American equivalents to be vastly inferior. Kings and covenants, princesses and protocol, trade and tribute, religion and ritual all were tailored to fit a European pattern: the pieces that did not fit became irrelevant scraps. The conceptual framework with which early Euro-Americans attempted to analyze native peoples simply could not encompass radically different lifeways and world-views.

The development of a new conceptual framework has come about only recently. For generations, scholars continued to assume that native diplomacy functioned on the same basis as that of Western Europe, that economic goals were similar, that some sort of universal principles of geography, kinship, gender, political power, communication, and monument construction applied, and that nineteenth-century locations and populations of native peoples correlated to precontact societies. Largely through the work of ethnohistorians who attempt to study the past in a culturally unbiased and interdisciplinary way, such an approach has fallen into disrepute. Scholars increasingly are attempting to analyze native societies on their own terms. The writings in this volume represent a significant step in that direction.

In *Powhatan's Mantle,* Peter Wood, Gregory A. Waselkov, and M. Thomas Hatley have assembled superb examples of how the history of southeastern Indians is being rewritten. Diversity is apparent: subjects range from a single individual to a village to the region as a whole, while the authors' approaches vary from demography to ecology to symbolism. Each chapter, however, reflects a careful and creative analysis of the sources by a scholar sensitive to ethnocentrism and to cultural nuances. The result is a volume that presents a new interpretation of the native southeast.

Theda Perdue and Michael D. Green

General Introduction

Scholars of the Americas have long been engaged in research regarding the peoples who inhabited this hemisphere in so-called pre-Columbian times, well before A.D. 1500,[1] and during the subsequent colonial era, up to roughly 1800. Such researchers have faced numerous and basic questions. Which continents did these people come from, and what were their numbers? How did they live, and how did they respond to drastic change? Despite its esoteric language and deliberate pace, this many-sided discussion constitutes more than a remote academic discourse. It contains a deep, and often hidden, significance for our present and future self-understanding.

In Latin America, where intensive contact between Indians and non-Indians began earliest and occurred on the largest scale, work has proceeded actively for generations. As early as 1950, much fresh knowledge had been consolidated in the Smithsonian Institution's six-volume *Handbook of South American Indians*. And research has progressed steadily since then, down to the impressive new studies of the present day.[2] Regarding North America, in contrast, modern research has proceeded more slowly. Only in recent decades has a sizable contingent of North American scholars begun systematically to sift through the work of their historian and anthropologist forebears, crossing the persistent geographical and disciplinary boundaries that have impeded general understanding. Beginning from many different quarters, these diverse scholars have slowly started to formulate a clearer picture of the Indians, Africans, and Europeans who peopled America by 1800, at the start of the demographic explosion that shaped our modern world.[3]

Underlying much of this work, where native populations are concerned, has been the gradual emergence of ethnohistory. This approach combines techniques from history and anthropology to study change over time in societies that did not write their own histories. The establishment of the Indian Claims Commission by the United States government in 1946 is often cited as sparking initial efforts in ethnohistory. Suddenly scores of anthropologists, called as expert witnesses, were obliged to interact with historians in making use of written documents to legitimate specific land claims. In the 1950s, regional meetings between anthropologists and historians led to the formation of the American Indian Ethnohistorical Conference, which later expanded into the American Society for Ethnohistory and began publication of the journal *Ethnohistory*.[4]

Predictably, the greatest North American advances to date regarding Indian inhabitants have involved the Southwest (with a sizable Native American population, a long tradition of anthropological study, and a climate suited to archaeology) and the Northeast (with its rich historical resources, its prestigious university centers, and its international scholarly community on both sides of the St. Lawrence). So it is not surprising that several of the earliest completed volumes of the Smithsonian Institution's new *Handbook of North American Indians* have covered these two separate areas. But interdisciplinary work in other regions has also proceeded at an encouraging pace, aided by improved field techniques, expanded research tools, and well-run resource centers.[5]

No single North American region stands to gain more from this renewed ground swell of scholarly interest than the South. Important overviews by anthropologist Charles Hudson and historian J. Leitch Wright, Jr., have appeared in recent years to summarize current knowledge and raise fresh questions. The forthcoming *Southeast* volume of the *Handbook of North American Indians* repeats this process on a broader scale. Current students therefore can still return to such pioneering authors as John Swanton, James Mooney, Frank G. Speck, and Verner W. Crane, but from now on they will have many more diverse and up-to-date monographic materials available to shape—and no doubt complicate—their endeavors.[6]

These fresh southern materials derive not only from history and anthropology, but from archaeology as well.[7] Careful fieldwork in the region got its first boost during the Great Depression, when shovels and trowels became tools of survival as well as research. And since then publicly funded archaeology has continued to concentrate on "salvage digs" near large construction projects (such as Tellico Dam) where the basic research materials are soon destroyed or covered over forever, after only a brief sampling of the site.

In some areas archaeological consciousness is moving faster than the Sunbelt developers, and funds for basic excavation and analysis are growing in certain states. But everywhere progress is slow and sporadic in comparison with wealthier parts of the country, and national funders have yet to realize the full extent of the archaeological potential that exists in the region. Nevertheless, we are now learning more about the South through scientific fieldwork than we have at any time since Thomas Jefferson dug his first test trench through an Indian mound near Monticello. And we can hope to learn a good deal more before the last free-flowing river is dammed up or diverted forever.

The earliest Southerners lived by their rivers. And this assertion contains more than one layer of truth, for over thousands of years these diverse people regularly lived beside, from, and through the myriad streams that shaped the southern environment. The incomparable Mississippi system, descending from the north, has divided and nurtured the South for eons. But even the Father of Waters—Walt Whitman's "spinal column" of the continent—can hardly overshadow the scores of smaller waterways that descend from interior slopes to the Gulf of Mexico and the Atlantic Ocean. From the Brazos and the Trinity in Texas to the Potomac and the Rappahannock on the Chesapeake, these numerous rivers follow relatively brief courses from the interior to the sea. All of them, long or short, derive from a series of confluences along the way, where several smaller branches come together to form the larger stream. For countless generations, the region's inhabitants regularly chose to locate their villages at these rich intersections.

In a sense this book is located at such an intersection, since it concerns several sets of convergences—disciplinary, chronological, and geographic. The most important confluence involves separate disciplines. This is reflected even in the backgrounds of the three editors, Gregory Waselkov, Thomas Hatley, and Peter Wood, for we have all pursued the study of the southern past in different ways—as archaeological anthropologist, environmental historian, and social historian, respectively. The other contributors to this volume also vary markedly in background and training, and all have suffered from the general tendencies inhibiting work across disciplinary lines. Hence all have hopes that a volume like this can help make amends.

Who is to say whether history or anthropology has been more recalcitrant about incorporating the insights of the other field? But we do know, according to a recent survey of nearly four thousand scholars by the American Council of Learned Societies, that historians are particularly "unlikely to collaborate with other members of their profession or even to exchange information," and that they "are also less likely to co-author articles or books than other scholars."[8] As editors, we have requested historical, rather than anthropological, notation throughout the book in a small concession to these conservative tendencies. But in selecting and arranging these original essays, we have tried to remind ourselves, our fellow contributors, and our readers of the potential insights to be gained from communication across disciplinary lines.

This collection also represents important convergences over time and space. Chronologically, it focuses for the most part upon the seventeenth and eighteenth centuries A.D. This era is more distant and less populous than the familiar "Antebellum" and "Civil War" periods, so inviting to historians, or than the subsequent parade of "New Souths." But it is not as remote and difficult to document as the many generations preceding Columbus, plus the first crucial hundred years of Spanish and French intervention, which have long absorbed many of the region's best anthropologists. Situated between a less tangible "prehistory" and a too familiar recent history, it constitutes a moment of enormous change, as the ensuing essays testify, and also an era of surprising continuity with what had gone before and what was still to follow.

Geographically, our focus here includes the whole southeastern section of North America, from the Ohio River to the Gulf of Mexico and the Florida Keys, from the East Texas timber country to the Sea Islands and the Outer Banks. Several essays extend over virtually the entire forest; others examine in greater detail some separate aspect or single portion of the whole. For many people working outside the region, who may know well the different nations of the Iroquois League or the separate mesa settlements of Pueblo culture, this presentation may help clarify both the parts and the whole of southeastern Indian life, reducing important aspects to manageable size. On the other hand, for the increasing numbers within the region, working on some local aspect of Indian life in the colonial era, this collection may help broaden their horizons beyond a specific excavation or archive, giving them a wider context for their ongoing work.

Whatever an initial glance at the title might suggest, this book concerns the *entire* geographic South. In fact, the title *Powhatan's Mantle* has been chosen consciously on the assumption that many readers, both laypersons and scholars, begin from a limited set of inherited images. For most of us, mention of Indians in the colonial Southeast still conjures up immediate recollections of Powhatan and Pocahontas on the Chesapeake; all else remains a void. In a literal sense, Powhatan's mantle is a fascinating artifact, pictured in the frontispiece and discussed in Gregory Waselkov's essay. But in a figurative sense it is much larger, an emblem for the Indian inheritance of the entire region, of which Powhatan's chiefdom, even at its height, embraced only a very small corner.

Indeed, the word "mantle" can be read to mean the land itself, the earth's surface and subsurface, which had one significance for the South's original inhabitants and quite another for the newcomers who gradually took control of the region, piece by piece, decade by decade. The same forces that removed Powhatan's literal mantle to the Ashmolean Museum eventually seized the inheritance of numerous chiefdoms larger than his. The southern land and its resources, "Powhatan's mantle" in the largest metaphorical sense, passed swiftly from Indian to intruder in the course of a few short generations.

This book, then, concentrates upon that momentous period of transition known as the "postcontact" or "colonial" era. It brings together original studies by scholars actively at work in this field, to suggest the complexity and importance of this portion of southern history when viewed from a fresh perspective. We hope that both the significance of the topic and the liveliness and diversity of current research will become clear through the twelve original essays that follow. They are not the product of any symposium or seminar; each was written independently, and taken together they reflect, we believe, the present state of research in this developing field. We have not arranged them in any linear manner but instead have grouped them, to borrow an Indian image, around three separate fires. Talk at the initial fire concerns population and geography, the diverse land and its changing peoples. Around the second fire, though specific subjects vary, politics and economics are the underlying matters of discussion. At the third fire, broad themes of social change and cultural continuity emerge from a series of case studies.

To bring together the voices represented around these fires has not proved nearly so quick and easy as first anticipated. We feel fortunate, therefore, to have had encouragement and advice from numerous friends and colleagues along the way. We are indebted to the series editors and advisers for taking an interest in this project. And we are particularly grateful to our fellow contributors for their support and confidence—and most of all for their patience. We thank all of them for their part in helping to kindle these council fires.

Peter H. Wood, Gregory A. Waselkov, M. Thomas Hatley

Notes

1. For recent basic overviews, see Michael Coe, Dean Snow, and Elizabeth Benson, *Atlas of Ancient America* (New York: Facts on File, 1986); Brian M. Fagan, *The Great Journey: The Peopling of Ancient America* (New York: Thames and Hudson, 1987); Stuart J. Fiedel, *Prehistory of the Americas* (Cambridge: Cambridge University Press, 1987).

2. Julian H. Steward, *Handbook of South American Indians*, 7 vols., Bureau of American Ethnology Bulletin 143 (Washington, D.C.: Government Printing Office, 1946–59). For review summaries from more recent decades, see Elman R. Service, "Indian-European Relations in Colonial Latin America," *American Anthropologist*, n.s., 57(1955): 411–25; Karen Spalding, "The Colonial Indian: Past and Future Research Perspectives," *Latin American Research Review* 7(1972): 47–76. An outstanding example of current research is the anthropology dissertation of Louise M. Burkhart, "The Slippery Earth: Nahua-Christian Moral Dialogue in Sixteenth-Century Mexico" (Ph.D. diss., Yale University, 1986).

3. For an introduction to the literature on Indians, see Henry F. Dobyns, *Native American Historical Demography: A Critical Bibliography* (Bloomington: Indiana University Press, 1976). Regarding Africans, see Joseph C. Miller, *Slavery: A Comparative Teaching Bibliography* (Waltham, Mass.: African Studies Association, 1977, with updates). Respecting aspects of Europe's colonizing population, see the project outlined in Bernard Bailyn, *The Peopling of North America* (New York: Alfred A. Knopf, 1986). Describing this project in 1981 (paper delivered to the Organization of American Historians in Dallas and furnished by the author), Professor Bailyn noted that his overview did "not involve to any significant extent . . . the native Americans and the Africans—whose histories are so central a part of the story. For we know as yet very little about their histories; we have nothing like the density of information about them that is available for all other groups." Bailyn added, "To uncover their histories in anything like the detail available for the European components of the early American popula-

tion is, in my view, the greatest challenge in this whole realm of research." But in revising the passage for his book, Bailyn deleted this encouraging sentence and substituted a more negative reference (p. 20) to "the mass of writing, most of it polemical, that is available on both of these groups."

4. Robert M. Carmack, "Ethnohistory: A Review of Its Development, Definitions, Methods, and Aims," *Annual Review of Anthropology* 1(1972): 227–46; James Axtell, "The Ethnohistory of Early America: A Review Essay," *William and Mary Quarterly*, 3d ser., 35(January 1978): 110–44; James Axtell, "Ethnohistory: An Historian's Viewpoint," *Ethnohistory* 26(1979): 1–13; Bruce Trigger, "Ethnohistory: Problems and Prospects," *Ethnohistory* 29(1982): 1–19; Francis Jennings, "A Growing Partnership: Historians, Anthropologists, and American Indian History," *Ethnohistory* 29(1982): 21–41.

5. The best index of progress in this area is the steady appearance of volumes in the American Indian Bibliographical Series of the Indiana University Press, Francis Jennings, general editor, such as the thirteenth volume: W. R. Swagerty, ed., *Scholars and the Indian Experience: Critical Reviews of Recent Writing in the Social Sciences* (Bloomington: Indiana University Press, 1984). The series is sponsored by the D'Arcy McNickle Center for the History of the American Indian at the Newberry Library in Chicago, which has played a crucial role in encouraging this scholarly resurgence. See, for example, the papers from a 1985 Washington conference in the Center's Occasional Papers in Curriculum Series, number 4, *The Impact of Indian History on the Teaching of United States History* (Chicago: Newberry Library, 1986). For evidence of the Smithsonian's continuing contribution, beyond publication of the multivolume *Handbook of North American Indians*, see William W. Fitzhugh, ed., *Cultures in Contact: The Impact of European Contacts on Native American Cultural Institutions, A.D. 1000–1800* (Washington, D.C.: Smithsonian Institution Press, 1985).

6. Charles Hudson, *The Southeastern Indians* (Knoxville: University of Tennessee Press, 1976); J. Leitch Wright, Jr. *The Only Land They Knew; The Tragic Story of the American Indians in the Old South* (New York: Free Press, 1981); J. Norman Heard, *Handbook of the American Frontier: Four Centuries of Indian-White Relationships*, vol. 1, *The Southeastern Woodlands*, Native American Resources Series 1 (Metuchen, N.J.: Scarecrow Press, 1987). Among the essay collections to appear recently on more focused topics, see Jerald T. Milanich and Samuel Proctor, eds., *Tacachale: Essays on the Indians of Florida and Southeastern Georgia during the Historic Period* (Gainesville: University Presses of Florida, 1978); Patricia K. Galloway, ed., *La Salle and His Legacy: Frenchmen and Indians in the Lower Mississippi Valley* (Jackson: University Press of Mississippi, 1982); R. Reid Badger and Lawrence A. Clayton, eds., *Alabama and the Borderlands: From Prehistory to Statehood* (University: University of Alabama Press, 1985); Nelson D. Lankford, ed., "'The Takinge Upp of Powhatans Bones': Virginia Indians, 1585–1945," special issue of the *Virginia Magazine of History and Biography* 95 (April 1987).

7. For example, see the latest contributions to the Ripley P. Bullen Monograph Series of the University of Florida Press and the Florida State Museum: Marvin T. Smith, *Archaeology of Aboriginal Culture Change in the Interior Southeast: Depopulation during the Early Historic Period* (Gainesville: University Presses of Florida, 1987);

John H. Hann, *Apalachee: The Land between the Rivers* (Gainesville: University Presses of Florida, 1987). For specialized essays and recent bibliography, also see *Structure and Process in Southeastern Archaeology*. ed. Roy S. Dickens, Jr., and H. Trawick Ward (University of Alabama Press, 1985).

8. *Perspectives* (American Historical Association), January 1987, 8.

Part One Geography and Population

Introduction by Peter H. Wood

Up until at least the time when Alaska and Hawaii received statehood in the middle of this century, general United States history texts—and even specialized demographic surveys—had a peculiar way of portraying American "expansion." A chronological series of blank maps showed a few population dots along the eastern seaboard in 1650, and they multiplied steadily, migrating across an otherwise empty continent as time progressed. The dots would stop mysteriously at any political border, only to burst out across a new region like a rash of measles when "territorial acquisition" occurred. So generations of students received the strong subliminal message that no one inhabited Appalachia or the Ohio valley until English-speaking settlers arrived. They were shown the Louisiana Territory as a huge void, an empty funnel in the center of the continent, before President Jefferson purchased it from the French. Accompanying text might suggest the story's greater complexity, but a picture—even a partially vacant outline map—can outweigh a great many words.

In creating such demographic pictures, did these textbook cartographers ignore the presence of Native Americans through ignorance, accident, or some conspiracy of silence? Had anyone asked them, and apparently few did, the responses would no doubt have varied. Some would invoke precedent: "We've always done it this way." Others would plead lack of hard evidence: "I'd like to show everyone, but I don't think reliable data exist." However plausible such excuses seemed at the time, these empty expanses stretching across historical population maps diminished to zero the significance of whole Indian societies and precluded the discussion of interaction between natives and newcomers. Moreover, whether inadvertently or not, they avoided the unsettling questions of Indian decimation and removal associated with the European colonization and conquest of North America.

But the fiction could not be maintained forever, and after midcentury the picture began to change as two competing influences came to bear. One model for population reconstruction came from farther south and west, where historical demographers, spurred on by anthropologists and archaeologists studying Latin America, had been asking questions about the resource productivity and "carrying capacity" of specific environments, using elaborate models for broad areas. Meanwhile, an alternative approach to population issues came from the north and east, where colonial historians began to apply the tools of localized historical demography developed in Europe to early English villages in the New World. Working with excellent written records at the parish level, they soon became sophisticated and precise about demographic processes, though for the most part they remained less interested in reconstructing whole populations over time.

Both perspectives are beginning to make valid contributions toward understanding the postcontact Southeast, though reconciling these different approaches cannot be swift for a region where demographic study regarding the colonial era has been slow to take hold. If black dots marching across an empty map are a thing of the past, more realistic population pictures have been slow to evolve. An atlas for the era of the American Revolution that appeared in 1976, for example, combined state-of-the-art cartography with segregation concepts from an earlier time. On maps of settlement the editors inserted a small disclaimer in parentheses: "(Indian population not included)." Then on other pages they introduced separate maps of some—by no means all—of the documented Indian towns of the East (although, as is customary with treatments of the Revolutionary era, they omitted Indians of the Mississippi valley and the Great West altogether). The map titled "Southern Indian Villages, 1760–94" was carefully prepared by Adele Hast and Helen Hornbeck Tanner. Despite its necessarily small scale, this summary overview approached again, after two centuries, the level of detail with regard to the names and locations of Native American towns that had appeared on the large-scale chart of the region drawn up before the Revolution by Joseph Purcell, under the direction of John Stuart, superintendent of Indian affairs for the Southern District.[1]

Helen Tanner has continued to pioneer in linking Indian history to geography through maps. Her recent *Atlas of Great Lakes Indian History* provides a model of what can be accomplished through painstaking research and innovative cartography.[2] As yet, the diverse region below the Ohio River has not been subjected to such careful scrutiny. But the materials now exist for such an undertaking, whenever the right match can be arranged between dedicated researchers and a supportive press. (The forthcoming Southeastern volume of the *Handbook of North American Indians* will provide innumerable kernels that could become further grist for such a mill.) Meanwhile, the articles in this section, focusing on the geography and demography of the postcontact South, offer some hint of what an *Atlas of Southeastern Indians* might portray in its presentation of the colonial era.

Fittingly, the initial essay is by Helen Tanner, providing a brief introduction to the system of communication that linked southeastern Indians by land and water. Tanner does not attempt to chart the whole elaborate network in all its complexity over time. Instead, she surveys the major patterns of communication and the dominant arteries of contact that shaped the societies of the South. Her chapter not only summarizes current knowledge and offers an introductory overview; it also opens the door to ethnographers with an interest in mental mapping. For as Gregory Waselkov demonstrates near the end of this volume, we are only beginning to understand Indian perceptions of the geographic world in which they lived.

However stationary it may appear from the twentieth century, there was nothing static about this world, as Tanner's lines of communication make clear. And more was in motion than warbelts and trade goods, crop gatherers and hunting parties. Shifts from shoreline to hillside as seasons changed, from old field to new field as soil became depleted, from townsite to townsite as a community grew or dwindled—all these local movements were a regular feature of precontact southern life. But so was large-scale migration, as numerous tribal myths of origin suggest.

The arrival of Europeans spurred further relocations, some of which are sketched in Marvin Smith's essay on the southern interior. It is important to remember that the widespread social and political reorganization that began after de Soto, and continued until Removal some three hundred years later, affected the entire Southeast, not just the area and time span Smith focuses on here. Indeed, all the major tribal entities of the historic period (Creeks, Choctaws,

Chickasaws, Catawbas, Cherokees, and later the Seminoles) were amalgams, to a greater or lesser degree, of numerous local and refugee groups that coalesced from the population remnants left after the ravages of virgin soil epidemics and the English-inspired slave wars of the late seventeenth and eighteenth centuries.

Not long ago, Smith's propositions might have seemed pure conjecture. But recent historical research into early Spanish documents, on one hand, and increasingly extensive and precise archaeological evidence, on the other, make it possible to suggest specific patterns of change. Physically and linguistically diverse groups moved to form loosely organized confederacies, unions of mutual convenience, that effectively restrained interethnic hostilities in the absence of the hierarchical social controls characteristic of prehistoric southeastern chiefdoms. Further research will test and modify these patterns, adding details for areas not covered in Smith's case study. But his hypothesis that population decline brought on by foreign diseases played a role in opening new prospects for relocation and reorganization seems likely to find support in future studies.

The population decline mentioned by Smith and subsequent authors becomes a central focus for Peter Wood's long chapter on the demography of the South during the final century of the colonial era. The causes and consequences, the extent and duration, of this overall decline—in the South and elsewhere—have absorbed and divided scholars for some time. But until now no one has attempted a systematic survey of change over time for the entire southern region, estimating arriving Europeans and Africans alongside the established Indian groups they would eventually displace. By focusing on the late colonial period, when the records are most complete, Wood has managed to create a framework that registers change from one decade to the next and from one subregion to another.

The results of this comparative overview are startling, to say the least, for it is precisely in this century, from the 1680s to the 1780s, that the population of the South undergoes its most dramatic transformation. Before 1700 the region is inhabited almost entirely by Native Americans, and their numbers are continuing to decline at a rate that more than offsets the growing influx of newcomers; the southern population as a whole—generations of colonial historians notwithstanding—is actually growing smaller year by year. Two generations later, on the eve of the American Revolution, all this has changed. The decline among Indian groups has slowed and even begun to reverse itself in places, Wood shows, but this severely diminished population is now heavily outnumbered, in one area after another, by the rapidly expanding and migrating population of whites and blacks from overseas.

The interactions of these three groups—Indians, Europeans, and Africans—has been a focus of the work of Daniel Usner, one of the new group of ethnohistorians represented in this volume. His essay on the Indians of colonial New Orleans, which concludes this initial section, zeros in on one small and little-known piece of the large demographic quilt displayed by Wood. By delving into the complex interracial origins of his home city in Louisiana, Usner reminds readers that there is nothing new about the people sociologists call "urban Indians." His detailed reconstruction of which native people were present in the French colonial port, and why, provides a suggestive reminder about the sheer diversity of the Indian experience in the long colonial era and the extent to which careful research can restore forgotten people to their complex world in a meaningful way.

Together, these four very different essays serve to introduce the varied landscapes and differing peoples who are the subject of this volume. Like the essays to follow, they draw upon generations of intriguing scholarship in long-separated fields and point the way toward more integrated research in the future. They attempt, so to speak, to "put southern Indians back on the map." This having been done, it will be possible in parts 2 and 3 to focus upon the changing worlds—political, economic, social, and philosophical—in which these indigenous Southerners lived out their lives during the first three centuries after steady transatlantic contact began.

Notes

1. Lester J. Cappon, ed., *Atlas of Early American History: The Revolutionary Era, 1760–1790* (Princeton: Princeton University Press, 1976), 19–21, 95–96; cf. disclaimer on p. 78. For details of the Stuart–Purcell map of about 1773 in the Ayer Collection of the Newberry Library in Chicago, see William P. Cumming, *The Southeast in Early Maps* (Princeton: Princeton University Press, 1958), 251.

2. Helen Hornbeck Tanner, ed., *Atlas of Great Lakes Indian History* (Norman: University of Oklahoma Press, 1987).

The Land and Water Communication Systems of the Southeastern Indians

Helen Hornbeck Tanner

The vitality of Indian community life in the southeastern section of the present United States was enhanced by a maze of intervillage contacts. The frequency of interaction depended upon the distance between townsites. Descriptions of southern Indian society include accounts of intertown ball games, itinerant peddling of goods in a barter economy, diplomatic councils, and gatherings for seasonal festivals. These lines of contact were engraved in the earth as pathways connecting associated towns.

But there were also intertribal contacts utilizing trails and canoe routes over distances of several hundred miles, extending in the case of war parties and diplomatic missions to 1,000 or 1,500 miles. These longer routes formed a network that also had a bearing on life in the individual villages. The entire communication system, composed of local subsystems, hubs or intermediate terminals, and connections with other networks, can be roughly outlined with the view of demonstrating the wide range of contacts accessible to southeastern Indians.

This outline deals primarily with the major population groups of the eighteenth century, the Cherokees, Creeks, Seminoles, Choctaws, and Chickasaws east of the Mississippi River and the Caddos of Louisiana and East Texas.[1] The overall area involved in this treatment of the Southeast is the region south of the Ohio River and southwest of the Great Kanawha River, a major southern tributary of the Ohio River flowing through West Virginia, and also southwest of the James River entering the Atlantic Ocean at the southern end of Chesapeake Bay. West of the Mississippi, the Arkansas River is a reasonable north-south dividing line. The Arkansas River marks the traditional northern border of the country of the Caddos, a people more similar to their eastern neighbors across the Mississippi River than to those living in any other direction. The western border of this definition of the Southeast is the Cross Timbers, originally a belt of forest that extended north and south in central Oklahoma, reaching into northern Texas.[2] Geographically, the Southeast ends near modern Dallas at the head of the Trinity River.

Most of the information about the details of traditional transportation routes in the southland comes from eighteenth-century sources, though some references date from both the early seventeenth century and the early nineteenth. Yet the persistence of the same transportation routes, in some cases evident from the time of the mastodon to the present highway and railroad era, makes it possible to use reports from different time periods in forming a coherent picture of a communications system for the Southeast.

Turning attention first to the trail system in the southeastern United States, it is important to distinguish between pathways chiefly used for local purposes, any series of short links, and the lengthy thoroughfares of interregional communication that are the ultimate concern of this discussion.[3] From maps already published, it is apparent that there were a number of trails developed solely to serve local population concentrations. Notable are the networks connecting fifty Choctaw towns in southeastern Mississippi and Alabama, the local pattern reflecting the tight formation of seven Chickasaw towns near modern Pontotoc in northeastern Mississippi, and the intricate maze crisscrossing the southern Appalachian Highlands in the Cherokee country of eastern Tennessee and adjacent sections of North Carolina and Georgia.[4]

In the total communication system of the Southeast, there are also hubs where important trails going in different directions crossed and branched. Significant examples of this feature of the communication system are present in Nashville and Chattanooga, Tennessee, and in Montgomery, Alabama—places that have always been geographic focal points. The Hiwassee River valley near Murphy, Tennessee, close to the Georgia–North Carolina border, was another focal point of aboriginal travel.[5] These townsites are all in the interior heartland of the Southeast, but the trail system spread out to touch points on both the Gulf and Atlantic coasts, frequently following paths from the highlands to the coastal plain along river valleys such as the Santee, Savannah, Chattahoochee, and Coosa.

The most comprehensive work on regional land trails is the monograph of William E. Myer, edited by John R. Swanton and published

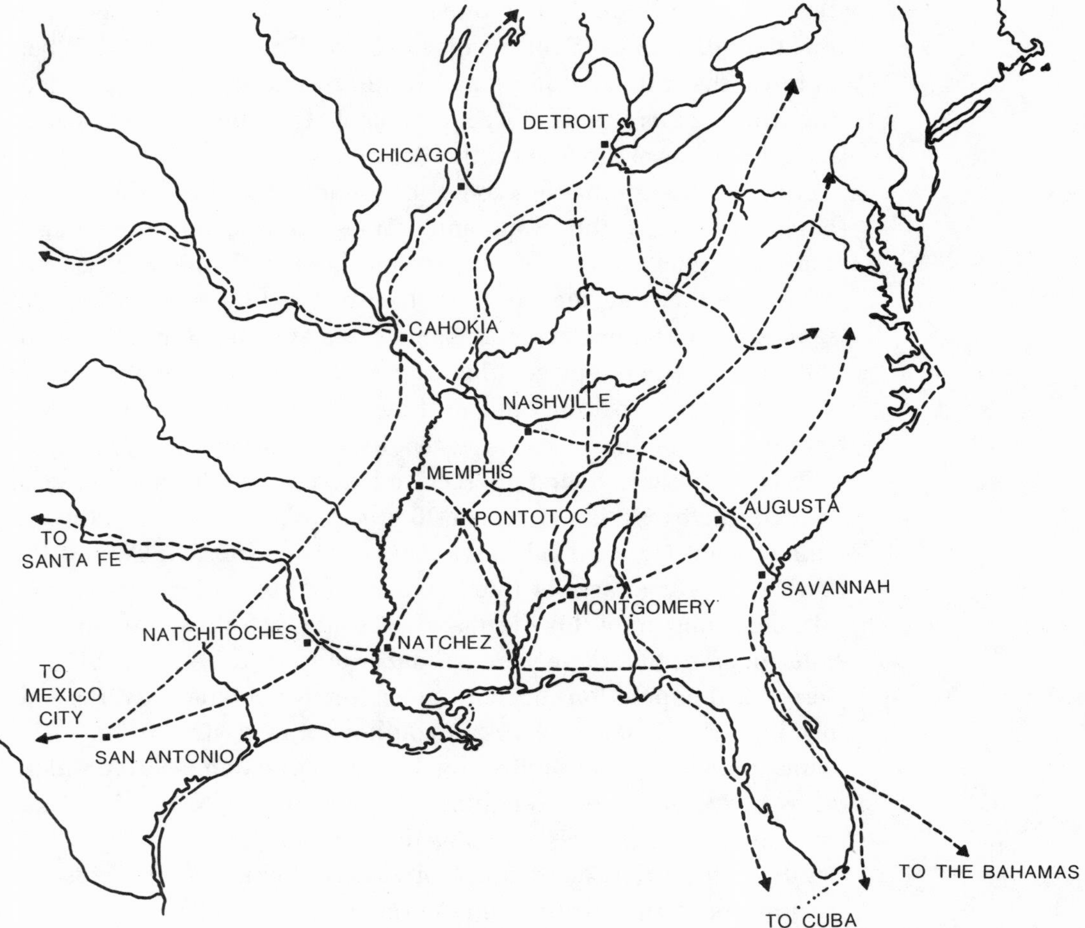

Figure 1 Communications network of the colonial Southeast. See the endpapers for the detailed map of which this is a simplified rendering.

in 1928.[6] In his summary of thirty-five years of research into the trail system of the southeastern United States, Myer identified 125 separate trails. His investigation of Tennessee and Kentucky was exceptionally thorough; the coverage of southern Georgia, Florida, and Louisiana was less complete. The more recent work of Utley and Hemperly augments Myer's original contribution.[7]

Myer became firmly convinced that Indian people throughout eastern North America, including the Southeast, often traveled well over a thousand miles on war and trading expeditions. He gave particular attention to the principal north-south artery "Great Indian Warpath" that extended southward from the Kanawha River of West

Virginia. The main prong of the Great Warrior Path led southeast up the Kanawha to the New River, then west to the Holston River's north fork and present Kingsport, Tennessee. One branch diverted east, to the Catawba country near Roanoke, Virginia, and followed the valley of the Shenandoah River. The main route continued through the east Tennessee Cherokee settlements, including the ancient capital of Echota, to present Chattanooga, Tennessee, and on south to the Upper Creek villages around present Montgomery, Alabama. A Pennsylvania branch of the Great Warrior Path was the route of Iroquois parties raiding southern Indian villages. In the opposite direction, it was the route of the Tuscaroras seeking refuge with the Iroquois in 1715.[8]

The Kanawha River mouth was actually the easternmost of three trails crossing the Ohio River within the boundaries of the present state of Ohio. They were all important in interregional relations between northeastern and southeastern Indians. The second notable crossing was at the mouth of the Scioto River, where a trail ran southwest through the Kentucky bluegrass district to the Cumberland Gap, there intersecting the main branch of the Great Warrior Path in the Holston valley of Tennessee.[9] The geological formation of the southern Appalachian Range offered a number of parallel routes running through valleys in a northeast to southwesterly direction.[10] The third important crossing in this section of the Ohio River was at the mouth of the Licking River opposite modern Cincinnati, an alternative route to present Chattanooga. Trails joining at that point led south to the country of the Creeks and Cherokees in Alabama and Georgia. North of the Ohio River, trails converged toward Detroit and the Upper Great Lakes crossroads at the Straits of Mackinac.

While the Great Warrior Path, with spreading prongs and feeder routes throughout its length, was probably used for war and trade in earlier eras, the documents of colonial times show that warriors, messengers, and tribal delegations traveled this path regularly in the eighteenth century. This trail system was used by Wyandots from Detroit in warfare against the Catawbas, and by Cherokees coming to the mouth of the Scioto River for conferences with the Shawnees in 1751 and 1752.[11] Chippewas from the Straits of Mackinac were also among the tribes that met for intertribal councils with the Shawnees of the Scioto valley, a significant point of interregional contact. Delawares living in the Muskingum valley of eastern Ohio in the

1770s sent a delegation to live with the Cherokees for several years; they returned home in 1779 with Cherokee representatives who brought articles to trade.[12] Following the American Revolution, Creek and Cherokee leaders traveled north to Detroit to join Great Lakes tribes in councils with British authorities.[13] These are examples of use of the communication system for interchange between southeastern Indians and Indian peoples living north of the Ohio River in the eighteenth century. Indian leaders and runners spending considerable time on intertribal business learned several languages.

Continuing with an examination of the transportation routes in the upper section of the Southeast, it is next important to observe the course of the Cumberland and Tennessee rivers. Both have their headwaters near the all-important Cumberland Gap through the Appalachian Range, where the southwestern tip of Virginia meets the Kentucky-Tennessee border. Their middle courses diverge widely, the Cumberland keeping to the north along both sides of the Kentucky-Tennessee border while the Tennessee River dips into northern Alabama. But downstream both rivers turn north to follow parallel courses, entering the Ohio River only about twenty miles apart near Paducah, Kentucky. Dam construction has obscured the original watercourses, but the relative position of the two rivers is still plain on a modern map.

From headwaters to river mouth, the Cumberland and Tennessee were channels of east-west communication, but segments of the Tennessee in particular also served as part of a north-south communication line. At the bend of the Tennessee River in the extreme northwestern corner of Alabama, near Muscle Shoals, a main trail ran south to the Chickasaw towns.[14] On the Illinois shore of the Ohio River, opposite the mouths of the Cumberland and Tennessee rivers, were the trails north to Cahokia, a location strategically situated to tap trade up the Missouri, Mississippi, and Illinois rivers. Recognizing the Cherokees' use of the entire course of the Cumberland and Tennessee Rivers, the French in 1757 built the "Cherokee Fort" on the lower Ohio by these river mouths.[15]

For traveling northeast from the mouths of the Cumberland and Tennessee rivers, water transportation was available all the way to Detroit except for a short portage at present Fort Wayne. This route ascended the Ohio for a short distance to the Wabash, continuing up the Wabash and down the Maumee to Lake Erie at present Toledo,

Ohio, then north to the entrance to the Detroit River. The Wabash, Ohio, Tennessee River route was probably the one used by the Miamis in their raids on the Chickasaws, and by the Chickasaws in attacks on French Vincennes in the 1730s.[16] The stretch of the Ohio River between the entrances of the Tennessee and the Wabash also was crossed by several land trails from southern Illinois converging at Nashville.

The east-west lines of communication across the lower southland were land trails. The most enterprising British trader in Charlestown, South Carolina, had reached the Mississippi before 1690, traveling more than eight hundred miles westward from his home base.[17] The British Indian trade also pushed across the Mississippi River very early in the colonial era. In 1698 a trader went beyond the Chickasaws to establish trade with the Quapaws near the mouth of the Arkansas River.[18] It is interesting that when the first French explorer with trade in mind penetrated the Indian country of central Oklahoma by way of the Red River in 1719, he found the inhabitants of a Wichita village already trading with a Chickasaw, who soon returned to the Yazoo River.[19] At that time Charlestown was the center of English colonial trade with the southern Indians, challenging the French trade based at Mobile beginning in 1702 as well as the less competitive Spanish traders from St. Augustine. Merchants from Savannah and Augusta later entered the system of existing Indian trails to trade with the Creeks and Choctaws east of the Mississippi. Although the Mississippi River was a formidable barrier during seasons of high water, the southeastern communication system crossed the river at present Memphis, Vicksburg, and Natchez. The main trail from present Birmingham, Alabama, to Greenville, Mississippi, had a branch looping north specifically to connect with the mouth of the Arkansas River.[20]

British traders began developing east-west trade routes through the interior country of the Southeast in the late seventeenth century. In 1685 a large convoy of traders with English goods arrived at Coweta, center of the Lower Creeks near the falls of the Chattahoochee River. The following spring, 150 Indian burdeners laden with deerskin packs returned to Charlestown, beginning an expanding trade network.[21] By the mid-eighteenth century, trains of packhorses replaced the Indian burdeners, creating a well-beaten trail pattern. The main path and a number of alternate routes to Oakfuskee, Upper Creek trade center on the Tallapoosa River, have been worked out by

John Goff. The Upper Creek path had an important branch to the Cherokees of northwest Georgia and northeast Alabama, and on the Coosa River it connected with trails leading westward to the Chickasaws and Choctaws.[22]

The most southerly east-west route originated on the Atlantic coast at St. Augustine, Florida. It headed toward the fording point at the bend in the lower St. Johns River (present Jacksonville), then continued by way of present Tallahassee to Mobile and on to the Mississippi River opposite the mouth of the Red River. Either ascending the Red River from its mouth, or crossing farther north at Natchez, the traveler arrived at Natchitoches, Louisiana, the gateway to the Caddo country. From Natchitoches the overland trail westward ran through the Caddo (or Hasinai) settlements in the Neches and Angelina valleys of East Texas to San Antonio, and through Presidio on the Rio Grande at the mouth of the Rio Conchos. The juncture of the two rivers was the sixteenth-century homeland of the Jumanos Indians, noted intermediaries in the regional trade network.[23] Here, on the present Mexican border, trails led southwest to Chihuahua in the direction of Casas Grandes, a thirteenth-century trade center, and to Mexico City.

The long overland route from the Atlantic coast of Florida eventually reaching Mexico City was primarily used in sections, with concentrated local traffic between the east coast of Florida and the Apalachee Bay area and also from Apalachee to Pensacola and Mobile Bay.[24] Mobile to Natchez, Mississippi, and Natchitoches, Louisiana, was another intermediate link. But the first ambitious French trader to locate in Mobile, before the founding of New Orleans in 1718, went back and forth over this land trail from Mobile beyond Natchitoches to the Texas border carrying on lucrative illegal trade with the Spaniards.[25] East-west contact across the Mississippi River between the Creeks and the Caddos continued into the early nineteenth century. The Creeks sought military aid from the Caddos at the time they were threatened by General Andrew Jackson's army.[26]

Natchitoches was also an important terminal in two other long-distance lines of communication besides the trans-Texas land route. Trading and exploring parties went up the Red River from Natchitoches or from the cluster of Caddo towns at the river bend near present Texarkana and continued to Santa Fe, New Mexico.[27] The last lap of course was overland. The Arkansas River by way of the

Canadian River was another largely water route from the Mississippi valley to Santa Fe.

From both modern Texarkana, Texas, and Natchitoches, trails headed northeast, meeting in southern Arkansas, with Cahokia as the ultimate destination. The route the Caddos used to take horses to the Illinois country is on an early map of Louisiana; and from documentary evidence it is apparent that this trade was well established before 1700.[28] By the late eighteenth century, of course, the marketing center on the upper Mississippi was St. Louis, across the river from Cahokia, the ancient Indian population center much diminished in comparison with its peak development about A.D. 1200. At this point it is probably important to interject the observation that the route from the Caddo country to Cahokia was undoubtedly used for other kinds of trade and interchange before the horse-trading era.

Considered as a whole, the land passage traced from present Jacksonville, Florida, to the Mexican border was essentially an inland circuit of the Gulf coast following the most geographically feasible line of travel just north of the numerous bays and marshes.[29] Crossing this east-west route were several north-south lines of communication. The points of intersection between the north-south and the east-west communication lines formed significant transportation terminals. East of the Mississippi River, three of these interchanges or terminals deserve special attention. These are Mobile Bay, Apalachee Bay, and the bay at the mouth of the St. John River that extends inland to present Jacksonville. The routes of travel outlined for the upper section of the Southeast all connected with those three southern terminals. First of all, there is a natural drainage along the Tombigbee and Coosa-Alabama rivers funneling into Mobile Bay. The trail system northwest of Mobile Bay, passing through the Choctaw and Chickasaw towns, extended to the Mississippi River at present Memphis. Similarly, direct trails connected the Upper Creek towns near the junction of the Tallapoosa and Coosa rivers with Mobile. As a terminal in the total network, Mobile Bay offered many transportation alternatives, including coastal waterways around the Gulf of Mexico.

Apalachee Bay to the east of Mobile Bay also offered diversified transportation opportunities. From St. Marks Creek at the head of Apalachee Bay, a trail led straight north through the Lower Creek country to the eastern Cherokee towns. Apalachee Bay was also a port of embarkation for coastal canoe traffic south to Tampa Bay. Northwest of the bay, the trail pattern led to the meeting ground where the Chattahoochee and Flint rivers converge to form the Apalachicola River, on the Georgia-Florida state boundary. In the late eighteenth century the main Lower Creek towns were situated along the Chattahoochee about a hundred miles north of this junction. East of Apalachee Bay, the trail pattern included alternative paths, one swinging south through the Seminole settlements in the Alachua prairie (present Gainesville, Florida) to St. Augustine. This section of northern Florida had been a more populous region in the sixteenth century.

Jacksonville, at the fording point on the St. Johns River, is the easternmost point of intersection between main east-west and north-south routes forming part of the basic southeastern communication system. West of Jacksonville, the long overland route to the Mississippi River and beyond has already been traced. But this fording point at Jacksonville was also near the southern end of the inland roadway along the south Atlantic coast terminating on the ocean shore at present St. Augustine.[30] Beyond St. Augustine, the sandy beach itself was available for foot travel but was not a principal transportation route. From Jacksonville south, the course of the St. Johns River was the main artery for travel throughout the interior of the Florida peninsula. The river itself is exceptional because it flows not south but northward from headwaters nearly two hundred miles away near Melbourne, Florida. From its upper waters, branches provided access via portages to both the Tampa and Miami regions.[31] The second important fording point on the St. Johns River, at Picolata directly west of St. Augustine, gave access to the fertile Alachua prairie region, in the eighteenth century a Seminole stronghold.[32]

Among the evidence of use of the north-south routes of Florida in the late seventeenth and eighteenth centuries is the narrative of Gabriel Arthur. As a prisoner of Indians in the region of the French Broad River of North Carolina between 1673 and 1675, he accompanied a contingent carrying warfare into Spanish Florida and also made a trip north to the Ohio River by way of the Kanawha. According to a contemporary French map, the Shawnees living in Tennessee in the 1680s, probably near Nashville, went to St. Augustine to trade with the Spaniards.[33] In the early eighteenth century, raids from South Carolina against the Florida Indians extended into the Kissimmee River region north of Lake Okeechobee. Raids of Yuchi

Indians from the north forced abandonment of an attempted mission on St. Lucie Inlet in 1743.[34] In 1785 ambassadors of the Northern Indian Confederacy attended spring councils of the Creek Nation in Alabama. A Creek delegation relayed their news to departing British officials and the incoming Spanish governor of East Florida.[35] Corresponding delegations of Creeks and Cherokees using the Great Warrior Path for more peaceful missions were present in both the Ohio country and Iroquois councils in New York in the late eighteenth century.

From the point of view of a communications network, Florida divides into two subsystems, one along the Atlantic coast and the other along the Gulf coast. Except for the trail already described across the northern neck of the peninsula and a water route along the Caloosahatchee River from the southern Gulf coast through Lake Okeechobee, there was little east-west travel across Florida. Finding good drinking water along the interior ridges was apparently a problem.[36]

Geographically, the Florida peninsula as a whole appears as an appendage to the southeastern United States, but for this very reason the area provides unique extensions to the total communications network. The southeast coast of Florida was connected with the Bahama Islands by canoe travel. Indian people congregated on the coast near the Indian River to gather turtle eggs in the proper season. People came from Providence Island in the Bahamas for turtle hunting as well. In the 1780s, when the adventurer William Augustus Bowles wanted to get from Providence Island to his Creek relatives, he and his followers landed near the Indian River inlet, went overland to the St. Johns River, and descended the river with the objective of reaching the Flint River by way of the Alachua prairie.[37] In the early nineteenth century, Seminoles from southern Florida fled in their cypress canoes to Andros Island, nearest of the Bahamas.

On the west side of the Florida peninsula, dugout canoes regularly carried Indian people from Tampa Bay back and forth to the Island of Cuba by way of Key West. Feathers and birds wings were lightweight but valuable items of commerce exported from Florida to Cuba.[38] There were also connections with the sparse population of the Keys. Matacumbe Key was particularly important for its fresh water supply.[39]

Tampa Bay served as a principal trading terminal with connections north and south along the Gulf coast and an entry into the interior of the peninsula. An allied channel was the Suwanee River entering the Gulf coast near Cedar Key. Spanish hacendados from the Apalachee and St. Johns River districts used the mouth of the Suwanee as a port of embarkation for shipping beef to Cuba before 1700.[40] In the early years of the American Revolution, Spanish guns and ammunition reached the Creek and Cherokee towns by way of Tampa, Apalachee Bay, and the Chattahoochee River.[41] Independent Indian voyages by cypress canoe continued between Florida and Cuba until the time of the Second Seminole War in 1840. All in all, the Florida peninsula should be considered a special subsystem furnishing two-way communication with the South Atlantic and Caribbean Islands.

The foregoing brief overview of a large communications network gives special emphasis to canoe routes because there is a tendency to overlook the importance of watercourses. Dugout canoes were not the only watercraft in use. On the Kanawha, Cumberland, and Tennessee river systems, canoes were constructed of a framework covered with elm or hickory bark. Sometimes these were used for only part of a long expedition and were hidden or buried in the water to be picked up on the return trip. Bark canoes were also built exclusively for one-way trips downriver and then discarded in favor of returning upstream on foot. While streams undoubtedly aided transportation in some directions, for overland travel in other directions they created time-consuming and hazardous problems. For example, stream crossings were a major impediment in traveling from the Upper Creek towns to St. Augustine, a trip that often required three weeks to accomplish.

A vivid description of triumph over natural difficulties in this part of the Southeast was recorded by an American agent returning in 1790 with a Creek delegation following negotiations for the Treaty of New York. Proceeding south on board ship, the Creeks asked to be let off at the mouth of St. Mary's River, the present Georgia-Florida border, to take a shortcut to their home communities. The party of travelers advanced upstream well past the first big bend, then followed a trail skirting the Okefenokee Swamp. Along the way they encountered one stream swollen and turbulent from fall rains. Confronted with this challenge, the Indians shot wild cattle and stretched the green hides over sapling hoops to form a bowl-shaped watercraft that was then used to ferry the American agent and the baggage across the stream. The power was supplied by Indian swimmers, who held the tow strings in their teeth and at intervals gave war whoops to frighten off the alligators, at the same time evading the tangled vines and branches being swept along by the current.[42]

A summary of the communication system of the southeastern Indians focuses first on the primary network consisting of interior trails and watercourses. On the perimeter of the interior networks are terminals supplying connections with other networks. Selected locations cited in this discussion were points on the Ohio River, Cahokia, Illinois; Natchitoches, Louisiana; Mobile, Alabama; and four places on the long shoreline of Florida: Apalachee Bay, Tampa Bay, St. John's River near the mouth, and the Indian River Inlet.

In the late eighteenth century, the communications network served a southeastern population east of the Mississippi estimated at well over 50,000 Indians living in more than one hundred towns.[43] Two centuries earlier, before penetration by Europeans, the population of the Southeast was much larger and included additional Indian provinces along the Atlantic coast south of Chesapeake Bay. Though the data used in this discussion are from the late colonial period, the same routes of travel had probably been in use for centuries. Indian people living in the highlands of the interior Southeast were not restricted to knowledge of their immediate areas; all made use of access to the seacoast. Those living along the coast were certainly not landlocked. The geographic panorama for a well-informed southeastern Indian extended north to the Great Lakes region, westward to the Great Plains, southwest to the Mexican border, and southeast to islands in the Atlantic and Caribbean.

Notes

1. See Adele Hast and Helen Hornbeck Tanner, "Southern Indian Villages, 1760–1794," in *Atlas of Early American History*, ed. Lester J. Cappon (Princeton: Princeton University Press, 1976), 19, and explanatory text, 95.

2. The significance of the Cross Timbers as a boundary zone is discussed in Helen Hornbeck Tanner, "The Territory of the Caddo Tribe of Oklahoma," in *Caddoan Indians*, vol. 4 (New York and London: Garland, 1974), 70–74.

3. See figure 1, "Communications network of the colonial southwest." To clarify geographical locations, present city names are used. It should be noted, however, that Cahokia in southwestern Illinois was supplanted in importance in the early nineteenth century by St. Louis, established across the Mississippi River on the west bank in 1764.

4. See map in Howard T. Malone, *Cherokees of the Old South, a People in Transition* (Norman: University of Oklahoma Press, 1956). See also William E. Myer, "Indian Trails of the Southeast," in *Forty-second Annual Report of the Bureau of American Ethnology for 1924–1925* (Washington, D.C.: Government Printing Office, 1928), plate 15.

5. Frank M. Setzler and Jesse D. Jennings, *Peachtree Mount and Village Site, Cherokee County, North Carolina*, Bureau of American Ethnology Bulletin 131 (Washington, D.C.: Government Printing Office, 1941), 7–10.

6. Myer, "Indian Trails."

7. Francis Lee Utley and Marion R. Hemperly, *Place Names in Georgia* (Athens: University of Georgia Press, 1975).

8. Myer, "Indian Trails," 765.

9. For discussion of the Great Warrior Path, see Myer, "Indian Trails," 749–57. The trade route from Petersburg in southwestern Virginia through the highlands to Augusta can be traced on a modern highway map. See Douglas L. Rights, "The Trading Path to the Indians," *North Carolina Historical Review* 8(1931): 404.

10. See Erwin Raisz, *Landforms of the United States*, 6th ed., rev. (Cambridge, Mass.: Erwin Raisz, 1957). Every American historian should have this map at hand.

11. Helen Hornbeck Tanner, "Cherokees in the Ohio Country," *Journal of Cherokee Studies* 3, no. 2 (1978): 94–95.

12. John Heckewelder, *A Narrative of a Mission to the United Brethren among the Delawares and Mohegan Indians* (Philadelphia: McCarty and Davis, 1820), 179–203.

13. Tanner, "Cherokees," 99. See also James G. Simcoe, Speech to the Indians, October 9, 1792, in *Collections and Researches Made by the Michigan Pioneer and Historical Society*, 40 vols. (Lansing: Thorp and Godfrey and others, 1874–1949), 24:499–500.

14. During the mid-nineteenth century slaves from Mississippi used a similar trail to escape up the Tombigbee and down the lower Tennessee River to the Ohio River and freedom. (Peter Wood kindly provided this additional information.)

15. Reuben Gold Thwaites and Louise P. Kellogg, *Frontier Defense on the Upper Ohio* (Madison: Wisconsin Historical Society, 1912), 202–3.

16. Ermine Wheeler Voegelin, *Miami, Wea, and Eel–River Indians of Southern Indiana* (New York: Garland, 1974), 85–86.

17. Wilbur R. Jacobs, ed., *The Appalachian Indian Frontier: The Edmund Atkin Report and Plan of 1755* (Lincoln: University of Nebraska Press, 1941), 16.

18. Verner W. Crane, "The Tennessee River as the Road to Carolina: The Beginnings of Exploration and Trade," *Mississippi Valley Historical Review* 3(June 1916): 8.

19. Ralph A. Smith, ed. and trans., "Account of the Journey of Bérnard de La Harpe," *Southwest Historical Quarterly* 62(1959): 533.

20. Myer, "Indian Trails," plate 15.

21. David H. Corkran, *The Creek Frontier, 1540–1783* (Norman: University of Oklahoma Press, 1967), 50–51.

22. See map in John H. Goff, "The Path to Oakfuskee: Upper Trading Route in Georgia to the Creek Indians," *Georgia Historical Quarterly* 39 (1955). To coordinate this detailed map with the system map, figure 1, note the position of Augusta, Georgia, on both maps. The site of Fort Toulouse in the southwestern corner of Goff's map is about ten miles north of present Montgomery, Alabama, shown on figure 1.

23. J. Charles Kelly, "Juan Sabeata and Diffusion," *American Anthropologist* 57 (1955): 55.

24. Joseph Purcell, "A Map of the Southern Indian District of North America, 1773," original in the Newberry Library, Chicago.

25. Herbert E. Bolton, *Athanase de Mézières and the Louisiana-Texas Frontier, 1768–1780*, 2 vols. (Cleveland: Arthur Clark, 1914), 1:36–37.

26. William C. Claiborne, *Official Letterbooks of W. C. C. Claiborne, 1801–1816*, ed. Dunbar Rowland, 6 vols. (Jackson, Miss.: State Department of Archives and History, 1917), 6:293.

27. Carlos E. Castaneda, ed., "Map of Texas, 1761–1810," in *The End of the Spanish Regime, 1780–1810*, vol. 5 of *Our Catholic Heritage in Texas*, 7 vols. (Austin: Von Boeckman–Jones, 1936–58), facing p. 514. For accounts of route up the Red River, see Noel H. Loomis and Abraham P. Nasatir, *Pedro Vial and the Roads to Santa Fe* (Norman: University of Oklahoma Press, 1967). For a detailed description of the river course to the vicinity of the "great bend" near present Texarkana, Texas, see Dan L. Flores, ed., *Jefferson and Southwestern Exploration: The Freeman and Custis Accounts of the Red River Expedition of 1806* (Norman: University of Oklahoma Press, 1984).

28. William Darby, *A Map of the State of Louisiana . . . from Actual Survey* (Philadelphia: John Melish, 1816). See also Charles Claude du Tisné, "Du Tisné chez les Missouri," in *Découvertes et établissements des Français dans l'ouest et dans le sud de l'Amérique Septentrionale (1614–1754)*, ed. Pierre Margry 6 vols. (Paris: Imprimérie D. Jouast, 1876–86), 6:312–15.

29. Myer, "Indian Trails," 831–32.

30. Charles L. Mowat, *East Florida as a British Province* (Berkeley: University of California Press, 1943), 123.

31. James Adair, *Adair's History of the American Indians*, ed. Samuel Cole Williams (Johnson City, Tenn.: Watauga Press, 1930), 489.

32. Lester J. Cappon, "Travels of John and William Bartram," in *Atlas of Early American History*, ed. Lester J. Cappon (Princeton: Princeton University Press, 1976), 33, 108. See also Mowat, *East Florida*, 25, 67–68.

33. Myer, "Indian Trails," 736. Jean Baptiste Franquelin, "Carte de Louisiana, ou des voyages du Sr. de la Salle, 1684," in *The Jesuit Relations and Allied Documents, 1610–1791*, 73 vols. (Cleveland: Burrows Brothers, 1896–1901), 70:63.

34. John M. Goggin, "The Indians and the History of the Matacumbe Region," in *Indian and Spanish Selected Writings*, ed. John M. Goggin (Coral Gables, Fla.: University of Miami Press, 1964).

35. Vicente Manuel de Zéspedes to Bernardo de Gálvez, June 12, 1785, in Joseph B.

Lockey, *East Florida, 1783–1785* (Berkeley and Los Angeles: University of California Press, 1949), 557.

36. Bernard Romans, *A Concise Natural History of East and West Florida* (New York: R. Aitkin, 1775), 38, 187–88.

37. Helen Hornbeck Tanner, *Zéspedes in East Florida, 1784–1790* (Coral Gables, Fla.: University of Miami Press, 1963), 189–95.

38. James W. Covington, "Trade Relations between Southwestern Florida and Cuba," *Florida Historical Quarterly* 39(1959): 114–28.

39. Goggin, "Indians."

40. Charles Arnade, "Cattle Raising in Spanish Florida, 1573–1763," *Agricultural History* 35(July 1961): 116–24.

41. Helen Hornbeck Tanner, "Pipesmoke and Muskets: Florida Indian Intrigues of the Revolutionary Era," in *Eighteenth Century Florida and Its Borderlands*, ed. Samuel Proctor (Gainesville: University of Florida Press, 1975), 18–19.

42. Henry R. Schoolcraft, *Archives of Aboriginal Knowledge*, 6 vols. (Philadelphia: J. B. Lippincott, 1868), 253–61.

43. See table 1 in Peter Wood's essay, later in this volume. For a more expansive contemporary estimate made during wartime, see Lachlan McIntosh, Letter to General George Washington, Savannah, April 13, 1777, "The Letter Book of Lachlan McIntosh, 1776–1777," *Georgia Historical Quarterly* 38(1954): 367. McIntosh reports the estimate of 20,000 gunmen for the combined southern tribes. At the usual ratio of five to one, this number of gunmen would imply a total population of 100,000, exclusive of the Caddos west of the Mississippi, estimated at about 5,000 at the time of the American Revolution.

Aboriginal Population Movements in the Early Historic Period Interior Southeast

Marvin T. Smith

Spanish exploration was particularly hard on southeastern Indians. Natives were killed or conscripted for forced labor, stored food supplies were stolen, and new diseases were introduced by the Spanish explorers, particularly Hernando de Soto (1540) and his men. Later English settlers established an organized slave trade using Indian middlemen.[1] The trauma of contact between Indians and Europeans during the sixteenth and seventeenth centuries set in motion complex population movements. Using historical and archaeological data, this brief essay seeks to describe and explain these movements in the interior Southeast. The area to be considered includes the Valley and Ridge and piedmont portions of Alabama, Georgia, Tennessee, and South Carolina, as well as portions of the Appalachian Summit of North Carolina. Chronologically, the period covered here stretches from the mid-sixteenth to the late seventeenth century.

This span of more than 150 years can be divided into three time segments, each with its own sources of data. Population movements that took place during the second half of the sixteenth century can be traced by two methods. Towns located by a reconstruction of the route of Hernando de Soto[2] can be compared with towns visited a generation later by the Juan Pardo[3] and Tristán de Luna[4] expeditions. Other sixteenth-century movements can be demonstrated archaeologically. During the first three-quarters of the seventeenth century, there were virtually no Europeans residing in the study area, and the lack of written records obliges scholars to rely solely on archaeological data in tracking possible population shifts.

Finally, European explorers again penetrated the interior in the late seventeenth century and left us valuable records of population movements. Besides giving firsthand accounts of contemporary shifts, they also reported new locations of towns mentioned by de

Soto and Luna. The sources do not suggest when these moves occurred or whether they took place in gradual stages or as single episodes. However, archaeological data allow us to construct some inferences that can be tested by further archaeological research. Many of the reconstructed population movements presented here should be considered as testable hypotheses to be investigated further.

The baseline knowledge of the location of aboriginal groups in the study area comes from the recent reconstruction of the routes of Hernando de Soto, Tristán de Luna, and Juan Pardo by Charles Hudson and his associates.[5] Population centers include the upper Coosa drainage, the Oconee drainage, the Santee-Wateree drainage, the upper Tennessee River, the Little Tennessee River, the middle Coosa River, the upper Alabama River, and many other areas. Archaeological knowledge suggests many other areas of dense population, among them the lower Tallapoosa valley,[6] the central Chattahoochee,[7] the upper Savannah,[8] and the Appalachian Summit area[9] for a few examples.

The expeditions of Luna and Pardo during the 1560s give us a further glimpse of the interior a few years after the de Soto entrada. Luna and Pardo visited many of the same towns as de Soto. Thus we know that Cofitachequi, Xuala, Chiaha, Coosa, Ulibahali, and probably Apica and Piachi remained in the same locations where de Soto had found them.[10] The Luna expedition also allows us to locate the Napochie villages at the Citico and Audubon Acres sites near Chattanooga, Tennessee (fig. 1). Conspicuously absent, however, are the Tascaloosa towns of the upper Alabama River and the Talisi towns of the middle Coosa. Apparently the Tascaloosa chiefdom collapsed after the battle of Mabila in 1540, perhaps moving down the Alabama River. Archaeological research by Knight and Wilson[11] suggests that the Talisi towns moved away from the Coosa River up Talledaga Creek to such sites as Hightower village.

By the beginning of the seventeenth century, archaeological data demonstrate more radical movements of people (see fig. 2). The Coosa chiefdom abandoned the upper Coosa drainage, moving downriver to the present Lake Weiss area of Alabama and later farther downstream.[12] Similarly, the Mouse Creek towns along the Hiwassee River were abandoned, and I have suggested that these groups moved north to the Tennessee River proper, to such sites as Upper Hampton and De Armond that were occupied during the seventeenth century, based on the presence of diagnostic European

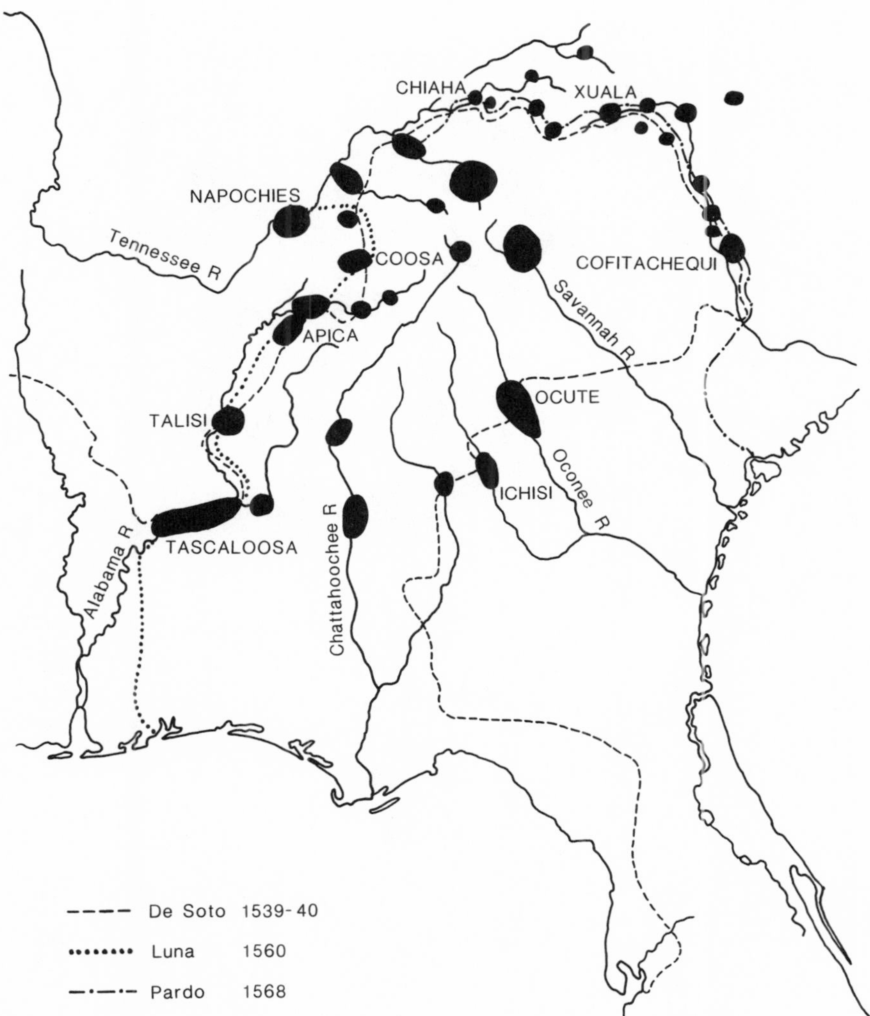

Figure 1 Sixteenth-century populations encountered by Spanish explorers or known through archaeological research.

trade goods.[13] Later these people may have moved south to Hiwassee Island, where there is evidence of mid- to late seventeenth-century burials placed into earlier Woodland period burial mounds, which were constructed in the first millennium A.D.[14]

The Little Tennessee River drainage also underwent demographic changes. The large Citico, McMurray, and Toqua mound sites appear to have been abandoned during the sixteenth century. Probable late sixteenth-century components are known from the Stratton, Brake-

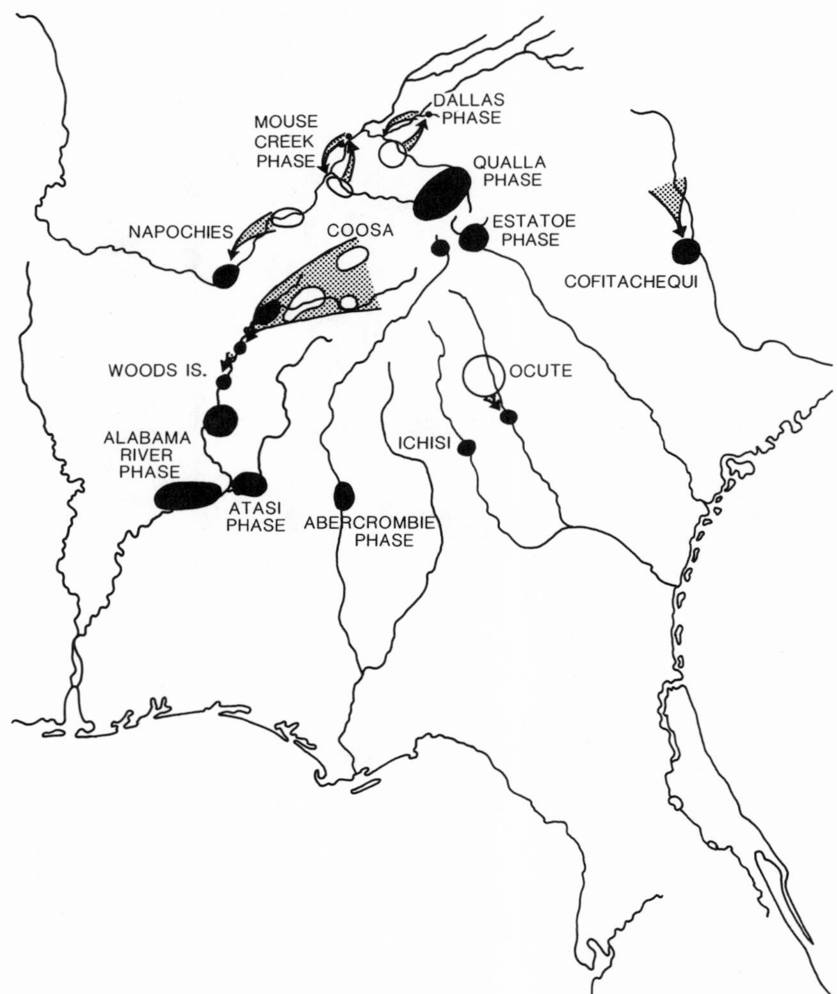

Figure 2 Seventeenth-century population movements from the southern Appalachian region.

bill, and McMahon sites on the Tennessee River proper, perhaps indicating a movement to the main river valley paralleling that hypothesized for the Hiwassee River groups. Early seventeenth-century materials have been reported from the Bussel Island and Tomotley sites on the Little Tennessee and the Post Oak Island site on the Tennessee River proper. That none of these sites contains the quantity of European goods seen on contemporary sites in Alabama may indicate that they were abandoned early in the seventeenth century or that access to European goods proved more difficult in this more northerly region. Late in the seventeenth century there appears to have been a sudden influx of people, based on the abundance of late seventeenth-century European trade material at such sites as Tallassee, Toqua, and Citico. I interpret this influx as a movement of Cherokee-speaking peoples into the valley.[15]

Archaeological evidence from the Chattanooga, Tennessee, area can be interpreted as follows. The Audubon Acres and Citico sites have been identified as two towns of the Napochies attacked by members of the Luna expedition and Coosa warriors in 1560.[16] Archaeological evidence suggests that Audubon Acres was abandoned before about 1575 and that Citico was abandoned shortly thereafter. Major late sixteenth/early seventeenth-century components are present on Williams Island and the Hampton Place site on Moccasin Bend across from Chattanooga,[17] and it seems reasonable to interpret these sites as Napochie towns that had moved north across the Tennessee River to put that barrier between them and the Coosa chiefdom and its apparent Spanish allies to the south. All sites in the Chattanooga area appear to have been abandoned by the mid-seventeenth century, just when several sites in the Guntersville Reservoir area appear to have been first settled. I have therefore suggested that the Napochies moved downstream southwest into Alabama, but this hypothesis needs additional testing.

The Oconee River valley (particularly the Wallace Reservoir area south to the fall line), part of the Ocute chiefdom described in the de Soto narratives, shows some population decline and settlement redistribution but remains occupied into the seventeenth century. Major mound centers all appear to have been abandoned by the beginning of the seventeenth century,[18] and population apparently became dispersed into smaller sites. By approximately 1630, the Wallace Reservoir area of the piedmont appears to have been abandoned. Elsewhere I have suggested that the population of this area moved south, eventually to be recorded in history as Oconee Old Town on the fall line of the river in the early eighteenth century,[19] but again this interpretation is merely a testable hypothesis. It also appears likely that some of the inhabitants moved to the coast, where an Oconee mission is recorded by the mid-seventeenth century.[20] Some of them may have moved to the Chattahoochee River, and it has been suggested that "Ocute" may be ancestral to "Coweta."[21]

Both de Soto and Pardo recorded a thriving population at Cofitachequi on the fall line of the Wateree River near present Camden, South Carolina. Pedro de Torres visited Cofitachequi again in 1628, and it was still important and apparently still in the same location when English explorers reached the area in 1670.[22] All references to Cofitachequi seem to relate to the same location, and archaeological research at the Mulberry site suggests occupation well into the seventeenth century.[23] I strongly suspect, although I do not have the data to demonstrate, that this area received a great population influx from the north during the sixteenth and seventeenth centuries, comparable to that recorded historically for the Tallapoosa valley.

The Tallapoosa valley was not visited by any of the three sixteenth-century Spanish expeditions, but archaeological research demonstrates that this area was a population center in the sixteenth and seventeenth centuries. Both the sixteenth-century Shine II phase and the seventeenth-century Atasi phase[24] sites are known to be concentrated along the lower valley.

The fall line area of the Chattahoochee River was also important throughout the period in question. Resurvey and analysis of the Walter F. George Reservoir[25] have yielded an excellent picture of the population dynamics of the region. Sixteenth-century Bull Creek phase population levels dropped dramatically during the subsequent Abercrombie phase, probably following the introduction of European diseases. By the late seventeenth century, a population recovery is noted. It is not clear whether this is a natural population recovery or simply an influx of other people. The presence of the Taskigis in the area in 1686 suggests that some in-migration occurred.[26]

The fall line area of the Ocmulgee River near present Macon, Georgia, was also an important population center during de Soto's day. Here he found the Province of Ichisi, consisting of several towns, with the capital probably at the Lamar archaeological site.[27] It is suggested that this site continued to be an important location up to the time Chattahoochee River groups moved east to the Ocmulgee in 1690. Three forms of evidence suggest this stability: the presence of late seventeenth-century European trade materials at the site; that the Creek groups of the area were known to the English by the name Ochese Creeks, an obvious corruption of the name Ichisi recorded by the Spaniards; and probable ceramic continuity.[28]

The upper Savannah River valley also appears to have been a major population center during the Mississippi and early historic periods (ca. 1000–1670). Current research[29] indicates that this area may not have been continuously occupied throughout the Lamar period (sixteenth and seventeenth-century Tugalo phase) into the historic eighteenth-century Cherokees (Estatoe phase). There may have been a gap in occupation at the major sites during the seventeenth century. It is not at present known whether the entire region was depopulated or only the major centers were abandoned. The abandonment of mound centers has been documented for other areas of the Southeast during the late sixteenth century.[30]

The Appalachian Summit area of North Carolina appears to have maintained population stability from the prehistoric Qualla phase to the historically documented eighteenth-century Cherokee presence.[31] Changes occurred in settlement pattern and location, but these were relatively minor shifts. In general there was a movement away from the French Broad River westward toward the Little Tennessee. Sites became smaller and more dispersed, but a large population was maintained. These villages became known to history as the Middle Towns of the Cherokees, and their numbers diminished steadily after 1700.

Late in the seventeenth century Europeans began to reenter the area, leaving records of actual movements of people and giving new locations for groups found by sixteenth-century Spanish exploratory expeditions. The slave trade out of Charlestown became an important factor in population movements. Early maps provide much information. These relocations are illustrated in figure 3.

For example, during the late seventeenth century, numerous groups from the north are known to have moved into the lower Coosa and Tallapoosa valleys. In 1675 Bishop Calderón reported that the Tuasis were in this area,[32] whereas their location during the de Soto period was in northeastern Alabama.[33] In 1686 Marcos Delgado reported that several northern groups had moved to the area around the junction of the Coosa and Tallapoosa rivers. For example, inhabitants of Qusate, the Coste of de Soto and Koasati of the eighteenth century, had moved from their sixteenth-century location at the mouth of the Little Tennessee River, fleeing English explorers and warlike Indians.[34] The Alabamas (Aymamu) were also reported to have fled to this area because of warfare. This group can be identified with the Alimamus of the de Soto period, when they had been situated in northern Mississippi. The Alabamas may have been responsible for some or all of the Alabama River phase sites on the

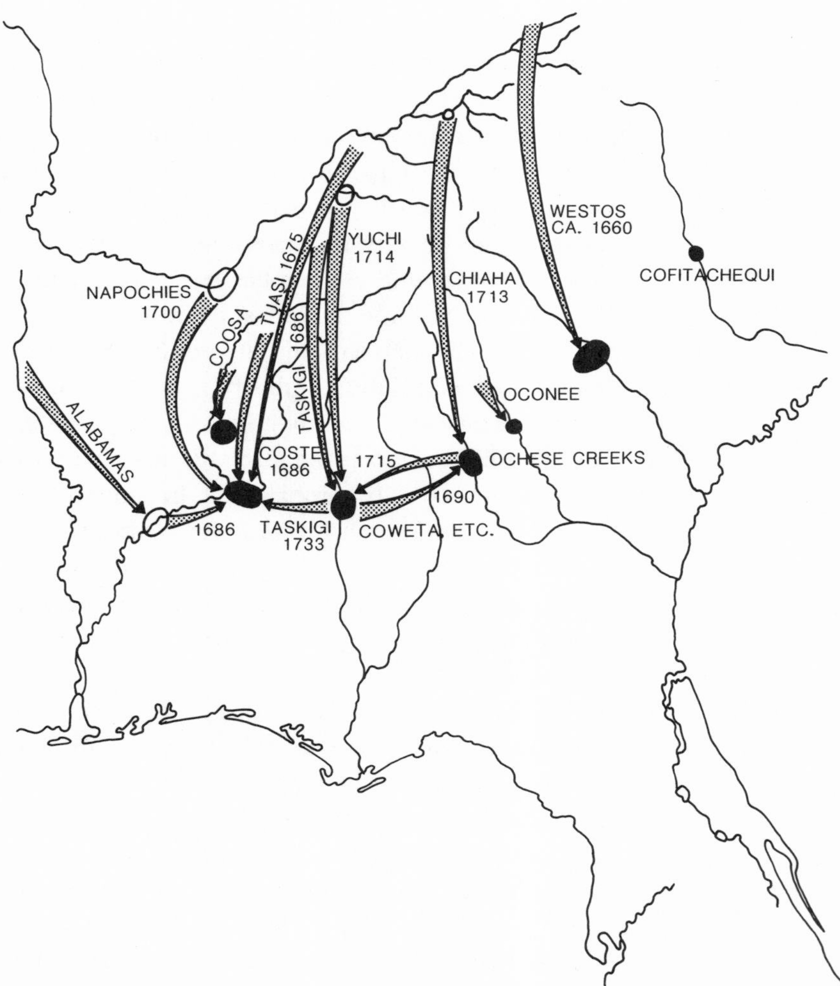

Figure 3 Documented Indian movements after the establishment of the Carolina colony, circa 1675–1715.

Alabama River during the seventeenth century.[35] By 1700 the Napochies were situated in this area (having moved from the Chattanooga area),[36] and by 1733 the Taskigis were also here—long removed from their north Georgia home documented by Pardo in 1568.[37] They did not move directly, however, since they are known to have been on the Chattahoochee River in 1686.[38] It is apparent that this fall line region of Alabama along the lower Coosa and Tallapoosa rivers was an important focal point for population resettlement.

Other seventeenth-century movements were recorded. Problems

with Spanish belligerence and the lure of English trade prompted several towns to abandon the Chattahoochee River area about 1690 to move to the fall line area of the Ocmulgee River near present Macon, Georgia. After the Yamasee War of 1715 these groups, joined by other refugees, moved back to the Chattahoochee.[39]

In 1712 the Yuchis were reported to be situated on the Hiwassee River at the Chestowe site. These may have been the same people who had previously inhabited the Mouse Creek sites and Hiwassee Island. This town was abandoned in 1714[40] when the Yuchis moved to the Chattahoochee River to join the Lower Creeks. Before 1715 Chiaha, whose sixteenth-century location is believed to have been on Zimmerman's Island in eastern Tennessee, was on the fall line of the Ocmulgee, again demonstrating the attraction of this zone.[41]

By the early eighteenth century, Coosas and Abihkas are known to have been situated on the middle reaches of the Coosa River, considerably downstream from their sixteenth-century home in northern Georgia.[42] It has been suggested that this was a gradual movement that took place in several stages.[43]

Several points can be made from these attempts to portray population movements. Warfare, famine, and disease brought about by the de Soto expedition did have effects on population. From the Luna accounts only twenty years later, we know that the powerful chiefdom of Tascaloosa was destroyed, or at least relocated, and the chiefdom of Talisi was also moved or possibly temporarily abandoned. Effects of disease and other disruptive factors seen archaeologically suggest that by the end of the sixteenth century dramatic changes in population centers had taken place. Thus northwestern Georgia, the lower Hiwassee River, and perhaps the Little Tennessee River in Tennessee were abandoned. Dramatic losses of population can be demonstrated for the central Chattahoochee and the central Oconee, where new diseases had an enormous impact.

Archaeological evidence suggests possible areas of migration during the seventeenth century that need to be tested by future research. Groups from northwestern Georgia apparently moved down the Coosa River; Little Tennessee and Hiwassee River groups may have moved to the main Tennessee River valley; the Napochies in the Chattanooga area apparently moved to the north side of the river, then later moved downriver to the southwest; Oconee River groups may have concentrated on the fall line; and Alabama River phase groups reoccupied the upper Alabama River.

By the late seventeenth and early eighteenth centuries, historical documentation is again available. Eastern Tennessee groups now appeared on the fall line area of the Coosa and Tallapoosa rivers. Chattahoochee River and Tennessee groups appeared on the fall-line area of the Ocmulgee River. Groups were appearing on the long-abandoned middle Savannah River near the fall line. The fall line areas of the Wateree River and the Oconee River were documented as important centers, and the fall line of the Chattahoochee River was reoccupied by groups following the Yamasee War of 1715, although it should be noted that it probably was never totally abandoned.

What was the draw of this fall line zone from central Alabama to central South Carolina? Certainly it is an area rich in natural resources suitable for aboriginal farming, hunting, and gathering. These areas of most southeastern rivers had been important population centers throughout the Mississippi period. With decreasing population density brought about by the introduction of European diseases, more groups were able to settle these choice locations. They were also closer to sources of European trade goods, a factor that became important at least as early as the first half of the seventeenth century. Later in the seventeenth century, Indian trails along the fall line became important routes for English traders out of Charlestown, and more aboriginal groups appeared to take advantage of this trade. The fall line was no doubt important in prehistoric trade routes as well.

It is also seems apparent from the writings of Marcos Delgado in 1686 that many northern (mostly eastern Tennessee) groups were moving south to flee English slave raiders and Indians armed with European weapons. Elsewhere I have argued that the fur trade wars of the Northeast set in motion a chain reaction of population movements that pushed other groups farther south.[44] Groups of northern Indians, already armed with firearms, were entering the Southeast before 1670, especially the Westos, who may have been an Erie Iroquois group.[45] These movements of well-armed Indians, some of whom participated in the English slave trade, caused many other population displacements.

Another important point can be made. It seems likely that the natives of areas that were spared direct European contact in the sixteenth century emerged by the beginning of the eighteenth century as the most important and powerful groups. Thus the lower Tallapoosa and Chattahoochee river valleys, bypassed by de Soto and Luna, became the important core areas of the Creek Confederacy—the Upper and Lower Creeks, respectively. These areas are historically documented as having received many refugee groups from farther north. The upper Savannah River was the center for the Lower Cherokee towns, and the Appalachian Summit of North Carolina was the center for the Middle towns of the Cherokees. These groups appear much stronger in eighteenth-century historical records than would have been expected given the simple chiefdoms seen archaeologically for the fifteenth and sixteenth centuries. Major chiefdoms—such as Coosa, Ocute, and Ichisi—documented by de Soto, had virtually disappeared or become relatively minor towns (or groups of towns) in the Creek Confederacy by the eighteenth century. Thus northwestern Georgia and much of eastern Tennessee were depopulated, allowing the movement of Cherokee speakers into the area during the late seventeenth, eighteenth, and nineteenth centuries.

One major exception is Cofitachequi, which apparently maintained its power in spite of repeated visits by Europeans. However, Cofitachequi was already situated on the favored fall line, and I suspect that further research will show that large groups of refugees amalgamated with the Cofitachequi core to maintain its importance. I suspect that the important complex chiefdom of the sixteenth century devolved into basically one town by about 1670. Within a few years the name Cofitachequi disappears from the colonial records, and Catawbas, Esaws, Waterees, and Waxhaws are the recorded inhabitants of the area.

I hope that this brief attempt to describe aboriginal population movements will stimulate further research. Many of the hypothesized population movements described in this chapter require archaeological confirmation. The dramatic population changes that took place following European contact are still poorly known, but they must be understood if we are to unravel the complexities of the contact-period Southeast.

Acknowledgments

This chapter is based on a paper originally delivered at the 1986 Southeastern Archaeological Conference. It has benefited greatly by comments from Charles Hudson, Gregory Waselkov, Vernon Knight,

David Hally, David Anderson, Peter Wood, and Thomas Hatley. I am grateful for their assistance.

Notes

1. J. Leitch Wright, Jr., *The Only Land They Knew* (New York: Free Press, 1981).

2. Charles Hudson, Marvin T. Smith, and Chester DePratter, "The Hernando de Soto Expedition: From Apalachee to Chiaha," *Southeastern Archaeology* 3 (Summer 1984): 65–77; Chester DePratter, Charles Hudson, and Marvin T. Smith, "The De Soto Expedition: From Chiaha to Mabila," in *Alabama and the Borderlands, from Prehistory to Statehood*, ed. Reid Badger and Lawrence Clayton (Tuscaloosa: University of Alabama Press, 1985), 108–27.

3. Chester DePratter, Charles Hudson, and Marvin T. Smith, "The Route of Juan Pardo's Explorations in the Interior Southeast, 1566–1568," *Florida Historical Quarterly* 62 (October 1983): 125–58.

4. Charles Hudson et al., "The Tristan de Luna Expedition, 1559–1561" (paper presented at the Forty-second Annual Southeastern Archaeological Conference, Birmingham, Alabama, November 8, 1985).

5. Hudson, Smith, and DePratter, "De Soto"; DePratter, Hudson, and Smith, "Juan Pardo's Explorations"; DePratter, Hudson, and Smith, "De Soto Expedition"; Marvin T. Smith, *Archaeology of Aboriginal Culture Change in the Interior Southeast: Depopulation during the Early Historic Period* (Gainesville: University Presses of Florida, 1987).

6. Vernon J. Knight, Jr., *Tukabatchee: Archaeological Investigations at an Historic Creek Town, Elmore County, Alabama, 1984*, Report of Investigations 45 (Moundville: University of Alabama, Office of Archaeological Research, 1985); Gregory A. Waselkov, "Lower Tallapoosa River Cultural Resources Survey: Phase 1 Report" (Alabama Historical Commission, Montgomery, 1981).

7. Vernon J. Knight, Jr., and Tim S. Mistovich, *Walter F. George Lake: Archaeological Survey of Fee Owned Lands, Alabama and Georgia*, Report of Investigations 42 (Moundville: University of Alabama, Office of Archaeological Research, 1984).

8. David J. Hally, "The Cherokee Archaeology of Georgia," in *The Conference on Cherokee Prehistory*, ed. David Moore (Swannanoa, N.C.: Warren Wilson College, 1986).

9. Bennie Keel, *Cherokee Archaeology* (Knoxville: University of Tennessee Press, 1976): Roy S. Dickens, Jr., *Cherokee Prehistory* (Knoxville: University of Tennessee Press, 1976); Roy S. Dickens, Jr., "Settlement Patterns in the Appalachian Summit Area: The Pisgah and Qualla Phases," in *Mississippian Settlement Patterns*, ed. Bruce D. Smith (New York: Academic Press, 1978), 115–40.

10. Charles Hudson et al., "Coosa: A Chiefdom in the Sixteenth Century Southeastern United States," *American Antiquity* 50 (October 1985): 723–37.

11. Vernon J. Knight, Jr., Gloria Cole, and Richard Walling, *An Archaeological Reconnaissance of the Coosa and Tallapoosa River Valleys, East Alabama: 1983*, Report of

Investigations 43 (Moundville: University of Alabama, Office of Archaeological Research, 1984); Robert C. Wilson, personal communication, 1986.

12. Marvin T. Smith, "The Coosa Chiefdom: Responses to European Contact" (paper presented at the Fifty-first Annual meeting of the Society for American Archaeology, New Orleans, Louisiana, April 25, 1986).

13. Smith, *Aboriginal Culture Change.*

14. T. M. N. Lewis and Madeline Kneberg, *Hiwassee Island* (Knoxville: University of Tennessee Press, 1946).

15. Smith, *Aboriginal Culture Change.*

16. Marvin T. Smith, "Depopulation and Culture Change in the Early Historic Period Interior Southeast" (Ph.D. diss., University of Florida, 1984); Hudson et al., "Tristan de Luna Expedition."

17. Marvin T. Smith, "The Route of De Soto through Tennessee, Georgia, and Alabama: The evidence from Material Culture," *Early Georgia* 4 (1976): 27–48; Smith, "Depopulation and Culture Change."

18. Marvin T. Smith, *Archaeological Investigations at the Dyar Site, 9Ge5,* Wallace Reservoir Project Contribution 11 (Athens: University of Georgia, Department of Anthropology, 1981); J. Mark Williams, "Archaeological Investigations at Scull Shoals, 9Ge4" (manuscript on file at the Laboratory of Archaeology, University of Georgia, Athens); J. Mark Williams, personal communication, 1986.

19. Smith, "Depopulation and Culture Change."

20. John R. Swanton, *Early History of the Creek Indians and Their Neighbors,* Bureau of American Ethnology Bulletin 73 (Washington, D.C.: Government Printing Office, 1922).

21. Charles Hudson, personal communication, 1987.

22. Swanton, *Creek Indians,* 217–20.

23. Chester DePratter and Chris Judge, "Wateree River: Regional and Temporal Variation in Material Culture" (paper presented at the LAMAR Institute Conference on South Appalachian Mississippian, Macon, Georgia, May 9, 1986).

24. Knight, *Tukabatchee;* Vernon J. Knight, Jr., and Marvin T. Smith, "Big Tallassee: A Contribution to Upper Creek Site Archaeology," *Early Georgia* 8 (1980): 59–74; Waselkov, "Lower Tallapoosa River." The term "phase" is used by archaeologists to describe a group of archaeological sites that have similar material culture, are found in a restricted area, and appear to date to a relatively restricted period (usually about a century or less). This term is used by prehistorians when precise tribal identifications are unknown.

25. Knight and Mistovich, *Walter F. George Lake.*

26. Manuel Serrano y Sanz, *Documentos históricos de la Florida y la Luisiana, siglos XVI al XVIII* (Madrid: Librería General de Victoriano Suárez, 1912), 194.

27. Hudson, Smith, and DePratter, "De Soto."

28. The ceramic continuity was recognized by David Hally, personal communication, 1986.

29. Hally, "Cherokee Archaeology."

30. Smith, "Depopulation and Culture Change."

31. Dickens, "Appalachian Summit."

32. Lucy Wenhold, *A Seventeenth Century Letter of Gabriel Diaz Vara Calderón. Bishop of Cuba, Describing the Indians and Indian Missions of Florida*, Smithsonian Miscellaneous Collections 95, pt. 16 (Washington, D.C.: Government Printing Office, 1936), 1–15.

33. DePratter, Hudson, and Smith, "De Soto Expedition."

34. Mark F. Boyd, "Expedition of Marcos Delgado, 1686," *Florida Historical Quarterly* 16 (July 1937): 26.

35. Craig T. Sheldon, Jr., "The Mississippian–Historic Transition in Central Alabama" (Ph.D. diss., University of Oregon, 1974), 54–65.

36. John Barnwell's map of 1722, illustrated in William P. Cumming, *The Southeast in Early Maps* (Princeton: Princeton University Press, 1958), pl. 48.

37. Smith, *Aboriginal Culture Change*.

38. Knight, *Tukabatchee*, 24; Serrano y Sanz, *Documentos Históricos*, 194.

39. Verner W. Crane, *The Southern Frontier, 1670–1732*, ed. Peter H. Wood (New York: W. W. Norton, 1981).

40. Lewis and Kneberg, *Hiwassee Island*, 14.

41. DePratter, Hudson, and Smith, "De Soto Expedition"; Swanton, *Creek Indians*, 169.

42. Knight, Cole, and Walling, *Archaeological Reconnaissance*.

43. Smith, "Coosa Chiefdom."

44. Smith, "Depopulation and Culture Change"; Smith, *Aboriginal Culture Change*.

45. Crane, *Southern Frontier;* Carol I. Mason, "A Reconsideration of Westo-Yuchi Identification," *American Anthropologist* 65 (December 1963): 1342–46; Smith, "Depopulation and Culture Change."

The Changing Population of the Colonial South: An Overview by Race and Region, 1685–1790

Peter H. Wood

It is hard to fathom the historical and cultural patterns of a region, especially in times of great demographic change, without understanding the basic size and distribution of the whole population. This may be one reason the overall history of the South in the eighteenth century has remained elusive and incomplete for so many generations. Surprisingly, almost no one has ever posed the basic question: How many people lived in the southern geographic region during the century before the formation of the United States? And nobody has tried, even in rough terms, to find the answer to this many-sided problem in any systematic and sustained way. In recent years, with help from others, I have explored numerical changes in the population of southeastern North America in the late colonial period. This chapter presents the picture that emerges from such an extended demographic survey.[1]

My goal has been to seek out and combine population data on Indians, Africans, and Europeans from the late seventeenth century through the late eighteenth century. Specifically, I took 1790, the year of the first federal census, as a final date and, more arbitrarily, 1685 as the starting point. Much of the most dramatic change in the Indian populations of the region had already occurred by that time, as is now well known. But written records covering the preceding century and a half of intermittent foreign intrusion do not touch all parts of the South and are neither frequent nor reliable. By examining the most accessible, and lowest, part of the downward demographic curve among southern Indians, I hoped to assist, indirectly, in the discussion of earlier and less well documented population change. At the same time, I wanted to integrate data concerning Indians with figures for the rapidly changing white and black populations of the region. Only then would it be possible for demographic maps to show for the first time, at least roughly, the actual distribution of people across the South over the course of the eighteenth century. To establish this distribution meaningfully, it proved necessary to divide the region into a set of logical subregions.

I began, therefore, by separating the entire domain east of the Great Plains and south of the Ohio and Potomac rivers into a workable number of distinct subregions. Some of these ten zones might be combined, such as North and South Carolina, while others could be further divided, such as the Choctaw/Chickasaw area. Plausibly, a "Maryland" subregion could be added on the periphery.[2] But as they stand here, each of the ten districts had a geographical, political, or social identity during the colonial era that was separate enough to distinguish it from the rest of the region. Within each broad district the settlements, both Indian and colonial, generally occurred in rather concentrated locales, separated by considerable open space or "hunting land" between different ethnic and economic clusters. These communities were by no means stationary, and occasionally families, villages, or whole groups relocated within the district or migrated from one subregion to another, temporarily or permanently. Only with the largest shifts, as when the Seminoles moved into Florida, have I noted these movements, for they generally had more social and political than demographic significance.

As treated successively in separate sections below and as shown on the accompanying table, the ten subregions include (I) Virginia, (II) North Carolina, and (III) South Carolina—all to the eastern edge of the mountains. Farther south lies (IV) Florida, following the boundary of the present state rather than the shifting borders imposed by eighteenth-century treaties. Touching the Atlantic coast between the Savannah and the St. Mary's rivers but extending inland to include all of modern-day Georgia and Alabama below the Appalachian chain and east of the Tombigbee River is (V) the Creek Confederacy. To its north, (VI) the Cherokee Nation occupies southern Appalachia. Still farther to the west lie (VII) the Choctaw and Chickasaw homelands in Mississippi and (VIII) the rich lowcountry of the greater Mississippi Delta in Louisiana, dominated first by the Natchez and their neighbors, later by the French and the Spanish. At the western edge of the geographic South, stretching to the Balcones Fault, was (IX) the sparsely inhabited trans-Mississippi area of East Texas and Arkansas, and stretching across the north lies (X) the vast interior crescent below the Ohio, frequently traversed by Shawnee Indians and others, that would become West Virginia, trans-Appalachian Kentucky, and Tennessee.

With these convenient boundaries in mind, I then sought out population figures for each area by race—red, white, and black. I used racial categories not only because the numbers that survive were recorded that way, but also because these divisions represent the three interdependent cultural worlds that made up the early South. From the time colonization began, these worlds were not isolated genetically, any more than they were in terms of trade or disease; considerable miscegenation had occurred before 1685, and a great deal more would follow.[3] Since on the surface these simple categories obscure that fact, it is necessary to keep in mind the more complex underlying reality. This is especially important because intervening generations of racist thought and practice in the South have made such interactions difficult for many to accept.[4] Needless to say, the simplified picture below does not single out the numerous offspring of French traders and their Choctaw wives, of Virginia planters and their African workers, or of black men and Indian women enslaved on Carolina plantations, but all these persons are incorporated in the statistics compiled here.

To avoid undue simplification on the one hand and unjustified precision on the other proved no easy matter. Beginning at 1685 and ending at 1790, I divided the period into fifteen-year intervals at 1700, 1715, 1730, 1745, 1760, and 1775. I then set out to determine population estimates for all three races, in all ten subregions, for each of these eight years—240 separate numbers in all. Knowing that credible data for such a regular and detailed grid would not be easily available, I started to dig in official and unofficial sources from the Spanish, French, and English colonies, using for guidance works by John R. Swanton and scores of other researchers, past and present. Eventually I recovered hundreds of figures (only a small portion are cited in this summary) that varied greatly in completeness, precision, and reliability. I discovered that for a variety of reasons—military, economic, religious, and scientific—plausible statistics still exist, or can be extrapolated with varying degrees of accuracy, on each group in every region over four generations.

Table 1 presents this general overview. Completing such a large grid proved rather like doing a crossword puzzle; once I could fill in certain items with confidence, it became more plausible to evaluate

Table 1 Estimated Southern Population by Race and Region, 1685–1790

	1685	1700	1715	1730	1745	1760	1775	1790
I. Virginia (east of the mountains)								
Red	2,900	1,900	1,300	900	600	400	300	200
White	38,100	56,100	74,100	103,300	148,300	196,300	279,500	442,100
Black	2,600	5,500	20,900	49,700	85,300	130,900	186,400	305,500
Total	43,600	63,500	96,300	153,900	234,200	327,600	466,200	747,800
II. North Carolina (east of the mountains)								
Red	10,000	7,200	3,000	2,000	1,500	1,000	500	300
White	5,700	9,400	14,800	27,300	42,700	84,500	156,800	288,200
Black	200	400	1,800	5,500	14,000	28,200	52,300	105,500
Total	15,900	17,000	19,600	34,800	58,200	113,700	209,600	394,000
III. South Carolina (east of the mountains)								
Red	10,000	7,500	5,100	2,000	1,500	1,000	500	300
White	1,400	3,800	5,500	9,800	20,300	38,600	71,600	140,200
Black	500	2,800	8,600	21,600	40,600	57,900	107,300	108,900
Total	11,900	14,100	19,200	33,400	62,400	97,500	179,400	249,400
IV. Florida								
Red	16,000	10,000	3,700	2,800	1,700	700	1,500	2,000
White	1,500	1,500	1,500	1,700	2,100	2,700	1,800	1,400
Black	—	—	—	100	300	500	3,000	500
Total	17,500	11,500	5,200	4,600	4,100	3,900	6,300	3,900
V. Creeks/Georgia/Alabama								
Red	15,000	9,000	10,000	11,000	12,000	13,000	14,000	15,000
White	—	—	—	100	1,400	6,000	18,000	52,900
Black	—	—	—	—	100	3,600	15,000	29,700
Total	15,000	9,000	10,000	11,100	13,500	22,600	47,000	97,600
VI. Cherokees								
Red	32,000	16,000	11,200	10,500	9,000	7,200	8,500	7,500
White	—	—	—	—	—	300	2,000	26,100
Black	—	—	—	—	—	—	200	2,500
Total	32,000	16,000	11,200	10,500	9,000	7,500	10,700	36,100
VII. Choctaws/Chickasaws								
Red	35,000	26,000	20,800	14,300	14,500	14,900	16,300	17,800
White	—	—	—	100	100	100	100	500
Black	—	—	—	—	—	—	—	300
Total	35,000	26,000	20,800	14,400	14,600	15,000	16,400	18,600

Continued

Table 1 *Continued*

	1685	1700	1715	1730	1745	1760	1775	1790
VIII. Natchez/Louisiana								
Red	42,000	27,000	15,000	8,000	5,000	3,600	3,700	4,000
White	—	100	300	1,700	3,900	4.000	10,900	19,400
Black	—	—	100	3,600	4,100	5,300	9,600	23,200
Total	42,000	27,100	15,400	13,300	13,000	12,900	24,200	46,600
IX. East Texas								
Red	28,000	21,000	17,000	14,000	12,000	10,000	8,300	7,000
White	200	—	300	600	900	1,200	1,500	1,800
Black	—	—	—	100	200	300	600	600
Total	28,200	21,000	17,300	14,700	13,100	11,500	10,400	9,400
X. Shawnee Interior								
Red	8,500	5,000	3,000	1,200	1,500	1,800	2,000	1,800
White	—	—	—	—	—	—	300	67,000
Black	—	—	—	—	—	—	—	13,800
Total	8,500	5,000	3,000	1,200	1,500	1,800	2,300	82,600
Totals for Areas I–X								
Red	199,400	130,600	90,100	66,700	59,300	53,600	55,600	55,900
White	46,900	70,900	96,500	144,600	219,700	333,700	542,500	1,039,600
Black	3,300	8,700	31,400	80,600	144,600	226,700	374,400	590,500
Total	249,600	210,200	218,000	291,900	423,600	614,000	972,500	1,686,000

differing evidence for the empty squares. Missing numbers between two known numbers could be projected. Divergent contemporary estimates could be weighed against established figures. Obvious mistakes, involving some clerical error or wild guess in the past, could be discarded. In reconciling conflicting estimates, I have tried to steer an informed middle course, but given the intricacy of the topic and the condensed nature of this survey, numerous adjustments remain ahead. Even more than most historical statistics, these population figures will continue to demand revision and to invite interpretation.

Both the geographical and the racial boundaries employed are by definition indistinct. Moreover, the separate numbers used here vary in accuracy from precise firsthand head counts to rough secondhand "guesstimates." So all primary-source figures, including those given down to the last significant digit, have been rounded off to the nearest hundred. Even that suggests much more precision than the records actually allow in many cases, for the statistical quilt presented here has been stitched together from hundreds of scraps of partial and conflicting evidence, few of which conformed neatly to the geographic, racial, and chronological lines laid out in table 1. Inevitably, therefore, this new quilt contains distortions owing to the inaccuracies of certain original records or of my own calculations and projections for any one group in any one year. But these are more than counterbalanced, I hope, by the opportunity to obtain a fresh overview of the demography of the entire region during a crucial transitional century.

I. Virginia

The Native American population of coastal and piedmont Virginia during the late colonial period consisted of small communities of Indian "tributaries," living on assigned lands and paying annual tribute to the local English government. They had been reduced to little more than reservation status by the early and extensive colonial invasion of the Chesapeake tidewater region. Though not so old as Spanish Florida, Virginia had become the first successful settler colony in the South, owing to Europe's infatuation with American tobacco. By 1685 more than 38,000 whites and roughly 2,600 blacks already lived in coastal Virginia. Though small compared with English colonies farther north that had grown more quickly, the Virginia settlement was by far the largest contingent of non-Indians in the seventeenth-century South. As this population base finally became more stable and healthy, its size began to increase rapidly through new births, longer lives, and increased migration. With the expanding slave trade, the number of blacks grew even faster than the figure for whites. Although Afro-Americans made up less than a quarter of Virginia's population in 1715, by 1760 they made up 40 percent. By 1790, only Virginia and the two Carolinas among the South's ten subregions contained 250,000 persons or more, and Virginia—with nearly 750,000—was almost twice as populous as North Carolina and three times more than South Carolina.

Within Virginia's expansive tobacco society, the recognizable Indian presence became small indeed. As the pressure for farmland intensified, colonial warfare destroyed some native inhabitants and forced others to flee. The Occaneechees, for example, who resided on an island in the Roanoke River, suffered heavy losses during Bacon's Rebellion in 1676 and withdrew south to the Eno River in North Carolina. Moreover, in Virginia, as in the later coastal colonies, innumerable individuals found themselves absorbed into the ranks of enslaved blacks and free whites, where their original racial and cultural identity often became obscured within several generations.[5] In 1669 the Virginia Assembly had listed eighteen groups of "Indian tributaries" that were to deliver so many wolves' heads annually in exchange for the right to remain in the region under colonial protection. Together they had 725 "bowmen," according to authorities. James Mooney accepted a ratio of four to one between total population and warriors among southern Indians near the Atlantic coast, and recent archaeological evidence seems to confirm this ratio, so we can estimate a Virginia Indian population of 2,900 in 1669. Several groups seem to have been missed, but their numbers would be roughly offset by the attrition of the next sixteen years, so we can put the Virginia Indian population of 1685 at 2,900 as well.[6]

Though the rate of decline over the next century varied from group to group and decade to decade, the overall reduction amounted to roughly one-third of the existing Indian population every fifteen years. Prominent colonial authors recorded this demise. "The Indians of Virginia are almost wasted," wrote Robert Beverley at the start of the eighteenth century. He listed "such Towns, or People as retain their Names, and live in Bodies," but he estimated that all these communities "together can't raise five hundred fighting men. They live poorly," he added, "and much in fear of neighboring Indians." At most, therefore, they must have totaled fewer than 2,000 in 1700, and a sampling of Beverley's comments upon individual towns makes clear their steadily declining condition:

—*Matomkin* is much decreased of late by the Small Pox, that was carried thither.

—*Gingoteque*. The few remains of this Town are joyn'd with a Nation of the *Maryland Indians*.

—*Kiequotank*, is reduc'd to very few Men.

—*Matchopungo*, has a small number yet living. . . .

—*Chiconessex*, has very few, who just keep the name. . . .

—*Wyanoke*, is almost wasted, and now gone to live among other *Indians*. . . .

—*Appamattox*. These Live in Collonel *Byrd*'s Pasture, not being above seven Families. . . .

—*Rappahannock*, is reduc'd to a few Families, and live scatter'd upon the *English* Seats. . . .

—*Wiccocomoco*, has but three men living, which yet keep up their Kingdom, and retain their Fashion; they live by themselves, separate from all other *Indians*, and from the *English*.[7]

Even those groups that prospered for a generation or two and gained from the attrition of their neighbors could not endure indefinitely. About 1700 Beverley said that the Nottoways (listed in 1669 as including ninety bowmen in two towns) "are about a hundred Bow men, of late a thriving and increasing People." But by 1764 a report of the Indian Superintendent for the South added Virginia's Nottoway and Sapony groups together for a total of "60 gun-men."[8] In his *Notes on the State of Virginia*, written at the end of the Revolutionary War and published in 1787, Thomas Jefferson recorded, "Of the *Nottoways*, not a male is left. A few women constitute the remains of that tribe." According to Jefferson, the Mattaponys and the Pamunkeys (who had had twenty and fifty hunters, respectively, in the statute of 1669) each absorbed remnants of the Chickahominys early in the eighteenth century. But by the 1780s, Jefferson stated:

> There remain of the *Mattaponies* three or four men only, and have more negro than Indian blood in them. They have lost their language, have reduced themselves, by voluntary sales, to about fifty acres of land, which lie on the river of their own name, and have from time to time, been joining the Pamunkies, from whom they are distant but ten miles. The *Pamunkies* are reduced to about ten or twelve men, tolerably pure from mixture with other colors. The older ones among them preserve their language in a small degree, which are the last vestiges on earth, as far as we know, of the Powhatan language. They have about three hundred acres of very fertile land on Pamunkey River.[9]

Hence, if identifiable Indians living apart from the Virginia settlers included no more than 2,000 at the start of the century, they probably numbered fewer than 200 by 1790. Nowhere else in the South had the native population been reduced so low, in either relative or absolute terms. By this time President Washington, grown wealthy upon lands once occupied by native Virginians, was concerned with suppressing Indians farther west: the strong alliance in the Ohio valley and the so-called Chickamaugas in south-central Tennessee, under the leadership of Dragging Canoe. Meanwhile Washington's secretary of state, the fellow planter from Monticello, had plunged into the debate about Indian origins and undertaken some of the first systematic excavations of Indian remains. Elsewhere in the South such abstract speculation and research would gain ground in the following century, after procedures for destruction and removal of Indian people became sanctioned elements of state and federal policy.

II. North Carolina

In contrast to Virginia, with its enormous bay and accessible rivers, North Carolina was protected from overseas colonization by the treacherous Outer Banks and the lack of suitable harbors. Separate contacts during the sixteenth century by the French (Verrazzano), the Spanish (de Soto and Pardo), and the English (Barlowe and White) had introduced foreign goods and diseases into the region, but lasting colonization did not occur until the second half of the seventeenth century, as land-hungry English settlers pushed south from the Chesapeake tidewater into the region of Albemarle Sound. The dynamics experienced by Powhatan's Virginia in the seventeenth century of a foreign influx, a strong and protracted resistance from the dominant Indians near the coast, and an eventual decline and dispersal of the native population would recur farther south in the early eighteenth century.

In 1586 English colonists at Roanoke Island had heard about the powerful Tuscaroras, a large Iroquoian-speaking group living to the west, between the Roanoke and Neuse rivers. The smaller Algonquian-speaking tribes along the coast referred to these rivals as the Rattlesnakes ("Mangoak"), "whose name and multitude besides their valor is terrible to all the rest of the provinces." During the ensuing generations the Tuscaroras extended their power through war and trade, so that the English who settled at Jamestown heard stories of a chief to the south who was "a greater weroance" than Powhatan. Dealing first with the Spanish and later with the English, the Tuscaroras established themselves as effective middlemen, occasionally carrying European goods as far as the Mississippi during the seventeenth century. In the 1660s and 1670s, they tolerated the movement of several thousand whites and a few hundred blacks into the area north of Albemarle Sound and east of the Chowan River, taking advantage of trade possibilities while preventing any further advance. In 1683 Lord Culpeper put the Tuscarora population at between 6,000 and 8,000 persons. Several thousand more Indians were dispersed nearer the coast in more than a dozen small groups, some of which had moved southward from the Chesapeake.[10]

Considering the Cape Fear and Catawba Indians with South Carolina and regarding the Cherokees in the mountains as inhabitants of a separate geographic region, the Indian population of North Carolina's piedmont and coastal plain must have come to roughly 10,000 persons in 1685, nearly twice the non-Indian population. But this ratio was shifting rapidly. In England in 1689, the proprietors of Carolina named a separate governor for the region stretching from Albemarle to Cape Fear, marking the beginnings of North Carolina as a distinct colonial entity, and migration from the north continued. When an epidemic devastated the Pamlico Indians in 1695, white settlers moved south to occupy the peninsula between Albemarle Sound and the Pamlico River. Modern estimates that this colonial population had reached 10,000 by 1700 may be somewhat too high, and the contemporary enumeration of Indian residents by John Lawson may have been too low, but by the start of the eighteenth century white and black newcomers probably outnumbered native inhabitants for the first time.[11]

John Lawson explored North Carolina soon after 1700, and his description of the region published in London in 1709 included a detailed account of the local Indian tribes and a summary of their numbers in terms of "Fighting Men." For the dominant Tuscaroras he named fifteen villages with a total of 1,200 men. Their neighbors included three smaller Iroquoian tribes: the Meherrins to the north, with 50 men in a town along the Meherrin River, and the Neusiocs and Corees to the south, with a total of 40 men in four villages on the Neuse River and Core Sound. Just south of the Tuscaroras a Siouan tribe, the Woccons, had two villages with 120 fighting men. Farther east, a series of small Algonquian-language tribes lined the coast from north to south, each reduced to a single village. North of Albemarle Sound lived the Chowanocs, Pasquotanks, and Poteskeets, with a total of 55 fighting men (plus the surviving Yeopims with only 6 persons in all). Below the sound lived the Pamlico, Hatteras, Matchapunga, and Bay, or Bear, River tribes, with a total of 111 fighting men. Lawson noted one village of Nottoway Indians from

Virginia, with 30 men, and added that "five Nations of the *Totero's, Sapona's, Keiauwee's, Aconechos,* and Schoccories, are lately come amongst us, and may contain, in all, about 750 Men, Women and Children."[12]

From this summary, Lawson put the total Indian population soon after the turn of the century at 4,780, but this estimate may be low on several counts. First of all, in dealing with the dominant Tuscaroras, Lawson's list of fifteen towns omits half a dozen in the north that show up several years later in other documents, so it appears, according to the best recent study, "that he underestimated Tuscarora strength." He also underestimated all the Indian women and children by guessing that they "probably" numbered three for every two fighting men, whereas it is likely that they made up about 75 percent, rather than 60 percent, of every village. In addition, Lawson seems to have reached his totals "not including Old Men." Perhaps he minimized Indian numbers because his book was intended to promote further migration from Europe. Or perhaps he simply wished to emphasize their drastic decline within two generations. "The Small-Pox and Rum have made such a Destruction amongst them," he wrote, "that, on good grounds, I do believe, there is not the sixth Savage living within two hundred Miles of all our Settlements, as there were fifty Years ago. These poor Creatures have so many Enemies to destroy them, that it's a wonder one of them is left alive near us."[13]

As was often the case elsewhere, such devastation helped prompt a desperate anticolonial war. Smallpox was spreading among the Tuscaroras by 1707, perhaps for the first time, and over the next few years, according to a later account, it "destroyed most of those Savages that were seized with it." When southern Tuscarora villages attacked the Pamlico settlers in 1711, colonial forces struck back with aid from their South Carolina neighbors. South Carolinians, eager to obtain Indian slaves and eyeing the prospect of plantations in the Cape Fear region, sent expeditions that made heavy use of Yamasee and Cherokee allies. By 1713 they had crushed the Tuscaroras, killing some 1,400 in battle and enslaving nearly 1,000 more. In 1717 the survivors were removed to a reservation on the north bank of the Roanoke River, and many abandoned North Carolina altogether, moving north to affirm their links to the Iroquois League. By 1715, therefore, the area's Indian population was scarcely 3,000, and a generation later it appeared little more than half that. "The Indians in North Carolina that live near the Planters, are few," John Brickell reported in the 1730s, "not exceeding *Fifteen* or *Sixteen* hundred Men, Women and Children, and those in good harmony with the *English*, with whom they constantly trade."[14]

By then the region's non-Indian population, according to the slightly optimistic estimate of Governor Burrington in 1732, had reached 30,000 whites and 6,000 blacks, and not all of the latter were consigned to slavery. "It is clear," William Byrd wrote in 1728, that "many Slaves Shelter themselves in this Obscure part of the World, nor will any of their righteous Neighbors discover them." As plantation agriculture expanded over the next half-century, particularly near the coast, the proportion of blacks to whites in North Carolina increased somewhat, but the rapid migration of white farmers from England and Scotland, Virginia and Pennsylvania kept the white population two or three times as large as the black. The transition of the native hunting lands and "old fields" into colonial farms, whether slave or free, ensured that North Carolina's unassimilated Indians would fall to statistical insignificance, probably fewer than 400 persons in a total population east of the mountains that was rapidly approaching 400,000 by 1790.[15]

III. South Carolina

The colony of South Carolina evolved rather differently from its sister province to the north. Significantly, the Sea Islands provided protection from ocean storms without hindering transatlantic shipping. Indeed, the harbor formed by the convergence of the Ashley and Cooper rivers provided the best Atlantic port south of Chesapeake Bay, and within a decade of their arrival in 1670, English settlers had begun to lay out the village of Charlestown on the peninsula between the two rivers. By 1685 there were almost 1,400 whites and nearly 500 blacks in the area, and fifteen years later, as would-be planters continued to arrive from overcrowded Barbados with their slaves, whites numbered roughly 3,800 and blacks 2,800. By 1700 it was becoming clear that with sufficient labor rice could be grown commercially in the lowcountry's freshwater swamps. Whites who initially made money by raising cattle and pigs in the woods and selling the meat to the West Indies could now invest their profits in workers to grow rice.

Some of the initial laborers were Indians captured in tribal wars or on deliberate slaving raids. Between 1703 and 1708, the number of Indian slaves in the English colony (not to be confused with the total number of Indians in the South Carolina region) jumped from 350 to 1,400, while the white population rose by less than 300, from 3,800 to 4,080. But the regional supply of enslaved Indians could not keep up with escalating demand for unfree labor, and besides, colonial aggression was creating diplomatic and strategic problems on the frontier. Africans, on the other hand, could be obtained in great numbers without local repercussions, especially since the monopoly of England's Royal African Company had given way to "independent" trade. Unlike indentured servants from Europe, West Africans and their offspring could be exploited in perpetuity, with little chance of escape. Moreover, they were less vulnerable to malaria than the Europeans, and many of them already had a valuable familiarity with rice cultivation. In the same five-year span before 1708, the enslaved black population rose from 3,000 to 4,100. Since men outnumbered women among the black newcomers and women exceeded men among the Indian slaves, miscegenation between these two races produced a considerable mixed-blood population. But in succeeding generations these "mustees" were, for the most part, absorbed back into the rapidly expanding Afro-American slave community, while the number of discernable Indian slaves—never more than a few thousand—gradually declined.[16]

By 1715 blacks in the colony numbered 8,600 and exceeded whites by more than 3,000. By 1730 (with the smaller ports of Georgetown and Port Royal now actively buying slaves via Charlestown and shipping back produce in return) the ratio had grown to more than two to one, and the sizable black majority continued in South Carolina through the American Revolution. In 1775 there were twice as many blacks in South Carolina as in North Carolina (107,300 to 52,300) and fewer than half as many whites (71,600 to 156,800). Over the next fifteen years the number of black South Carolinians increased very little. War interrupted the trade from Africa; rich loyalists emigrated with their slaves; and adventuresome planters began transporting human property to the Georgia frontier. The census of 1790 showed 107,094 slaves in South Carolina, along with 1,801 free blacks, bringing the total recorded Afro-American population to 108,895. In contrast, the white population had virtually doubled since Independence, reaching 140,178 according to the 1790 census. Most of these newcomers had arrived from farther north, taking up land in the backcountry once controlled by Indians. But as had been true for more than a century, South Carolina's total white population still did not equal half that of its northern neighbor.[17]

Despite the contrasts in their non-Indian populations during the eighteenth century, the demographic histories of the Indian occupants in the two Carolinas have much in common. As in North Carolina, the small tribes near the South Carolina coast were decimated within several generations after foreign colonization. An exhaustive recent study by Gene Waddell has reconstructed this demise in unique detail. Already reduced by sickness and slave raiding during the era of Spanish dominance, they numbered scarcely 1,000 by 1685. In 1686, St. Helena and Edisto Indians in the vicinity of Port Royal died during a Spanish raid on the colony. Sometime during the next decade a party of Sewee Indians put out to sea in canoes, hoping to avoid colonial middlemen by establishing direct contact with England somewhere beyond the horizon; most drowned in a storm and others were taken up by an English ship and sold into slavery in the Caribbean.[18] But as usual, disease caused the greatest destruction. Afra Coming probably referred to the Wando tribe northeast of Charlestown when she wrote in 1699 that smallpox was "said to have swept away a whole neighboring nation, all to 5 or 6 which ran away and left their dead unburied, lying on the ground for the vultures to devouer." In the righteous words of Governor Archdale, "the Hand of God was eminently seen in Thining the Indians, to make room for the English."[19]

Numbering perhaps 800 at the outbreak of the Yamasee War in 1715, most of these coastal Indians sided with the colonists and suffered because of it. The Wimbee, Combahee, Kussah, and Ashepoo tribes (all of whom resided south of Edisto Island in the Port Royal area, where the warfare was most intense) never appear again in the records, and the groups that survived were now so dependent as to be called "Indians residing within the Settlement." By 1730 they numbered scarcely 500 in all, and the St. Helena, Edisto, Kiawah and Kussoe tribes are last mentioned in 1743. An Anglican minister in St. Paul's Parish west of Charlestown, where the Kussoes resided, reported in that year that they numbered "about 65 Men Women and Children in all; though formerly they consisted of about 1000, as they say." By 1751 only the Etiwans appear by name in English records, and by 1760 the coastal survivors numbered 250 or fewer, though some still held together in groups. "There are among our Settlements several small Tribes of *Indians*, consisting only of some few Families each," reported Governor Glen in 1761.[20]

Groups that resided to the north or farther inland fared only slightly better, as can be seen from a list prepared at the beginning of 1715 to document the "Strength of all the Indian Nations that were subject to the Government of South Carolina, and solely traded with them." This "Exact Account" listed more than half a dozen Siouan tribes of various sizes living north of Charlestown. Some 57 Sewees survived following the effort to cross the Atlantic; 106 Winyahs remained after a generation of slaving raids. The Santee and Congaree tribes, situated in three towns near the fall line on the Santee River, numbered only 125 persons together, while the Cape Fears totaled 206 people in five small towns near the Cape Fear River. Two larger groups had recently moved southward as a result of disruptions farther north. The Saras, or Cheraws, who had earlier moved north to the Dan River to avoid the Spanish, now inhabited a single large town of 510 near the Pedee River. The Waccomassees, or Waccamaws, totaling 610 persons in four villages, were new arrivals who—several years earlier as the Woccon Indians—had been neighbors of the Tuscaroras.[21]

This census had scarcely been compiled before a new conflict erupted in April 1715. Just as the Tuscaroras, linked to the Iroquois, lost a desperate war in North Carolina and then eventually withdrew to the north, so the Yamasees, tied to the Creeks, launched a major campaign against South Carolina. When they failed, just barely, in their efforts to dislodge the English and African newcomers, they removed to the south and took up residence near the Spanish in Florida, but the struggle changed the face of South Carolina. In June 1715, for example, a combined force of Siouan warriors raided plantation outposts and captured the colonial garrison on the Santee River, but the English launched an immediate counterattack, taking slaves where possible, and gradually regained the upper hand. By the end of 1716 a Charlestown official could report of the "Northward Indians" that "several Slaughters and Blood Sheddings" had "lessened their numbers and utterly Extirpated some little tribes as the Congarees, Santees, Seawees," and others.[22] But the largest of these Siouan tribes remained intact, and for the rest of the eighteenth century by far the most numerous native group between the edge of the Cherokee hunting domain and the Atlantic coast would be the Catawba Indians.

Adair's assertion that the Catawbas had "mustered fifteen hundred fighting men" when South Carolina "was in its infancy" seems well founded, for in 1682 the English had estimated Catawba warriors at 1,500—"or about 4,600 souls," according to Swanton's extrapolation.[23] The "Exact Account" of 1715 put their population at only 1,470, with 570 men in seven villages. But the dislocations of the Yamasee War added to their total, so that two years later on a visit to Charlestown "the Catawba Chief King" could claim 700 gunmen.[24] This unique piedmont nation was centered on a nucleus of towns near the confluence of Sugar Creek and the Catawba River. These villages, 200 miles north-northwest of Charlestown, had their own "eastern Siouan" language. But they were joined over time by a score of smaller groups drawn from all directions, the remnants of other tribes, who spoke a variety of languages and took up residence nearby.

To foster trade with this considerable nation, Carolina arranged in 1717 "for a garrison to be built at Congarees," near the site of modern Columbia. For several years Congaree Fort served as a government trading post, securing the northern trail between Charlestown and the Cherokees and guarding the fork where the path to the Catawbas (now U.S. 21) branched off to the north.[25] When he surveyed the Catawbas' homeland a decade later, Virginian William Byrd took note of their antagonisms with the Tuscaroras and the other members of the Iroquois Confederacy, saying the Catawbas had formerly been "a very Numerous Powerful People. But the frequent Slaughters made upon them by the Northern Indians, and, what has been still more destructive by far, the Intemperence and Foul Distempers introduc'd amongst them by the Carolina Traders, have now reduc'd their Numbers to little More than 400 Fighting Men, besides Women and Children."[26] According to James Adair, "About the year 1743, their nation consisted of almost 400 warriors, of above twenty different dialects."[27]

Catawba numbers continued to decline, and by midcentury a debate, sparked by the Cheraw desire to withdraw and relocate, led to bloodshed. Outbreaks of smallpox, one in 1738 and another in 1760, added to the destruction. Noting their "bitter war" with the Iroquois League since "time immemorial," James Adair wrote before the Revolution that "the Katahba are now reduced to very few above one hundred fighting men—the smallpox, and intemperate drinking, have contributed however more than their wars to their great decay."[28] But he noted that unlike other coastal and piedmont tribes that had suffered even greater decimation, the Catawbas still maintained a distinct territory of their own, "bounded on the north and north-east, by North-Carolina—on the east and south, by South-Carolina—and about west-south-west by the Cheerake nation."[29] During the Revolution the Catawbas remained loyal to the Patriot cause, providing men at Fort Moultrie in 1776 and Guilford Court House in 1781. Yet their land base and their population continued to diminish, and by the 1790s whites claimed the Catawbas once had been "numerous but were now a very small and despised nation" of several hundred inhabitants.[30]

Overall, the sharp decline in the Indian population of coastal and piedmont South Carolina since the late 1600s had run a course comparable to that of North Carolina, though no doubt less similar than indicated by the rounded estimates of table 1. In the northern district the impact of the Tuscarora War preceded 1715, and to the south the disruptions of the Yamasee conflict came several years later. But in each of these similar and adjoining regions the number of Indian inhabitants dropped from at least 10,000 to only a few hundred in the course of a century.

IV. Florida

Closest to the Caribbean, Florida became the first portion of North America to be invaded by the Spanish, beginning in 1513. During the initial five or six generations of contact with slave raiders, European viruses, and Christian missionaries, Florida's native population declined enormously. The most recent study of this decline, by Henry Dobyns, is also the most expansive in estimating its horrendous scope. But even if one modifies Dobyns's upper-limit calculations, a more conservative reading of the evidence still suggests that during the first 170 years after Spanish arrival, Florida's population may have fallen by a factor of ten, from several hundred thousand to fewer than 20,000. The debate sparked by Dobyns's projections belongs, of course, to the larger controversy over the size of America's entire pre-Columbian population and over the causes, timing, and extent of its subsequent decline. Regardless of where that broader argument may lead, no one disputes that in the Southeast Florida sustained the earliest severe losses owing to the arrival of outsiders.[31]

The seventeenth century marked the height of Spanish missionary activity in northern Florida, but death outstripped conversions. A letter of February 2, 1635, claimed 30,000 Christian Indians associated with forty-four missions, but within forty years this number would be only half as great. In October 1655 Governor Rebelledo described "a high mortality rate" in Timucua province as a result of a "series of small-pox plagues which have affected the country for the last ten months . . . and of the trials and hunger which these unfortunate people have suffered." These conditions brought on a major rebellion in Timucua the following year that Rebelledo brutally suppressed, compounding the destruction. In 1657 he reported that Timucua and the province of Guale farther north had been annihilated—"wiped out with the sickness of the plague and small-pox which has overtaken them in the past years."[32]

Two decades later, in 1675, Bishop Calderón of Cuba made a lengthy expedition through the region. He asserted that nearly all of the surviving Indians of northern Florida had been nominally Christianized, but they now totaled scarcely 13,000 in all. Along the Atlantic coast north of St. Augustine, the province of Guale had eight missions, and just west of St. Augustine the smaller province of Timucua included eleven missions. Farther west the Apalaches, with a population of about 6,000 people, inhabited thirteen missions. In the northwestern province of Apalachicola, Calderón reported that the 130 residents in two Chatot villages near Pensacola Bay had received baptism in 1674, and the bishop himself claimed to have "converted to our holy faith" several leaders of the neighboring Lower Creeks, setting up a mission at their southernmost town of Sabacola el Menor. In all, Bishop Calderón reported 13,152 Christian Indians in these four provinces, an inclusive census that appears to some scholars to represent an actual enumeration.[33] Since the Spanish presence in north Florida at this time totaled 1,500 at most, primarily in the vicinity of St. Augustine, these priests and soldiers were outnumbered nearly ten to one by their native allies.[34]

Estimating the population for 1685, we can assume that those not counted in 1675 offset those lost in the intervening decade. And while roughly 13,000 Indians remained in northern Florida, another several thousand persons inhabited the coastlines of the peninsula farther south. Less familiar to the Spanish, they constituted more than a dozen small nonagricultural tribes, such as the Ais and the Tequestas along the Atlantic coast. In 1675 Bishop Calderón had characterized these coastal groups as "savage heathen Carib Indians, in camps, having no fixed abodes, living only on fish and roots of trees." Both culturally and numerically, the dominant group in South Florida remained the once-powerful Calusas, living between Lake Okeechobee and the Gulf of Mexico. A report from an expedition through five Calusa villages in 1680 counted 960 persons, representing a persons/town ratio of 192:1. Since they had other villages as well, the Calusas still numbered more than 1,000, but all the inhabitants of southern Florida probably constituted no more than 3,000 persons. This would bring the total Florida Indian population in 1685 to roughly 16,000 persons.[35]

Though documentation is scarce, that population clearly continued to drop. According to William Sturtevant, another "period of depopulation—perhaps better called disintegration and annihilation—begins about 1680," as slave-seeking Englishmen start trading guns to their Indian allies. For southern Florida, we can apply a crude average rate of decline of 500 persons every fifteen years. Before 1715, raiders from Carolina had probably reduced the Calusas and their neighbors to 2,000, including refugees from the north, and thirty years later the number was perhaps half that. In 1763, about eighty Calusa families evacuated Florida with the Spanish, and remnants of the southernmost tribes were seeking refuge on the Florida Keys from the Lower Creek newcomers who became known as Seminoles.[36]

In northern Florida, where native inhabitants had allied with the Spanish, the latest round of devastation arrived abruptly and can be closely documented. After a Spanish effort to dislodge the English from Charlestown failed in 1686, the Guale Indians withdrew southward from their exposed mission towns on the Georgia coast, taking up residence below the St. Mary's River by 1692. Between 1702 and 1713, during the War of the Spanish Succession, repeated assaults by Englishmen from Carolina and their Indian allies destroyed almost all of northern Florida's remaining Indian missions. These raids, mounted to disrupt the Spanish borderland and obtain profitable slaves, forced Indian survivors in the Timucua and Apalache provinces to take permanent refuge near St. Augustine. The largest attack, a brutal thrust into western Florida by the English and their

Creek allies in 1704, resulted in death for hundreds of Apalache Indians and enslavement for hundreds more. To avoid slavery, another 1,300 agreed to resettle near the English (at the falls of the Savannah River); 400 more sought protection near the French at Mobile Bay; while another 100 formed a new town near Pensacola. A Spanish report claimed that by 1705 Carolina forces had destroyed thirty-two Indian towns in all.[37]

And the devastation continued. Thomas Nairne, at the center of Carolina's aggressive policy, could boast in 1709 that "the garrison of Saint Augustine is by this warr reduced to the bare walls, their castle and Indian towns all consumed either by us in our invasion of that place or by the Indian subjects since who in quest of booty are now obliged to goe down as far as the point of Florida as the firm land will permitt." The Indian raiding parties, Nairne concluded, "have drove the Floridians to the islands of the Cape, have brought in and sold many hundreds of them and daily now continue that trade." When these same Yamasee and Lower Creek raiders turned against the English in 1715, the Spanish sought to claim them as allies, and the Indian population of northern Florida was slightly renewed by the dislocations of the Yamasee War. A census of the ten remaining missions near St. Augustine in 1717 counted 1,591 Indians, including Apalache, Timucua, and Yamasee refugees. But even this number, plus the 100 Apalaches at Pensacola, suggests a total of fewer than 1,700 Indians in northern Florida, a drop of 87 percent in thirty years. They scarcely outnumbered the Spanish, who had added a small garrison at Pensacola in 1699 and who continued to average roughly 1,500 inhabitants (though the main population center at St. Augustine may have been slightly reduced.)[38]

During the next generation Florida's small Spanish population showed an upward turn, to roughly 1,700 in 1730, 2,100 in 1745, and 2,700 by 1760. The total of black residents, enslaved and free, rose over the same time, from scarcely 100 in 1730 to nearly 500 in 1760, as new migrants brought Negroes from Cuba and as the number of runaways escaping from the neighboring English slave colonies increased. In contrast, the small Indian population continued to decline. If we estimate the Calusas and others in southern Florida as shrinking from 1,500 in 1730 to 500 in 1760, we can add more detailed data for the northern regions. At Pensacola, the Apalache refugee village established in 1715 apparently persisted, for evacuation figures from that Gulf coast port in 1763 indicate that 108

Christian Indians left with the Spanish. Farther east, at San Marcos de Apalache, the Indian inhabitants dropped from 160 in 1730 to 25 three decades later. But the largest decline was in the St. Augustine region, where the number of Indians—by Spanish count—fell from 1,011 in 1729 to 79 in 1760. All told, Florida's Native Americans decreased from nearly 2,800 in 1730 to scarcely 700 thirty years later. (An estimated middle figure for 1745 would be 1,700).[39]

After the British acquired Florida in 1763, the non-Indian population rose to nearly 5,000 before the American Revolution, as white immigrants brought some 3,000 slaves to the new colony in hopes of establishing plantations. But many of these endeavors failed, and by 1790, following the departure of British loyalists and their slaves and the reimposition of Spanish colonial rule, only 1,400 whites and 500 blacks remained. The young naturalist William Bartram was among those who attempted to use slaves to start a frontier plantation in the mid-1760s, but he soon gave up, returning to explore the South a decade later. In Florida, as elsewhere, he observed clear signs of the diminished native population, and he illustrated the decline of Spanish power through his description of the road that had once connected St. Augustine to St. Mark's on Apalache Bay. Traveling across northern Florida in the summer of 1774, Bartram noted that the historic route had been "unfrequented for many years past, since the Creeks subdued the remnant tribes of ancient Floridans, and drove the Spaniards from their settlements in East Florida into St. Augustine, which effectually cut off their communication between that Garrison and St. Mark's." Therefore, he reported, "this ancient highway is grown up in many places with trees and shrubs; but yet has left so deep a track on the surface of the earth, that it may be traced for ages yet to come."[40]

This portion of Bartram's extensive travels put him in an excellent position to observe the expansion of the Seminoles, Lower Creek Indians who had been gradually drifting into Florida and filling the void left by previous tribes. "The Siminoles are but a weak people with respect to numbers," Bartram wrote after his journey in the 1770s. "All of them, I suppose, would not be sufficient to people one of the towns in the Muscogulge; for instance, the Uches on the main branch of the Apalachucla river, which alone contains near two thousand inhabitants. Yet this handful of people possesses a vast territory; all East Florida and the greatest part of West Florida." The Seminoles, who assimilated the remnants of local groups and added runaway slaves to their number, may have included 1,500 by 1775 and 2,000 by 1790. They continued to spread out after the turn of the century, and we know that by 1822 Florida's Indian population, dispersed among some thirty-five towns, had again reached 5,000 persons, the highest total in more than a century.[41]

V. Creeks/Georgia/Alabama

The broad inland domain just above the eastern Gulf Coast differed markedly from neighboring Florida in its eighteenth-century population profile. Geographically, it included most of what is now Alabama and Georgia, minus the Appalachian foothills in the north, the Choctaw hunting grounds beyond the Tombigbee River in the west, and the Mobile Bay area to the south, which became associated with French Louisiana. The Muskogee Indians, later known as the Creeks, had dominated this region for hundreds of years when the first Europeans arrived in the sixteenth century. After surviving the incursions of de Soto (1540) and Luna (1559), the Muskogees consolidated their enviable position between southern Appalachia and the sea, much as other Indian nations were attempting to do farther east. Like the Tuscaroras, they proved astute traders and aggressive warriors, and like the Catawbas, they maintained a loose confederacy of towns that readily absorbed refugees from other areas. But unlike the eastern piedmont tribes, they found themselves one step removed from the colonizing pressures of the English and strategically situated between two, then three, rival European forces. Taking advantage of this unique location through aggressive military and diplomatic policies, they managed to enhance both their power and their population during the late colonial period, in the face of dramatic demographic and political shifts taking place around them.

By the late seventeenth century, the numerous villages on the Tallapoosa and Coosa, near where these rivers combine to make the Alabama, were being pressured from the west by the more numerous Choctaws and by the Mobilian tribes near the coast. Farther east, along the Chattahoochee (the modern-day border between southern Georgia and Alabama) north of where it joins the Flint River to form the Apalachicola, similar communities found themselves vulnerable to the Westo Indians of Carolina, newly armed with guns from Charlestown. As a last resort, some of these towns sought aid and protection from the Spanish in Florida. But others objected strenuously, and in 1685 pro-English factions helped Henry Woodward erect a stockade near the falls of the Chattahoochee so they could begin direct trade with Carolina. Within five years a number of towns had moved east to the Altamaha and settled along its western branch, the Ocmulgee River, the upper portion of which was known to the English as Ochese Creek. Soon the English were calling these Ochese Creek Indians simply Creeks, and the name quickly came to include the entire confederation. The eastern portion, living in the valleys of the Chattahoochee, Flint, and Ocmulgee rivers in Georgia, became known as Lower Creeks. Those residing farther "up" the trading path from Charlestown, on the Coosa, Tallapoosa, and Alabama rivers in central Alabama, were designated Upper Creeks.[42]

Long resentful of Choctaw incursions from the west and Spanish intimidation from the south, the Creeks, now armed and encouraged by English traders, struck back. They took Choctaw captives for sale in Charlestown's growing slave trade, and they stole horses from Spanish missions to sell to Carolina traders. With the arrival of the French in Mobile at the turn of the century, regional politics became increasingly complex. Agents from Charlestown failed in their efforts to move additional Creek allies eastward to help Carolina resist her Spanish and French enemies. But the English did convince Creek warriors to spearhead attacks on St. Augustine (1703), the Apalache missions (1704), and the Spanish fort at Pensacola (1707 and 1708). These raids were followed by forays against French Mobile (1709) and France's Choctaw allies (1711) before the Creek-English alliance broke down.[43]

A gradual increase (less steady than suggested in table 1) in the region's Indian population during the eighteenth century can be established from numerous sources. But it is harder to estimate seventeenth-century numbers; just how sharply native towns had been reduced by initial Spanish contacts, and how fully they had recovered after several generations, remains uncertain. The few European reports surviving from the late seventeenth century, such as Bishop Calderón's 1675 letter, give evidence for the interior that is secondhand or incomplete.[44] Moreover, as noted above, whole towns occasionally relocated—often preserving their names—when new pressures prevailed. So the few estimates made by competing European empires conflict, omitting some groups and exaggerating or double-counting others. In table 1 I have put the region's Indian population at 15,000 persons for 1685, but this figure is even more speculative than most. The actual number may have been nearly half again as high but declining rapidly owing to increased English contact. Or it may have been scarcely half that number but already rising slowly as it would continue to do over the next century.

By 1700 the Indian population probably hovered somewhere around 9,000 persons. In 1708 the governor of South Carolina wrote that 150 miles west from Charlestown "are settled on ochasee River eleven Towns of Indians consisting of six hundred men." Highly pleased by his allies, Nathaniel Johnson added: "These people are great Hunters & Warriors & consume great quantity of English goods." Farther west, on the Chattahoochee River, Johnson noted another community that provided a "very serviceable" stopping point for English traders on their way to the Upper Creek settlements "of the Tallabousees & the Alabamees." He noted vaguely that these more western groups reside in "many Towns," and their 1,300 men "are Great Warriors & Trade with this Government for a great quantity of goods."[45] Johnson seems to suggest a sum of 1,900 Creek men, which, if multiplied by the accepted figure of 3.5, gives a total population of 6,650. To this number can be added several thousand people from the smaller adjacent groups noted in the next paragraph.

Johnson's numbers are similar to, though slightly smaller than, the figures submitted in 1715 as part of a South Carolina census of neighboring Indians that had been in preparation for several years. The document listed ten villages of the Ochese Creeks, containing 731 men and 2,406 persons in all. (As with Johnson's 1708 figures, a contingent of Lower Creeks remaining on the Chattahoochee may have been overlooked in the calculations.) The census recorded 1,352 adult men among the three divisions of the Upper Creeks, giving the following breakdown of their overall population: 1,773 Abeikas in fifteen towns, 2,343 Tallapoosas in thirteen towns, and 770 Alabamas in four towns. So the census offers totals of 2,083 men and 7,292 inhabitants living in forty-two villages. Although the towns obviously varied considerably in size and composition, according to these figures the average Creek townsite in 1715 had 50 men and 174 residents. (This confirms a total population/warrior ratio of 3.5:1, which I have applied to other Creek data as well.) Additional precise figures were given for villages of the Yamasees (10), Apalachicolas (2), Apalaches (4), Savannahs (3), and Yuchis (2), totaling another

2,700 inhabitants. This would mean some 10,000 Indians resided in the region in 1715, on the eve of the Yamasee War.[46]

If the Creek population had fallen below 10,000 persons in the decades before 1715, it began to rise again in succeeding generations. As a new phase of diplomacy began, refugees from power struggles elsewhere sought protection in Creek territory. The nation that had assimilated Apalachicola Indians from Florida added Taensas from Louisiana; after 1730 Natchez survivors arrived from the Mississippi. Creek scholar David Corkran notes that by the 1740s, "Several score Chickasaws, faltering under the pounding that nation had taken from the French and Choctaws, had settled in the upper reaches of the Abeika country at a town to be known as the Breed Camp and had become part of the Creek confederacy . . . , and in 1744 a village of Shawnees from the Ohio country came to settle among the Upper Creeks."[47] An English estimate made in 1749 and published in 1755 put the number of Creek fighting men at 1,200 in the "Lower Nation" and 1,365 in the "Upper Nation," a total of 2,565 warriors, or nearly 9,000 Creeks in all. At the same time, non-Creeks in the area had diminished somewhat, having migrated, died out, or been absorbed.[48]

Meanwhile, James Oglethorpe's small Georgia colony was establishing a foothold near the Atlantic coast, aided by a local village of several hundred Yamacraw Indians, who had been banished by the Creeks during the 1720s and had settled near the Savannah River shortly before Oglethorpe arrived. By 1745 there were nearly 1,400 whites in the colony, plus some runaway Negroes from South Carolina and some illegally enslaved black workers—probably fewer than 100 in all. By 1760, with steady immigration, improved living conditions, and decreased mortality, the white population had risen to roughly 6,000 persons. In addition, following the legalization of slavery in 1751, several thousand blacks had been imported to clear coastal plantation sites. But farther west the Creek population also continued to grow, and it still remained the dominant numerical presence in the region as a whole. One English estimate from 1764 put the number of Creek fighting men at 3,655, while another census report from the same year showed an equivalent figure of 3,683 gunmen in fifty-nine villages. So the total Creek population may have approached 13,000 by 1760, and it probably continued to expand somewhat despite the turbulence of the ensuing decades.[49] James

Adair wrote of the Creeks in 1775, "This nation is generally computed to consist of about 3500 men fit to bear arms; and has fifty towns, or villages," his appraisal may have been slightly dated, secondhand, and incomplete, though Bernard Romans published the same rough estimate in the same year.[50]

Even if the region's Indian population had risen slightly, to perhaps 14,000, by 1775, the non-Indian populations had grown much more rapidly. Migration into the expanding English colony—both free and forced, by land and sea—had brought the number of black and white Georgians to 15,000 and 18,000 respectively. According to the census of 1790, the new state of Georgia included 52,886 whites, plus 29,264 slaves and 398 free blacks. Creek numbers too increased during the fifteen years after American Independence, though at nowhere near the same rate. An estimate from 1780 (which included the roughly 1,500 Seminoles in Florida) put the Creek total at 17,280, of whom 5,860 were said to be gunmen.[51] Five years later a report to Richard Henry Lee put the gunmen of the "Upper and Lower Creek nation" (excluding the Seminoles) at 5,400, and in 1791 Creek leader Alexander McGillivray was said to estimate "the number of gun-men to be between 5000 and 6000, exclusive of the Seminolies."[52] A report to the governor of West Florida and Louisiana for the Spanish in 1793 recorded 8,715 people in thirty-one Upper Creek towns and 6,445 persons in twenty-five Lower Creek towns, for a total of 15,160 within the Creek Nation, roughly double the number that had lived there eighty years before.[53]

Although this upward trend seems clear, individual estimates remain uncertain, for the ratio of total population to warriors varied depending on conditions and methods of counting, and whole communities shifted in size, location, and importance over time. Whereas the English census of 1715 shows a ratio of 3.5:1, a report to the secretary of war in 1789 put the "number of old men, women, and children, in the proportion as four to one of the warriors." As for villages, the same report conceded, "The number of towns in each district, could not be ascertained, probably about eighty in the whole, of which about forty-five are in the upper country. The towns are very different in magnitude; and a few, of what are called the mother towns, have the principle direction of national affairs."[54]

Caleb Swan, writing two years later, reported a similar number of towns, varying in size from twenty houses to two hundred. He put the number of whites in the nation at 300, and with regard to the overall population, he expressed what earlier observers had also felt. "From their roving and unsteady manner of living," Swan wrote, "it is impossible to determine, with much precision, the number of Indians that compose the Creek nation." But he added a succinct explanation for their demographic rise. "It appears long to have been a maxim of their policy, to give equal liberty and protection to tribes conquered by themselves, as well as those vanquished by others," he observed, briefly rehearsing the nation's history. "The Alabamas and Coosades are said to be the first who adopted the ceremonies and customs of the Creeks, and became part of the nation. The Natchez, or Sunset Indians, from the Mississippi, joined the Creeks about fifty years since, after being driven out of Louisiana, and added considerably to their confederative body. And now," he noted in 1791, "the Shawanese, called by them Sawanes, are joining them in large numbers every year, having already four towns on the Tallapoosee river, that contain near 300 war men, and more are soon expected." In short, Swan concluded, "Their numbers have increased faster by acquisition of foreign subjects, than by the increase of the original stock."[55]

VI. Cherokees

According to "An Exact Account of the Number and Strength of all the Indian Nations that were subject to the Government of South Carolina" in 1715, the Cherokee Nation at that time contained 11,210 persons living in sixty villages. (This would be an average of 187 persons per village, though scholars believe the median town size not long before had been twice as great, suggesting a much larger overall population.)[56] Broken down by locality, the census—clearly using slightly rounded numbers—lists 2,100 people in eleven Lower towns, 6,350 people in thirty Middle towns, and 2,760 people in nineteen Upper towns. Divided by age and sex, this document shows 7,600 adults plus 3,610 children; 5,750 men and boys plus 5,460 women and girls. Since it records 4,000 adult men in all, the ratio of total population to male warriors in this census comes to 2.8:1. This approaches the ratio of 3:1 that emerges from later records and that I have applied to counts of Cherokee warriors from other years.[57]

The first such military count by the English had appeared seven

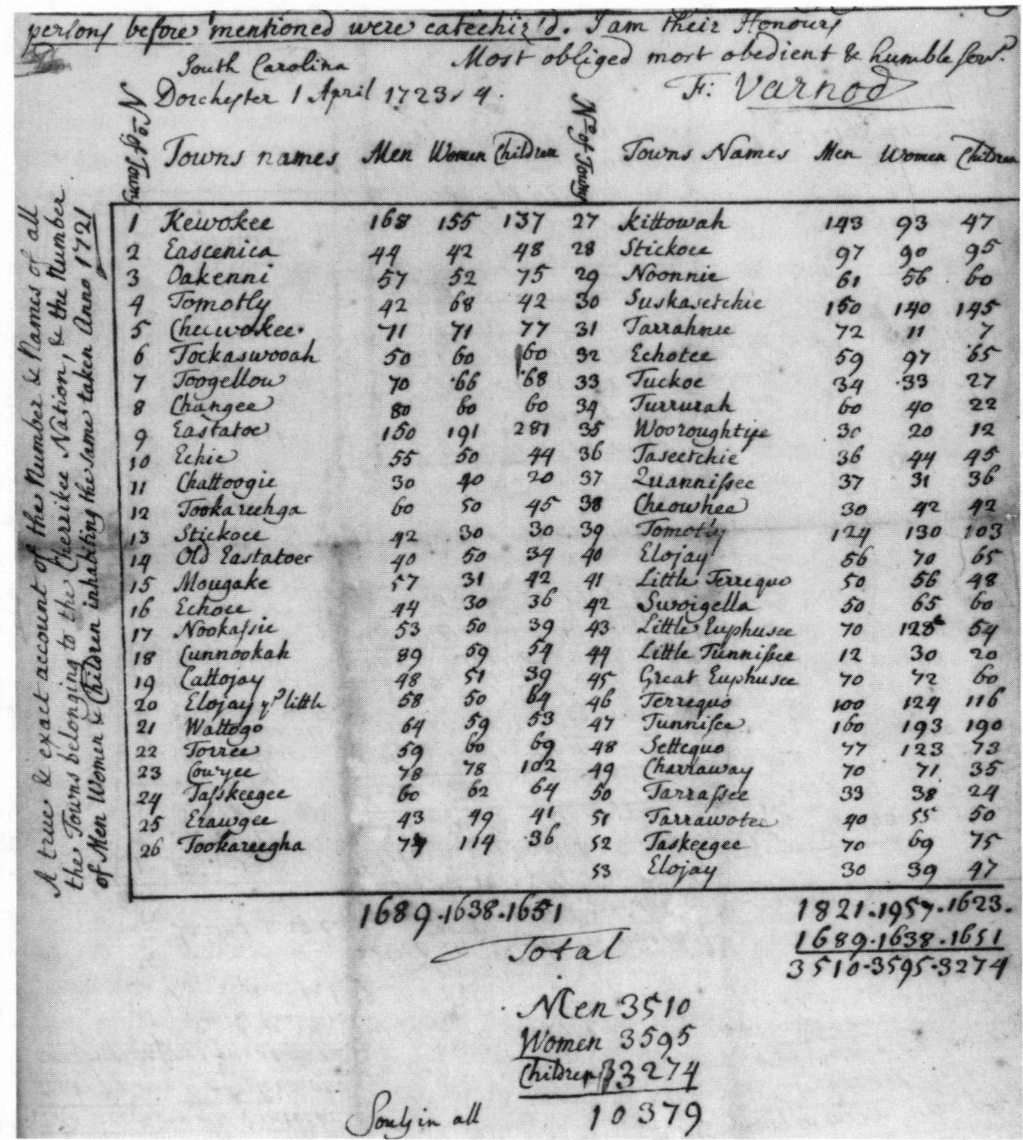

persons before mentioned were catechiz'd. I am their Honours
Most obliged most obedient & humble Servt.
F: Varnod

South Carolina
Dorchester 1 April 1723/4.

A true & exact account of the Number & Names of all the Towns belonging to the Cherrikee Nation, & the Number of Men Women & Children inhabiting the same taken Anno 1721

No. of Towns	Towns names	Men	Women	Children	No. of Towns	Towns Names	Men	Women	Children
1	Kewokee	168	155	137	27	Kittowah	143	93	47
2	Eascenica	44	42	48	28	Stickoee	97	90	95
3	Oakenni	57	52	75	29	Noonnie	61	56	60
4	Tomotly	42	68	42	30	Suskasetchie	150	140	145
5	Cheewokee	71	71	77	31	Tarrahnee	72	11	7
6	Tockaswooah	50	60	60	32	Echotee	59	97	65
7	Toogellow	70	66	68	33	Tuckoe	34	33	27
8	Changee	80	60	60	34	Turrurah	60	40	22
9	Eastatoe	150	191	281	35	Wooroughtye	30	20	12
10	Echie	55	50	44	36	Taseetchie	36	44	45
11	Chattoogie	30	40	20	37	Quannissee	37	31	36
12	Tookareehga	60	50	45	38	Cheowhee	30	42	42
13	Stickoee	42	30	30	39	Tomotly	124	130	103
14	Old Eastatoe	40	50	34	40	Elojay	56	70	65
15	Mougake	57	31	42	41	Little Terrequo	50	56	48
16	Echoee	44	30	36	42	Suwoigella	50	65	60
17	Nookassie	53	50	39	43	Little Euphusee	70	128	54
18	Cunnookah	89	59	54	44	Little Tunnissee	12	30	20
19	Cattojay	48	51	39	45	Great Euphusee	70	72	60
20	Elojay ye little	58	50	64	46	Terrequo	100	124	116
21	Wattogo	64	59	53	47	Tunnissee	160	193	190
22	Torree	59	60	69	48	Settequo	77	123	73
23	Couyee	78	78	102	49	Charraway	70	71	35
24	Tasskeegee	60	62	64	50	Tarrassee	33	38	24
25	Erawgee	43	49	41	51	Tarrawotee	40	55	50
26	Tookareegha	74	114	36	52	Taskeegee	70	69	75
					53	Elojay	30	39	47
		1689	1638	1651			1821	1957	1623
							1689	1638	1651
	Total						3510	3595	3274

Men 3510
Women 3595
Children 3274
Souls in all 10379

Figure 1 Francis Varnod's census of Cherokee towns, 1721 (courtesy of the Rhodes House Library and the United Society for the Propagation of the Gospel in Foreign Parts).

years earlier, in 1708, when South Carolina governor Nathaniel Johnson reported from Charlestown: "The Chereky Indians live about Two hundred & fifty miles northwest from our Settlement on a Ridge of Mountains." He described them as "a numerous people . . . settled in sixty Towns," and he estimated their warriors "are at least Five thousand men." At a ratio of 3:1, this would put the total population at 15,000 (2.8:1 would yield 14,000). Johnson's figures may not have been entirely accurate or up to date, and the drop during the seven years preceding 1708 may well have differed from the decline during the seven following years. Nevertheless, a conservative extrapolation backward from these two totals would put the Cherokee population above 16,000 in 1700.[58]

Projecting further back, into the preceding century, the population size becomes even more sketchy. James Mooney estimated long ago that the Cherokees numbered 22,000 in 1650, but his undocumented figure was probably too low. If sixteenth-century Spanish incursions had caused serious depopulation in the mountains, the relatively isolated Cherokees may well have recovered within a century. Their constant exposure to Europeans began only in the late seventeenth century, with the opening of the deerskin trade to Charlestown, and the first documented smallpox epidemic to reach their settlements arrived in 1697. We know from comparable situations that this dread disease often destroyed half or three-quarters of all the inhabitants in previously unexposed Indian populations. By applying a smallpox death rate of 50 percent to the postepidemic estimate of 16,000 Cherokees in 1700, we can project backward to a much larger preepidemic population of between 30,000 and 35,000 in 1685.[59]

Projections forward in the generations after 1715 are scarcely easier, for though the documentary estimates become more numerous, they remain hard to reconcile. For example, in his report of 1755, Edmond Atkin estimated that the Cherokees numbered "above three Thousand Men," suggesting a total population exceeding 9,000 persons.[60] But the same year Governor Arthur Dobbs of North Carolina sent the Board of Trade an account of Cherokee warriors broken down by locality that showed a total of only 2,590 men, suggesting an overall population of 7,770. Twenty years later James Adair, publishing his *History of the American Indians* in 1775, remarked:

> Formerly, the Cheerake were a very numerous and potent nation. Not above forty years ago, they had 64 towns and villages,

populous, and full of women and children. According to the computations of the most intelligent old traders of that time, they amounted to upwards of six-thousand fighting men; a prodigious number to have so close on our settlements, defended by blue-topped ledges of inaccessible mountains.[61]

At face value, Adair's comment leads to the often-cited figure of 18,000 Cherokees for 1735, and it fits with his recollection that in "about the year 1738, the Cheerake received a most depopulating shock, by the small pox, which reduced them almost one half, in about a year's time." Adair was correct about the date of the smallpox scourge—and perhaps about its awesome extent as well, for he had been a trader among the Cherokees as early as 1736—but his population estimate remains ambiguous.[62] If correct, this relatively high number would suggest that previous counts had missed a substantial percentage of these mountain people. Cherokee population figures at the time of English contact would be pushed higher, and the rate of decline would become even steeper (leading downward to lower estimates after midcentury, such as that of Governor Dobbs). On the other hand, Adair (or his London editor) may have conflated his own forty years among the Indians from 1735 to 1775 with the preceding forty years of contact that he heard about from "intelligent old traders," combining the devastating epidemic of 1697–98 with that of 1738–39. A population of 6,000 warriors and 18,000 inhabitants among sixty-four villages in the mid-1690s, four decades before his first arrival in the mountains, would square very well with the estimates given above for 1708 and 1715.

The epidemic of 1738 was followed by a continued decline in population through warfare, first with Indian neighbors and then with the encroaching Europeans. Between 1759 and 1761 the Cherokees fought a destructive war against the English, made worse by the cyclical return of smallpox to strike a new generation. "We learn from the Cherokee country," wrote an informant in mid-1760, "that the People of the Lower Towns have carried smallpox into the Middle Settlement and Valley, where that disease rages with great Violence, and that the Upper Towns are in such dread of the Infection, that they will not allow a single Person from the above named places to come amongst them."[63] At the end of the Cherokee War, according to Adair, "the traders calculated the number of their warriors to consist of about two thousand three-hundred, which is a great diminution for so short a space of time."[64] This suggests a total community of about 6,900, down from an overall population in 1755 of just below 8,000, estimating from Dobbs (or at least 1,000 more, judging from Atkin). Therefore Cherokee numbers may have dropped to perhaps 7,200 by the middle of the war in 1760 and to a nadir of fewer than 7,000 persons several years later.

In the following decades the Cherokee Nation apparently rebounded somewhat, though recollections of their numbers may have been slightly exaggerated by one "Mr. Purcell, who, in the year 1780, resided among them." Fifteen years later he provided David Ramsay with the intelligence that at that time the Cherokee had numbered 8,550, of whom 2,800 "were gun-men" (a total population/warrior ratio of just over 3:1). If this was more than an inflated estimate of wartime power during the Revolution, any such demographic renewal probably derived mostly from the assimilation of traders and Indian refugees, plus a further withdrawal from expanding colonial settlements. The so-called Chickamauga Cherokees—some 500 warriors and their families who relocated to a mountain fastness in south-central Tennessee, under the leadership of Dragging Canoe, in March 1777—drew to them diverse Indians committed to waging a serious resistance struggle against mounting white encroachment.[65]

But in 1783 the Cherokees experienced yet another smallpox epidemic, and conflicts with white newcomers took an increasing toll that could not be offset by the continued assimilation of refugees or resistance fighters. In November 1785, at the time of the Hopewell Treaty, Indian commissioners put Cherokee strength "at 2,000 warriors, but they were estimated, in 1787, by Colonel Joseph Martin, who was well acquainted with them, at 2,650." In reporting these figures to President Washington in 1789, his secretary of war added, "it is probable they may be lessened since, by the depredations committed on them."[66]

While the native population of the Cherokee region oscillated somewhere between 7,000 and 8,500 persons during the last third of the century, the non-Indian population jumped dramatically. By 1760, 93 colonial soldiers were garrisoned at Fort Prince George, built in 1753 next to the Cherokee town of Keowee on a tributary of the Savannah River, and 136 men were stationed at Fort Loudoun, erected in 1757 five miles west of the Indian town of Chota. Assuming that some women and children accompanied these men and that other families and isolated traders already resided in the area, there were perhaps 300 white settlers living beyond the piedmont in the fringes of Appalachia in 1760. South Carolina laws prohibited Negro participation in the deerskin trade and offered bounties to Indian "slavecatchers" for the return of black runaways, dead or alive. So the number of Afro-Americans in the region who were not passing as red or white must have remained negligible.[67]

After 1768 colonists from North Carolina and Virginia began to migrate into the Watauga valley. The Watauga, Holston, and Nolachucky settlements constituted the earliest core of white population in the Cherokee territory, and from there the newcomers spread out through northeastern Tennessee. To avoid eviction by the Cherokees and to evade the royal proclamation of 1763 against purchasing Indian lands, the Wataugans and their neighbors leased the land they occupied from the Cherokee chief Attakullakulla in 1772. By 1776 these Appalachian settlers could muster between 700 and 800 riflemen, according to Moses Fisk, and many of these occasional soldiers helped defeat the British—particularly at King's Mountain in 1780. George Imlay, who traveled in the Watauga valley at the time of the Revolution, put the number of settlers there at about 2,000.[68] A handful may have brought black servants with them to help clear the land, and the dislocations of the decade may have contributed small bands of runaway slaves, spurred by rumors of pending freedom in the West. But the black population could hardly have exceeded several hundred.[69]

After the War of Independence the rush westward began in earnest. In the 1790 census, five counties of east Tennessee (Washington, Sullivan, Greene, Hawkins, and South of French Broad) already contained 26,100 whites. In addition, 293 "other free persons" and 2,256 slaves gave a total of 2,549 blacks. Together these non-Indians scattering through the mountains (hundreds more of whom must have gone uncounted) suddenly made up more than three-quarters of the population of southern Appalachia. And this number does not even include figures from the mountain fringes of modern-day Alabama, Georgia, and the Carolinas that had been a part of the Cherokee domain.[70]

VII. Choctaws/Chickasaws

West of the Alabama River and east of the Mississippi, two Indian nations dominated what is now central and eastern Mississippi and western Alabama throughout the colonial period. By the Choctaws' own account, their ancestors had entered the region from the west centuries earlier, settling at Nanih Waiya near the Pearl River in central Mississippi and erecting a large temple mound at this sacred center. From the great curve of the Pearl they expanded their settlements eastward to the next two rivers that ran south to the Gulf, the Chickasawhay (or Pascagoula) and the longer Tombigbee, with its westward tributary the Noxubee. Meanwhile their genetic and cultural kinsmen, the Chickasaws, had separated themselves completely, establishing towns farther north, not far from the Mississippi, between the upper reaches of the Yazoo River and the headwaters of the Tombigbee. With their common heritage, adjoining hunting grounds, and mutually intelligible languages, it makes sense to associate the Choctaws and Chickasaws for demographic purposes. But throughout the colonial period they were generally bitter rivals, the allies of competing European powers, and frequently enemies in open war.

The Chickasaws were probably the smaller of the two groups from the time of their separation, and they may have suffered more heavily in the mid-sixteenth century from greater direct contact with de Soto's forces. Considering what happened to their western neighbors the Quapaws at the end of the seventeenth century (see next section), presumably the Chickasaws also experienced severe losses during the generation of early French and English contact following La Salle's descent of the Mississippi. But the exact scale of this Chickasaw decline remains unclear, since the earliest population references are vague. "They seem to be the remains of a populous nation," commented a French writer, noting that the Choctaws continued to "speak the Chickasaw language, though somewhat corrupted, and those who speak it best value themselves upon it." Antoine Le Page du Pratz who lived among the neighboring Natchez in the 1720s, after a full generation of Chickasaw slaving raids inspired by English traders, believed that their "warlike disposition had prompted them to invade several nations, whom they have indeed destroyed, but not without diminishing their own numbers by those expeditions." "Their tradition says they had ten thousand men fit for war, when they first came from the west, and this account seems very probable," wrote James Adair in the eighteenth century, since—along with the Choctaws and the smaller Chokchoomas—they originally "came together from the west as one family."[71]

The first French visitors in the 1680s, associated with La Salle's exploration, varied in their estimates of Chickasaw population. "This nation is very numerous," Father Anastasius Douay noted in 1687; "they count at least four thousand warriors; have an abundance of peltry." Tonti, in contrast, recalled that they had "2,000 warriors" at the time of his first contact, but this may have referred to only several villages. French estimates after 1700 remained vague. In 1702 Iberville thought the Chickasaws had at least "2,000 families," and two years later La Vente thought they might be "as numerous as the Choctaw," with 700 to 800 cabins.[72] But the earliest English estimates were lower. In part this is because they were made later, at a time when the population was falling rapidly, but in part it is because the English had established themselves as trading allies and had obtained ready access to Chickasaw villages. In 1708 a report from Charlestown attributed at least 600 warriors, while another from 1715 showed 700 men and 1,200 others, for a total population of 1,900 (and a total population/warrior ratio of 2.7:1).

Swanton, who first accumulated these figures, concluded there must have been roughly 2,000 Chickasaws in 1715, and 3,000 to 3,500 fifteen years earlier. Projecting back further in time at a similar rate of decline would mean the population in 1685 had been between 4,500 and 6,125 persons. But the firsthand French estimates from that time would put the number higher no matter which figures one uses. On the low side, Tonti's 2,000 warriors at a ratio of 3.5:1 yields a total of 7,000; while at the opposite extreme, Douay's 4,000 warriors at 3.5:1 suggests 14,000 inhabitants. Applying the lower ratio of 2.7:1 that appears in the English tally of 1715 would yield between 5,400 and 10,800. While 7,000 falls inside all these limits, it is probably a conservative estimate for 1685. Round numbers of 5,000 for 1700 and 4,000 for 1715, though above the estimates from Swanton and English sources, may not be unreasonable. At the time of Chickasaw Removal back across the Mississippi 120 years later, that nation's population, with the addition of black slaves, would again exceed 6,000, but for much of the eighteenth century it was scarcely half that size.[73]

A combination of factors forced Chickasaw numbers below 4,000 for roughly a century. Recurrent disease continued to take its toll, as did bitter warfare with the French and their Choctaw allies, more bloody than the traditional boundary skirmishes of earlier times. "As long as the Chickasaws exist we shall always have to fear that they shall entice away the others from us in favor of the English," Bienville wrote to the French Ministry in 1734. "The entire destruction of this hostile nation therefore becomes every day more necessary to our interests and I am going to exert all diligence to accomplish it." Equipped with English weapons, the Chickasaws managed to repulse concerted attacks in 1736, 1739, and 1752. But their alliance with the English not only incurred French animosity, it also applied significant centrifugal forces to Chickasaw society. As time passed, warriors roamed ever more widely in search of deerskins to trade with the English, along with other items obtained in the West and valued in Carolina: captive slaves and "Chickasaw" horses. Probably to maximize that trade and to protect it, one band under the Squirrel King moved all the way to the Savannah River in 1723, while another migrated to Creek territory, near the head of the Coosa River. Given these diverse pressures, the Chickasaw nucleus in northern Mississippi probably fell to 3,100 in 1730, 2,300 in 1745, and 1,600 in 1760, before rebounding—after the removal of the French—to 2,300 in 1775, and 3,100 in 1790.[74]

In contrast to the Chickasaws, their rival kinsmen to the south and east, the Choctaws, appear to have been a far larger and more stable population throughout the late colonial era. Indeed Swanton, after compiling various contrasting estimates, settled for a rough and unchanging total of 15,000 for more than a century, stating that the "numbers of Choctaw seem to have varied little from the period of first white contact, though earlier figures sometimes disagree very considerably." Like James Mooney before him, Swanton guessed at "a population of about 15,000 in 1650" and went on to speculate that "we shall not be far wrong if we assume" the same number for 1700. "The figures for the Choctaw appear to tell a simple story," Swanton wrote. "It would seem from the figures given us by travelers and officials that during the eighteenth century the tribe had a population of about 15,000. Only a few small tribes were added to it during the historic period. Toward the end of that century and during the first three decades of the nineteenth the population appears to have increased gradually."[75]

Swanton exaggerated Choctaw stability and the ease with which the nation's size can be determined across time, but his basic estimate points to the appropriate range. As with other southeastern groups, European enumerations for the Choctaws did not always include all the villages, and the total population/warrior ratio could fluctuate. For example, consider two Choctaw censuses from 1795 compiled for officials of Spanish Louisiana, not available to Swanton. These summaries, now in the Bancroft Library at Berkeley, list more than 11,200 persons living in fifty-three villages, but only two of the three Choctaw districts seem to be covered adequately. The towns named on the lists vary in size from several dozen persons to 765 inhabitants; in some locations men outnumber women while in others the reverse is true. All told, the lists report 3,230 warriors (plus 186 chiefs and captains), along with 3,500 women and 3,377 children. Since the Choctaws had "war towns" and "peace towns," the total population/warrior ratio varied from less than 3:1 to more than 4:1, averaging out to slightly below 3.5:1.[76]

Additional problems exist for determining population figures among the Choctaws. The French, their trading and military partners throughout most of the period, rarely made detailed census counts and sometimes exaggerated the numbers of their Indian allies for government and religious officials at home. To the English, with more limited firsthand knowledge of the Choctaws, such estimates often seemed like deliberate misinformation spread by the French to keep their more numerous colonial rivals at bay. According to James Adair, "The French, to intimidate the English traders by the prodigious number of their red legions in West-Florida, boasted that the Choktah consisted of nine thousand men fit to bear arms: but we find the true amount of their numbers, since West-Florida was ceded to us, to be not above half as many as the French report ascertained. And indeed," Adair added pointedly, "if the French and Spanish writers of the American Aborigines, had kept so near the truth, as to mix one half of realities, with their flourishing wild hyperboles, the literati would have owed them more thanks than is now their due."[77]

Though much work on the colonial Choctaws remains to be done, it seems likely that their population line over time was less flat than Swanton surmised and more in keeping with the downward curves of other groups. In the late seventeenth century the overall community was probably as large as or larger than the Cherokees, declining almost as far and as fast after French and English began to enter the region. Assuming a constant ratio of 3.5:1 for total population/warriors, there could have been as many as 8,000 bowmen and 28,000 inhabitants in 1685, 6,000 fighters and 21,000 persons by 1700, and 4,800 warriors and 16,800 individuals in 1715. In 1702 Iberville, with little firsthand knowledge as yet, appears to have put the number of Choctaw warriors too low, at "about 3800 to 4000 men" (though a year earlier, on the basis of discussions with coastal Indians, he had guessed "there must be more than six thousand men" in over fifty Choctaw villages).[78] On the other hand, French estimates several decades later may have ranged too high. A 1723 letter from Louisiana refers to the "the war we have stirred up between the Choctaws and the Chickasaws," suggesting the need "to maintain this war" through aid to "the Choctaws, a nation that contains nearly eight thousand men."[79]

Still later, Le Page du Pratz observed vaguely that this "great nation" was reckoned at 25,000 warriors.[80] But it is hard to say whether he was mistaking warriors for total inhabitants, referring to some earlier time, exaggerating greatly—or some combination of these. Setting such "wild hyperboles" aside, it appears that the Choctaw population may have reached its nadir in the 1730s, gradually renewing somewhat over succeeding generations, despite occasional setbacks from war and disease. A Frenchman named Lusser who compiled a census after a visit to Choctaw villages in 1730 recorded 3,010 men bearing arms, and a summary drawn up by Régis du Roullet two years later showed 2,728 warriors.[81] Both lists were undoubtedly incomplete, but the population may well have declined to some 3,200 warriors, or 11,200 inhabitants, by 1730 before leveling out in the subsequent decade.

If Choctaw numbers dipped this low at the time of the Natchez War, they had begun to recover slightly by midcentury, despite the internal conflict that flared for several years after 1746. In the winter of 1743–44, the new governor of Louisiana, Marquis Vaudreuil, "welcomed more than 3,000 members of the Choctaw tribe" to Mobile, and one of his subsequent reports to the French secretary of state, which fell into the hands of the British, contained a town-by-town census that showed 3,600 Choctaw men.[82] Louis Billouart de Kerlérec, who arrived in Louisiana in 1753 and governed the French colony in its final decade, gave various estimates of Choctaw strength, ranging from 3,000 to 4,000 men bearing arms, as he worked to retain these crucial allies. Jean-Bernard Bossu, writing from Tombigbee late in 1759, reported that the Choctaws "can muster four thousand warriors who would be happy to fight."[83] From these conflicting numbers, a rough working estimate would be 3,600 fighters and 12,200 persons in 1745, rising to perhaps 3,800 warriors and 13,300 inhabitants in 1760.

Figures on the Choctaws seem no more consistent or reliable after French removal from the Gulf, and few observers were as candid as the Reverend Elam Potter in 1768, who followed his low estimate of "8 or 900 fighting men" with the warning, "I could get no certain account of their number, it being very lately that any traders have gone amongst them." In contrast, Mr. Purcell's account for 1780 implied complete, if unfounded, accuracy. "The Chactaw nation, at that time," he wrote confidently to David Ramsay fifteen years later, "consisted of 13,423 of which were gun-men . . . 4,141." Summing up conflicting intelligence on the Choctaws from the 1780s, Secretary of War Knox wrote in July 1789, "This nation of Indians were estimated by the commissioners of the United States, at 6,000 warriors; other opinions state them at 4,500 or 5,000." That same year a vague report told the secretary, "We think . . . the Choctaws about 3,000" gunmen. But twelve years later a more informed estimate for a new secretary of war claimed the Choctaw population "exceeds fifteen thousand."[84] A tentative estimate reconciling some—but not all—of the existing numbers would be 4,000 warriors and 14,000 people in 1775 (following a decade of wars with the Creeks), with 4,200 gunmen and 14,700 people in 1790.

Like the Cherokees, the Choctaws were a numerous people well situated to withstand the European invasion of the South, and they were initially more remote from the economic and military designs of the expansive English. The same relative isolation and independence that prevented foreigners from obtaining a reliable overview of Choctaw numbers also allowed the population to rebound sooner and more rapidly than smaller or less protected groups. For the Chickasaw and Choctaw region as a whole, therefore, the Indian population probably reached its lowest in the middle decades of the eighteenth century, with fewer than 15,000 people, and then rose gradually. By 1790 Indian numbers were still barely half what they had been in 1685 (though they were approaching seventeenth-century levels again by the time of forced removal in the nineteenth century). From the beginning of the century, occasional black runaways entered the region, and during the generations after 1715 the number of French and English traders and agents in the area probably exceeded 50 at any given time. The other non-Indians who began to enter the region after the Revolution—perhaps 500 whites and 300 blacks by 1790—would soon transform cornfields, ball grounds, and hunting preserves into extensive cotton plantations.

VIII. Natchez/Louisiana

To the west and south of the Choctaw-Chickasaw region, well-established Indian communities of various sizes had long inhabited the fertile lands of the enormous Mississippi Delta and the adjacent shores of the central Gulf coast. During the colonial period these groups were of moderate and decreasing size; their life-style was mobile, their mortality rate was desperate, and the population estimates made by European colonizers were inconsistent at best. In analyzing demographic data for his *Indian Tribes of the Lower Mississippi Valley*, Swanton observed at one point that the surviving historical "figures are so fragmentary and conflicting that it is nearly impossible to base any satisfactory conclusions upon them." That situation still persists, but it is possible, using Swanton's somewhat low estimates and the research of more recent scholars, to put together a rough profile of demographic change in the region during the century after La Salle's exploration of the Mississippi in 1682.[85]

As we have seen, Indians on the eastern slope of the Appalachian chain often divided into small and vulnerable shore communities, larger groups somewhat removed from the coast, and stronger and more stable nations in the protected interior. Similarly, the Indians near the Mississippi Delta can be separated into three geographic groupings for the purpose of estimating overall native population. The location of small coastal tribes, such as the Biloxis, Pascagoulas, and once-numerous Mobilians, would prompt the French colonizers to use their names to identify bays and rivers along the Gulf. Meanwhile, the Houmas, Chitimachas, and others resided near the base of the Mississippi, where it flowed southeastward across the delta (and where the French would establish the town of New Orleans between Lake Pontchartrain and the river in 1718). Farther upstream, between where the Red River and the Arkansas enter the Mississippi, lived several larger nations, particularly the Natchez and the Quapaws.

Unlike most of the South's subregions, Louisiana did not provide relative geographical isolation and protection for its sizable interior nations, delaying and blunting the impact of invasion from abroad. On the contrary, the extraordinary highway of the Mississippi meant that Louisiana was explored and colonized from the north as well as from the south, so by the start of the eighteenth century not only the native inhabitants of Biloxi Bay and Mobile Bay, but also residents of the Yazoo Basin more than three hundred miles inland, were experiencing foreign diseases and colonial-inspired slaving raids. The pattern was not new. When de Soto's huge expeditionary force had spread disease and destruction across the region in the 1540s, they not only massacred several thousand Mobilians near the coast but brought incalculable devastation to interior nations along the banks of the Mississippi as well. La Salle, carrying maps and chronicles of de Soto's venture with him in 1682, doubted whether he was on the same river the Spaniards had crossed, because the Indian populations he encountered seemed so much smaller than those his predecessor had described.

Having mistaken the latitude of the mouth of the Mississippi in 1682, La Salle failed to locate the river again when he returned to the Gulf by sea in 1685. The explorer led several hundred French colonists to the latitude on the Texas coast where he thought he would find the Mississippi, and he was killed by disheartened followers several years later while still struggling to rectify his error. When local Indians destroyed La Salle's colony near Matagorda Bay, French plans to occupy the Mississippi were delayed by more than a decade. Finally, in 1699 a Canadian-born adventurer found the mouth of the river by sailing along the Gulf coast. But Iberville and his younger brother Bienville chose to establish the initial French outposts near sheltered coastal bays well east of the delta—first at Biloxi, later at Mobile.[86]

When some Mobile and Tohome Indians arrived at Fort Biloxi from their towns on the Mobile River in August 1699, they were said to represent "nations together numbering more than seven hundred men," or roughly 2,500 persons. Soon after that, the local Pascagoula Indians told Iberville that these two groups each had about 300 warriors, but when he visited their villages for himself in 1702, he estimated their combined total of fighting men at no more than 350. Their numbers continued to drop rapidly, so that in 1725–26 Bienville (including the Little Tohomes, or Naniabas) put the warrior total at 150, while stating that he could remember a time at the turn of the century when it had been roughly 800 men. An estimate from 1730 put the number of Mobile, Tohome, and Naniaba Indians at 140, and by 1758 Kerlérec estimated that these groups had scarcely 100 warriors. Assuming that fighting men remained a stable proportion of the population but declined in number from approximately 750 in 1700 to 150 in 1725 and 100 in 1750, this represents an 80 percent population drop during the first quarter of the eighteenth century and an additional 33 percent decline during the second quarter. The other small coastal tribes, such as the Biloxis, Pascagoulas, Moctobis, and Capinas, probably equaled in combined size the once-powerful Mobiles and their Tohome neighbors and undoubtedly diminished at a comparable rate.[87]

This steep demise of the small coastal population can be estimated over fifteen-year intervals, as shown on the first line in table 2 below. The second line summarizes the decline of the Lower River groups, and the third line projects the reduction of the Central River nations. The final line (also shown in table 1) offers combined totals for the native inhabitants of the Natchez/Louisiana region as a whole, situated between the Choctaws, Chickasaws, and Upper Creeks to the east and the various inhabitants of East Texas and the Red River area to the west. All told, the region's Indian population seems to have dropped by more than 90 percent in seventy-five years, recovering very slightly, at least among some of the Mississippi River communities, during the last third of the eighteenth century.

Groups along the Lower River were roughly twice as numerous as the coastal peoples when the French arrived; they included the Ouachas, Chaouchas, Mongoulachas, Bayogoulas, Chitimachas, Atakapas, Opelousas, Houmas, and Acolapissas. Here, as along the coast, scanty records suggest crushing declines in population. The recent calculations of Daniel Usner, upon which I have relied considerably for the estimates in table 2, suggest nearly 10,000 for these Lower River groups in 1700; fewer than 3,000 by 1725; well under 1,000 by midcentury; and only slightly more than that in 1775. (As noted below, at least 100 Indians residing in the Lower River area in 1760 were enslaved.)[88]

The full weight of French colonization was felt slightly later along

Table 2 Indian Population of the Natchez Louisiana Region, 1685–1790

	1685	1700	1715	1730	1745	1760	1775	1790
Gulf coast	8,000	5,000	2,000	1,500	1,000	700	450	300
Lower River	16,000	10,000	5,000	2,500	1,300	900	1,150	1,400
Central River	18,000	12,000	8,000	4,000	2,700	2,000	2,100	2,300
Total	42,000	27,000	15,000	8,000	5,000	3,600	3,700	4,000

the Lower River, but foreign diseases, coupled with warfare and alcohol, took an enormous toll within several generations. Timing varied from village to village, but no group escaped. Some disappeared entirely, the survivors melting into neighboring communities. Others relocated closer to the growing town of New Orleans, which had come under Spanish control in 1763, where they managed to subsist by marketing provisions. Table 2 reflects the fact that some of these diminished groups began to increase in numbers during the last third of the century. Their resistance to foreign diseases grew, and they absorbed additional Indians from decimated towns elsewhere.

The Houmas, one of the larger and better-documented groups in the areas, are apparently typical in the rate and extent of their demise. They occupied a large village on the Mississippi just south of the Bayogoulas. (A tall red stake on the east bank marked the line between Houma and Bayogoula hunting grounds; the site would become known in French as Baton Rouge.) Smallpox was already ravaging the Houma town when Iberville arrived there in 1699. Conflicting initial estimates by the French suggest more than 250 warriors at the start of the century. La Harpe reported 200 fighting men in 1718, while a 1739 report found only 90 to 100 warriors, though the dwindling Houmas had been joined by remnants of the Acolapissas and Bayogoulas. By 1758 Kerlérec noted 60 warriors in the entire group, and in 1784 Thomas Hutchins wrote that the Houmas, "once a considerable nation of Indians," were "reduced now to about 25 warriors," while their neighbors, the Chitimachas, "reckon about 27 warriors."[89]

The so-called Central River nations farther north, including the Quapaws and Taensas, the Tunicas and Natchez, and the Upper and Lower Yazoos, were the largest of the groupings in the region. But they too had been touched by the early Spanish incursion and were dramatically affected by the arrival of the French via the Great River, first from the north and then from the south. Moreover, English traders and slave-raiding parties appeared in the Central River area before the end of the seventeenth century, and they may have been responsible for the major epidemic that swept the area in 1698. Within three generations after La Salle's appearance, the number of local Indians had plummeted by nearly 90 percent, from at least 18,000 in the 1680s to scarcely 2,000 in the middle of the eighteenth century. Consolidation with other groups may have brought a slight rise of a few hundred persons over the ensuing decades.[90]

The plight of the Quapaw Indians, or "Downstream People," is representative. In 1682, according to historian David Baird, they numbered somewhere between 6,000 and 15,000 persons, settled in four large towns on the Mississippi near the mouth of the Arkansas. But the epidemic of 1698 reduced their population by two-thirds, and English-sponsored slave raids took an additional toll. When a French priest established a mission among them in 1727, they had withdrawn to three small villages along the Arkansas and numbered scarcely 1,200 persons. Further epidemics followed in 1747 and 1751. By 1763 fewer than 700 people survived, of whom only 160 were men of fighting age. "Their use as raiders and auxiliary troops by the French accounted for some of the decrease, but their reduction was mostly a consequence of European introduced disease," explains Baird. "The governmental organization of the Downstream People had reflected the four-part division" of their original towns, "hence it too was altered. Rather than four chiefs who acted in concert only when national interests required it, a great chief emerged to claim special hereditary prerogatives." Baird concludes that, as with so many southern Indian groups, the Quapaws' social structure must have been "altered in other ways by the decimation of the population."[91]

The Tunicas suffered similar heavy losses at the end of the seventeenth century and continued to decline from several thousand to only a few score. "Sickness was among them when we arrived there," wrote a French visitor in 1698. "They were dying in great numbers." The Tunicas, Thomas Hutchins stated in 1784, were "formerly a numerous nation of Indians; but their constant intercourse with the white people, and immoderate use of spirituous liquors, have reduced them to about twenty warriors." In fact, disease constituted the primary cause of decline, as it did with the Taensas as well. When Iberville visited their locale in March 1700, he reported that this nation had previously been numerous but that at present it had no more than 300 men.[92]

That same month Iberville's party visited the Natchez Indians, who possessed far more elaborate ceremonial traditions and retained strong memories of a once-formidable demographic presence. "According to the Natchez, there were formerly . . . more than two hundred thousand persons," La Harpe explained vaguely. If such numbers ever existed, they occurred generations earlier, perhaps even before the Natchez settled beside the Mississippi, but during the seventeenth century the nation remained one of the larger ones in the region. By 1704, however, a newly arrived clergyman wrote regarding the Natchez that during the past six years their "number has diminished a third." Father Charlevoix, who visited the Natchez in 1721, testified to their continuing demise, though he may have overstated their population somewhat. The French priest reported that "about six years ago they reckoned among them four thousand warriors. It appears that they were more numerous in the time of M. de la Salle, and even when M. d'Iberville discovered the mouth of the Mississippi. At present," Charlevoix continued, "the Natchez cannot raise two thousand fighting men. They attribute this decrease to some contagious diseases, which in these last years have made a great ravage of them."[93]

Soon pestilence was joined by war, for in 1729 bitter Natchez warriors attacked the French outpost of Fort Rosalie and killed 237 people, after being told by a contemptuous officer that they would have to move their villages. The French retaliated, and the next two years saw the virtual destruction of the Natchez nation. Some 450 captives were taken to New Orleans and sold into slavery in St. Domingue. Only a few hundred Natchez survived in the vicinity, taking refuge among the Chickasaws. As suggested in the third line of table 2, the Indian population of the Central River area as a whole was roughly 12,000 persons in 1700 and already declining rapidly. Over the next two generations this population was reduced by five-sixths, before increasing slightly during the era of the American Revolution.[94]

Compared with English settlements on the east coast, Louisiana's non-Indian population grew slowly. At the start of 1700, a small and sickly French vanguard of scarcely 80 men under Bienville inhabited the newly built Fort Maurepas on Biloxi Bay, awaiting the return of Iberville from France with reinforcements. They had already encountered a few Englishmen and several half-starved runaways from the rival Spanish outpost at Pensacola. But even as Canadian voyageurs and French missionaries began to appear along the Mississippi, the total number of whites in the region may not have exceeded 100 persons. By 1715, after the uphill battle to locate a settlement at Old Mobile, hardly 300 French and Canadians remained in the area, along with a few dozen African slaves (a rounded figure of 100 is no doubt too large). In contrast, the shift of colonization efforts to the Mississippi and the founding of New Orleans made the next fifteen years a period of rapid growth, creating new pressures for Indian groups along the river. By the time of the French-Natchez War, the number of whites had risen at least to 1,700, and perhaps considerably higher. Through forced importation, the total of blacks had climbed faster, approaching 3,600 by 1730.[95]

The defeat of the Natchez, coupled with the earlier decimation of neighboring tribes through disease, meant that during the 1730s the combined colonial population came to exceed the number of Indians in the region for the first time, though the total figure for the area probably continued to decline slightly, rising again only after the political shifts of 1763. By 1745 there were roughly 8,000 newcomers—4,100 Africans and 3,900 Europeans—in Louisiana, and by 1760 the colony still did not exceed 10,000, with an estimated 5,300 blacks and 4,000 whites plus 100 Indian slaves. While overall Indian numbers may have revived slightly after 1760, the totals for non-Indians during the subsequent generation of Spanish control approximately doubled during the first fifteen years and doubled again in the fifteen years after that. The white census had reached nearly 11,000 persons by 1775, and as Acadians continued to arrive, it was approaching 20,000 by 1790. For a brief span (after a generation of numerical dominance), Afro-Americans represented less than 50 percent of the non-Indian population, climbing only to 9,600 by 1775. But by 1790, as the Haitian Revolution began to unfold in the Caribbean, blacks in Louisiana numbered over 23,000, roughly equaling the combined total of Native Americans and Euro-Americans residing in the region.[96]

IX. East Texas

The final two regions, though large and significant geographically, remained relatively inaccessible to European settlement until late in the eighteenth century, so records regarding the size and location of Indian groups during earlier generations remain somewhat tentative and sketchy. Neither the timberland of western Louisiana and East Texas nor the huge swath of land stretching from the banks of the Arkansas to the headwaters of the Potomac witnessed an extended colonizing onslaught during the century before the American Revolution. However, there was enough contact, both direct and indirect, during this era to prompt Indian numbers to decrease markedly in these regions and to allow for crude estimates of that decline.

In the late seventeenth century, three loose confederacies of Caddo Indians, including more than two dozen groups in all, dominated what is now western Louisiana and eastern Texas. They lived in separate clusters of towns and spoke different dialects of the same Caddo language. They were connected linguistically to the Pawnee and Wichita peoples farther north who spoke related, though very different, Caddoan languages. But culturally they had more in common with southeastern Indian nations. Like the Natchez, they were productive agriculturalists who developed substantial ceremonial centers during the centuries before de Soto's sudden arrival. And their flat-topped temple mounds, like those of the Natchez, suggest a significant population density before the colonial period. As with the Natchez, there are indications, according to W. W. Newcomb, Jr., "that the culture of the historic Caddoes was in some respects the disintegrating shadow of something which had once been more spectacular."[97]

Their first major confrontation with Europeans had occurred in October 1541, with the appearance of de Soto's army, shortly before the leader's death. The next year de Soto's successor returned briefly, but further contacts were minimal until La Salle's party entered the region well over a century later. When the French encountered the Caddos in the 1680s, there were three distinct groupings, plus several independent Caddo communities (the Yatasi, the Adais, and the Eyeish—or Hais). First, along the lower reaches of the Red River in central Louisiana, resided the Natchitoches Indians, near the site of the modern-day town that bears their name. Second, several hundred miles upstream where the Red River flows west to east above the present city of Texarkana, stretched the towns of the Kadohadacho confederacy, which included the upper Natchitoches, the Nanatsohos, the Nasonis, and the Kadohadachos or Caddos proper. The third and largest grouping was the Hasinais, or Cenis, consisting of eight or ten neighboring groups along the streams that come together to form the Neches River in East Texas. (They called each other "*teyshas*," or "allies," and when they applied the same term of friendship to Spaniards arriving from the southwest, the newcomers used this word for the area, and eventually for the whole state of Texas.)[98]

"Although it is true that even as early as the seventeenth and eighteenth centuries the Caddoes appear to have passed their zenith," Newcomb writes of these groupings, "they remained, nonetheless, the most productive, advanced, and populous peoples of Texas." But their demise was imminent, he states, and "seems to have been primarily brought about by epidemics rather than by war. The collapse of these confederacies was so rapid, and their decline in numbers so great that the onrushing American frontier hardly took notice of the Caddoes, the dregs of what had been two centuries earlier rich, splendid, barbaric theocracies."[99]

To the south of the Caddos, in the valley of the Trinity River and beyond, lived the Atakapan peoples. Closest to the Caddos geographically and culturally were the Bidais and Deadoses, residing more than a hundred miles inland. The little-known Patiris lived nearer to the coast, not far north of modern-day Houston. The Akokisas inhabited the north side of Galveston Bay and may have been the "Hans" with whom the Spaniard Cabeza de Vaca lived in 1528. To their east, the Atakapas proper occupied the coastal littoral near Sabine Lake, between present-day Beaumont and the Gulf. These small groups, linked by language to the Tunicas farther east in the Yazoo River area, were much less culturally impressive than the Caddo confederacies, and they were less numerous as well. Newcomb, drawing on Swanton, estimates their total population at fewer than 3,500 persons during the colonial period. More than 200 Atakapan speakers from the interrelated Bidais, Deadoses, and Akokisas were attracted west to the new Spanish mission of San Ildefonso on the San Gabriel River in 1749. But within six years Apache raids and internal dissent had caused the demise of this and neighboring missions in the vicinity of present Rockdale, Texas.[100]

From the west side of Galveston Bay, the Karankawas occupied several hundred miles of coastline, stretching toward the southwest. These nomadic bands of tattooed hunters and fishermen resisted the arrival of several hundred would-be colonizers under La Salle who disembarked at Matagorda Bay in 1685. Within several years they had successfully destroyed the isolated French outpost of Fort St. Louis on Garcitas Creek, absorbing a few young survivors into their tribe. A generation later, Europeans again met a hostile reception. Bernard de La Harpe's French expedition entered Karankawa territory briefly in 1720, and in response the Spanish attempted to set up a fort and a mission in the area two years later. But by 1726 the

Spanish presidio and mission had withdrawn westward to the San Antonio River, and this small coastal group continued to resist cultural intrusion throughout the century.[101]

By the 1770s the Karankawas were being joined by remnants of the Tonkawan bands that had long been their inland neighbors to the immediate north. The Tonkawas, like the Karankawas, occupied the ecological and cultural transition area between the South and the West. Weakened in the seventeenth century, whether by rivals or disease, these Indians living between the Brazos and the Colorado rivers sought protection from Spanish newcomers, and they may have paid a high demographic price for contact with the foreign missionaries and soldiers. "The number of Tonkowas must have declined considerably during the eighteenth century," Newcomb writes, "though information is sparse on this point."[102]

The non-Indian population of East Texas had scarcely reached 1,200 persons by the mid-eighteenth century. In 1685 La Salle's settlers at Fort St. Louis numbered several hundred. But many died of smallpox, according to Spanish reports, and the rest were killed by Indians, except for a handful of deserters and children. By 1694 the first Spanish missions, designed to counteract the French intrusion, had also failed, and for two more decades non-Indians were virtually absent from East Texas for the last time. After 1715 new missions were established at San Antonio, giving Spanish clerics a forward base for carrying their message farther east. At the same time the French consolidated their hold on Natchitoches and pushed farther up the Red River. In rounded numbers, however, the combination of Spanish missionaries and soldiers, plus French traders and planters, probably amounted to no more than 300 in 1715, 600 in 1730, 900 in 1745, and 1,200 in 1760. (Several hundred black and mulatto slaves, runaways, and freedmen were also present by midcentury.) After France relinquished its land west of the Mississippi to Spain in 1763, the small non-Indian population continued to grow, as more enslaved blacks were imported to work on frontier plantations along the Red River.

Though relatively small, these colonial incursions had a devastating effect on the native population of East Texas, which may well have been between 25,000 and 30,000 in 1685. Mooney estimated the region's Indians at just below 14,000 in 1690, with 8,500 Caddoans making up more than half the total. But a modern authority, John C. Ewers, stated in 1973 that "Mooney's estimates for the Indian tribes of Texas appear to be conservative." Ewers increased some of Mooney's local estimates by 50 percent and his general totals by nearly 20 percent. (An analysis of East Texas demography for the late eighteenth century, published the following year by Alicia V. Tjarks, suggests indirectly that these early numbers should be even higher.) Ewers pointed out that Mooney cited only two "great epidemics" between 1685 and 1790: a sickness that killed some 3,000 Caddoans in 1691 and a smallpox outbreak that swept most tribes in 1778. Examining colonial records in greater detail, Ewers found evidence for more than a dozen other epidemics among East Texas Indians during these years.[103]

The scale of the decimation is suggested by a French report of 1715 that a Yatasi group had lost four-fifths of its people, reduced from 2,500 to 500 by sickness and Chickasaw raids. Even if other groups suffered less severely, it seems likely that the overall population by 1730 may have been scarcely half what it had been forty or fifty years earlier. In 1739 smallpox and measles devastated the new missions at San Antonio, and Indians who fled this destruction apparently carried the diseases eastward among the Tonkawan and Atakapan peoples. Twenty years later, in 1759, smallpox and measles were rampant among the Caddoan nations. By 1760 the region's total Indian population had probably been reduced to roughly 10,000 persons. After that, expanding interracial contact meant a further rise in persons of mixed ancestry, and uncertain geographic boundaries and crude census methods compound the problems of calculating total inhabitants by simplified racial category. Still, the frequency and accuracy of population estimates increased as the Spanish extended their colonial control over the area, and it is possible to weigh these figures both for contemporary totals and for a baseline in gauging the larger Indian population of previous times.[104]

After 1760 Indian numbers continued to decrease, though the small communities of non-Indians probably remained in the minority when all the native inhabitants are considered.[105] Unfortunately, historians have often focused only on the carefully enumerated mission Indians, a tradition Tjarks invoked when analyzing colonial census records in 1974. She took the practical but misleading position that "roaming Indian tribes cannot be included in the general estimate of the Texan population. Some information about them exists," Tjarks conceded, but available figures "are merely approximate or rough estimates, notwithstanding that they resulted from commendable efforts." Opting for precision over inclusiveness, she focused only upon some 1,000 Christianized Indians and mestizos living near the Spanish. "To proceed otherwise—that is, trying to add into the calculations a minimum of 6,000 pagan Indians (Croix mentioned 7,280 in 1778) to some 3,000 inhabitants of the three Spanish towns—would lead to extreme ambiguity and lack of precision."[106]

Taken together, the Indians of East Texas had roughly equaled the Cherokees in number during the seventeenth century. But they were more widely dispersed and farther removed from the new sicknesses of Europeans, so their population seems to have reached its lowest point at a somewhat later date. In 1764 a severe smallpox epidemic devastated a mission west of San Antonio, and in 1777, according to Elizabeth John, a "virulent epidemic ravaged the populations of eastern Texas and western Louisiana" and returned to do more damage the following summer. During the mid-1770s some 1,500 Spaniards and 600 blacks and mulattoes lived near the established missions, along with nearly 1,000 Indians and mestizos, while another 7,300 Native Americans subsisted outside Spanish control. Further outbreaks of disease occurred in the 1780s, and by 1790 there were probably no more than 7,000 Indians, Christianized or pagan, in the whole East Texas region, along with 2,400 non-Indians. For the first time in centuries the area had fewer than 10,000 total inhabitants, and its overall population would not begin to increase again until after 1800.[107]

X. The Shawnee Interior

The tenth and final southeastern region, which I have broadly termed the Shawnee Interior, was both the largest and, from the coastal perspective of intruding Europeans, the most remote. So demographic estimates are scarce for this broad arc, spreading over the South like a wide umbrella from the Arkansas River in the west to the headwaters of the Potomac in the east. But there can be little doubt that in terms of both relative density and absolute numbers, this was by far the least populous area of the entire South in the century before the American Revolution. Despite its geographic size, its permanent inhabitants were few until the dramatic influx across the Appalachian chain in the decades after Independence.

For the most part, the region served as a vast buffer zone and hunting ground between the Iroquois and their dependent allies to the north and the Cherokees and other nations to the south. Numerous salt licks throughout what is now Kentucky (along the Salt River and the Licking River, for example), attracted deer and buffalo. The Indian hunters who frequented such locations found that they could nurture these herds and direct their movements by killing trees and allowing the extensive grasslands to expand, providing enhanced grazing spots to which the animals would return at predictable times, especially when undergrowth was burned off to prompt tender new growth for browsing. As competition for skins increased during the eighteenth century, so did conflict within this arena. The trail that crossed the Ohio at what is now Maysville, Kentucky, and curved south in two branches toward Cumberland Gap and Pound Gap, was known, significantly, as the Great Warrior Path. This same name was applied to the portion of the trail on the eastern side of the Appalachian Divide, where the much-traveled route stretched along the Shenandoah River as it flows northeastward to its confluence with the Potomac.

In March 1762 Lieutenant Henry Timberlake witnessed the return of Cherokee warriors to their town of Tommotly after attacking "a party of Shawnese, hunting buffaloes" several hundred miles away near the Ohio River. Such hostile encounters in this valuable hunting region had become commonplace in recent generations, and the danger involved in seeking skins limited the resident Indian population, prompting herds to increase further. Nevertheless, those most familiar with the area appear to have been the much traveled and widely dispersed Shawnees, an Algonquian-speaking people who had moved gradually eastward from Illinois to Pennsylvania after the French appeared in the Mississippi valley. They migrated back into the Ohio region a generation later in response to English pressure, while repeatedly dispersing small contingents to reside in the Deep South. In fact, their name derived from the Algonquian words *shawan* for "south" and *shawunogi* meaning "southerner." According to Jerry E. Clark, "They probably numbered between 2,000 and 4,000 individuals during the early historic period," though that estimate may be too low for all five divisions of this peripatetic nation.[108]

Exactly when, where, and how many Shawnees—and other groups—inhabited the zone between Cherokee country and the Ohio River remains uncertain. Perhaps as early as the 1680s, and certainly by the 1730s, members of the Piqua division of the Shawnees occupied the village of Eskippakithiki, or "blue lick place," less than fifty miles south of the Ohio on the Great Warrior Path, and slightly east of modern-day Lexington. (A French census from 1736 recorded 200 men in the town.) At times the Shawnees also inhabited sites farther east along the various tributaries flowing northwest to the Ohio: the Big Sandy, the Kanawha, the little Kanawha, and the Monongahela. But as Clark points out, "It is not certain whether many of the settlements in eastern Kentucky were permanent or whether they were merely seasonal hunting and warring encampments."[109]

Though increased trade and protection offered by the French drew many of the Shawnee settlements to the north side of the Ohio River by the eighteenth century, this highly mobile nation, like the neighboring Delawares, maintained a presence in the southern Ohio valley. When King George's War broke out in 1744, the British navy was able to harass French shipping on the Atlantic and disrupt the trade of Canadian merchants with their Indian allies in the Ohio valley. In 1748 at Logstown, on the upper Ohio just west of modern Pittsburgh, Conrad Weiser and George Croghan convinced Shawnee, Delaware, and other chiefs to pledge allegiance to England and open the area to traders from the British colonies. The Iroquois League continued to claim control over the Ohio valley by right of conquest, but its leaders ceded the area to the British at the Treaty of Fort Stanwix in 1768, much to the dismay of the Shawnees.[110]

Notwithstanding the royal proclamation of 1763 prohibiting settlement west of the Appalachian Divide, migration westward from the English colonies began in earnest. Indian occupants of the trans Appalachian region resisted, and mutual reprisals escalated. When white newcomers killed the family of Logan, a Cayuga or Mingo leader married to a Shawnee woman, warfare erupted in 1774. Some 300 Shawnee warriors under Cornstalk, having tried to drive the invaders out of their traditional hunting grounds, were eventually defeated by 1,100 of Lord Dunmore's Virginia militiamen at Point Pleasant near the mouth of the Kanawha River in October. (Puckeshinwa, father of Tecumseh and Tenskwatawa, was among those who died.) By the spring of 1775, the floodgates for westward migration into the interior had been opened wide. Nearly 80,000 non-Indians poured into the region over the next fifteen years. Nevertheless, the Shawnees did not relinquish their claims to land south of the Ohio until the Treaty of Greenville in 1795, following General Anthony Wayne's victory at Fallen Timbers the previous year.[111]

The demographic picture of this interior zone, therefore, is both atypical and cloudy. In the late seventeenth century, when La Salle was encountering Shawnees as far west as the Illinois, we might assume that this region below the Ohio had at least 8,500 inhabitants, many of whom were situated near the Mississippi. Since these occupants had steady contact with hunters and warriors from outside the region, it must be assumed that they did not entirely escape the dangerous diseases that were reducing Indian numbers in other areas. On the other hand, they were widely dispersed, and the rate of decline in this well-protected area was no doubt minor compared with other parts of the South. Perhaps numbers in the interior dropped to 5,000 by 1700 and to 3,000 by 1715. Out-migration by Shawnees to both north and south, plus warfare and sickness, may have reduced the total population to as low as 1,200 during the following decades. But by 1745 it was probably beginning to rise slightly with the arrival of small refugee groups from all directions, perhaps reaching 1,800 by 1760 and 2,000 again by 1775. Continuing warfare and the onslaught of non-Indian migration may have reduced this small population somewhat, to perhaps 1,800, in the years during and after the American Revolution.

Even if these tentative figures for native inhabitants of the interior region are considerably off base for some years, as they may well be, this would not change the dimensions of the extraordinary demographic shift in the eastern portion of this region during the late eighteenth century. When Daniel Boone set out from Hillsborough, North Carolina, in 1775 there were almost no African Americans and only a few hundred European Americans residing beyond the mountains. But soon the trickle became a torrent as settlers from Pennsylvania and Maryland followed those from North Carolina and Virginia. In the spring of 1780 alone, three hundred boatloads of migrants reached the Falls of the Ohio. Census figures for 1790 showed 66,946 whites and 13,773 blacks in what would become Tennessee and Kentucky. In other words, more than 80,000 persons, both free and enslaved, had poured into one segment of the vast interior region within fifteen years (not to mention thousands more who were now residing in the mountains of extreme western Virginia and North Carolina). Suddenly the total population had jumped more than twenty-five times in little over a decade, and this proved only a prologue to the influx that was still to come.[112]

Conclusion

The process of revising, confirming, and interpreting the data presented here remains an extended task to which numerous scholars will lend their expertise. For a demographic foundation such as the one laid out in table 1 becomes strong and useful only when other builders test its validity and reduce its shortcomings. Various researchers will arrange and explain these numbers in different ways, using them to alter traditional narratives and open up new lines of inquiry. Treated with due care and skepticism, as a set of interlocking estimations in a field where we have had no prior overview, these population figures can provide a background and framework for much that anthropologists and historians are discovering about the colonial South. Behind these seemingly innocuous quantitative estimates lie broad expanses of history—social and cultural, economic and military—waiting to be written or rewritten.

Though the period examined here has long received only passing attention, few will deny that it marked a crucial transition and deserves more than cursory reexamination. As George Fredrickson noted in his comparative study of South Africa and the American South:

> The process of stripping the indigenes of their patrimony and reducing them to subservience or marginality was, from the historian's perspective, a complex and uneven one that cannot be fully appreciated . . . merely by looking at the final outcome as the predetermined result of white attitudes, motivations, and advantages. Not only did the indigenous peoples put up a stiff resistance that at times seemed capable of stalling the white advance indefinitely, but the lack of a firm consensus of interests and attitudes within the invading community, or between the actual settlers and the agents of a metropole or mother country, could lead to internal disagreements concerning the character and pace of expansion and even on whether it should continue at all. Ultimate white hegemony may have been virtually inevitable, especially in the American case, but this outcome was less clear to the historical actors than to future generations.[113]

The numbers themselves cannot tell this complicated and significant story. Nevertheless, in conclusion it is worth pointing out several patterns that emerge from an overview of this kind. First of all, the colony of Virginia, which has so often been used by colonial historians to represent the early South, is actually an aberration in the region as a whole. Though not as old as Spanish Florida, Virginia had been the first successful settler colony in the region, and by 1685 approximately four-fifths of all the whites (38,100 of 46,900) and blacks (2,600 of 3,300) in the entire South lived in coastal Virginia. On the eve of the American Revolution in 1775, Virginia east of the mountains still contained more than half the people with European and African ancestry in the whole region (some 465,900 of an estimated 916,900). Even in 1790, when the exodus westward via Cumberland Gap and other routes was well under way, white and black Virginians numbered nearly 750,000 within a southern non-Indian population that had reached 1,630,000. Within the geographic South as a whole, therefore, Virginia's growth after the 1680s makes it the exception rather than the rule. The long shadow cast by the world of Williamsburg has obscured our view of the wider southern world beyond.

When Virginia is removed, the figures for the rest of the region look strikingly different. The total population by race for the nine subregions south and west of Virginia over the course of the eighteenth century appears in table 3 (totals II–X). Across that whole domain in 1685, from the Outer Banks to the Texas pine forests, 95 of every 100 people were Native Americans (some 196,500 out of 206,000). Even when Virginia is put back in the balance (totals I–X), four out of every five persons (almost 200,000 of nearly 250,000 inhabitants) were Indians in 1685—not a statistic that our standard approaches to early southern history have reflected in a serious way.

But if this composite overview reveals a striking preponderance of Indians in the late seventeenth-century South, it also documents their rapid, ongoing demise. The region's Native American population had already been suffering a steep decline for nearly two centuries, particularly among the coastal tribes, though the early figures are far harder to recover and therefore much more tentative and controversial. During the generation after the 1680s, where we begin to have access to somewhat more reliable and comprehensive statistics, it is clear that disaster was again spreading inland, as it had during the Spanish incursions of the mid-sixteenth century. Be-

Table 3 Comparison of Population Totals for Different Parts of the South, 1685–1790

	1685	1700	1715	1730	1745	1760	1775	1790
Totals for Areas I–X								
Red	199,400	130,600	90,100	66,700	59,300	53,600	55,600	55,900
White	46,900	70,900	96,500	144,600	219,700	333,700	542,500	1039,600
Black	3,300	8,700	31,400	80,600	144,600	226,700	374,400	590,500
Total	249,600	210,200	218,000	291,900	423,600	614,000	972,500	1686,000
Totals for Areas II–X (Excluding Virginia)								
Red	196,500	128,700	88,800	65,800	58,700	53,200	55,300	55,700
White	8,800	14,800	22,400	41,300	71,400	137,400	263,000	597,500
Black	700	3,200	10,500	30,900	59,300	95,800	188,000	285,000
Total	206,000	146,700	121,700	138,000	189,400	286,400	506,300	938,200
Totals for Areas III–X (Excluding Virginia and North Carolina)								
Red	186,500	121,500	85,800	63,800	57,200	52,200	54,800	55,400
White	3,100	5,400	7,600	14,000	28,700	52,900	106,200	309,300
Black	500	2,800	8,700	25,400	45,300	67,600	135,700	179,500
Total	190,100	129,700	102,100	103,200	131,200	172,700	296,700	544,200
Totals for Areas IV–X (Excluding Virginia and North and South Carolina)								
Red	176,500	114,000	80,700	61,800	55,700	51,200	54,300	55,100
White	1,700	1,600	2,100	4,200	8,400	14,300	34,600	169,100
Black	—	—	100	3,800	4,700	9,700	28,400	70,600
Total	178,200	115,600	82,900	69,800	68,800	75,200	117,300	294,800

tween 1685 and 1730, the South's native population was further reduced by a full two-thirds, from roughly 200,000 to fewer than 67,000. Warfare, enslavement, and migration, but most of all epidemic disease, ravaged the major peoples of the Southeast.

As the smallpox virus spread along lines of broadening intercultural trade, the drop in numbers between 1685 and 1730 became cataclysmic: the Cherokees—32,000 to 10,500; the Choctaws—28,000 to 11,200; the Natchez and their neighbors—42,000 to 8,000. Since such groups dominated the Deep South's landscape, their decimation meant that the overall population of the South beyond Virginia declined by fully one-third over these forty-five years, despite a steady influx from Europe and Africa. Indeed, as revealed in totals II–X of table 3, the drop during the generation before 1715 was even steeper, from 206,000 to 121,700. Contrary to popular imagery, the greater South in the early eighteenth century was a region in demographic decline.

If we have underestimated the rapidity and significance of this regional pandemic among Native Americans, we tend to exaggerate the ease and rapidity of non-Indian expansion. By 1730 the combined white and black population of the non-Virginia South had come to slightly surpass the Indian population of the same area—a dramatic shift from fifteen years before, when Indians still outnumbered non-Indians more than eight to three. But the geographic distribution of the recent arrivals remains striking. Of more than 72,000 southern blacks and whites outside Virginia in 1730, all but 8,000 lived along a thin strip of land within one hundred miles of the coast of North and South Carolina. In other words, if Virginia's population skews the demography of the entire South most dramatically, the rapidly growing colonies of North and South Carolina also have a significant effect.

This can be seen in table 3 when first one (totals III–X) and then both of the Carolinas are removed from consideration, along with Virginia. Focusing on the rest of the South (totals IV–X), it is evident that in 1685 seven out of eight southern Indians reside in this wide domain away from the Atlantic coast claimed by England, and the proportion increases much further during the ensuing century. In contrast to coastal and piedmont Virginia and the Carolinas, the overall population in this domain is far less dense, and it is also far more indigenous. Here non-Indians do not begin to outnumber Indians until the decade before the American Revolution, and even in 1790, despite the flood of postwar migration, more than one person in six is still a Native American. But it also follows that when the largest English colonies are removed, the extent of population loss for the rest of the South appears all the more dramatic. For areas IV to X, the total population did not cease its absolute decline until the 1740s, having fallen by more than three-fifths in scarcely two generations.

It is clear from the aggregate calculations presented above that the rate of decline within the southern Indian population slowed during the eighteenth century and eventually reversed itself, achieving a slight net increase in the era of the Revolution after centuries of decline. Whether one examines the region as a whole or the somewhat smaller portions also shown in table 3, the number of Native Americans reaches its nadir about the time of the Cherokee War with the English in 1760, and overall numbers begin to rise again slowly over the next generation. The timing for the shift was not uniform, for local situations varied, but the general pattern is undeniable.

Several recent writers have suggested an epidemological explanation for this pattern. When Old World disease organisms first entered the Southeast in the sixteenth century, the effects were devastating. Sporadic exposure, perhaps no more often than once in a generation, prevented native groups from acquiring natural immunities, so entire populations suffered equally during repeated onslaughts. But as contacts with European traders became more extensive in the late seventeenth century, southern Indians gradually began to adapt to the shifting disease environment. More frequent exposure to a contagious illness such as smallpox meant that increasingly it became a childhood disease, having its greatest impact upon the newest members of the society. Among the Creeks, for example, research suggests that health status improved during the eighteenth century as occasional epidemics gave way to more common, but less devastating, endemic illnesses focused on young children. This first slowed the rate of population decline, then led to a gradual numerical increase, as confirmed by ethnohistorical and archaeological evidence. This upswing that appears clearly in the eighteenth-century southern data reflects a pattern found elsewhere in North America at different times, coinciding with the inception of regular direct contact by Indians with Europeans and Africans.[114]

Though a crucial demographic trend, this slowing and reversing of the population decline among southern Indians did not occur soon enough or fast enough, given the enormous influx of non-Indians into the region during the late colonial era. The overall population of the South had already begun to rebound during the first quarter of the eighteenth century, owing to new arrivals along the Atlantic coast. Over the next several generations these newcomers would slowly, then rapidly, intrude across the entire South, achieving both demographic and cultural hegemony. The region's main language would become English; its dominant religion would become Protestant Christianity; and its emergent political economy would become tied to free-market capitalism. These multiple transformations were by no means simple or predetermined, but until we comprehend the demographic context in which they occurred, we can never begin to understand the eighteenth-century South in all its dimensions.

Notes

1. The collaboration of Janice Blinder and Daniel H. Usner, Jr., in early stages of this project proved invaluable. I am indebted to them and to others who have provided references, suggestions, and criticism. A brief preview of this research, with graphs, appeared in *Southern Exposure* 16(Summer 1988).

2. One might also include Maryland, either separately or along with Virginia as part of a larger Chesapeake zone, for the two colonies had very similar demographic profiles. But while scholars still frequently discuss that area as "typifying" the colonial South, in terms of population makeup and density the Chesapeake differed markedly from the geographic South as a whole.

3. See, for example, David D. Smits, "'Abominable Mixture': Toward the Repudiation of Anglo-Indian Intermarriage in Seventeenth-Century Virginia," *Virginia Magazine of History and Biography* 95(April 1987): 157–92. This repudiation came much earlier in Virginia than throughout most of the South.

4. This can be seen in the "better-dead-than-red" approach to the disappearance of the English settlement at Roanoke in the 1580s, where the belief that the colony was "lost" persists in the face of evidence that many of the English were absorbed into local Indian populations.

5. Ben C. McCary, *Indians in Seventeenth-Century Virginia* (Charlottesville: University Press of Virginia, 1957), 81–82; Judith Reynolds, "Marriage between the English and Indians in Seventeenth-Century Virginia," *Quarterly Bulletin* (Archeological Society of Virginia) 17(1962): 19–25. Cf. Wesley Frank Craven, *White, Red and Black: The Seventeenth-Century Virginian* (Charlottesville: University Press of Virginia, 1971); Lynn E. Kauffman, James C. O'Neill, and Patricia A. Jehle, *Bibliography of the Virginia Indians* (Fredericksburg: Archeological Society of Virginia, 1976). Also see J. Frederick Fausz, "The Invasion of Virginia: Indians, Colonialism, and the Conquest of Cant, a Review Essay on Anglo-Indian Relations in the Chesapeake," *Virginia Magazine of History and Biography* 95(April 1987): 133–56; and Helen C. Rountree, "The Termination and Dispersal of the Nottaway Indians of Virginia," *Virginia Magazine of History and Biography* 95(April 1987): 193–215.

6. "An Act for Destroying Wolves," October 1669, in William W. Hening, *The Statutes at Large: Being a Collection of All Laws of Virginia, from the First Session of the Legislature in the Year 1619*, 13 vols. (Richmond: Samuel Pleasants, 1809–23), 2: 274–75; Douglas H. Ubelaker, *Reconstruction of Demographic Profiles from Ossuary Skeletal Samples: A Case Study from the Tidewater Potomac* (Washington, D.C.: Smithsonian Institution Press, 1974), 69.

7. Robert Beverley, *The History and Present State of Virginia* (1705), ed. Louis B. Wright (Chapel Hill: University of North Carolina Press, 1947), 232–33. Cf. Christian F. Feest, "Virginia Algonquians," in *Handbook of North American Indians*, vol. 15,

Northeast, ed. Bruce G. Trigger, gen. ed. William C. Sturtevant (Washington, D.C.: Smithsonian Institution Press, 1978), 253–70.

8. Beverley, *History*, 232; Clarence Carter, ed., "Observations of Superintendent John Stuart and Governor James Grant of East Florida on the Proposed Plan of 1764 for the Future Management of Indian Affairs," *American Historical Review* 20(July 1915): 825.

9. Thomas Jefferson, *Notes on the State of Virginia* (1787; New York: Harper and Row, 1964), 91–92. Cf. Helen Rountree, "The Termination and Dispersal of the Nottaway Indians of Virginia."

10. Thomas C. Parramore, "The Tuscarora Ascendency," *North Carolina Historical Review* 59(Autumn 1982): 307–15.

11. Ibid., 317; James W. Clay et al., *North Carolina Atlas: Portrait of a Changing Southern State* (Chapel Hill: University of North Carolina Press, 1975), fig. 1.2, p. 14; Christian F. Feest, "North Carolina Algonquians," in Trigger, *Handbook of North American Indians: Northeast*, 271–81.

12. John Lawson, *A New Voyage to Carolina*, ed. Hugh T. Lefler (London, 1709; Chapel Hill: University of North Carolina Press, 1967), 242–43; E. Lawrence Lee, *Indian Wars in North Carolina, 1663–1763* (Raleigh: Carolina Charter Tercentenary Commission, 1963), 3–5; Clay et al., *North Carolina Atlas*, 13.

13. Parramore, "Tuscarora Ascendancy," 315; Lawson, *New Voyage*, 232, 243.

14. Parramore, "Tuscarora Ascendancy," 315; Thomas C. Parramore, "With Tuscarora Jack on the Back Path to Bath," *North Carolina Historical Review* 64(April 1987): 115–38; John Brickell, *The Natural History of North-Carolina* (Dublin: James Carson, 1737; reprint, Murfreesboro, N.C.: Johnson, 1968), 253, 282; Patrick H. Garrow, *The Mattamuskeet Documents: A Study in Social History* (Raleigh: Archaeology Branch, North Carolina Division of Archives and History, 1975).

15. Elizabeth A. Fenn and Peter H. Wood, *Natives and Newcomers: The Way We Lived in North Carolina before 1770* (Chapel Hill: University of North Carolina Press, 1983), 31; James Mooney, *The Siouan Tribes of the East*, Bureau of American Ethnology Bulletin 22 (Washington, D.C.: Government Printing Office, 1894), 8.

16. Peter H. Wood, *Black Majority: Negroes in Colonial South Carolina from 1670 through the Stono Rebellion* (New York: Alfred A. Knopf, 1974), 37–42, 143–44; idem, "Indian Slavery in the Southeast," in *Handbook of North American Indians*, vol. 4 (Washington, D.C.: Smithsonian Institution Press, forthcoming).

17. Wood, *Black Majority*, 145–55; Donald B. Dodd and Wynelle S. Dodd, *Historical Statistics of the South, 1790–1970* (University: University of Alabama Press, 1973), 46.

18. Gene Waddell, *Indians of the South Carolina Lowcountry, 1562–1751* (Spartanburg, S.C.: Reprint Company, 1980), 14, 292–93.

19. Afra Coming to her sister, 6 March 1698/99, in Edward McCrady, *The History of South Carolina under the Proprietary Government, 1670–1719* (1897; reprint New York: Russell and Russell, 1969), 308; John Archdale, *A New Description of That Fertile and Pleasant Province of Carolina* (London: John Wyat, 1707), reprinted in *Nar-*

ratives of Early Carolina, 1650–1708, ed. Alexander S. Salley, Jr. (New York: Charles Scribner's Sons, 1911), 285.

20. Waddell, *Indians of the Lowcountry*, 6, 14, 269; James Glen, *A description of South Carolina: Containing many curious and interesting Particulars relating to the Civil, Natural and Commercial History of that Colony* (London: R. and J. Dodsley, 1761), 68.

21. Chapman J. Milling, *Red Carolinians*, 2d ed. (Columbia: University of South Carolina Press, 1969), 219–20, 222; Lee, *Indian Wars*, 47.

22. Lee, *Indian Wars*, 39–45; Milling, *Red Carolinians*, 222–23.

23. Samuel Cole Williams, ed., *Adair's History of the American Indians* (London, 1775; reprint, New York: Argonaut Press, 1966), 235; John R. Swanton, *The Indians of the Southeastern United States*, Bureau of American Ethnology Bulletin 137 (Washington, D.C.: Government Printing Office, 1946), 105.

24. Milling, *Red Carolinians*, 222, 235. See also James H. Merrell, "The Indians' New World: The Catawba Experience," *William and Mary Quarterly*, 3d ser., 41(October 1984): 537–65.

25. Verner W. Crane, *The Southern Frontier, 1670–1732* (Durham, N.C.: Duke University Press, 1928; reissued with a new preface by Peter H. Wood, New York: W. W. Norton, 1981), 129, 188; Larry E. Ivers, *Colonial Forts of South Carolina, 1670–1775* (Columbia: University of South Carolina Press, 1970), 43–44.

26. William K. Boyd, ed., *William Byrd's Histories of the Dividing Line betwixt Virginia and North Carolina* (New York: Dover, 1967), 300.

27. Williams, *Adair's History*, 235.

28. Ibid.

29. Ibid., 233.

30. Milling, *Red Carolinians*, 253–54; "Report of the Journey of the Brethren Abraham Steiner and Frederick C. De Schweinitz to the Cherokees and the Cumberland Settlements (1799)," in Samuel Cole Williams, ed., *Early Travels in the Tennessee Country, 1540–1800* (Johnson City, Tenn.: Watauga Press, 1928), 460.

31. Henry F. Dobyns, *Their Number Become Thinned: Native American Population Dynamics in Eastern North America* (Knoxville: University of Tennessee Press, 1983); William M. Denevan, ed., *The Native Population of the Americas in 1492* (Madison: University of Wisconsin Press, 1976); Douglas H. Ubelaker, "Prehistoric New World Population Size: Historical Review and Current Appraisal of North American Estimates," *American Journal of Physical Anthropology* 45(1976): 661–66; James H. Merrell, "Playing the Indian Numbers Game," *Reviews in American History* 12(1984): 354–58.

32. Swanton, *Indians of the Southeastern United States*, 194; John H. Hann, "Demographic Patterns and Changes in Mid-Seventeenth Century Timucua and Apalachee," *Florida Historical Quarterly* 64(April 1986): 378–81; Kathleen A. Deagan, "Cultures in Transition: Fusion and Assimilation among the Eastern Timucua," in *Tacachale: Essays on the Indians of Florida and Southeastern Georgia during the Historic Period*, ed. Jerald T. Milanich and Samuel Proctor (Gainesville: University Presses of Florida, 1978), 89–119.

33. J. G. Johnson, "The Spanish Southeast in the Seventeenth Century," *Georgia Historical Quarterly* 16(March 1932): 23; Lucy L. Wenhold, trans., *A Seventeenth-Century Letter of Gabriel Diaz Vara Calderón, Bishop of Cuba, Describing the Indians and Indian Missions of Florida*, with an introduction by John R. Swanton, Smithsonian Miscellaneous Collections 95, no. 16 (Washington, D.C.: Government Printing Office, 1936), 8–12; Mark F. Boyd, Hale G. Smith, and John W. Griffin, *Here They Once Stood: The Tragic End of the Apalachee Missions* (Gainesville: University of Florida Press, 1951), 8. Native resistance and English interference prevented Spanish conversion of the Creeks, so Calderón's total does not include thirteen Lower Creek villages along the Apalachicola River or fourteen Upper Creek villages farther north and west. These towns, and others not named in the bishop's initial listing, are included in the Indian population estimates for the Creek-Georgia-Alabama area. This is also true for Calderón's "more than 4,000 heathen called Chiscas," or Yuchis, "who sustain themselves with game, nuts and roots of trees" in the same area.

34. For evidence on Florida's non-Indian populations, see John R. Dunkle, "Population Change as an Element in the Historical Geography of St. Augustine," *Florida Historical Quarterly* 37(July 1958): 3–22; Kathleen A. Deagan, "*Mestizaje* in Colonial San Augustine," *Ethnohistory* 20(1973): 55–65; Theodore G. Corbett, "Population Structure in Hispanic St. Augustine, 1629–1763," *Florida Historical Quarterly* 54 (January 1976): 263–84; W. H. Siebert, "Slavery and White Servitude in East Florida, 1726–1776," *Florida Historical Quarterly* 10(July 1931): 5; Kenneth W. Porter, "Negroes on the Southern Frontier, 1670–1763," *Journal of Negro History* 33(1948): 53–78; John J. TePaske, "The Fugitive Slave: Intercolonial Rivalry and Spanish Slave Policy, 1697–1764," in *Eighteenth Century Florida and Its Borderlands*, ed. Samuel Proctor (Gainesville, University of Florida Press, 1975), 1–12; Jane Landers, "Spanish Sanctuary: Fugitives in Florida, 1687–1790," *Florida Historical Quarterly* 62(January 1984): 296–313; Joseph B. Lockey, *East Florida, 1783–1785: A File of Documents Assembled and Many of Them Translated* (Berkeley: University of California Press, 1949), 10–11, 420–21.

35. Wenhold, *Seventeenth-Century Letter*, 11; Swanton, *Indians of the Southeastern United States*, 102; Lewis H. Larson, *Aboriginal Subsistence Technology on the Southeastern Coastal Plain during the Late Prehistoric Period* (Gainesville: University Presses of Florida, 1980), 23–34; Clifford M. Lewis, "The Calusa," in Milanich and Proctor, *Tacachale*, 19–49.

36. William C. Sturtevant, "Spanish-Indian Relations in Southeastern North America," *Ethnohistory* 9(Winter 1962): 68–71; James W. Covington, "Migration of the Seminoles into Florida, 1700–1820," *Florida Historical Quarterly* 46(April 1968): 341–44.

37. Lewis H. Larson, Jr., "Historic Guale Indians of the Georgia Coast and the Impact of the Spanish Mission Effort," in Milanich and Proctor, *Tacachale*, 120; Crane, *Southern Frontier*, 80; Milling, *Red Carolinians*, 170–74; John Jay TePaske, *The Governorship of Spanish Florida, 1700–1763* (Durham, N.C.: Duke University Press, 1964), 197.

38. Thomas Nairne to the Earl of Sunderland, July 10, 1709, in Great Britain, Public Record Office, Colonial Office 5/382, no. 11 (hereafter cited as BPRO, CO); Sturtevant, "Spanish-Indian Relations," 71.

39. Theodore G. Corbett, "Migration to a Spanish Imperial Frontier in the Seventeenth and Eighteenth Centuries: St. Augustine," *Hispanic American Historical Review* 54(August 1974): 428–30; Robert L. Gold, *Borderland Empires in Transition: The Triple Nation Transfer of Florida* (Carbondale: Southern Illinois University Press, 1969), 76; Sturtevant, "Spanish-Indian Relations," 71; John R. Swanton, *Early History of the Creek Indians and Their Neighbors*, Bureau of American Ethnology Bulletin 73 (Washington, D.C.: Government Printing Office, 1922), 423; Covington, "Migration of the Seminoles," 342.

40. William Bartram, *Travels through North and South Carolina, Georgia, East and West Florida* (facsimile of the 1792 London edition; Savannah: Beehive Press, 1973), 206–7.

41. Ibid., 209; Clarence E. Carter, ed., *The Territorial Papers of the United States*, vol. 22, *The Territory of Florida, 1821–1824* (Washington, D.C.: Government Printing Office, 1956), 463–65; Henry A. Kersey, Jr., *The Seminole and Miccosukee Tribes: A Critical Bibliography* (Bloomington: Indiana University Press, 1987). On Seminole population, cf. Swanton, *Early History of the Creek Indians*, 400, 456, and idem, *Indians of the Southeastern United States*, 181.

42. Crane, *Southern Frontier*, 33–36. A suggestive current dissertation makes a convincing case for referring to these diverse peoples as the Muscogulges and to their homeland, encompassing most of the region described here, as Muskogee. Joel Wayne Martin, "Cultural Hermeneutics on the Frontier: Colonialism and the Muscogulge Millenarian Revolt of 1813" (Ph.D. diss., Duke University, 1988).

43. David H. Corkran, *The Creek Frontier, 1540–1783* (Norman: University of Oklahoma Press, 1967), 48–56.

44. Wenhold, *Seventeenth-Century Letter*, 9–10; Mark F. Boyd, "Expedition of Marcus Delgado from Apalache to the Upper Creek Country in 1686," *Florida Historical Quarterly* 16(July 1937): 3–32; Vernon J. Knight, Jr., and Sherée L. Adams, "A Voyage to the Mobile and Tomeh in 1700, with Notes on the Interior of Alabama," *Ethnohistory* 28(1981): 179–94.

45. "Letter from N. Johnson, Thomas Broughton, Robt. Gibbs, George Smith, and Richard Beresford," September 17, 1708, in A. S. Salley, indexer, *Records in the British Public Record Office Relating to South Carolina, 1701–1710* (Columbia, S.C., 1947), 208.

46. "An exact Account of ye Number and Strength of all the Indian Nations that were subject to the Government of South Carolina, and solely traded with them in ye beginning of ye year 1715 . . . ," in *A Chapter in the Early History of South Carolina*, ed. William J. Rivers (Charleston, 1874), 94.

47. Corkran, *Creek Frontier*, 114. Cf. Bernard Romans, *A Concise Natural History of East and West Florida* (1775), facsimile reproduction, ed. Rembert W. Patrick (Gainesville: University Presses of Florida, 1962), 90–91.

48. Wilber R. Jacobs, ed., *Indians of the Southern Colonial Frontier: The Edmond Atkin Report and Plan of 1755* (Columbia: University of South Carolina Press, 1954), 43.

49. "Names of the Villages inhabited by the Creek Indians & the No in each Village. in

Majr Farmar's letter of 24th Jany 1764," in *Mississippi Provincial Archives, 1763–1766: English Dominion*, vol. 1 (Nashville: Brandon Printing Company, 1911), 94–97; Report of Francis Ogilvie, July 8, 1764, in volume 21 of the Papers of General Thomas Gage, Clements Library, Ann Arbor, Michigan, cited in Corkran, *Creek Frontier*, 6.

50. Williams, *Adair's History*, 274; Romans, *Concise Natural History*, 90–91.

51. Dodd and Dodd, *Historical Statistics*, 18; "Observations on the Indians in the southern Parts of the United States, in a Letter from the Hon. Dr. Ramsay, corresponding Member of the Historical Society, March 10, 1795," including Mr. Purcell's 1780 estimate, *Collections of the Massachusetts Historical Society*, 1st ser., 4 (1795): 99–100.

52. "General Knox, Secretary of War, to the President of the United States," July 7, 1789, including letter from Hawkins et al., to Richard Henry Lee, December 2, 1785, in *American State Papers*, Class II, Indian Affairs, 1:38–39; Caleb Swan, "Position and State of Manners and Arts in the Creek, or Muscoggee Nation in 1791," in *Historical and Statistical Information Respecting the History, Condition, and Prospects of the Indian Tribes of the United States*, ed. Henry Rowe Schoolcraft, 6 vols. (Philadelphia: Lippincott, Grambo, 1851–57; reprint, New York: Paladin Press, 1969; New York: AMS, 1977), 5:263.

53. "Statement of the towns of the different tribes of Indians which today compose the nation known under the name of Creek or Maskoke," enclosed in a letter from Pedro Olivier to Carondelet, December 1, 1793, in *Spain in the Mississippi Valley, 1765–1794*, ed. Lawrence Kinnaird (Washington, D.C., 1946–49), part 3, 229–32. Cf. Albert S. Gatschet, "Towns and Villages of the Creek Confederacy in the XVIII. and XIX. Centuries," *Publications of the Alabama Historical Society, Miscellaneous Collections* 1, part 5 (1901): 386–415. The map "Southern Indian Villages, 1760–1794," in *Atlas of Early American History: The Revolutionary Era, 1760–1790*, ed. Lester J. Cappon et al. (Princeton: Princeton University Press for the Newberry Library, 1976), 19, shows only ten Creek towns.

54. "The Commissioners to the Secretary of War," November 20, 1789, in *American State Papers*, Class II, Indian Affairs, 1:78–79. A decade later Benjamin Hawkins listed the major "old towns" and elaborated on the system of satellite villages that made town counts vary so greatly. Besides the seven Seminole towns in Florida, Hawkins reported, "There are thirty-seven towns in the Creek nation, twelve on the waters of the Chat-to-ho-che, and twenty-five on the waters of Coo-sau and Tal-la-poo-sa. The small towns or villages belong to some one of these." Hawkins also commented upon population fluctuations within individual towns. Discussing the village of "Autosse" on the Tallapoosa, he wrote in 1799: "In the year 1766 there were forty-three gun men, and lately they were estimated at eighty. This is a much greater increase of population than is to be met with in other towns! They appear to be stationary generally, and in some towns are on the decrease; the apparent difference here, or increase, may be greater than the real; as formerly men grown were rated as gun men, and now boys of fifteen, who are hunters, are rated as gun men; they have for two years past been on the decline; are very sickly, and have lost many of their inhabitants; they are now rated at fifty gun men only." Benjamin Hawkins, "A Sketch of the Creek

Country in the Years 1798 and 1799," *Collections of the Georgia Historical Society*, 3, part 1 (1848): 24–25, 32.

55. Swan, "Position and State of Manners," 259–63.

56. Gary C. Goodwin, *Cherokees in Transition: A Study of Changing Culture and Environment prior to 1775* (Chicago: University of Chicago Department of Geography, 1977), 41.

57. "Exact Account," 94. If the breakdowns are correct, then the total of 11,530 given in the original document (BPRO, CO 5:1265, Q 201) is in error and should be 11,210 as presented in Rivers.

58. Letter from Governor Nathaniel Johnson and Council to Proprietors, September 17, 1708, in *Records of the British Public Record Office Relating to South Carolina, 1663–1710*, 5 vols., comp. W. Noel Sainsbury (Atlanta and Columbia, 1928–47), 5:209.

59. James Mooney, *The Aboriginal Population of America North of Mexico*, Smithsonian Miscellaneous Collections 80, no. 7 (Washington, D.C.: Government Printing Office, 1928), 8. On Indian smallpox death rates, see Conrad Heidenreich, *Huronia: A History and Geography of the Huron Indians, 1600–1650* (Toronto: McClelland and Stewart, 1971), 97–98.

60. Jacobs, *Indians*, 42.

61. Williams, *Adair's History*, 238.

62. Ibid., 244, 327.

63. Pennsylvania *Gazette*, September 4, 1760. I am indebted to Suzanne Krebsbach for this reference. Cf. Peter H. Wood, "The Impact of Smallpox on the Native Population of the Eighteenth-Century South," *New York State Journal of Medicine* 87(January 1987): 30–36.

64. Williams, *Adair's History*, 239.

65. "Observations," *Collections of the Massachusetts Historical Society*, 1st ser. 4 (1795): 99–100; James Paul Pate, "The Chickamauga: A Forgotten Segment of Indian Resistance on the Southern Frontier" (Ph.D. diss., Mississippi State University, 1969), 80–82.

66. "Gen. Henry Knox to the President," July 7, 1789, *American State Papers*, Indian Affairs, 1:38.

67. Robert L. Meriwether, *The Expansion of South Carolina, 1729–1765* (Kingsport, Tenn.: Southern Publishers, 1940), 217, 232; Larry E. Ivers, *Colonial Forts of South Carolina, 1670–1775* (Columbia: University of South Carolina Press for the South Carolina Tricentennial Commission, 1970), 16.

68. Max Dixon, *The Wataugans* (Nashville: Tennessee American Revolution Bicentennial Commission, 1976), 26; Evarts B. Greene and Virginia D. Harrington, *American Population before the Federal Census of 1790* (New York: Columbia University Press, 1932), 193.

69. Peter H. Wood, "'Impatient of Oppression': Black Freedom Struggles on the Eve of White Independence," *Southern Exposure* 12(November/December 1984): 10–16; and

Theda Perdue "Red and Black in the Southern Appalachians," in "Liberating Our Past: Four Hundred Years of Southern History," *Southern Exposure* 12(November/December 1984): 17–24.

70. Stella H. Sutherland, *Population Distribution in Colonial America* (New York: Columbia University Press, 1936), 209.

71. Antoine Le Page du Pratz, *The History of Louisiana*, facsimile reproduction of the 1774 translated British edition, ed. Joseph Tragle, Jr. (Baton Rouge: Louisiana State University Press, 1975), 310–11; Williams, *Adair's History*, 377.

72. Williams, *Early Travels in the Tennessee Country*, 62; Benjamin Franklin French, *Historical Collections of Louisiana*, 5 vols. (New York: Lamport, Blakeman and Law, 1846–53), 1:60.

73. Swanton, *Early History of the Creek Indians*, 449, 456. A roll prepared by federal officials in the mid-1830s showed a population of 6,070, made up of 4,914 Chickasaws and 1,156 slaves. Arrell M. Gibson, *The Chickasaws* (Norman: University of Oklahoma Press, 1971), 179.

74. Gibson, *Chickasaws*, 39–57, 63–64; Bienville to Maurepas, August 26, 1734, is quoted on p. 50.

75. Swanton, *Indians of the Southeastern United States*, 123; idem, *Early History of the Creek Indians*, 456, 450–51.

76. Jack D. L. Holmes, "The Choctaws in 1795," *Alabama Historical Quarterly*, 30(Spring 1968): 33–50. The totals on page 38 contain an error in addition or transcription.

77. Williams, *Adair's History*, 302–3.

78. Richebourg Gaillard McWilliams, ed. and trans., *Iberville's Gulf Journals* (University: University of Alabama Press, 1981), 174, 141. In a 1702 speech to several chiefs of the warring Chickasaws and Choctaws (p. 172), Iberville repeated what he had learned of their recent attrition. "You Chicacha can observe that during the last eight to ten years when you have been at war with the Chaqueta at the instigation of the English, who gave you ammunition and thirty guns for that purpose, you have taken more than 500 prisoners and killed more than 1,800 Chaqueta. Those prisoners were sold; but taking those prisoners cost you more than 800 men, slain on various war parties."

79. Letter of August 3, 1723, by LeBlond de la Tour, in "Minutes of the Superior Council of Louisiana," in *Mississippi Provincial Archives: French Dominion*, trans. and ed. Dunbar Rowland and Albert Sanders, 3 vols. (Jackson: Mississippi Department of Archives and History, 1927–32), 357–58.

80. Le Page du Pratz, *History of Louisiana*, 309.

81. Rowland and Sanders, *Mississippi Provincial Archives*, 1:115–17, 150–54.

82. Patricia Dillon Woods, *French-Indian Relations of the Southern Frontier, 1699–1762* (Ann Arbor: UMI Research Press, 1980), 148; Jacobs, *Indians*, 43–44. For overzealous estimates of Choctaw strength by English colonial officials seeking to win a powerful new ally against the French in the late 1730s, see Allen D. Candler and

Lucian Lamar Knight, eds., *The Colonial Records of the State of Georgia*, 24 vols. (Athens, Ga., 1904–16), 5:56, 190–91.

83. Woods, *French-Indian Relations*, 168; "Rapport du Chevalier de Kerlérec," *Compte Rendu du Congrès International des Américanistes*, 15th sess., 1:76n; Seymour Feiler, ed. and trans., *Jean-Bernard Bossu's Travels in the Interior of North America, 1751–1762* (Norman: University of Oklahoma Press, 1962), 163.

84. "An Account of Several Nations of Southern Indians. In a Letter From Rev. Elam Potter to Rev. Dr. Stiles, A.D. 1768," *Collections of the Massachusetts Historical Society*, 1st ser., 10(1795): 119–21; "Observations on the Indians in the Southern Parts of the United States, in a Letter from the Hon. Dr. Ramsay, Corresponding Member of the Historical Society. March 10, 1795," Ibid., 1st ser., 4:99; *American State Papers*, Documents, legislative and executive, of the Congress of the United States, Class II, Indian Affairs (Washington, D.C., 1832), 1:39, 49, 659.

85. John R. Swanton, *Indian Tribes of the Lower Mississippi Valley and Adjacent Coast of the Gulf of Mexico*, Bureau of American Ethnology Bulletin 43 (Washington, D.C.: Government Printing Office, 1911), 43. For a new overview, see Fred B. Kiffen, Hiram F. Gregory, and George A. Stokes, *The Historic Indian Tribes of Louisiana from 1542 to the Present* (Baton Rouge: Louisiana State University Press, 1987).

86. Peter H. Wood, "La Salle: Discovery of a Lost Explorer," *American Historical Review* 89(April 1984): 294–323.

87. Jean-Baptiste Bernard de La Harpe, *The Historical Journal of the Establishment of the French in Louisiana* (Lafayette: University of Southwestern Louisiana Press, 1971), 23; Swanton, *Indian Tribes of the Lower Mississippi Valley*, 41, idem, *Early History of the Creek Indians*, 425.

88. Daniel H. Usner, Jr., "Frontier Exchange in the Lower Mississippi Valley: Race Relations and Economic Life in Colonial Louisiana, 1699–1783" (Ph.D. diss., Duke University, 1981), 69.

89. Swanton, *Indians of the Southeast*, 140; Thomas Hutchins, *An Historical Narrative and Topographical Description of Louisiana, and West-Florida*, facsimile reproduction of 1784 edition, ed. Joseph G. Tragle, Jr. (Gainesville: University Presses of Florida, 1968), 39.

90. Usner, "Frontier Exchange," 69.

91. W. David Baird, *The Quapaw Indians: A History of the Downstream People* (Norman: University of Oklahoma Press, 1980), 31, 37.

92. "Letter of Mr. Thaumur de la Source," in *Early Voyages up and down the Mississippi*, ed. John D. G. Shea (Albany: Joel Munsell, 1861), 81; Hutchins, *Historical Narrative*, 44; Pierre Margry, *Découvertes et établissements des Français dans l'ouest et dans le sud de l'Amérique Septentrionale (1614–1754): Mémoires et documents origineaux*, 6 vols. (Paris: Imprimérie D. Jouast, 1876–86), 4:414.

93. La Harpe, *Historical Journal*, 33–34; Letter of Roulleaux de La Vente, September 20, 1704, quoted in Swanton, *Indian Tribes of the Lower Mississippi Valley*, 39; "Historical Journal of Father Pierre François Xavier de Charlevoix," in French, *Historical Collections of Louisiana*, 3:162.

94. Woods, *French-Indian Relations,* 95–110; Usner, "Frontier Exchange," 69.

95. Marcel Giraud, *A History of French Louisiana* (Baton Rouge: Louisiana State University Press, 1974), 277–79; Daniel H. Usner, Jr., "From African Captivity to American Slavery: The Introduction of Black Laborers to Colonial Louisiana," *Louisiana History* 20 (Winter 1979): 25–48.

96. Usner, "Frontier Exchange," 122, 140, 146; Andrew Walsh and Robert Wells, "Population Dynamics in the Eighteenth-Century Mississippi River Valley: Acadians in Louisiana," *Journal of Social History* 11(Summer 1978): 521–45.

97. W. W. Newcomb, Jr., *The Indians of Texas from Prehistoric to Modern Times* (Austin: University of Texas Press, 1961), 283. See also the four volumes of *Caddoan Indians* (New York: Garland, 1974) in the American Indian Ethnohistory Series, ed. David Agee Horr, containing expert testimony submitted to the Indian Claims Commission, such as Helen Hornbeck Tanner, "The Territory of the Caddo Tribe of Oklahoma," 4:9–144.

98. See Herbert Eugene Bolton, *The Hasinais: South Caddoans as Seen by the Earliest Europeans,* ed. Russell M. Magnaghi (Norman: University of Oklahoma Press, 1987).

99. Newcomb, *Indians of Texas,* 313.

100. Ibid., 315–29; Herbert Eugene Bolton, *Texas in the Middle Eighteenth Century: Studies in Spanish Colonial History and Administration* (Austin: University of Texas Press, 1970), 196–203, 219–40. (This book was originally published in 1915 as volume 3 of the University of California Publications in History.)

101. Newcomb, *Indians of Texas,* 59–81. On the Atakapas and Karankawas, also see Lawrence E. Aten, *Indians of the Upper Texas Coast* (New York: Academic Press, 1983).

102. Newcomb, *Indians of Texas,* 136.

103. John C. Ewers, "The Influence of Epidemics on the Indian Population and Cultures of Texas," *Plains Anthropologist* 18(May 1973): 104–15, esp. 105–7; Alicia V. Tjarks, "Comparative Demographic Analysis of Texas, 1777–1793," *Southwestern Historical Quarterly* 77(January 1974): 291–338.

104. Elizabeth A. H. John, *Storms Brewed in Other Men's Worlds: The Confrontation of Indians, Spanish, and French in the Southwest, 1540–1795* (College Station: Texas A&M Press, 1975), 204–5; Ewers, "Influence of Epidemics," 108.

105. Non-Indian numbers regarding East Texas before 1775 have not yet been adequately documented. For several estimates larger than those given in table 1, see Tjarks, "Comparative Demographic Analysis of Texas," 299.

106. Ibid., 295–96.

107. Ibid., 301, 324–25; John, *Storms,* 369, 499, 523, 540–41.

108. Samuel Cole Williams, ed., *Lieut. Henry Timberlake's Memoirs, 1756–1765* (1927; reprint Marietta, Ga.: Continental Book Company, 1948), 113–16; Charles Callender, "Shawnee," in Trigger, *Handbook of North American Indians: Northeast,* 623, 630–31; Jerry E. Clark, *The Shawnee* (Lexington: University Press of Kentucky, 1977), 3.

109. Clark, *Shawnee*, 15–16, 18; Lucien Beckner, "Eskippakithiki: The Last Indian Town in Kentucky," *Filson Club History Quarterly* 6(1932): 355–82; Ernest H. Howerton, "Logan, the Shawnee Capital of West Virginia—from 1760 to 1780," *West Virginia History* 16(July 1955): 313–33.

110. Michael N. McConnell, "Peoples 'In Between': The Iroquois and the Ohio Indians, 1720–1768," in *Beyond the Covenant Chain: The Iroquois and Their Neighbors in Indian North America, 1675–1775*, ed. James H. Merrell and Daniel K. Richter (Syracuse: Syracuse University Press, 1987).

111. R. David Edmunds, *The Shawnee Prophet* (Lincoln: University of Nebraska Press, 1983), 10; idem, *Tecumseh and the Quest for Indian Leadership* (Boston: Little, Brown, 1984), 20.

112. James H. Pauley, "Early North Carolina Migrations into the Tennessee Country, 1768–1782: A Study in Historical Demography" (Ph.D. diss., Middle Tennessee State University, 1969): Patricia Watlington, "The Partisan Spirit: Kentucky Politics, 1779–1792" (Ph.D. diss., Yale University, 1964), 49.

113. George M. Frederickson, *White Supremacy: A Comparative Study in American and South African History* (New York: Oxford University Press, 1981), 5.

114. Jeanne Kay, "The Fur Trade and Native American Population Growth," *Ethnohistory* 31(1984): 265–87; Kenneth R. Turner, "Health, Illness, and the People of Hoithlewaulee," in *Culture Change on the Creek Indian Frontier*, ed. Gregory A. Waselkov, Final Report to the National Science Foundation, Grant Award #BNS-8305437, pp. 55–82.

American Indians in Colonial New Orleans

Daniel H. Usner, Jr.

So much of the scholarship on American Indians in colonial North America has concentrated on the populous nations inhabiting the interior that relatively little is understood about those smaller Indian groups situated in the midst of colonial settlements and towns. The praying towns of New England and the mission reserves of Canada are the most familiar of such communities, thanks to recent investigations into the refugees and survivors of seventeenth-century wars.[1] Since so much research is needed on southeastern Indians in general, one is hard pressed to urge emphasis on any particular category of colonial-Indian relations. The large picture of geopolitical, economic, and cultural interaction demands closer attention to the Cherokees, Creeks, Choctaws, Chickasaws, and Caddos before we can afford the luxury of studying smaller, more enclosed Indian communities. Yet to ignore the latter would exclude Indian peoples living within sizable parts of the Southeast—like the tidewater and piedmont Atlantic areas, the Florida panhandle, and the alluvial plain of the Mississippi River—who experienced colonialism differently, but no less importantly, than did interior tribespeople.[2]

Colonial towns serve as especially informative foci for examining forms of Indian adaptation and persistence different from those that occurred within Indian nations situated in the backcountry of European colonies. In diverse eighteenth-century towns across the Southeast, Indians frequently lived and visited in an array of circumstances. An inestimable number of Indians from many tribes found themselves either being shipped away as slaves from colonial ports or working as slaves in and around them. Charlestown merchants waged slave-raiding expeditions that brought captive Timucuans, Apalaches, Tuscaroras, Yamasees, and Choctaws to households in their town as well as to plantations in Virginia and Carolina.

Intimate contact with Europeans and Africans and coercive labor at entirely new tasks undoubtedly changed life for Indian servants and slaves inhabiting colonized areas while channeling Indian influences to the colonial populace. The colonial capitals of Williamsburg, Charlestown, Savannah, and St. Augustine, and eventually such interior centers as Augusta, Fort Toulouse, and Natchez, became important meeting places for Indian diplomats, many of whom traveled long distances to exchange words and gifts with European officials. More regularly these emerging cities were frequented by Indian villagers who lived nearby and, though reduced to tributary or subordinate status by war or flight, participated actively in the social and economic rhythm of town life as boathands, packhorsemen, interpreters, day laborers, and peddlers.[3] All these types of activity were experienced by American Indians in another southern colonial town, named by its French founders "Nouvelle Orléans."

Traveling up the Mississippi River in early March 1699, Pierre Le Moyne d'Iberville was shown by his Bayogoula Indian guide "the place through which the Indians make their portage to this river from the back of the bay where the ships are anchored. They drag their canoes over a rather good road, at which we found several pieces of baggage owned by men that were going there or were returning."[4] Situated between a chain of lakes and the Mississippi, the crescent-shaped bend at what became New Orleans had been mainly used by Indians for transport between waterways and seasonal gathering of food sources. Yet natural conditions that made this site ideal for portage and fishing reduced its potential for permanent occupation.[5] Now a metropolis slowly sinking inside artificial levees and spillways, New Orleans sits on a natural levee, created by sediment deposited during seasonal flooding, that slopes down from a crest of fifteen feet above sea level to almost five feet below sea level. The city's vulnerability to flooding is exacerbated by Lake Pontchartrain to the north and Lake Borge to the east.[6]

Before European contact Indians used the four-to-eight-mile-wide strip of swampland as a fishing/hunting/gathering station and as a portage between the lakes and the river. The most habitable sites were along Bayou St. John, a few miles long and about twenty feet wide when Iberville traveled it, and on the Metairie ridge, which linked that bayou with Bayou Chapitoulas. From this junction Indians reached the Mississippi by a three-mile portage.[7] Since René-Robert Cavalier de La Salle's voyage down the Mississippi in 1682, this had been a highly volatile area. A Tangipahoa village a few miles above the portage road was destroyed, perhaps by Quinipissas from upriver. By 1699 a group of Acolapissas occupied Metairie ridge, but during the first decade of the eighteenth century some Biloxis and then some Houmas moved in temporarily. English slave raids upriver to the north and French war against the Chitimachas kept the lower Mississippi Delta in turmoil until Jean-Baptiste Le Moyne de Bienville began construction of New Orleans in 1718.[8]

Largely in consequence of this early conflict, enslaved Indians constituted the core of the resident Indian population in French New Orleans, resembling the earlier presence of Native American slaves in such colonial towns as Boston, New York, and Charlestown. French and English colonies in North America allowed and periodically encouraged the enslavement of Indian people from enemy tribes or distant territories. Most captives were transported from one region to another, but many enslaved Indians remained in their locale to be joined by black and Indian slaves imported from abroad. By November 1721 fifty-one Indian slaves lived in the vicinity of New Orleans—twenty-one in town and the rest on farms at Bayou St. John, Gentilly, Chapitoulas, Cannes Bruslée, and Chaouchas. Louisiana's total slave population at the time numbered 161 Indians and 680 Africans.[9]

Indian slaves in the colony belonged to several tribes. "Panis," an epithet for Indians captured above the Arkansas River, were present, but Alibamon, Taensa, and Chitimacha slaves—captives in local wars—also lived in colonial households. Suffering more enslavement than other local tribes, the Chitimachas of Bayou Lafourche became a significant ethnic component in the early slave population of lower Louisiana. Late in 1706 some Chitimachas assassinated Jean François Buisson de Saint-Cosmé, a priest of the Foreign Missions, and subsequent French and allied-Indian warfare against the tribe lasted more than a decade, with scores of captured Chitimachas being sold into slavery in Louisiana and the Caribbean. When he arrived at Bayou St. John in the winter of 1718–19, Antoine Le Page du Pratz purchased a Chitimacha woman from another settler "in order to have a person who could dress our victuals."[10]

Before New Orleans was founded, the presence of Indian slave women in Louisiana households had generated a great deal of controversy. While some marriages between Frenchmen and Indian women were blessed by priests at Mobile and Kaskaskia, where few white women lived during the early colonial period, most officials and clergymen condemned soldiers and settlers who cohabited with their female servants. Accusations of laxness toward this practice flew across factional lines in the colonial government. In a memoir written after his return to France in 1710, the former pastor of the colony's main settlement at Mobile denounced many Louisianians for preferring over legitimate marriage "to maintain scandalous concubinages with young Indian women, driven by their proclivity for the extremes of licentiousness. They have bought them under the pretext of keeping them as servants, but actually to seduce them, as they in fact have done."[11] The immigration of more European women to Louisiana after 1717 created a more balanced gender ratio within the colonial population and made intimacy with Indian women less threatening to the colony's order. The Black Code issued for Louisiana in 1724, furthermore, prohibited sexual intercourse between slaves and colonists. But interracial cohabitation, like so many other acts forbidden by that law, certainly did not end. While the census taken in January 1726 did not designate the sexual identity of the 229 Indians and 1,540 Negroes in the colony's rapidly growing slave population, a large proportion were women, many of whom were obliged to live among the French as mistresses or common-law wives. Although "the number of those who maintain young Indian women or negresses to satisfy their intemperence is considerably diminished," Père Raphael reported that same year, "there still remain enough to scandalize the church and to require an effective remedy."[12]

Complaints of concubinage, although it undoubtedly existed in some cases, should not divert attention from other services rendered by Indian men and women who worked for families and artisans. Dispersed among urban households and neighboring farms by the 1720s, Indian slaves influenced material life in early New Orleans. The 1726 census showed thirty Indian slaves inside the city residing in diverse household arrangements. On the Rue Royalle two Indian and four Negro slaves lived with carpenter Thomas Dezery, and one slave lived in the household of a locksmith named Sulpice L'Evique with his wife and three children. Seven Indian slaves lived in another conjugal household on the Rue St. Louis, that of François St. Amand, his wife, and his two children. On the Rue du Quay a slave lived with Sieur Duval and his family, and another inhabited the house of Reboul, a hunter, perhaps as a female companion or a male assistant. At Chapitoulas, just above New Orleans along the Mississippi, eleven Indian slaves lived on four separate plantations along with eleven European servants and 302 Negro slaves. At Bayou St. John and Gentilly, on the northeastern outskirts of the city, eight Indian slaves also worked beside white and black laborers on several farms.[13]

The recalcitrance of Indian slaves intensified the colonial government's anxiety over the potential for a slave revolt in Louisiana, where enslaved blacks outnumbered the white populace by the 1730s. Given their knowledge of the region, runaway Indian slaves around New Orleans seriously threatened the property and security of slaveowners, even alarming officials into discouraging further enslavement of Louisiana Indians. Following reports of *marrons sauvages* raiding cattle and attacking the Negro public executioner, a maroon camp called *Natanapallé* was discovered in 1727. Sancousy, an Indian slave who lost his owner's ox, fled to this makeshift village, where he met about fifteen black and Indian fugitives. These escaped slaves possessed enough guns and ammunition to defend themselves against any pursuers. The arrest of other runaways who had apparently seen this community influenced Governor Etienne Boucher de Périer to request that the trade for Indian slaves be terminated. Not only did this traffic incite costly wars between tribes, but "these Indian slaves being mixed with our negroes may induce them to desert with them, as has already happened, as they may maintain relations with them which might be disastrous to the colony when there are more blacks."[14]

A conjunction of circumstances that Louisiana shared with other North American colonies slowed the rate of Indian enslavement. The decimation of neighboring tribes by disease, the desire to secure stable trading relations, and the ease with which Indian captives could abscond all contributed to this decline. The increased availability of Africans by the 1720s reinforced the racial categorization of slaves as Negro and mulatto. Major conflicts with the Natchez in 1729–30 and with the Chickasaws over the following decade produced hundreds of slaves, mostly Natchez, but the abatement of warfare elsewhere in the lower Mississippi valley reduced the general incidence of captivity. Some of the five hundred or more men, women, and children captured in the Natchez war remained in Louisiana as slaves and others were executed, but most were shipped by the Company of the Indies to the Caribbean. The New Orleans census of January 1732 lists only six Indian women and five Indian men amid a town population of 626 Euro-Americans and 258 Afro-Americans, while fewer than fifty Indian slaves inhabited farms below and above the city.[15]

Fear of Indian and black cooperation combined with stable Indian-French relations to reduce the number of Indian slaves in and around the colonial capital, but the economic interests of slaveowners managed to maintain an Indian slave population of 120 persons in Louisiana by 1771. The number of Indian slaves recorded in New Orleans had actually increased to forty-two females and nineteen males of different ages. One also should conjecture that liaisons between Indian and Afro-American slaves produced children who were ascribed by owners to Negro and mulatto identities and that some offspring of Indian women and white men grew up free. As in other early towns, therefore, a portion of the Indian population was assimilated by the colonial society through slavery.[16]

Only with its transfer to Spain in 1766 did laws prohibiting the enslavement, purchase, or transfer of Indians reach the colony. During the Spanish period the Indian slave populace in the city and the colony at large virtually disappeared. Avenues to emancipation available under Spanish law contributed slightly to this diminution, and undecided petitions by some slaves claiming Indian ancestry were inherited by the Orleans Territory courts of the United States. "It is reported to me," wrote Governor William Claiborne to Secretary of State James Madison in 1808, "that in this Territory, there are now several hundred persons held as slaves, who are descended of Indian families."[17] But by then the inhabitants of New Orleans fell into a rigid tripartite division of racial identity: free whites, enslaved blacks (some actually being mulatto), and free people of color. Nearly 20 percent of the city's 8,500 people were classified as *gens de couleur*, which was synonymous with mixed ancestry. And in the process of making blacks and slaves the same category, the Louisiana Supreme Court ruled in 1810 that "persons of color may be descended from Indians on both sides, from a white parent, or mulatto parents in possession of their freedom."[18] The fascinating legal and social ramifications of this kind of decision aside, continuing absorption into a rapidly growing non-Indian population and a tightening racial structure together caused the apparent disappearance of Indian slaves in New Orleans by the nineteenth century.

More conspicuous than the presence of Indian slaves in colonial

New Orleans were diplomatic visits by chiefs and delegates from various Indian nations. The ritual protocol of Native American diplomacy created dramatic spectacles in many North American towns. The location of a port and the security of concessions along the lower Mississippi hinged upon securing peace with the Chitimachas, who were raiding newly established plantations at Chapitoulas. Upon receiving an overture from the French in 1718, the beleaguered tribe agreed to meet Bienville at the site where construction of New Orleans had just begun. Chitimacha delegates solemnly marched to the cadence of their own voices from the riverbank to Bienville's cabin. After they sat on the ground and poised their faces in their hands, the wordbearer rose to light the sacred calumet. He puffed the pipe and passed it to the governor and then to everyone assembled. After presenting Bienville with the pipe and a gift of deerskins, the elderly Chitimacha bemoaned the years of warfare with the French, when "our women wept unceasingly, our children cried with fright, the game fled far from us, our houses were abandoned, and our fields uncultivated." Then, as translated for Le Page du Pratz by his Chitimacha slave, the Indian diplomat voiced the joy of his people "to see that we will walk along the same road as you, Frenchmen."[19]

Throughout the eighteenth century, the Chitimachas and other *petites nations* sent annual delegations to New Orleans to receive gifts from French and, after 1766, Spanish governors. Other official visits involved providing military assistance to Louisiana, returning runaway slaves, and even requesting pardons for deserting soldiers. The Tunicas were the most visible allies among the small tribes in the French war against the Natchez. After the first campaign of 1730, Governor Périer permitted Tunica warriors to burn a Natchez woman at the stake in New Orleans, "before the whole city, who flocked to witness the spectacle." As she underwent a slow torture, according to one witness, the captive taunted her tormentors for their unskillfulness and threatened revenge by her tribe. Her prophecy was fulfilled a year later, when a party of Natchez struck the Tunica village by surprise, burning it down and killing its chief along with many other residents. Testifying to the Tunicas' military importance to Louisiana, Diron d'Artaguette feared that this great tragedy would expose New Orleans and the colony's most lucrative plantations to enemy attack.[20] Local Indians served regularly as scouts and soldiers to defend Louisiana colonists. In 1750 Governor Pierre François Rigault de Cavagnal et Vaudreuil persuaded a group of Indians, probably some Bayogoulas or Ouachas, to settle opposite the German Coast for the sole purpose of guarding that settlement against attacks by rebellious Choctaws. The Tunicas and other small nations closer to New Orleans fought in later French campaigns against the Chickasaws and in the Spanish seizure of English West Florida posts during the American Revolution.[21]

While deployment of allied Indian warriors against hostile groups helped the colonial government by discouraging unified opposition among Indian nations, paying local Indians to capture runaway slaves promoted hostility between blacks and Indians. Familiarity with the countryside and the promise of rewards made Indians effective bounty hunters. A group of Indians on patrol for Governor Bienville in the spring of 1738 caught a runaway Negro named La Fleur, who accused his owners of not giving him enough food. In 1748 Jean Deslandes of the German Coast hired an Indian to accompany ten of his slaves on an attack against a camp of armed runaways. The Indian fired at the planter's command and seriously wounded one of the *marrons*. For killing a Negro highwayman outside the city, an authorized posse of Indians received one hundred pesos from the New Orleans cabildo in 1785.[22]

Louisiana Indians did not hesitate to visit New Orleans in pursuit of their own interests and desires, as when an entourage of Quapaws under Guedelonguay met with Governor Louis Billouard de Kerlérec at the government house on June 20, 1756. Guedelonguay requested pardons for four French soldiers who had deserted from the Arkansas fort and taken refuge in the Indians' temple. He explained that anyone finding sanctuary in the sacred cabin of his people "is regarded as washed clean of his crime." He then warned with bowed head that if the soldiers "were put to death, he would not answer for the dangerous attacks and the rebellions that the chief of the sacred cabin could bring about." The Quapaw chief also reminded the governor "that his nation having lately been at war against the Chickasaws as a mark of affection for the French, his son was killed there and his daughter wounded, and it is because of this that he asks that the loss of the one and the spilled blood of the other be repaid by the pardon that he asks for the four soldiers." Kerlérec grudgingly granted Guedelonguay's request in exchange for a promise "to hand over to him in the future all deserting soldiers or malefactors or other culprits, with no restriction or condition whatever."[23]

Diplomatic journeys from the Choctaw nation, most populous and powerful Indian ally of French Louisiana, were annually made to Mobile instead of New Orleans. The proximity of the older colonial port to the Choctaw towns influenced this pattern, but French anxiety over the security of the New Orleans area made it official policy. When Governor Périer invited Choctaw chiefs to the city in 1729–30, recruiting their military services against the rebellious Natchez, he was chastised by company officials for familiarizing them with the unfortified capital and the scattered plantations along the Mississippi River. In 1748 raids just upriver from New Orleans by Choctaw rebels intensified fear of Choctaw access to the area, yet negotiations terminating the Choctaw revolt brought a delegation of fourteen leaders from the upstart western villages to New Orleans for meetings with the governor. The Choctaws periodically visited the city on their own initiative, and seven "honored men" welcomed a new governor in early March 1753 with seven Chickasaw scalps. "After two days of speeches as long as [they were] bad," an unappreciative and novice Governor Kerlérec "expressly forbade them to make a habit of coming to New Orleans, assuring them that I would not fail to go to Mobile every year." During the 1750s and 1760s complaints against delayed distributions of gifts provoked more diplomatic missions by Choctaws to the capital, causing repeated consternation among New Orleanians. News of Louisiana's transfer to Spain and of English dominion in West Florida generated further excited journeys of Choctaw chiefs to the city.[24]

New Orleans hosted a series of ceremonial visits in the autumn of 1769, when Alexandro O'Reilly summoned lower Mississippi River tribes after completing the military occupation of Louisiana for Spain. On September 30, chiefs, interpreters, and other persons from the Tunicas, Taensas, Pacanas, Houmas, Bayogoulas, Ofogoulas, Chaouchas, and Ouachas approached the general's house with song and music. Inside he greeted them under a canopy in the company of prominent residents of New Orleans. Each chief placed his weapon at O'Reilly's feet and waved a feather fan over his head. O'Reilly accepted their fans, smoked their pipes, and clasped their hands. Then the Bayogoula leader spoke for the delegation, offering loyalty to the Spanish and requesting that they "grant us the same favors and benefits as did the French." After exhorting the Indians to treat both the English in West Florida and the Spanish in Louisiana peaceably, O'Reilly placed medals hanging from scarlet ribbons around the chiefs' necks and had presents distributed. This procedure was repeated when the Chahtos, Biloxis, Pascagoulas, and Mobilians arrived on October 22, the Chitimachas on October 29, and the Quapaws on November 16.[25]

After the American Revolution, Indian diplomacy in New Orleans entered a new era. Spanish Louisiana contended against the United States for Indian allies, while the Creek, Chickasaw, and Choctaw nations maneuvered to preserve their sovereignty. Indian missions to New Orleans came frequently and in large numbers during the 1790s, including delegations of Cherokees, but the tribes avoided showing signs of exclusive allegiance and therefore refused to make visits to the Spanish governor an obligatory routine. Chiefs often excused themselves from traveling to the city because of bad weather or poor health and, whenever they did complete a junket, complained about inadequate provisions and insulting treatment. "They don't say anything in the City," reported Juan de la Villebeuvre from the Choctaw village of Boukfouca, "but in the Nation they murmur very much."[26] At the time Spain ceded Louisiana to the French Republic in 1800, the intensity of intrigue and diplomacy in the city led Pierre-Clément de Laussat, prefect charged with overseeing the transfer, to "count on there descending, after the expression of the country 2 to 3,000 Indians per year to New Orleans: others say 3 to 400 chiefs."[27]

Purchase of Louisiana by the United States in 1803 suddenly decelerated Indian political activity in New Orleans. Agencies established near the large interior nations—at Fort St. Stephens, Chickasaw Bluffs, and Natchitoches—virtually ended their diplomatic ties to the Crescent City. For another decade, the small nations in the area continued making formal visits to territorial officials. In 1806 Governor Claiborne of the Orleans Territory presented uniform coats to two representatives from the Houma tribe in Ascension Parish, and in 1811 he distributed $100 worth of articles to Chief Chac-Chouma of the Houmas and his attendants. "From the different Governors of Louisiana," Claiborne summarized their diplomatic relationship with New Orleans, "they were accustomed to receive marks of friendly attention. At the present day, the number of this Tribe is greatly diminished; it does not exceed 80 souls, but their conduct is exemplary and the late visit of the Chief being the first paid to me, I thought it a matter of policy to make him a small present." This meeting marked the beginning of the Houma Indians' struggle for official recognition by the United States government. But they and other *petites nations* along the lower Mississippi and Red rivers were denied the political protection needed to secure their small land bases. After a century of alliance with colonial governments in New Orleans, the Chitimachas, Houmas, Tunicas, and others were finally pressured into the backcountry of Louisiana. The federal government indifferently lost sight of them, for the time being.[28]

Neither the severence of diplomatic ties with New Orleans nor the dissipation of resident Indian slaves by the nineteenth century ended the presence of American Indians in the city. A more continuous and lasting relationship had evolved over the colonial period through an array of informal economic activities, especially the marketing of food in town by neighboring Indians. In their 1718 treaty with the French, the Chitimachas agreed to move their village from Bayou Lafourche closer to the incipient town, a few miles below the Paris brothers' plantation. Other tribes also migrated toward New Orleans. From the backcountry south of the town site, the Chaouchas settled within several miles on the east bank of the Mississippi and the Ouachas about twenty miles above New Orleans on the west bank. The Acolapissas moved from the north shore of Lake Pontchartrain to the east bank of the Mississippi some fifty miles above town. "All these nations are highly industrious," observed André Pénicaut, "and all are quite helpful in furnishing food to the French, to the troops as well as to the people on the concessions."[29]

In addition to these newly relocated Indian settlements, villages of Houmas, Tunicas, and Bayogoulas also occupied the banks of the Mississippi near New Orleans. In 1706–9 Tunica refugees from upriver drove the Houmas from their village 150 miles above the Bayou St. John portage and occupied the spacious bluff east of the river themselves. After a brief stay on Bayou St. John, the Houmas by 1718 resettled several miles below Bayou Lafourche. All these people suffered severe population loss, from epidemics more than warfare, but in 1725 they still composed a substantial percentage of the total population along the Mississippi south of the Red River. Interspersed among one thousand European settlers and another thousand African slaves within this area, seven Indian communities totaled approximately three thousand men, women, and children.[30]

Indians in the New Orleans area provided important goods and services to the colonial town. Indian men frequently visited as packhorsemen accompanying traders or as crewmen paddling or rowing boats. As already seen, French and later Spanish governors recruited auxiliaries from neighboring villages for military campaigns and paid bounties to Indians who captured and returned runaway slaves and soldiers. During the Natchez revolt, however, the Chaoucha village was virtually destroyed when Périer dispatched a group of armed Negro slaves against it, hoping to alleviate fear in New Orleans over local attacks and to generate black-Indian antagonism. Commending the slaves for their prompt and secret mission, the governor boasted, "If I had been willing to use our negro volunteers I should have destroyed all these little nations which are of no use to us, and which might on the contrary cause our negroes to revolt." He did not further employ these black soldiers "for fear of rendering [them] . . . too bold and of inclining them perhaps to revolt after the example of those who joined the Natchez." Defying customary practices more than once during his troublesome governorship, Périer was criticized for his genocidal assessment of local Indians, who in fact proved very useful to colonial Louisiana.[31]

Provisioning early New Orleans with food, more than any other activity, integrated Indians into the social and economic life of the colonial town. In the mid-1720s Bienville acknowledged that the farming, hunting, and fishing skills of lower Louisiana Indians produced food supplies for the colony. Estimating their population at fifty men, he reported that the Houmas "have rendered us good services in the famines that we have experienced in recent years by the abundance of provisions that they have furnished us." Bernard de La Harpe had earlier observed that the Houma village of some sixty cabins "busies itself in raising hens and in the culture of maize and beans." The one hundred men of the Acolapissas, Bienville noted, "furnish us almost all the fresh meat that is consumed at New Orleans without however their neglecting the cultivation of their lands which produce a great deal of corn."[32]

The continuous presence of Indians in New Orleans—whether as slaves, guides, boatmen, or peddlers—affected how the colonial government regulated interaction among social groups. Like their counterparts in Boston, New York, and Charlestown, New Orleans officials associated both free and enslaved Indians with blacks, free people of color, and lower-class whites in efforts to police behavior on the city's streets and behind its closed doors. In all of these towns Indians were subject during the eighteenth century to the same ordinances that prohibited slaves and free Negroes from carrying firearms, congregating, owning livestock, trading without special permission, and walking the streets after curfew—ordinances intended to reduce insolence and theft aimed at white property owners. In New Orleans much insubordination was attributed to the consumption of alcohol by soldiers as well as by Indians and blacks. In 1751 the Louisiana Superior Council tried to reinforce the Black Code and a series of other regulations on drinking, gambling, and assemblies by issuing a new set of police regulations. Among articles mostly restricting the social and economic activities of slaves and free Negroes, there was a prohibition against the six newly licensed taverns' selling wine or liquor to soldiers, Indians, and Negroes.[33]

Face-to-face contact with settlers, soldiers, and slaves posed special problems for Indians who frequented New Orleans. Trade had a debilitating effect on the *petites nations*, Governor Kerlérec explained, "mainly because of the quantity of drink that has been traded to them." Contagious diseases continued to strike down lower Louisiana Indians and by midcentury reduced their number to about two hundred warriors or seven hundred people. As in other colonial regions, those Indian groups experiencing the longest and most intimate contact with colonists suffered more drastically from exposure to viruses and alcohol than did the interior tribes, many becoming extinct or being absorbed by other peoples. "The Chaouchas, the Washas, [the] Acolapissas, and also the Avoyelles and the Bayogoulas were so many different nations," Kerlérec wrote in 1758, "which the proximity of the French and the trade in drink have likewise destroyed." Only through their own resilience and resourcefulness, especially in their capacity to adopt refugees and other outsiders into community life, did any Indian enclaves survive within colonial society.[34]

Attrition among the Indian populace around New Orleans was actually reversed in the mid-1760s when villagers from the Mobile Bay area and from the Choctaw Nation began resettlement on the north shore of Lake Pontchartrain and along the banks of the Mississippi River. After Great Britain occupied West Florida, the Apalaches, Taensas, Pacanas, Mobilians, Alibamons, Biloxis, Chahtos, and Pascagoulas—many of them Roman Catholic in religion—migrated to the French settlements in lower Louisiana, then discovered that the colony belonged to Spain. Kerlérec realized the benefits to be derived from the approximately eighty Apalache Indians, "being hunters and farmers," and in September 1763 he decided to locate them at the rapids of the Red River. "There," recorded general commissioner Jean-Jacques Blaise d'Abbadie, "they will be useful for aiding vessels ascending the river towards Natchitoches. Moreover, through their hunting, they will be able to supply New Orleans."[35] As they extended authority over the east side of the Mississippi River, above the chain of lakes and bayous that made New Orleans a Spanish island, the English also vied for the services of these immigrant Indians. During the spring of 1768, Montfort Browne met a group of Chahtos and Mobilians building a new village on the Amite River and was welcomed at the palmetto-covered house of chief Mattaha with a calumet dance. The Indians had already supplied the English at Fort Bute with three boats and, "as I found them a great deal disgusted against the Spaniards' late behavior," Browne persuaded them to settle closer to Baton Rouge after the year's harvest. "As these Savages are a good deal civilized, industrious and excellent Hunters," he wrote, "the acquisition will be the greater."[36]

By the early 1770s at least eight villages were interspersed among colonial settlements between New Orleans and the Red River, totaling more than one thousand Indians. The colonial population within this stretch (see fig. 1) included about 2,750 Negroes and 2,300 whites (New Orleans itself containing 1,000 Negroes and 1,800 whites), and the plantations below New Orleans included 1,600 Negroes and 450 whites. "The Houma, Chitimacha, and other Indian communities that were dispersed among the plantations," cartographer and naturalist Bernard Romans noted, "serve as hunters, and for some other laborious uses, something similar to subdued tribes of New England."[37] In 1773 the main town of the Houmas, consisting of some forty gunmen, stood on the east bank of the Mississippi sixty miles above New Orleans. Another Houma village was situated across the river. A league below Manchac the Taensas, Pacanas, and Mobilians lived on the west bank in a single town of about thirty gunmen. The Alibamons counted thirty-seven gunmen and lived just above Manchac on the east side. While some Chitimachas were moving down Bayou Plaquemine, about fifteen gunmen and their families remained along the Mississippi. Down the bayou other Chitimachas and some Atakapas and Opelousas totaled another fifty gunmen. The Tunicas still occupied their town, numbering about thirty-five gunmen, on the east bluff above the Pointe Coupée plantations. Above Tunica stood a village of ten to twelve Chahto gunmen and another of fifteen Pascagoula gunmen on the west bank. The

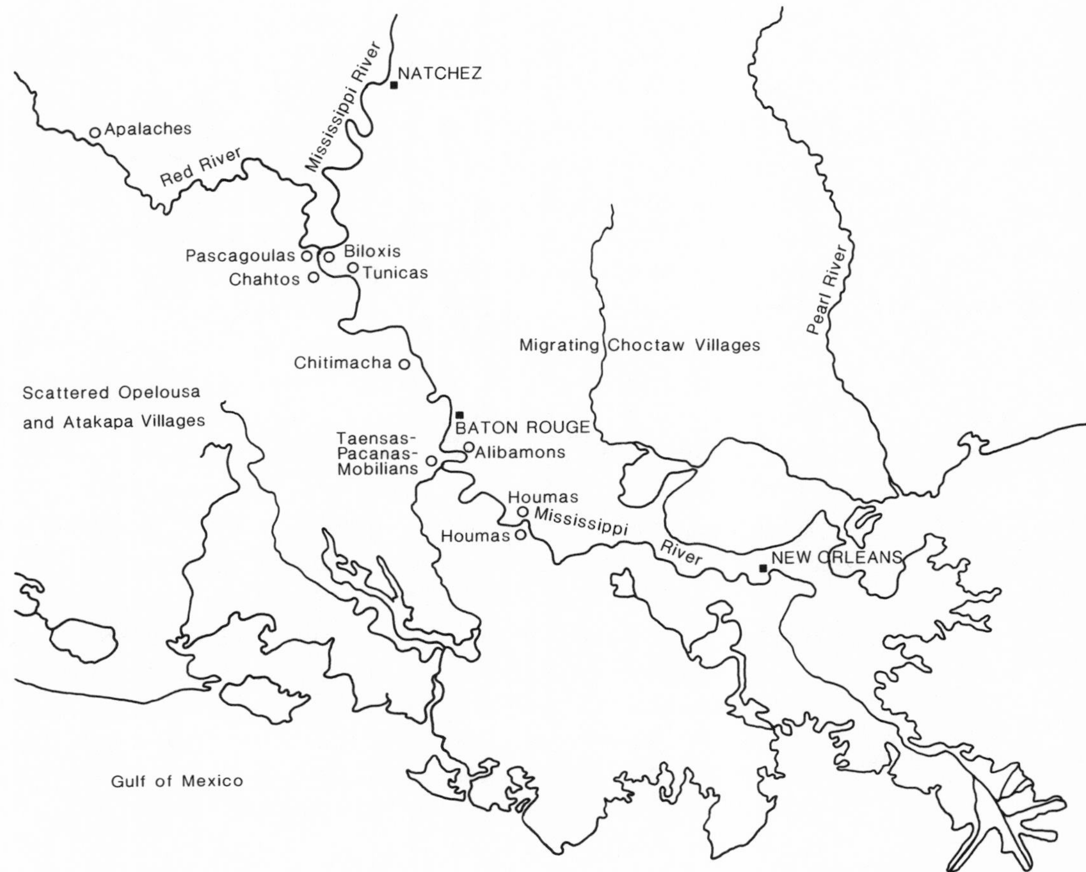

Figure 1 Indian villages on the banks of the Mississippi and Red rivers, 1773.

Biloxis, numbering nearly one hundred gunmen, had just moved from the west to the east bank a short distance below the Red River.[38] Over the next few decades most of these communities migrated from the Mississippi River either to the Red River habitat of the Apalaches or down Bayous Plaquemine and Lafourche. Also during the 1790s more groups of Choctaws and Coushattas were migrating west of the Mississippi River into Louisiana, though their numbers were overshadowed by the contemporaneous immigration of Anglo-American settlers and Afro-American slaves.[39]

The migration of some Choctaws into the New Orleans area, which began during the 1760s, was more volatile than that of others.

Yet in the long run their proximity proved to be the most enduring in New Orleans history. After Great Britain assumed control over West Florida's trade with interior tribes, many Choctaws—especially from the Six Towns district—attempted to maintain ties with the French. They complained of abuses committed by English traders, carried on illicit trade with inhabitants of Louisiana, and committed acts of banditry against settlers in West Florida. General Frederick Haldimand reported in 1768 to General Thomas Gage, "The continual depredations of the Choctaw Indians of the six villages, who hunt in and frequent continually the neighborhood of lakes Pontchartrain and Maurepas where they pillage the inhabitants, kill their animals, and introduce French traders in their country, require that there should be some one of confidence and authority among them who would repress their outbreaks."[40] Groups of Choctaws were then settling farther down Pearl River, around Pass Christian, and on the north shore of Lake Pontchartrain, where many French settlers also lived resentfully under British rule. As hunting and trading increased in this thickly pine-forested area, colonial residents at Spanish Galveztown and English Baton Rouge exchanged rum, ammunition, and corn for pelts, game, and bear oil produced by traveling Choctaw families. Although it perturbed merchants in Pensacola and Mobile with privileged rights over Choctaw trade and antagonized farmers and planters vulnerable to pilferage, this commerce germinated several new Indian communities across Lake Pontchartrain from New Orleans.[41]

The movement of Choctaws and other groups toward the Crescent City after 1763 discloses how some Indians relied on cities in their adjustment to new political and economic circumstances. By the late eighteenth century, New Orleans had become an important station for the seasonally varied strategies Indians devised to cope with a decline in diplomatic and commercial leverage. Faced with diminishing opportunity in the deerskin trade—manifested by falling prices for pelts and mounting debts to merchants—and with growing numbers of Anglo-American immigrants, Indians in the lower Mississippi valley resorted to a seasonal cycle of itinerant economic activities.[42] Camps of extended families, formerly the units that spent only winter hunting seasons away from their villages, sojourned more frequently along waterways and roads, trading small quantities of goods with other travelers, farmers, and slaves. While the men hunted to supply local meat markets, women sold leaves and roots, baskets and mats, and even began to pick cotton during the harvest season.[43]

On the outskirts of New Orleans, groups of Houmas, Chitimachas, and Choctaws camped along Bayou St. John and Bayou Road. Hundreds of Indians gathered in late winter to request gifts from officials and to join in the celebration of carnival.[44] On the city's streets and in the marketplace, Indian women peddled baskets, mats, sifters, plants, herbs, and firewood; their men sold venison, wildfowl, and cane blowguns and occasionally earned wages as day laborers and dockworkers. On his way to a Choctaw camp behind the city gates, Fortescue Cuming met on a March afternoon in 1799 "numbers of Indian women with large bundles of wood on their backs, first tied together and then held by a strap carried over their foreheads." A few years later Paul Alliot observed that the Indian men "kill game with great dexterity, and sell it for excellent prices" and that the women "busy themselves in making reed baskets which they sell at good prices."[45]

The impact of Indians upon the culture of New Orleans, through their diversified presence in the colonial city, is not easily measured. Many New Orleanians, identified as white, black, or free colored by the end of the eighteenth century, possessed various degrees of Indian ancestry. Inside urban households and in the marketplace, Indian women influenced cuisine not only through their uses of corn and beans but through a knowledge of the region's wild plants and animals.[46] On the outskirts of town or around its taverns, Indians also shared music, dance, and other cultural expressions with colonists and slaves. Perhaps the most fascinating Indian contribution to New Orleans social life was the ball game called *toli* by the Choctaws and *raquettes* by the French, the city's most popular spectator sport until the arrival of baseball. Before United States acquisition of New Orleans, contests had become Sunday afternoon events behind the city gates. Spectators assembled on the "Communes de la Ville," also called Congo Plains, where players carrying short sticks in both hands tossed the small buckskin ball between two goalposts sometimes placed a half-mile apart. As described by Pierre Clément de Laussat, two prominent black teams in 1803 were the "Bayous," players from the Bayou St. John area, and the "La Villes," those from the city proper. They competed against white teams as well as against each other, and some Indians reportedly belonged to the

"Bayous." The particular circumstances in which New Orleanians adopted this ancient Indian ball game are obscure, but its performance over the eighteenth century by Indians in and around the city must have been influential.[47]

For Indians living in the eighteenth-century Southeast, contact with colonists and slaves produced a variety of new settings in which they made decisions and had choices forced upon them.[48] Life in or around colonial settlements was filled with a multitude of challenges, and in an urban setting different kinds of exchange and struggle converged. Colonial towns proved to be destructive intrusions for many Indian groups. The largest tribe in the Mississippi Delta by the early eighteenth century, the Chitimachas, suffered a protracted war as the French tried to establish a permanent base on the river. The beginning of construction at New Orleans in 1718 marked the end of their struggle, but not before many Chitimachas had been captured and enslaved. Colonial towns like New Orleans became hotbeds of anxiety over Indian and slave rebellions. The Chaoucha village just below New Orleans was destroyed in 1729, during the Natchez revolt, when the governor decided to alleviate fear in town and avert a black-Indian coalition—which had already occurred at Natchez—by sending a small army of Negro slaves against the closest community of Indians. The New Orleans experience also shows how dangerous an alliance with colonists could be, when the well-armed Tunica village was devastated by Natchez attackers after it supplied vital military assistance to the French army. Small Indian nations along the lower Mississippi, including the surviving Tunicas, continued to provide valuable defense for New Orleans and its surrounding plantations.

Many Indian tribes found towns to be places for engaging in diplomacy rather than warfare. Throughout the eighteenth century, Indians traveled to New Orleans from near and far to negotiate agreements that helped them adjust to the European presence. Issues discussed in the government house ranged from the return of runaway slaves and soldiers to the defense of Louisiana against other European colonies and their Indian allies. Indian diplomatic protocol constituted a dramatic form of public interaction in which colonial officials received processions of singers, smoked the calumet, and presented gifts. These very formal displays of reciprocal alliance were as much a part of the city's calendar as were Easter, Christmas, and the king's birthday, and even the most ethnocentric of European observers were impressed by the dignity and importance of Indian diplomacy.[49]

At the level of daily life, Indian experiences in New Orleans varied widely. There were some Indian men, women, and children who worked as slaves in households and shops. Employment in long-distance trade and transportation brought Indian men regularly through the city, while the growing urban populace provided a market for foods and other goods produced by neighboring Indian villages. Even in taking advantage of this opportunity, however, Louisiana Indians faced difficulties in the city. Disease and alcohol endangered their health and took the lives of countless individuals. Government efforts to control the behavior of Indians, slaves, and soldiers created mounting vigilance against the activities of Indians inside and outside the city walls. But as the political and economic status of Indian nations continued to decay toward the end of the eighteenth century, New Orleans did not witness a declining Indian presence. Instead, many Indian families turned to the city as a useful way station in a new pattern of adjustment and survival.

Notes

1. For samples of, and bibliographical guidance to, the literature on New England and Canadian settlement Indians, see Laura E. Conkey, Ethel Boissevain, and Ives Goddard, "Indians of Southern New England and Long Island: Late Period," and William N. Fenton and Elisabeth Tooker, "Mohawk," both in *Handbook of North American Indians*, vol. 15, *Northeast*, ed. Bruce G. Trigger (Washington, D.C.: Smithsonian Institution Press, 1978), 177–89, 466–80. Documents and scholarship have been combed for the religious dimensions of these northeastern communities in James Axtell, *The Invasion Within: The Contest of Cultures in Colonial North America* (New York: Oxford University Press, 1985). For socioeconomic and environmental elements, see William Cronon, *Changes in the Land: Indians, Colonists, and the Ecology of New England* (New York: Hill and Wang, 1983).

2. An exemplary, and the most comprehensive, study of a South Atlantic coastal tribe is James Merrell, "Natives in a New World: The Catawba Indians of Carolina, 1650–1800" (Ph.D. diss., Johns Hopkins University, 1982). Some southeastern coastal communities of Indians are partly covered for the eighteenth century in Christian F. Feest, "Nanticoke and Neighboring Tribes," idem, "Virginia Algonquians," idem, "North Carolina Algonquians," and Douglas W. Boyce, "Iroquoian Tribes of the Virginia-North Carolina Coastal Plain," all in Trigger, *Handbook of North America Indians: Northeast*, 240–89.

3. These town experiences of southeastern Indians are gleaned from Verner W. Crane, *The Southern Frontier, 1670–1732* (Durham, N.C.: Duke University Press, 1928); Peter

H. Wood, *Black Majority: Negroes in Colonial South Carolina from 1670 through the Stono Rebellion* (New York: Alfred A. Knopf, 1974); Phinizy Spalding, *Oglethorpe in America* (Chicago: University of Chicago Press, 1977); Charles H. Fairbanks, "From Missionary to Mestizo: Changing Culture of Eighteenth-Century St. Augustine," in *Eighteenth-Century Florida and the Caribbean*, ed. Samuel Proctor (Gainesville: University Presses of Florida, 1976), 88–99; J. Leitch Wright, Jr., *The Only Land They Knew: The Tragic Story of the American Indians in the Old South* (New York: Free Press, 1981); and Kathleen A. Deagan, *Spanish St. Augustine: The Archaeology of a Colonial Creole Community* (New York: Academic Press, 1983).

4. Richebourg Gaillard McWilliams, trans. and ed., *Iberville's Gulf Journals* (University: University of Alabama Press, 1981), 57.

5. Marco J. Giardino, "Documentary Evidence for the Location of Historic Indian Villages in the Mississippi Delta," in *Perspectives on Gulf Coast Prehistory*, ed. Dave D. Davis (Gainesville: University Presses of Florida, 1984), 232–57.

6. Peirce F. Lewis, *New Orleans: The Making of an Urban Landscape* (Cambridge, Mass.: Ballinger, 1976), 17–30; Rod E. Emmer and Karen Wicker, "Sedimentary Environments, Ecological Systems, and Land Use in Southwestern Louisiana," and Fredrick W. Wagner, "Development Problems in the New Orleans Coastal Zone," in *A Field Guidebook for Louisiana*, ed. Richard E. Kesel and Robert A. Sauder (Washington, D.C.: Association of American Geographers, 1978), 48–53, 124–27.

7. McWilliams, *Gulf Journals*, 111–12; Richard J. Shenkel and Jon L. Gibson, "Big Oak Island, an Historical Perspective of Changing Site Function," *Louisiana Studies* 13(Summer 1974): 173–86; Richard J. Shenkel, *Oak Island Archaeology: Prehistoric Estuarine Adaptations in the Mississippi River Delta* (New Orleans: Jean Lafitte National Historical Park, 1980).

8. Marc de Villiers du Terrage, "A History of the Foundation of New Orleans (1717–1722)," trans. Warrington Dawson, *Louisiana Historical Quarterly* 3(April 1920): 157–251, at 161–79; John R. Swanton, *Indian Tribes of the Lower Mississippi Valley and Adjacent Coast of the Gulf of Mexico*, Bureau of American Ethnology Bulletin 43 (Washington, D.C.: Government Printing Office, 1911), 274–84, 297–301. Also see Henry C. Bezou, *Metairie: A Tongue of Land to Pasture* (Gretna, La.: Pelican, 1973), 35–36; and Edna B. Freiberg, *Bayou St. John in Colonial Louisiana 1699–1803* (New Orleans: Harvey Press, 1980), 26–27.

9. Charles R. Maduell, Jr., comp. and ed., *The Census Tables for the French Colony of Louisiana from 1699 through 1732* (Baltimore: Genealogical Publishing Company, 1972), 16–27. Almon Wheeler Lauber, *Indian Slavery in Colonial Times within the Present Limits of the United States* (New York: Columbia University, 1913), is still the most comprehensive treatment of enslaved Indians in North America.

10. Richebourg Gaillard McWilliams, ed. and trans. *Fleur de Lys and Calumet: Being the Pénicaut Narrative of French Adventure in Louisiana* (Baton Rouge: Louisiana State University Press, 1953), 101–2, cited hereafter as *Pénicaut Narrative;* Antoine Le Page du Pratz, *The History of Louisiana*, ed. Joseph Tregle, Jr., facsimile of 1774 London edition (Baton Rouge: Louisiana State University Press, 1975), 20–21; Marcel Giraud, *A History of French Louisiana*, vol. 1, *The Reign of Louis XIV, 1698–1715*,

trans. Joseph C. Lambert (1953; reprint Baton Rouge: Louisiana State University Press, 1974), 177–80.

11. Archives des Colonies, Paris, ser. C13A, vol. 3, fol. 390, cited hereafter as AC, C13A, volume number:folio number; Giraud, *History of French Louisiana*, 278–80; Charles Edwards O'Neill, *Church and State in French Colonial Louisiana: Policy and Politics to 1732* (New Haven: Yale University Press, 1966), 86–92, 248–55; Carl A. Brasseaux, "The Moral Climate of French Colonial Louisiana, 1699–1763," *Louisiana History* 27(Winter 1986): 27–41.

12. AC, C13A, 10:46; Carl A. Brasseaux, "The Administration of Slave Regulations in French Louisiana, 1725–1766," *Louisiana History* 21(Spring 1980): 139–58.

13. Maduell, *Census Tables*, 50–76.

14. "Records of the Superior Council," *Louisiana Historical Quarterly* 1(January 1918): 109, 3(July 1920): 414, 443–44; Dunbar Rowland and Albert Sanders, trans. and ed., *Mississippi Provincial Archives: French Dominion*, 3 vols. (Jackson: Mississippi Department of Archives and History, 1929–32), 2:573–74, cited hereafter as *MPAFD*.

15. "Records of the Superior Council," *Louisiana Historical Quarterly* 13(April 1930): 329, 14(July 1931): 458, 14(October 1931): 580; Maduell, *Census Tables*, 113, 123; Patricia Kay Galloway, ed., *Mississippi Provincial Archives: French Dominion*, vols. 4 and 5 (Baton Rouge: Louisiana State University Press, 1984), 4:79, 102–5; cited hereafter as *MPAFD* (1984).

16. Lawrence Kinnaird, trans. and ed., *Spain in the Mississippi Valley, 1765–1794*, 3 vols. (Washington, D.C.: American Historical Association, 1946–49), 1:125–26, 196; Wright, *Only Land They Knew*, 126–50, 248–78. For discussions of Indian slavery in the Northeast, see A. Leon Higginbotham, Jr., *In the Matter of Color. Race and the American Legal Process: The Colonial Period* (New York: Oxford University Press, 1978); and John A. Sainsbury, "Indian Labor in Early Rhode Island," *New England Quarterly* 48(September 1975): 378–93.

17. Dunbar Rowland, ed., *Official Letter Books of W. C. C. Claiborne, 1801–1816*, 6 vols. (Jackson: Mississippi Department of Archives and History, 1917), 4:179–81. Hans Baade, "The Law of Slavery in Spanish Louisiana, 1769–1803," in *Louisiana's Legal Heritage*, ed. Edward F. Haas (New Orleans: Louisiana State Museum, 1983), 43–86, and Stephen Webre, "The Problem of Indian Slavery in Spanish Louisiana, 1769–1803," *Louisiana History* 25(Spring 1984): 117–35, are important analyses of slavery during the Spanish period.

18. Charles L. Thompson, ed., *New Orleans in 1805: A Directory and a Census* (New Orleans: Pelican Gallery, 1936); Ira Berlin, *Slaves without Master: The Free Negro in the Antebellum South* (New York: Pantheon Books, 1974), 108–32; Virginia R. Dominguez, *White by Definition: Social Classification in Creole Louisiana* (New Brunswick, N.J.: Rutgers University Press, 1986), 23–26.

19. *Pénicaut Narrative*, 216–18; Antoine Le Page du Pratz, *Histoire de la Louisiane*, 3 vols. (Paris: De Bure, La Veuve et Lambert, 1758), 1:106–14.

20. *MPAFD* (1984) 4:37, 77; "Historical Memoirs of M. Dumont," in *Historical Collec-*

tions of Louisiana, ed. Benjamin Franklin French, 5 vols. (New York: Lamport, Blakeman and Law, 1846–53), 5:98–97.

21. *MPAFD* (1984), 4:40, 49; Patricia D. Woods, *French-Indian Relations on the Southern Frontier, 1699–1762* (Ann Arbor: UMI Research Press, 1980), 139; J. Barton Starr, *Tories, Dons, and Rebels: The American Revolution in British West Florida* (Gainesville: University Presses of Florida, 1976), 142–60.

22. "Records of the Superior Council," *Louisiana Historical Quarterly* 3(July 1920): 414, 5(October 1922): 593–94, 19(October 1936): 1087–88; Records and Deliberations of the Cabildo, November 25, 1785 (Louisiana Division, New Orleans Public Library).

23. *MPAFD* (1984), 4:187–88, 5:173–78.

24. *MPAFD* (1984), 4:46–47, 81–82, 5:38–44, 122, 183, 273–74.

25. Kinnaird, *Spain in the Mississippi Valley*, 1:101–2, 154–55.

26. Kinnaird, *Spain in the Mississippi Valley*, 2:185, 258, 3:141–43, 151–52; Miró to Luis de las Casas, September 10, December 26, 1790, June 28, 1791, Dispatches of the Spanish Governors of Louisiana, WPA typescript in Louisiana Historical Center, New Orleans; Villebeuvre to Carondelet, January 16, February 7, March 30, 1793, *East Tennessee Historical Society Publications* 29(1957): 142–43, 152, 30(1958): 101–2.

27. Laussat to Minister of Navy, September 27, 1802, Claude Perrin Victor Papers, the Historic New Orleans Collection, New Orleans; James Wilkinson to William Claiborne, Fort Adams, April 13, 1803, Indian Department Journal, Mississippi Department of History and Archives, Jackson: "I have received the following information from a confidential source in New Orleans, viz: 'Mingo poos Coos has been here, and thro the Interpreter has been invited to bring his people to meet their old friends the French, the Indians are daily comeing in, and the Interpreter has gone over the lake [Pontchartrain] to provide for their accommodation.'"

28. Rowland, *Official Letter Books of W. C. C. Claiborne*, 5:275, 322–23. For an overview of the Houmas since the eighteenth century, see Jan Curry, "A History of the Houma Indians and Their Story of Federal Nonrecognition," *American Indian Journal* 5(February 1979): 8–28.

29. *Pénicaut Narrative*, 216–20; *MPAFD*, 3:527–28, 535.

30. Jean-Baptiste Bernard de La Harpe, *The Historical Journal of the Establishment of the French in Louisiana*, trans. Joan Cain and Virginia Koenig, ed. and annotated Glenn R. Conrad (Lafayette: University of Southwestern Louisiana Press, 1971), 60–79; *MPAFD*, 3:526–35.

31. *MPAFD*, 1:64–65, 71.

32. La Harpe, *Historical Journal*, 75–76; *MPAFD*, 3:527–29, 535.

33. AC, C13A, 35:39–52. Patterns of control affecting Negroes and Indians in other eighteenth-century colonial towns are best examined in Wood, *Black Majority;* and Higginbotham, *In the Matter of Color.*

34. *MPAFD* (1984), 5:212–13.

35. Carl A. Brasseaux, trans., ed., and annotator, *A Comparative View of French Louisiana, 1699 and 1762; The Journals of Pierre Le Moyne d'Iberville and Jean-Jacques-*

Blaise d'Abbadie (Lafayette: University of Southwestern Louisiana Press, 1979), 100–102, 107, 112.

36. Browne to Hillsborough, Pensacola, July 6, 1768, English Provincial Records, Mississippi Department of Archives and History, Jackson.

37. Bernard Romans, *A Concise Natural History of East and West Florida* (1775; reprint New Orleans: Pelican, 1961), 69–71.

38. List of the Several Tribes of Indians inhabiting the banks of the Mississippi, Between New Orleans and Red River, with their number of gun-men and places of residence, January 1, 1773, William Haldimand Papers, British Museum (microfilm in Louisiana Division, New Orleans Public Library). Other population estimates of these Indian communities for this period can be found in Jacqueline K. Voorhies, trans. and comp., *Some Late Eighteenth-Century Louisianians: Census Records of the Colony, 1758–1796* (Lafayette: University of Southwestern Louisiana Press, 1973), 164–66; Eron Dunbar Rowland, ed., "Peter Chester: Third Governor of the Province of West Florida under the British Dominion, 1770–1781," *Publications of the Mississippi Historical Society: Centenary Series* 5(1925): 97; Philip Pittman, *The Present State of the European Settlements on the Mississippi*, ed. Robert Rea, facsimile of 1770 edition (Gainesville: University Presses of Florida, 1973), 24, 35–36.

39. The migration of Indians into the Atchafalaya and Red River basins can be traced in Daniel Clark, "An Account of the Indian Tribes in Louisiana, New Orleans, Sept. 29, 1803," in *The Territorial Papers of the United States*, ed. Clarence E. Carter, 26 vols., (Washington, D.C.: Government Printing Office, 1934–62), 9:62–64; John Sibley, "Historical sketches of the several Indian Tribes in Louisiana, south of the Arkansas river, and between the Mississippi and river Grand," in *Annals of the Congress of the United States*, 9th Cong., 2d sess. (Washington, D.C.: Gales and Seaton, 1852), 1076–88; Sibley, *A Report from Natchitoches in 1807*, ed. Annie Heloise Abel (New York: Museum of the American Indian, 1922). For a history of the Choctaws who settled permanently in central Louisiana, see Hiram F. Gregory, "Jena Band of Louisiana Choctaw," *American Indian Journal* 3(February 1977): 2–16.

40. Brasseaux, *Comparative View*, 11; Clarence W. Alvord and C. E. Carter, eds., *The Critical Period, 1763–1765* (Springfield: Illinois State Historical Library, 1915), 200–201, 413–14.

41. Kinnaird, *Spain in the Mississippi Valley*, 2:382–84, 3:53–54; William Panton to Carondelet, Pensacola, April 16, 1792, *Georgia Historical Quarterly* 22(December 1938): 393; John Forbes to Carondelet, October 31, 1792, Panton to Carondelet, November 6, 1792, *East Tennessee Historical Society Publications* 28(1956): 131–33; James A. Robertson, ed., *Louisiana under the Rule of Spain, France, and the United States, 1785–1807*, 2 vols. (Cleveland: Arthur H. Clark, 1911), 2:103.

42. The economic strategies devised by lower Mississippi valley Indians in the late eighteenth and early nineteenth centuries are discussed in Richard White, *The Roots of Dependency: Subsistence, Environment, and Social Change among the Choctaws, Pawnees, and Navajos* (Lincoln: University of Nebraska Press, 1983), 97–110, and Daniel H. Usner, Jr., "American Indians on the Cotton Frontier: Changing Economic Relations with Citizens and Slaves in the Mississippi Territory," *Journal of American History* 72(September 1985): 297–317.

43. John A. Watkins Manuscript on Choctaw Indians, Howard-Tilton Memorial Library, Tulane University, New Orleans; Fortescue Cuming, *Sketches of a Tour to the Western Country* (1810; reprint Cleveland: Arthur H. Clark, 1904), 351–52.

44. Berquin-Duvallon, *Travels in Louisiana and the Floridas, in the Year, 1802, Giving a Correct Picture of Those Countries*, trans. John Davis (New York: Isaac Riley, 1806), 96–99; Christian Schultz, Jr., *Travels on an Inland Voyage through the States of New-York, Pennsylvania, Virginia, Ohio, Kentucky and Tennessee, and through the Territories of Indiana, Louisiana, Mississippi and New-Orleans*, 2 vols. (New York: Isaac Riley, 1810), 2:198.

45. Cuming, *Sketches of a Tour*, 365–66; Robertson, *Louisiana under the Rule of Spain, France, and the United States*, 2:81–83.

46. Indian influences on Louisiana foodways are explored in Daniel H. Usner, Jr., "Food Marketing and Interethnic Exchange in the Eighteenth-Century Lower Mississippi Valley," *Food and Foodways* 1(1986): 279–310.

47. Pierre Clément de Laussat, *Memoirs of My Life to My Son during the Years 1803 and After*, trans. Sister Agnes-Josephine Pastwa and ed. Robert D. Bush (Baton Rouge: Louisiana State University Press, 1978), 53–54; Dominique Rouquette, "The Choctaws" (typescript of a manuscript written in 1850, Louisiana Historical Center, New Orleans), 51–54; George W. Cable, "The Dance in Place Congo," *Century Magazine* 31(February 1886): 518–19.

48. The broad spectrum of Indian experiences produced by contact with colonial settlers and slaves is skillfully examined in James Merrell, "The Indians' New World: The Catawba Experience," *William and Mary Quarterly*, 3d ser., 41(October 1984): 537–65.

49. Francis Jennings, William N. Fenton, Mary A. Druke, and David R. Miller, eds., *The History and Culture of Iroquois Diplomacy: An Interdisciplinary Guide to the Treaties of the Six Nations and Their League* (Syracuse: Syracuse University Press, 1985), offers a collection of useful approaches to the form as well as the content of Indian-European diplomacy.

Part Two Politics and Economics

Introduction by Gregory A. Waselkov

"Count the lying black marks of this one," exclaimed Attakullakulla (Little Carpenter), paper in hand, as he detailed the hypocrisies and half-truths contained in a stack of letters the colonial governor of South Carolina had sent him. The Cherokee leader "kept them regularly piled in a bundle, according to the time he received them," James Adair recalled, "and often shewed them to the traders, in order to expose their fine promising contents." The Indian elder conceded that the earliest messages from Governor James Glen "contained a little truth," according to Adair, "and he excused the failure" of the governor's subsequent letters on the ground that "much business might have perplexed him, so as to occasion him to forget complying with his strong promise." But eventually Attakullakulla, like Adair himself, "repented of trusting to the governor's promises" and admitted that his patience was exhausted. The governor's letters, he proclaimed, "were an heap of black broad papers, and ought to be burnt in the old years fire."[1]

Adair's scene presents two contrasting forms of evidence for understanding this distant time: written—and often misleading—European documents on the one hand and pointed—but rarely preserved—opinions of native leaders on the other. Unfortunately, the heaps of black broad papers that now constitute our principal source for constructing interpretive narratives of the colonial past are seldom accompanied by the first-person Indian perspectives so essential to a balanced picture of the period. Keenly aware of this bias, the authors of the following five chapters have metaphorically invoked the purifying fires of the busk in their critical studies of documentary and archaeological evidence. They have revealed long-stilled native voices speaking to issues of political and economic interaction, the same realms that colonial agents and officials sought most eagerly to dominate.

Amy Turner Bushnell discusses the dual political systems that functioned effectively for a century in Spanish Florida. Native leaders retained much of their authority at the village level, providing a basis for long-term stability. By means of a complex web of mutual obligations, sedentary Florida Indians managed to coexist relatively peacefully with Franciscan friars and secular Spanish colonists. This little-known experiment in Indian-European interaction deserves much more attention from ethnohistorians, who, as Bushnell correctly states, have generally regarded French and (especially) English colonization of the Southeast as "the central story."[2]

As familiar as we are with the English colonial adventure in Virginia, the next two chapters contain some startling revelations on the Native American response to that invasion. By focusing on Cockacoeske, successor to Powhatan and Opechancanough, Martha McCartney explains in the third chapter of this section how the "Queen of Pamunkey" adroitly manipulated colonial treaty negotiations in an ingenious (though ultimately unsuccessful) attempt to reestablish the dominance of her people in a reconstituted Powhatan chiefdom. In the process, McCartney also provides us with a rare commodity, a biographical depiction of an Indian woman in the colonial era.[3]

McCartney's portrait of Cockacoeske clearly indicates the weakness of chiefly authority that characterized Virginia's Algonquian political scene in the late seventeenth century. How the chiefs' influence declined is the subject of Stephen Potter's essay, the second chapter in this section. Since the earliest historical sources describe nearly total control by the chiefs over the acquisition of prestige items, including newly available European trade goods, Potter looks at the changing distribution of these objects in graves to pinpoint the first signs of lessening chiefly authority. As the availability of formerly scarce, high-status items rapidly increased with an accelerating intercultural trade in corn and furs, trade goods were acquired by—and buried with—a broader cross section of Indian society. Because possession of these valued goods originally served to validate the chiefs' claims to privileged rank, Potter argues, their gradual acquisition by other elements of the population mirrored the weakening authority of the chiefs.[4]

Copper, particularly in the form of gorgets (a type of pendant), served as a symbol of rank exclusively reserved for the Virginia Algonquian chiefs. When English-made buttons, bells, and other objects of copper and brass suddenly became available through trade, these too were incorporated directly into the traditional belief system, carrying a symbolic import similar to those items produced locally of native copper.[5] In applying conventional meanings to a new empirical environment, however, the Powhatan elite discovered that the pragmatics of trade led to practical revaluations.[6] Because chiefs no longer could effectively control the source of copper, the social power they had ascribed to its possession now became accessible to anyone with English trading connections. A depreciation of the metal's symbolic content ultimately occurred, at the expense of chiefly prestige.

Changes in cultural meanings and social contexts through the pragmatics of trade are the subject of James Merrell's chapter. In his survey of intercultural exchange in the Carolina piedmont between 1650 and 1750, Merrell looks beyond the objects of trade—slaves and deerskins, cloth and guns—to the "code of conduct" that, by scrupulous observance, permitted peaceful exchange. During the first half-century, trading activities depended upon the establishment of formal relationships between trade partners typical of those found in native southeastern gift economies. Transactions had simultaneous economic, social, and religious implications, differing in almost every regard from the unidimensional commodity exchange typical of European market economies.[7] Merrell traces the decline in gift-economy transactions, which coincided with a growing dependence (and a growing awareness of dependence) on manufactured trade goods by the Catawbas and other piedmont tribes. By 1750 the old code of conduct that had once proved indispensable for productive commerce now survived only in token gift exchanges signifying patron/client relationships, which were the reality of the late colonial period.

English demand for deerskins affected village life in many ways, with ramifications extending far beyond the immediate trade relationship. Thomas Hatley explores Cherokee economic ecology—the interconnectedness of human demographics, land use, labor commitments, sex roles—and the unanticipated changes in settlement pattern and subsistence strategy that resulted from increasing pressures on domestic production. By drawing a distinction between men's trade and women's trade, Hatley elucidates one important aspect of Cherokee sexual politics.[8] Through their control of surplus corn, women reinforced cultural boundaries, maintained subsistence independence, and—perhaps of greatest significance for the long-term survival of Cherokee culture—defended their own central place in the village economy, providing a needed balance to the male-dominated deerskin production and trade.

Most discussions of colonial-period deer hunting by southeastern Indians end with the native economies in ruins owing to the improvident extermination of deer herds by hunters blind to their own self-interest.[9] In fact, while overhunting undoubtedly occurred locally, there are no documented instances of extirpated white-tailed deer populations until the nineteenth century. Hatley's analysis of the complexities of Cherokee village economics demonstrates how a variety of alternative subsistence strategies developed during the long decline of the increasingly unprofitable deerskin trade. The Cherokee response to the European presence was a lengthy adaptive process guided primarily by the desire to maintain biological, economic, and spiritual links with an environment they had come to know intimately.[10]

Notes

1. James Adair, *History of the American Indians*, ed. Samuel Cole Williams (Johnson City, Tenn.: Watauga Press, 1930), 350–51. Cf. James Axtell, "The Power of Print in the Eastern Woodlands," *William and Mary Quarterly*, 3d ser., 44(April 1987): 300–309.

2. For much of interest on Indian-Spanish relations and trade, see Kathleen A. Deagan, "Spanish-Indian Interaction in Sixteenth-Century Florida and Hispaniola," in *Cultures in Contact*, ed. William W. Fitzhugh (Washington, D.C.: Smithsonian Institution Press, 1985); Amy Bushnell, *The King's Coffer: Proprietors of the Spanish Florida Treasury, 1565–1702* (Gainesville: University Presses of Florida, 1981), passim; and John Jay TePaske, *The Governorship of Spanish Florida, 1700–1763* (Durham, N.C.: Duke University Press, 1964), 193–226.

3. For some recent examples of men profiled in this genre, see J. Frederick Fausz, "Opechancanough: Indian Resistance Leader," in *Struggle and Survival in Colonial America*, ed. David G. Sweet and Gary B. Nash (Berkeley: University of California Press, 1981), 21–37; James H. Merrell, "Minding the Business of the Nation: Hagler as Catawba Leader," *Ethnohistory* 33(January 1986): 55–70.

4. Eric Wolf has pointed out how frequently chiefs "proved to be notorious collaborators of European fur traders and slave hunters on two continents. Connection with the Europeans offered chiefs access to arms and valuables, and hence to a following

outside of kinship and unencumbered by it." Eric Wolf, *Europe and the People without History* (Berkeley: University of California Press, 1982), 96.

5. The interpretation of newly imported artifact forms according to traditional ideology and a priori structural categories has been frequently noted; see Christopher L. Miller and George R. Hamell, "A New Perspective on Indian-White Contact," *Journal of American History* 73(1986): 315, 317; Gregory A. Waselkov and R. Eli Paul, "Frontiers and Archaeology," *North American Archaeologist* 2(1981): 316. For a discussion of archaeological measures of material culture change, see Jeffrey P. Brain, *Tunica Treasure*, Papers of the Peabody Museum of Archaeology and Ethnology 71 (Cambridge: Harvard University, 1979), 270–82.

6. The "pragmatics of trade" is one topic dealt with by Marshall Sahlins, *Islands of History* (Chicago: University of Chicago Press, 1985), 138, 145.

7. Marshall Sahlins, *Stone Age Economics* (Chicago: Aldine, 1972), 185–314; Lewis Hyde, *The Gift* (New York: Random House, 1983); Daniel H. Usner, Jr., "The Frontier Exchange Economy of the Lower Mississippi Valley in the Eighteenth Century," *William and Mary Quarterly*, 3d ser., 44(April 1987): 165–92.

8. Cf. Sahlins, *Islands of History*, 7.

9. Two articles that present alternative perspectives to the overhunting model are by Richard L. Haan, "The 'Trade Do's Not Flourish as Formerly': The Ecological Origins of the Yamassee War of 1715," *Ethnohistory* 28(Fall 1981): 347–51; and Charles H. Hudson, Jr., "Why the Southeastern Indians Slaughtered Deer," in *Indians, Animals, and the Fur Trade*, ed. Shepard Krech III (Athens: University of Georgia Press, 1981), 155–76. More balanced economic analyses can be found in Daniel H. Usner, Jr., "American Indians on the Cotton Frontier: Changing Economic Relations with Citizens and Slaves in the Mississippi Territory," *Journal of American History* 72(September 1985): 297–317; and Kathryn E. Holland Braund, "Mutual Convenience—Mutual Dependence: The Creeks, Augusta, and the Deerskin Trade, 1733–1783" (Ph.D. diss., Florida State University, 1986).

10. Calvin Martin, "Epilogue," in *The American Indian and the Problem of History*, ed. Calvin Martin (New York: Oxford University Press, 1987), esp. 212–17; for a useful survey of this topic, see Richard White, "Native Americans and the Environment," in *Scholars and the Indian Experience*, ed. W. R. Swagerty (Bloomington: Indiana University Press, 1984).

Ruling "the Republic of Indians" in Seventeenth-Century Florida

Amy Turner Bushnell

In the literature on colonial North America, scholars commonly contrast the English colonists, who courted the Indians through trade goods while holding them at a distance, with the French, who converted the Indians to Christianity and themselves to native life. Historians and anthropologists alike tend to discount Spanish and Indian interaction, regarding it as marginal to the central story—that of the French and English.[1] Yet the Spanish presence in eastern North America lasted more than three centuries, irrevocably altering the lives of thousands of Spanish-speaking colonists and many thousands of American Indians.

An examination of the ways Spanish and native cultures adapted to each other in the New World can provide a third model to lay against the better-known French and English ones. In the Spanish model, Indians accepted vassalage along with Christianity and were turned, through the agency of their own leaders, into a labor reserve. It was a system the Spanish applied with success throughout Central and South America wherever they encountered natives who were agricultural, sedentary, and with leaders they could co-opt. In due course they brought the system to North America to use in the self-contained polity of the provinces of Florida. This chapter introduces the native leadership of those provinces and examines the means by which Indians and Spaniards shared authority, as well as the reasons why authority could be seen as something to share.

Spaniards arrived in the Southeast with a sober respect for the formalities of conquest, developed over centuries of reconquering Spain from the Moors and generations of experience in the New World. The sweatiest of *entradas* into unknown territory was a matter of order and record, with banners flying and notaries at the ready. If the entrada resulted in the extension of the king's domains, the royal coat of arms was left as evidence in every town, mounted on the council house.[2] Religious entradas were equally formal, and more than a little military looking when the friars had an armed escort and carried the cross painted on a banner.[3] Anywhere the friars gained access they erected a cross, added a saint to the town's name, and gave directions for building a church.[4] To raise a cross was to found a *visita*, or a stop on the missionary circuit, which in the course of time could develop into a *doctrina* complete with resident friars.[5] Indians, recognizing the symbols of occupation, often signaled a rebellion by pulling down coats of arms and crosses and burning them.[6]

Besides the secular and church officials, a third power existed in the provinces of Spanish Florida, that of the region's chiefs, who survived the foreign invasion to become integral to the governmental system that developed out of it. Their underlying, continuing authority could well have been symbolized by the ball poles of their towns. Raising a ball pole in the Southeast was tantamount to founding a town, which was not so much a place as a corporate entity. Although the townsite had to be relocated periodically as the fertility of surrounding soil became exhausted and firewood gave out, the town's playing field and ball pole remained in place as a sign of ownership and continuity.[7] Aware that the Indian ball game had non-Christian significance, some of the friars would have had the natives take down their ball poles and raise crosses, but other Spaniards said that the playing leagues and the gatherings for games were necessary to the functioning of native government.[8]

As always, what the chiefs had to say on the subject remains open to question. Although some of them became literate in their own languages, they did not often resort to writing.[9] Officers and friars occasionally wrote for a chief's signature, and interpreters were used to translate their statements for recording by notaries, yet one can seldom be sure of what a native ruler really said, much less what he or she had in mind.[10] Nevertheless, we cannot allow the difficulty of the sources to make us underestimate the importance of these rulers or omit them from the provincial picture.

It had not been easy to bring them into line. In the sixteenth century the Spanish tried an array of tactics: wholesale enslavement, wars, trade alliances, conversion with and without force, and intermarriage. The first official expedition to touch Florida, that of Juan Ponce de León in 1513, was little more than a legalized slave raid.

Explorers Pánfilo de Narváez and Hernando de Soto in subsequent decades, seeking other Mexicos and other Perus, took slaves to serve their large armies as they penetrated the southern interior. The natives retaliated in kind. The Dominicans who came to Tampa Bay in 1547 were martyred on the beach, while the castaways from shipwrecks along the Florida coast, if not slaughtered, became slaves. The mutual ransoming of captives, called *rescate*, evolved into a wary sort of barter similar to that between Caribbean colonists and the French and English corsairs who ventured into their ports.[11]

In 1557 Philip II decided that Florida had strategic importance for the return route of the treasure fleet and must be occupied. After an unsuccessful attempt by the viceroy of New Spain to plant a colony at Pensacola, Pedro Menéndez de Avilés sailed directly from Spain in 1565 to surprise French Fort Caroline and establish a colony on the west coast.[12] The king of Spain might want Spaniards in Florida, but the Indians did not. Although Menéndez founded three settlements and put a Jesuit and a fort at nearly every deepwater harbor, the price in Spanish lives was high. He finally declared that one could do nothing with the "treacherous" Indians of Florida except wage a "just war" on them, transport them to the islands, and sell them.[13]

This drastic a solution the Crown forbade. Menéndez and his successors had to pull in the borders, withdrawing isolated garrisons and unprotected missionaries. The three original settlements contracted to two, then one: St. Augustine. From that single outpost the Spanish slowly "pacified" the Indians of Florida as they had the Chichimecos of northern New Spain, by a combination of "wars of fire and blood" on the one hand and presents on the other.[14] One after another, as the Spanish conquered the various tribes or maneuvered them into treaties of alliance, the rulers were forced to agree to a monopoly of their trade, to cooperation in time of war, to the levying of tribute upon their vassals, and not least, to the presence in their towns of Franciscans, who had replaced Jesuits as the indoctrinating agents in Florida.

In return, the new allies received access to the royal largesse. Every year, when the chiefs came to kiss the governor's hands, he distributed lengths of cloth, axes, felt hats, and other gifts among them in the name of the king, while the king's coffer outfitted their churches with altar furnishings and bells.[15] The expense of the gifts to the chiefs rose from 1,500 ducats in 1615 to four times as much in 1650. They accepted this bounty as no more than their due, and when presents were delayed, loyalty faltered.[16]

Franciscans urged their converts to live year-round in towns "like rational beings," within reach of the sacraments. In Florida this met with varying success. The wandering Ais and Tequesta Indians of the coast south of St. Augustine, "possessionless as deer," were never Hispanicized, nor were the nonagricultural Calusas of the southwestern coast.[17] The Guales and eastern Timucuans, hunters and gatherers as well as corn growers, took to the woods seasonally, abandoning both friars and "reductions"—the new towns formed at Spanish instance through a process of aggregation. One anticlerical governor said that if he were an Indian, he would run away too.[18] Only those natives who were both agricultural and sedentary, the Apalaches and western Timucuans, were what a friar could call "Indians of sense and satisfaction."[19]

In the sixteenth century the Spanish, thinking it possible to absorb sensible Indians into their own society through Christian association, encouraged close ties. Priests performed marriages between soldiers and high-ranking native women, and Menéndez himself accepted an Indian consort. Concubinage was common—the traditional Spanish form of union with a woman of lesser rank.[20] Governors served as godfathers to chiefs, bestowing their surnames with their baptismal gifts, so that the frontier of conversions might be traced by matching names of chiefs to names of governors. Native nobles sent their children to be raised in St. Augustine; painted warriors fought side by side with soldiers in padded cotton doublets, and at least one chief was favored with a military pension.[21] Expectations for trade were idyllic, and priests foresaw a time when happy natives would paddle downriver to the towns of Spaniards, bringing canoeloads of chickens and taking back civilization.[22]

Efforts toward an integrated polity ended at the close of the sixteenth century with the Guale Rebellion, which showed how far from idyllic Indians could be. One governor pronounced the conversion of the natives a chimera.[23] The seventeenth century saw the development of the far different system of social order known as the two republics.[24] The Republic of Spaniards and the separate Republic of Indians were to be united in allegiance to the Crown and obedience to the "law of God"; otherwise they were intended to stay strictly apart.

The two republics occupied different territories of the same country. Until the refounding of Pensacola in 1698, St. Augustine remained Florida's one authorized Spanish municipality, whereas there were up to forty towns of Christian Indians, divided by language group into the provinces of Guale (on the Georgia coast), Timucua (in central Florida), and Apalache (around present Tallahassee).[25] Indians were not to come to St. Augustine without a pass.[26] Spaniards, blacks, mestizos, and mulattoes traveling on the king's business could stay no more than three days in an Indian town and must sleep in the council house.[27]

The Franciscans would willingly have quarantined the converts they instructed in doctrine and provided with the consolations and discipline of their religion[28]—and discipline it was, for the natives of the "lower sort" attended mass with regularity out of fear of a whipping.[29] The missionaries asked only to live peaceably in their convents, meeting in chapter at St. Augustine every three years to elect a *padre provincial* as administrator and spokesman. But the king did not intend the friars to create theocracies. Through a series of papal concessions known as the *patronato real*, the Crown had long since gained control of the Spanish church and clergy in all but matters of doctrine, and the governor represented royal authority to the friars, as he often reminded them.[30]

To show the flag and keep track of the friars, the governor stationed in every province a detachment of troops under a *teniente* or deputy governor. Because married soldiers imposed less of a burden on the Indians, many of the soldiers brought along dependents, some of them mixed-bloods. In the garrison town of San Luis de Apalache a rough frontier settlement emerged, far to the west of the Spanish center of order and government in St. Augustine.[31] The soldiers and Florida-born creoles, called *floridanos*, tried the patience of missionaries with their incorrigible swearing, womanizing, mass skipping, and gambling at the ball games. Yet the system itself was clearly stable, for in the seventeenth century there were never more than two or three hundred able-bodied, armed Spaniards in all Florida to hold in check up to 26,000 Christian Indians.[32]

The Republic of Indians remained less centralized than the Spanish republic. Each town had its government of chief (*cacique*) and headmen (*principales* or *mandadores*), whom the Spanish interpreted as a town council (*cabildo*).[33] Sometimes a larger town would have subsidiary or satellite towns with subchiefs or tolerate a settlement of refugees from another tribe within its jurisdiction. The chiefs of the principal towns in a province met as needed to deal with defense and other intertown problems. The Spanish governor addressed them familiarly as "my sons and cousins."[34]

The formal means of communication was the yearly *visita*, a tour of inspection by the governor or his representative. As the *visitador* traveled from place to place the chiefs spoke to him one at a time, then gathered at an appointed location in the province to address him in council. The visita notary recorded their complaints about soldiers in debt to their vassals, floridanos running cattle across their fields, friars interfering with their games and dances, deputies treating them with disrespect, and other offenses to the Republic of Indians of which they were the acknowledged rulers. In the hundreds of pages of testimony one fact becomes clear. The chiefs were a force to reckon with in the provinces; they could have deputies withdrawn and friars reassigned.[35]

They had this power because to Spaniards it was unthinkable for them not to have it. According to medieval rationale, the right way to govern a country was to obtain the allegiance of its natural lords and through them the loyalty of their vassals. In Florida those Indian nobles who accepted Christianity and paid homage to the king of Spain could not reasonably be set aside, for that would have destroyed legitimacy in government. Instead they were drawn into alliances, favored, and supported in their rights as the natural lords (*señores naturales*) of the land. The rights of such leaders before contact varied from tribe to tribe. But during the Spanish hegemony their rights, as seen through Spanish eyes, were seigneurial. Equally with a Spanish *señor*, an Indian noble had the right to inherit title and position, the right to the preeminences of rank, the right to enjoy lands and rule vassals, and the right to combine with other lords and make war.

Like most Europeans, Spaniards traced descent patrilineally, from father to son. Southeastern natives, in contrast, were matrilineal. This meant that a chief's successor would be not his son but his nephew, son of his eldest sister. At first the Spanish found this system unnatural and lent their support to the "rightful heirs," particularly when the chief was a *cacica* married to a Spanish soldier.[36] In time, however, they came to understand that the imposition of Spanish inheritance patterns would undermine chiefs and disrupt clans, and so they accepted matriliny as the norm for the Republic of Indians.[37]

Because of the impermanent nature of townsites in Florida, a native title of nobility based itself upon a body of vassals rather than a tract of land. Don Patricio de Hinachuba, for instance, held the title chief of Ivitachuco, a town in Apalache province. He retained the appellation after leading an exodus of his vassals and their cattle to a place called Abosaya, far into Timucua province.[38] Such a title could be valid even without the vassals. Owing to the fortunes of war, disease, and famine, doña María, cacica of San Francisco, no longer had vassals of her own. She and her Cuban husband entered the historical record in the 1670s by trying unsuccessfully to persuade the subjects of another cacica to join her and form a new town.[39]

From a European standpoint, chiefs and headmen formed the equivalent of a Second Estate. They did not pay head tax or tribute; they were not subject to corporal punishment; they lived off the labor of commoners. Like their Spanish counterparts, the *hidalgos*, they were entitled to wear swords and ride horses.[40] Some chiefs of Apalache traded horses to the chiefs of Apalachicola, who in turn traded them to the English for guns. Determinedly heathen, the chiefs of Apalachicola told the Spanish governor that if God ever wanted them to accept Christianity they would let the Spanish know.[41]

Government in the Republic of Indians was financed by what might be called the "*sabana* system." Once or twice a year the common people of a town cleared, dug, and planted a sabana, or field, for their chief and each of their headmen, as well as the medicine man or woman, the best ballplayers, and the interpreter. There was one large communal field to provide for widows, orphans, and travelers and to put away a reserve.[42] Church expenses were met by another sabana, although friars were not impressed by the Indians as husbandmen and said that for the things of this world they were not ones to kill themselves.[43]

Chiefs and headmen did no manual labor, and neither did their families. Common women were expected to shuck and smoke oysters, parch cassina leaves for tea, shell and grind corn, and extract hickory oil, but an outraged chief of Guale threatened in writing to abandon his post on the frontier and bring all his people to be fed in

St. Augustine if his daughter was called to such tasks at the convent.[44]

A chief convicted of rebellion or another crime could forfeit his or her position but not the preeminences of rank, which were a birthright. A ruler was sentenced to a term of exile rather than to hard labor.[45] Hence Governor Rebolledo made a serious mistake in 1655 when he ordered up the Timucuan militia to reinforce St. Augustine—for who knew where the piratical English would attack after capturing Jamaica—and peremptorily told them all, including the headmen, to bring three *arrobas* of corn, a backpack load of seventy-five pounds. The Franciscans tried to enlighten him on social stratification. In the provinces, they explained, chiefs were the same as lords, sometimes absolute lords, and principales were the same as hidalgos; they were not of the "vile" (in other words "common") people who carried burdens on their backs. Rebolledo ignored this wise counsel, whereupon the rulers rose in rebellion. Rebolledo executed eleven of them, and the Council of the Indies had him arrested for provoking the lords of the land to revolt and then cruelly hanging them.[46]

Spaniards tended to confuse the communal lands or properties of a town with its chief's patrimony. (Perhaps a better word would be "matrimony," with both title and property coming by way of the mother.) They referred, for instance, to the old fields of the *chief* of Asile when they meant of the *town*. This was because a chief frequently did speak for his or her town in matters of land use, whether to grant hunting rights within its jurisdiction or grazing rights to its fallow fields.[47] The Laws of the Indies stipulated that no cattle ranches were to be situated nearer than three leagues from any native settlement, but in both republics there were ways to get around a law. The Crown objected to chiefs who leased their lands for money, not because the land was being alienated but because rents were a form of tribute, and tribute remained a royal prerogative.[48] In time, the depopulation of the provinces left more and more vacant lands where there had once been people,[49] but these lands did not revert to the royal domain as long as there was an heir of the chief's line.

Land was plentiful; without improvements it had little value. A town had other properties that were worth more, such as the herd of individually owned cattle (not to be confused with the cattle belonging to the chief)[50] and the food reserve in the town's several public granaries. In a good year the combined contents of all the granaries of all the towns could amount to a sizable surplus for the province and might become the subject of bitter dispute among Spaniards. The governors expected to purchase the corn and beans at low prices to feed St. Augustine. They instructed their deputies to enforce extra plantings to that end. The Franciscans, believing they were the ones who had taught double-cropping to the Indians, wanted to sell the same surplus in Havana to reduce their chapter's debts and beautify the native sanctuaries.[51] A large amount of money went into the competitive adorning of churches; the value of chrismatories, diadems, and other religious treasure in Apalache province once amounted to 2,500 pesos per town, more than a single Indian could earn in a lifetime of work at the king's wages.[52]

A town granary was double-locked, with Spanish locks and keys. Whoever might be fighting over the second of the locks, the key to the first remained in the hands of the chief, who upon the advice of his headmen might choose not to sell the town's surplus at all.[53] Officers and friars quarreled similarly over who held jurisdiction over the church confines. For the Indians this too was a moot point. The church structure they had built; the contents they had either purchased or been given by the Crown.[54] One friar who had to close down a mission was sued by his erstwhile parishioners for carrying off their church ornaments and bell. To represent them the governor appointed a "defender of the Indians," as was required when natives appeared in a Spanish court, and the decision was in their favor.[55]

Just as in Spain each kingdom preserved its ancient *fueros*, or privileges, the Republic of Indians governed itself according to established law and custom which the Crown saw no need to alter.[56] Only the practices contrary to the "law of God," such as magical cures and multiple wives, could be forbidden. (In their innocence the Indians had imagined that sororate polygyny, in which one's wives were close relatives of each other, was no worse than Spanish concubinage.)[57] A chief retained considerable power over his or her vassals,[58] and if they obeyed poorly, the governor could be called upon to help subdue them even if heathen mercenaries had to be brought in to do it. It was one of the ways the Spanish made themselves indispensable in the provinces.[59]

The relationship between chiefs and governor was symbiotic. He guaranteed their authority; they provided him with labor, and as far as the Spanish were concerned this was their principal function. Communities in the Republic of Indians were liable to a head tax based on the number of married males in the census the friars made every Lenten season. Soon this tribute was commuted to a labor levy, the *repartimiento*.[60] The Spaniards made themselves the cobeneficiaries of the sabana system described earlier by having workers sent to the city in relays to clear, dig, and plant the "king's" sabana, do the first, second, and third hoeings, and guard the ripening corn for the harvest.[61] These field hands, called *indios de cava*, were given rations only. The chiefs who sent them to St. Augustine received tools and other items needed by the town.[62]

From time to time authorities asked the chiefs to send additional workers for the king's service to unload ships, paddle canoes, cut firewood, carry messages, and be servants to important people. These *indios de servicio* got their rations plus a daily wage in trade goods originally figured to be worth one real per day, an eighth of a peso. The choices ran to beads, knives, and half-blankets.[63] One subset of the indios de servicio was the *indios de fábricas* assigned to public works projects, usually building fortifications such as the stone Castillo de San Marcos. When the public works were in their own province the chiefs sometimes donated their vassals' labor and paid for materials out of provincial tithes, which were apparently theirs to administer.

A second subset of the indios de servicio was the *indios de carga*, who carried heavy loads of supplies or trade goods on their backs for long distances. The Crown repeatedly prohibited this use of Indians without addressing the cause, which was the lack of mules and packhorses in Florida. The use of indios de carga became another heated issue between the friars and the governors, each side—with justification—accusing the other of abuses. Still, Spaniards believed that the Indians of Florida were not ill treated compared with the natives in the rest of the Indies. As a contemporary compiler pointed out, in Florida there were no *encomiendas* or factories or mines in which the natives could be occupied, and they did not pay tribute.[64]

The labor quota of a town was adjusted if its inhabitants had soldiers quartered on them, operated a ferry, or moved to a new place on the frontier or along the king's highway to accommodate the Spanish.[65] The quota was not adjusted to account for the Indians who had left the town to become craftsmen or apprentices or to work for private persons (at a better wage than the Crown paid), whether by the day, by the job, or on yearly contract. This is why Spanish and Indian authorities united to oppose peonage. A peon on a ranch was likely to be a man evading his turn on the labor levy and letting his neighbors support his family.[66]

If the Spanish took advantage of the sabana system, they also profited by the native inclination to war. Again, the chiefs were the agency. The vassals they supplied were used at first for couriers and indios de carga. Later, as the Spanish learned respect for Indian archers, their allies were enjoined to keep fifty arrows in their quivers. By the middle of the seventeenth century the Christian Indians were organized into companies of militia under their chiefs. When called to service they received rations and sometimes firearms. If after King Philip's War in 1675 and the Pueblo Revolt of 1680 the Crown had reservations about putting guns in the hands of Indians,[67] the Florida governors usually felt this was justified. The Indians fought more bravely than the Spanish did, they said, and with greater readiness.[68] Prowess in battle allowed an Indian warrior to advance through the ranks to *noroco* or *tascaya*, dancing in the council house with a fine string of scalps and exempt from the labor levy.[69]

Chiefs and Spanish officers might have joint command, as on the expeditions sent northward in the 1620s to locate de Soto's lagoon of pearls.[70] Or the chiefs might go out on their own. In 1680 the chief of Santa Fé took warriors out the Suwanee River in canoes and down the west coast to Charlotte Harbor to rescue Spaniards held captive by the powerful Calusas; two years later Timucuan chiefs rescued a floridano rancher and his people being held for ransom by French buccaneers.[71] The chiefs legalized their campaigns in the Spanish manner, meeting in junta and listing the provocations that called for retaliation and entitled them to take booty. Sometimes a few soldiers went with the Indians; more and more often toward the end of the century they were not invited because of what was called "*la mala unión*."[72]

Relations between the Republic of Spaniards and the Republic of Indians were becoming strained, and the cause was Carolina, founded in 1670. True to the English model, the initial colonists of Charlestown wanted only to trade with the natives. Governor James Colleton ingenuously expressed their policy in these words to his counterpart, Florida governor Diego de Quiroga y Losada: "As for the Yamassees, . . . they have nothing to do with our government nor do we trouble ourselves about them . . . showing no profit but of a few deerskins for which we sell them powder, guns and shot as we do to all Indians indifferently."[73]

In the 1680s, Indians equipped with English firearms and ammunition began to raid Florida towns to take slaves for the markets of Charlestown. This onslaught intensified during Queen Anne's War, when Colonel James Moore twice led armies of Creeks and Carolinians into Florida to destroy the provinces. Martyrologist accounts of the invasion of Apalache relate how Christians were burned on their own crosses, coats of arms defaced, and ball poles uprooted.[74]

The Spanish in the provinces recognized that in addition to invasion they and the chiefs faced a vassals' rebellion. Provincial and town government broke down. Mixed-bloods turned to brigandage. Native warriors demanded that soldiers dismount and fight beside them with ammunition equally divided, while officials became reluctant to issue firearms to Indians who were probably going to defect.[75] Among the several thousand Florida natives who accompanied Moore back to Carolina many went voluntarily, unaware that they would all be sold into servitude. Others headed for the new Spanish fort at Pensacola, for French territory, or for parts unknown, saying they would not stay to die with Spaniards.

Faced with wholesale desertion, the teniente at San Luis spiked the cannons, packed up the salvaged church treasure, and carted it to St. Augustine. In the end only one chief of importance, don Patricio de Hinachuba of the town of Ivitachuco, remained an ally. Having compounded with Moore to spare his town at the expense of its sacred treasure, he settled his vassals and their livestock on the empty savannas of Timucua, far from the Spanish capital.[76]

In the eighteenth century little was left in the provinces to remind one of the time of the two republics or of the rulers who had shared sovereignty with Spaniards. It was the English system that survived. With sadness the Spanish acknowledged that the southeastern Indians had become interested only in guns and gewgaws and that they gave their vassalage to no one. Baptism they might consent to for the sake of the presents, but once out of sight they made a mockery of it, striking their foreheads and calling, "Water, begone! I am no Christian!"[77]

Notes

1. James Axtell, who treats both French and English cultural interaction in *The Invasion Within: The Contest of Cultures in Colonial North America* (New York: Oxford University Press, 1985), x, pleads the demands of stylistic economy for leaving out the Spanish.

2. Alonso de las Alas and Juan Menéndez Marquez to the Crown, St. Augustine, 12–13–1595, *Archivo General de Indias, ramo Gobierno: Santo Domingo, legajo 229, número 18.* (Hereafter cited as SD; unless otherwise noted, origin is St. Augustine and addressee the Crown.)

3. Fr. Francisco Pareja, 1-17-1617, SD 235.

4. Friars in chapter, 10-16-1612, SD 232/61.

5. Fr. Alonso del Moral, [summary seen in Council 9-18-1676], SD 235/102.

6. Francisco Menéndez Marquez and Pedro Benedit Horruytiner, 7-27-1647, SD 235.

7. John R. Swanton, *Modern Square Grounds of the Creek Indians*, Smithsonian Miscellaneous Collections 85, no. 8 (Washington, D.C.: Government Printing Office, 1931), 38.

8. Amy Bushnell, "'That Demonic Game': The Campaign to Stop Indian *Pelota* Playing in Spanish Florida, 1675–1684," *The Americas* 35(July 1978): 1–19.

9. Father Luis Gerónimo de Oré, a contemporary observer, said that the Indians, men and women, learned to read easily and wrote letters to one another in their own languages. *The Martyrs of Florida, 1513–1616*, ed. and trans. Maynard Geiger, O.F.M., Franciscan Studies 18 (New York: Joseph F. Wagner, 1936), 103.

10. On the reliability of interested parties see Gov. Alonso de Aranguíz y Cotes, 11-14-1661, SD 225.

11. Irene Wright, "*Rescates:* With Special Reference to Cuba, 1599–1610," *Hispanic American Historical Review* 3(August 1920): 336–61; Paul E. Hoffman, *The Spanish Crown and the Defense of the Caribbean, 1535–1585: Precedent, Patrimonialism and Royal Parsimony* (Baton Rouge: Louisiana State University Press, 1980), 112–22.

12. Eugene Lyon, *The Enterprise of Florida: Pedro Menéndez de Avilés and the Spanish Conquest of 1565–1568* (Gainesville: University Presses of Florida, 1976), is definitive on this expedition and the first years of conquest.

13. The contemporary arguments for and against Menéndez's plan can be found in Jeannette Thurber Connor, trans. and ed., *Colonial Records of Spanish Florida*, 2 vols. (DeLand: Florida Historical Society, 1925, 1930), 1:31–37, 77–81; Cédula to Gerónimo de Montalva, Governor of Cuba, 8-10-1574, in "Registros: Reales órdenes y nombramientos dirigidos a autoridades y particulares de la Florida. Años 1570 a 1604," typescript, [1907], P. K. Yonge Library of Florida History, 70–74.

14. Juan Menéndez Marquez, 3-14-1608, SD 229/58; Gov. Juan Fernández de Olivera, 10-13-1612, SD 229/74.

15. Domingo de Leturiondo, in *Auto* on Mayaca and Enacape, 3-15-1682 to 9-7-1682, SD 226/95.

16. For a discussion of the fund for the "expense of Indians" (*gasto de indios*) see

Amy Bushnell, *The King's Coffer: Proprietors of the Spanish Florida Treasury, 1565–1702* (Gainesville: University Presses of Florida, 1981), 66.

17. Friars in chapter, 12-5-1693, SD 235/134, and 10-16-1612, SD 232/61; Gov. Laureano de Torres y Ayala, 9-19-1699, SD 228/155.

18. Francisco Menéndez Marquez and Pedro Benedit Horruytiner, 3-18-1647, SD 229; Informe against Gov. Juan Marques Cabrera, Havana, 8-4-1688, SD 864/8.

19. Fr. Juan de Paiva, Pelota Manuscript, San Luis de Talimali, 9-23-1676, in the Domingo de Leturiondo Visita of Apalache and Timucua, 1677–78, Residencia of Gov. Pablo de Hita Salazar, ramo Escribanía de Cámara 156–A, fols. 568–83 (hereafter cited as EC).

20. Stephen Edward Reilly, "A Marriage of Expedience: The Calusa Indians and Their Relations with Pedro Menéndez de Avilés in Southwest Florida, 1566–1569," *Florida Historical Quarterly* 59(April 1981): 395–421; Kathleen A. Deagan, "*Mestizaje* in Colonial St. Augustine," *Ethnohistory* 20, no. 1(Winter 1973): 55–65.

21. Don Gáspar Marquez, Chief of San Sebastian and Tocoy, 6-23-1606, SD 232/47; Catalina de Valdés, 1606, SD 19; idem, [1616], SD 232/76; Gov. Melchor de Navarrete, 11-15-1749, SD 2541/101.

22. In Informe on St. Augustine, 9-16-1602, SD 235/10.

23. Fr. Francisco Pareja, 1-17-1617, SD 235.

24. The ordering of the two republics is described by Lyle N. McAlister in *Spain and Portugal in the New World, 1492–1700* (Minneapolis: University of Minnesota Press, 1984), 391–95.

25. Mark F. Boyd, "Enumeration of Florida Spanish Missions in 1675," *Florida Historical Quarterly* 27(October 1948): 181–88. A *provincia* in Florida was the same as a *partido* in Honduras, according to Gov. Juan Marques Cabrera, 6-14-1681, SD 226.

26. Junta of Guale chiefs, Santa María, 2-7-1701, and Orders for Guale and Mocama, San Juan del Puerto, 2-11-1701, Residencia of Gov. Joseph de Zúñiga y Cerda, SD 858/4, fols. 179–85; Juan de Pueyo Visita of Guale and Mocama in 1695, Residencia of Gov. Laureano de Torres y Ayala, EC 157-A.

27. Orders for Timucua, San Francisco de Potano, 12-24-1694, in the Joachin de Florencia Visita of Apalache and Timucua, 1694–95, Residencia of Gov. Laureano de Torres y Ayala, EC 157-A.

28. Fr. Juan de Pareja, 1-17-1617, SD 235; Friars in chapter to Gov. Diego de Rebolledo, 5-10-1657, in idem, 9-10-1657, SD 235; Junta de Guerra, [Spain], 7-15-1660, SD 839; Gov. Juan Marques Cabrera, 5-10-1681 to 5-30-1681, SD 226.

29. The mission beadle, a native known as a *fiscal*, administered the punishment. See friars in chapter vs. Gov. Juan Marques Cabrera, 5-10-1681 to 5-30-1681, SD 226.

30. Gov. Pedro de Ybarra to Fr. Pedro Bermejo, 12-13-1605, SD 232; Gov. Juan Marques Cabrera, 12-8-1680, SD 226/68.

31. For discussions of Spanish settlers in the provinces see Amy Bushnell, "The Menéndez Marquez Cattle Barony at La Chua and the Determinants of Economic Expansion in Seventeenth-Century Florida," *Florida Historical Quarterly* 56(April 1978):

407–31; idem, "Patricio de Hinachuba: Defender of the Word of God, the Crown of the King, and the Little Children of Ivitachuco," *American Indian Culture and Research Journal* 3(July 1979): 1–21; idem, *King's Coffer*, 14.

32. In 1655 the Franciscans reported 70 friars, 38 doctrinas, and 26,000 Christian Indians in Florida. See Michael V. Gannon, *The Cross in the Sand: The Early Catholic Church in Florida, 1513–1870* (Gainesville: University of Florida Press, 1967), 57.

33. These are terms the Spanish brought with them. In the Indian languages, words for chiefs were *mico, inija, usinjulo,* and *alayguita.*

34. Gov. Joseph de Zúñiga y Cerda to the chiefs and principales of Vitachuco and San Luis, 4-24-1704, SD 858/B.

35. For accounts of visitas see Fred Lamar Pearson, Jr., "The Florencia Investigation of Spanish Timucua," *Florida Historical Quarterly* 51(October 1972): 166–76; idem, "Spanish-Indian Relations in Florida, 1602–1675: Some Aspects of Selected *Visitas*," *Florida Historical Quarterly* 52(January 1974): 261–73; Bushnell, "That Demonic Game"; idem, "Patricio de Hinachuba," 4–5.

Ecclesiastical visitas were also made, usually by the padre provincial. See Gov. Francisco de la Guerra y de la Vega, 2-28-1668, SD 233/68; Gov. Juan Marques Cabrera, 12-8-1680, SD 226/68.

36. Kathleen A. Deagan, "Cultures in Transition: Fusion and Assimilation among the Eastern Timucua," in *Tacachale: Essays on the Indians of Florida and Southeastern Georgia during the Historic Period*, ed. Jerald T. Milanich and Samuel Proctor (Gainesville: University Presses of Florida, 1978), 103–4; don Gáspar Marques, Chief of San Sebastian and Tocoy, 6-23-1606, SD 232/47.

37. Leturiondo Visita of 1677–78, EC 156-A; Florencia Visita of 1694–95, EC 157-A; Patricio, Chief of Ybitachuco [at Abosaya], to Gov. Joseph de Zúñiga y Cerda, 5-29-1705, SD 858/4.

38. Bushnell, "Patricio de Hinachuba."

39. Reported petition of María de Jesús, Cacica of San Francisco de Potano, 1-25-1678, acted upon at Salamototo, 1-30-1678, in the Leturiondo Visita of 1677–78, EC 156-A.

40. Florencia Visita of 1694–95, EC 157-A.

41. Gov. Joseph de Zúñiga y Cerda, 9-30-1702, SD 840/58; Gov. Juan Marques Cabrera, 9-20-1681, SD 226/95.

42. Gov. Juan Marques Cabrera, 6-14-1681, SD 226; Florencia Visita of 1694–95, EC 157-A; Orders for Guale and Mocama, San Juan del Puerto, 2-11-1701, SD 858/4, fol. 179; Teniente Antonio Mateos to Gov. Juan Marques Cabrera, [San Luis de Talimali], 3-14-1686, SD 839/82.

43. "Por las cosas deste mundo no se matan mucho" (Friars in chapter vs. Gov. Juan Marques Cabrera, 5-10-1681 to 5-30-1681, SD 226).

44. Chief of Guale to Gov. Juan Marques Cabrera, Sápala, 5-5-1681, SD 226.

45. Gov. Pablo de Hita Salazar, 7-5-1677, EC 158.

46. Fr. Juan Gómez de Engraba to Fr. Francisco Martínez, Havana, 3-13-1657 and 4-4-1657, SD 225; Investigation of Gov. Diego de Rebolledo by the Council of the Indies,

7-7-1657, included with Anon., Informe against Gov. Diego de Rebolledo, 6-15-1657, SD 6/17; Friars in chapter, 9-10-1657, SD 235.

47. Friars in chapter, 9-10-1657, SD 235; Pedro Benedit Horruytiner, 11-10-1657, SD 233/55.

48. For discussions of land grants and use in Florida see Bushnell, *King's Coffer,* 80–82, 113, and idem, "Menéndez Marquez Cattle Barony."

49. Henry F. Dobyns examines Timucuan depopulation as a representative case in *Their Number Become Thinned: Native American Population Dynamics in Eastern North America* (Knoxville: University of Tennessee Press, 1983), but his conclusions on total figures should be used with care. David Henige, in "Primary Source by Primary Source? On the Role of Epidemics in New World Depopulation," *Ethnohistory* 33(Summer 1986): 293–312, shows Dobyns to be incautious in his handling of the sources.

50. Florencia Visita of 1694–95, EC 157-A. Owners identified their stock by ear notching.

51. Bushnell, *King's Coffer,* 11–12, 24, 70, 99; Gov. Pablo de Hita Salazar, 9-6-1677, SD 839/46; Gov. Juan Marques Cabrera to Teniente Juan Fernández de Florencia, 1-20-1681, SD 226/76; Friars in chapter vs. Gov. Juan Marques Cabrera, 5-10-1681 to 5-30-1681, SD 226.

52. See Bushnell, "Patricio de Hinachuba," 12.

53. Orders for Guale and Mocama, San Juan del Puerto, 2-11-1701, SD 858/4, fol. 179; Florencia Visita of 1694–95, EC 157-A.

54. Gov. Juan Marques Cabrera to Fr. Blas de Robles, 5-10-1681, SD 226/76.

55. Domingo de Leturiondo, n.d., in Auto on Mayaca and Enacape, 3-15-1682 to 9-7-1682, SD 226/95; idem, 8-26-1682, with Gov. Juan Marques Cabrera, 10-7-1682, SD 226/95. On the defender of the Indians in Florida see Bushnell, *King's Coffer,* 40, 111. Cf. Charles R. Cutter, *The Protector de Indios in Colonial New Mexico, 1659–1821* (Albuquerque: University of New Mexico Press, 1986).

56. Captain Antonio de Argüelles, 2-24-1688, SD 234/87; Fiscal of the Council of the Indies, 7-23-1700, with Gov. Laureano de Torres y Ayala, 9-16-1699, SD 228/151.

57. Florencia Visita of 1694–95, EC 157-A; Lewis H. Larson, Jr., "Historic Guale Indians of the Georgia Coast and the Impact of the Spanish Mission Effort," in Milanich and Proctor, *Tacachale,* 120–40; Bushnell, "That Demonic Game," 8.

58. Jerald T. Milanich and William C. Sturtevant, eds., *Francisco Pareja's 1613 "Confessionario": A Documentary Source for Timucuan Ethnography,* trans. Emilio Moran (Tallahassee: Florida Department of State, 1972), 34–35.

59. Friars, Informe on St. Augustine, 9-16-1602, SD 235/10; Gov. Juan Fernández de Olivera, 10-13-1612, SD 229/74; Florencia Visita of 1694–95, EC 157-A.

60. On the tribute and repartimiento see Bushnell, *King's Coffer,* 11–13, 16–25, 37–46, 97–99, 106, 110–11, and idem, "Patricio de Hinachuba," 8; Florencia Visita of 1694–95, EC 157-A; Francisco Menéndez Marquez and Pedro Benedit Horruytiner, 7-27-1647, SD 235.

61. Friars to Gov. Diego de Rebolledo, 5-10-1657, with Friars in chapter, 9-10-1657, SD 235.

62. Bartolomé de Argüelles, 10-31-1598, SD 229/25; Fr. Antonio de Somoza, Commissary General of the Indies, [Spain], 5-2-1673, SD 235/97; Teniente Antonio Mateos to Gov. Juan Marques Cabrera, 2-8-1686, SD 839/82.

63. Apparently the blanket fabric was woven on a narrow backstrap loom, and a full blanket had a seam down the middle.

64. Juan Díez de la Calle, *Memorial y noticias sacras y reales del imperio de las Indias occidentales* (Madrid, 1646).

65. Friars in chapter to Gov. Diego de Rebolledo, 5-10-1657, in idem, 9-10-1657, SD 235; Florencia Visita of 1694–95, EC 157-A. For examples of town relocation to serve the communications network, see Leturiondo Visita of 1677–78, EC 156-A, fols. 568–83, and Bushnell, "Menéndez Marquez Cattle Barony," 420.

66. Fr. Alonso del Moral, [summary seen in Council 11-5-1676], SD 235/104; Auto on the abuses of the friars, 6-28-1683, SD 226/105; Florencia Visita of 1694–95, EC 157-A.

67. Francisco Menéndez Marquez and Pedro Benedit Horruytiner, 7-27-1647, SD 235; Fr. Miguel de Valverde and Fr. Rodrigo de la Barrera, San Nicolás de Tolentino, 9-10-1674, SD 234; Gov. Pablo de Hita Salazar, 5-14-1680, SD 839/63; Cédula, 3-22-1685, SD 852/34; Florencia Visita of 1694–95, EC 157-A.

68. Gov. Juan Marques Cabrera, 3-30-1686, SD 852.

69. Gov. Joseph de Zúñiga y Cerda, Orders on scalp taking, 3-14-1701, SD 858/B-252; Bushnell, "That Demonic Game," 11–12, 16; idem, *King's Coffer*, 96–97.

70. Bushnell, *King's Coffer*, 92.

71. Gov. Pablo de Hita Salazar, 3-6-1680, SD 226; Bushnell, "Menéndez Marquez Cattle Barony," 428.

72. Juntas de Guerra, St. Augustine, 11-3-1694, and San Luis de Talimali, 10-22-1702, SD 858/B-14.

73. Gov. James Colleton of Carolina, Charlestown, n.d., to Gov. Diego de Quiroga y Losada, translation sent to the Crown on 4-1-1688, SD 839.

74. See Charles W. Arnade, *The Siege of St. Augustine in 1702* (Gainesville: University of Florida Press, 1959); Mark F. Boyd, Hale G. Smith, and John W. Griffin, eds., *Here They Once Stood: The Tragic End of the Apalachee Missions* (Gainesville: University of Florida Press, 1951).

75. Bushnell, "Patricio de Hinachuba," 10; Captain Francisco Romo de Uriza, San Luis de Talimali, 10-22-1702, SD 858/B-14.

76. Bushnell, "Patricio de Hinachuba," 7–14.

77. Gov. Francisco del Moral Sánchez, 6-8-1734, SD 844/28; "Florida in the Late First Spanish Period: The 1756 Griñán Report," ed. Michael C. Scardaville and trans. Jesús María Belmonte, *El Escribano* 16(1979): 16; Francisco de Buenaventura, Bishop of Tricale, 4-29-1736, SD 863/119.

Early English Effects on Virginia Algonquian Exchange and Tribute in the Tidewater Potomac

Stephen R. Potter

Not long after an unsuccessful attempt to destroy the English colonists at Jamestown, in May of 1607, the paramount chief, or *mamanatowick*, of the Virginia Algonquians and his chiefs, or *werowances*, entered a period of trade with the English. In a scene replayed countless times, Indian maize was exchanged for European goods.[1] Such exchanges were more than ritual expressions of professed friendship—they were attempts by both Europeans and Indians to control and benefit from one another through trade.

From the perspective of the Algonquian werowances, this trade was a conscious effort to incorporate the strangers, or *tassantasses*, into the native system of exchange and tribute. It is my thesis that during earliest Anglo-Indian contact in Tidewater Virginia, the Algonquian werowances sought to control the flow of European goods into aboriginal society, much as they controlled the flow of luxury and status items gathered through tribute from their own people. As Anglo-Indian contact continued, Algonquian responses to the English differed depending upon their political relations with the Powhatan chiefdom of the James-York river basins and their distance from the earliest permanent English settlements. Among groups such as the Patawomekes, farther from both the Powhatan chiefdom and the Virginia English, the process of culture change was initially different even though the end result was the same—the collapse of centralized Algonquian political authority. This is most apparent in the English effects upon native systems of tribute and exchange, especially among peripheral chiefdoms like the Patawomekes.

In the late 1500s and early 1600s, the southeastern Algonquian groups blanketed the temperate coastal plain of the mid-Atlantic from the shores of the Chesapeake Bay and the tidewater regions of Maryland and Virginia to Albemarle and Pamlico sounds in North

Carolina.[2] They consisted of a series of ranked, kin-oriented societies living in semipermanent villages and hamlets composed of arborlike structures made of poles covered with bark or cane mats. The villages, situated near streams and rivers, were surrounded by extensive fields of maize and beans, maintained through slash-and-burn techniques. Smaller garden plots of squash, pumpkins, gourds, sunflowers, and tobacco were tended near the longhouses. Agricultural harvests were supplemented by communal deer hunts, solitary stalking of game, harvesting marine and estuarine fish and mollusks, and gathering a host of plant foods. Their social and political organization featured rank-differentiated roles and functions, dress, and burial customs; polygyny; matrilineal descent of chieftains; tribute systems; and trade monopolies.[3] Although the degree of social and political centralization varied among these groups, all of them manifested what Marshall Sahlins describes as "a system of chieftainship, a hierarchy of major and minor authorities holding forth over major and minor subdivisions of the tribe: a chain of command linking paramount to middle range and local level leaders."[4]

The largest and most centralized of the southeastern Algonquian polities was the Powhatan chiefdom, named for the paramount chief who ruled the majority of Virginia Algonquians at the time of English colonization in 1607. The apical status position of paramount chief was occupied by Powhatan, or Wahunsonacock, from about 1572 until 1617. Subordinate to Powhatan were the werowances who ruled the local groups. If there was more than one village in a group's territory, then subchiefs, or "lesser werowances," governed the villages where the werowance did not reside. Nonchiefly, high-status positions included advisers, priests, and distinguished warriors. Commoners and war captives occupied the bottom two positions within the social hierarchy.[5]

Although the position of werowance was hereditarily ascribed (at least by the early seventeenth century), social rank was maintained and reaffirmed by the accumulation and control of wealth.[6] Indeed, the Algonquian word *werowance* has been variously interpreted as meaning "he is rich," "he is of influence," or "he is wise."[7] Among the Virginia Algonquians, the primary means of wealth acquisition by the paramount chief and the werowances of the petty chiefdoms was through a hierarchical system of tribute. Powhatan received a diversity of tribute items from his werowances, including "skinnes, beades, copper, pearle, deare, turkies, wild beasts, and corne."[8] One of the early Virginia chroniclers, William Strachey, discussed tribute collection in some detail in an often-cited passage.

> Every Weroance knowes his owne Meeres and lymitts to fish fowle or hunt in (as before said) but they hold all of their great Weroance Powhatan, unto whome they paie 8. parts of 10. tribute of all the Commodities which their Countrey yeildeth, as of wheat [i.e., corn], pease, beanes, 8. measures of 10. (and these measured out in little Cades or Basketts which the great king appoints) of the dying roots 8. measures of ten; of all sorts of skyns and furrs 8. of tenne, and so he robbes the poore in effect of al they have even to the deares Skyn wherewith they cover them from Could, in so much as they dare not dresse yt and put yt on untill he have seene yt and refused yt; for what he Comaundeth they dare not disobey in the least thing.[9]

More than likely, Powhatan's assessment of eight parts out of every ten was made against the total tribute collected by each werowance from his respective local group and was not an assessment made against all the economic yields and goods produced by each group.[10]

The goods collected were usually stored in or near the house of each werowance, although Powhatan's main storehouse was near a village at the core of his chiefdom and not near his primary place of residence in 1607. Tribute items were used to support the werowances, their families, and the priests, to entertain visiting personages, and for communal feasts and religious activities. The werowances and their immediate supporters were the principal recipients of any luxury or prestige goods. Diffusion to society at large was mainly limited to those status items that could be easily regulated in number and size, such as strands of beads and pearls, or sheet copper in the form of small geometric pieces or rolled tubular beads. The werowances used these items to reward warriors for bravery, to repay individuals who helped plant and harvest their fields, and possibly to dispense to commoners after certain funeral rites.[11]

Of all the prestige goods, the one the werowances seem to have coveted most was copper—so much so that they strictly controlled its trade. Large gorgets, made from sheet copper cut in a variety of geometric shapes, were reserved for the werowances and other individuals of high status. They were worn either about the head or suspended from the neck. The shiny red metal was used to purchase assistance in warfare and was buried with the werowances in their mortuary temples.[12]

The formation of the Powhatan chiefdom began sometime during the 1570s when Powhatan inherited six to nine groups occupying territories that formed a crescent from the fall line of the James River, north-northeast to the York River (fig. 1). Urged on by his priests and their prophecy that "from the Chesapeack Bay a Nation should arise, which should dissolve and give end to his Empier," Powhatan expanded his chiefdom eastward to the coast.[13] By the end of 1608, through intimidation and warfare, Powhatan controlled almost all (at least fourteen) of the petty chiefdoms between the falls of the James and York rivers, and Chesapeake Bay.[14]

A notable exception to Powhatan's conquests were the Chickahominys, who thwarted his efforts to appoint a werowance to rule them. The Chickahominys were the only group of Virginia Algonquians not governed by a werowance. Instead, they were ruled by a council of eight priests or elders (or both). This different form of governance may explain why individual Chickahominy families were able to trade their baskets of maize for Captain John Smith's goods.[15] Describing his "discovery of the country of Chikhamania," Smith wrote "[I] shewed them what copper and hatchets they shuld have for corne, each family seeking to give me most content: so long they caused me to stay that 100 at least was expecting my comming by the river, with corne."[16]

When the English established Jamestown in 1607, Powhatan was preoccupied with consolidating his strategic hold over the remaining Tidewater Virginia Algonquians. This was especially true of those petty chiefdoms in northern Virginia, between the Rappahannock and Potomac rivers (e.g., the Patawomekes), and on Virginia's Eastern Shore (e.g., the Accomacs). Beyond the York and James rivers, Powhatan's authority diminished as the distance from the center of his chiefdom increased, a fact not lost on the English invaders.[17]

Despite the abrupt intrusion of the English in the midst of Powhatan's James River territories, the colonists and Powhatan natives attempted to accommodate one another during the period from July 1607 to 1609. William Strachey observed that the Indians were "generally Covetous of our Commodities, as Copper, white beades for their women, Hatchetts, . . . Howes to pare their Corne ground, knyves and such like."[18] Captain John Smith added "they were no lesse desirous of our commodities then we of their Corne."[19] Thus,

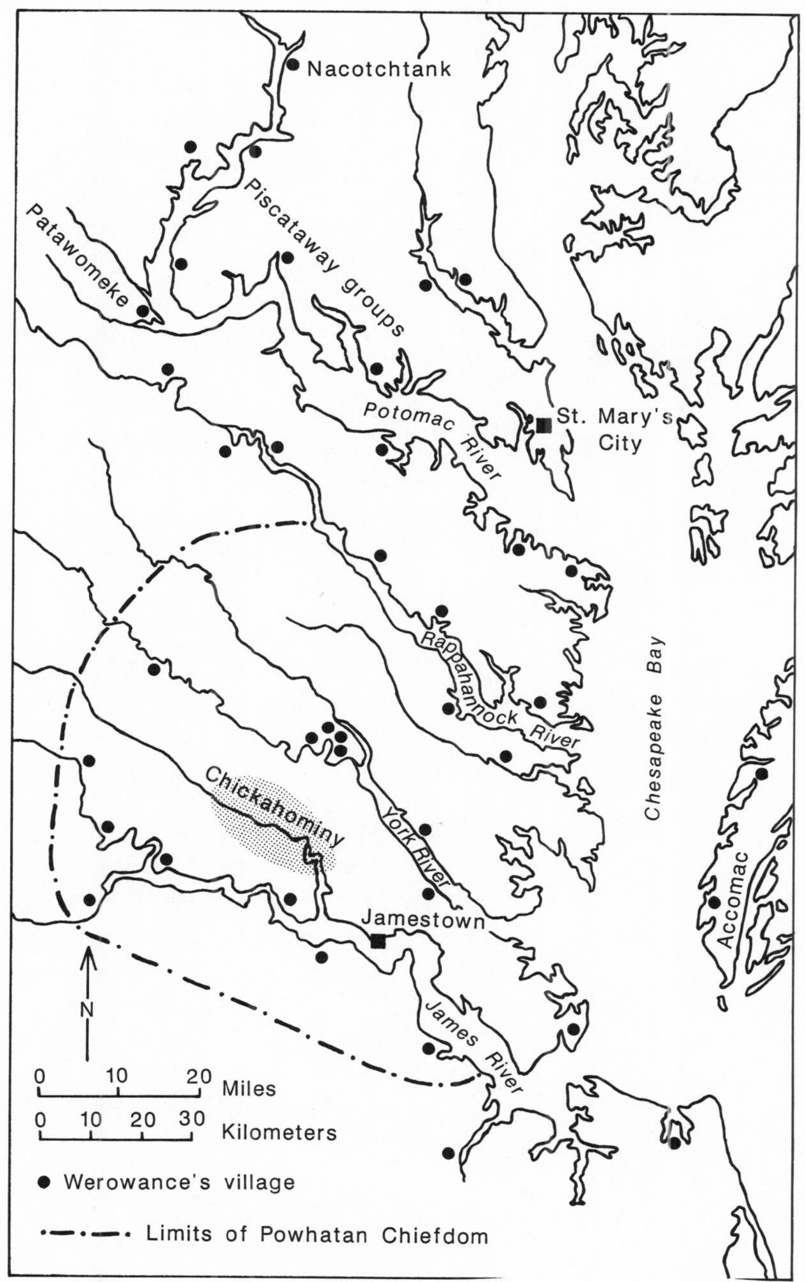

Figure 1 Map of Algonquian groups bordering Chesapeake Bay at the beginning of English occupation.

only occasional outbreaks of violence marred the trade of European goods for Indian maize.

During the early years of the Jamestown settlement, it was the paramount chief and his werowances who controlled, for the most part, the distribution of European goods among their people, particularly prestige items. On one occasion the paramount chief Powhatan told Captain Newport, "It is not agreeable to my greatnesse, in this pedling manner to trade for trifles, and I esteeme you also a great Werowance. Therefore lay me downe all your commodities together; what I like I will take, and in recompence give you what I thinke fitting their value."[20] Moreover, Powhatan attempted to "monopolize all the Copper brought into Virginia by the English: and whereas the English are now content, to receave in Exchange a few measures of Corne for a great deale of that mettell . . . Powhatan doth againe vent some smale quantety thereof to his neighbour Nations for 100. tymes the value, reserving notwithstanding for himself a plentiful quantety."[21]

In the course of their initial trading with the Jamestown colonists, the werowances were usually the ones who conducted the trade. Even items stolen from the English were taken to the werowance for first refusal, as mentioned by Captain John Smith:

> At our Fort, the tooles we had, were so ordinarily stolen by the Indians, as necessity inforced us to correct their braving theeverie. . . . Their custome is to take any thing they can ceaze off . . . but what others can steale, their King receiveth. . . . From Nansamond, which is 30. miles from us, the King sent us a Hatchet which they had stollen from us at our being there.[22]

Twenty-two years before the settling of Jamestown, Sir Walter Raleigh's colonists had similar experiences trading with the North Carolina Algonquians. Regarding the Roanoke Indians, Arthur Barlowe penned the following:

> The next day there came unto us divers boates, and in one of them the Kings brother, accompanied with fortie or fiftie men. . . . When hee came to the place, his servants spread a long matte uppon the grounde, on which he sat downe, and at the ende of the matte, foure others of his companie did the like. . . . After wee had presented this his brother, with such things as we

> thought he liked, we likewise gave somewhat to the other that sate with him on the matte: but presently he arose, and tooke all from them, and put it into his owne basket, making signes and tokens, that all things ought to be delivered unto him, and the rest were but his servants, and followers.[23]

Given the authority of the werowances to levy tribute, it should come as no surprise that they sought to control the flow of European goods into aboriginal society.

By 1609, private trading between English mariners (who came to the Jamestown colony on supply ships) and members of the Powhatan chiefdom flooded the James River chiefdoms with copper, potentially diminishing its value among the Algonquians as well as the prestige of the werowances. With copper aplenty, Powhatan now asked for English arms in exchange for Indian maize.[24] Unwilling to trade in arms and backed by a new charter charging the English colonists with "the conversion and reduccion of the [native] people in those parts unto the true worshipp of God and Christian religion," the Jamestown government launched attacks against the Powhatans to destroy their priesthood and obtain the precious corn by force.[25]

For most of the next quarter-century, members of the Powhatan chiefdom and their English neighbors engaged in "vengeful perpetual warre," interspersed with short-lived periods of peace.[26] The First Anglo-Powhatan War (1609–14) ended in English victory. Three years later Powhatan abdicated his position as paramount chief in favor of his brothers Opitchapam and Opechancanough. The following year Powhatan died, and eventually Opechancanough assumed the position of mamanatowick. By 1622 Christian missionary fervor and forced adoption of English "Fassions" seriously threatened Powhatan culture. These factors, coupled with loss of land, led Opechancanough to launch the Powhatan Uprising of 1622. Ten years later the Second Anglo-Powhatan War officially ended, leaving the Powhatan chiefdom in a state of near collapse. Over the next dozen years, further territorial expansion by the English triggered the Powhatan Uprising of 1644. In two years the war was over, Opechancanough was dead, the Powhatan chiefdom was destroyed, and *all* Virginia Algonquian groups were made tributary to the colony.[27]

As Anglo-Indian relations on the James and York rivers were being forged in the crucible of war, English relations took a different form with the Virginia Algonquians farther from both the English and the Powhatans. In May 1609, before the outbreak of hostilities, members of the Virginia Company of London advised the Jamestown leaders:

> If you make friendship with any of these nations as you must doe, choose to doe it with those that are fartherest from you and enemies unto those amonge whom you dwell, for you shall have least occasion to have differences with them and by that meanes a suerer league of amity, and you shalbe suer of their trade partely for covetousnes and to serve their owne ends, where the copper is yett in his primary estimacion which Powhatan hath hitherto engrossed.[28]

Advice became policy and distance from English settlements the means of distinguishing Indian friend from foe.

Hastening to put policy into action, in 1610 Captain Samuel Argall established a lucrative trade with the werowance of Patawomeke, "A King as great as Powhatan" and "a Person of great Interest and Authority, throughout the whole [Potomac] River."[29] The Patawomekes were the largest and most powerful of the northern Virginia Algonquian chiefdoms and had been key players in the native trade network before the English invasion—indeed, the name Patawomeke has been interpreted as "trading center."[30] Between 665 and 850 Patawomekes lived in ten villages near the southern shore of the Potomac River, with several of the minor villages or hamlets governed by Japazaw, a lesser werowance and brother to the great werowance of Patawomeke.[31]

As the First Anglo-Powhatan War raged in the lower reaches of the James and York rivers, Captain Argall, "trading for corne, with the great king of Patawomeck [Patawomeke], from him obteyned well neere 400. bushells of wheat [i.e., corn], pease and beanes (besyde many kind of furrs) for 9. poundes of Copper, 4. bunches of beades, 8. dozen of hatchetts, 5 dozen of knives, 4 bunches of bells, 1. dozen of sizers, all not much more worth than 40s. English."[32] Capitalizing on his earlier success, Argall returned to the Patawomekes in 1612, obtained 1,100 bushels of maize, and, more important, sealed a defensive military alliance with them against Powhatan.[33]

Yet Argall's greatest coup in the maize trade with the Patawomekes occurred in 1613. To quote another Jamestown chronicler, Ralph Hamor:

> It chaunced Powhatans delight and darling, his daughter Pocahuntas . . . tooke some pleasure . . . to be among her friends at Pataomecke . . . imploied thither, as shopkeepers to a Fare, to exchange some of her Fathers commodities for theirs, where residing some three months or longer it fortuned upon occasion either of promise or profit, Captain Argall to arrive there.[34]

With the aid of Japazaw and the approval of the werowance of Patawomeke, Argall succeeded in kidnapping Pocahontas for the price of "a small Copper kettle and som other les valuable toies."[35] This action, plus a devastating English raid on the Pamunkeys a year later, helped force an end to the First Anglo-Powhatan War.[36]

The maize trade with the northern Virginia Algonquians and Piscataway groups along the Potomac River slackened after the end of the war in 1614, as the colonists became more self-sufficient. Viewing the cessation of hostilities as an opportunity to Christianize the Indians, the Virginia Company of London promoted the metamorphosis of Algonquians into Anglicans while the Virginia English promoted the growth of tobacco. As the profitable tobacco market grew during the next seven years, English land acquisition and Christian missionary efforts helped precipitate the Second Anglo-Powhatan War of 1622–32.[37]

Acutely aware of the Patawomekes' invaluable services in the past and their nonparticipation in Opechancanough's attack of March 22, 1622, the Jamestown government realized the necessity of maintaining good relations with those Virginia Indians who were not in league with Opechancanough. In 1622 the English built a fort adjacent to the village of Patawomeke and the werowance of Patawomeke provided "40. or 50 choise Bow-men to conduct and assist" the English in a raid to seize maize from the Patawomekes' enemies, the Nacotchtanks.[38] Near summer's end, the beneficial alliance with the Patawomekes was severed for a time when Captain Isaac Maddison acted rashly on false information and brutally killed thirty or forty Patawomekes.[39]

The following March, Captain Henry Spelman and twenty-one Englishmen were killed somewhere on the Potomac River, within approximately thirty miles of present-day Washington, D.C. Some say the Nacotchtanks were responsible, others the Patawomekes. Both certainly had reason to want revenge on the English. Regardless of the group responsible, Governor Wyatt sought to renew the English alliance with the Patawomekes by leading an expedition against their enemies, the Nacotchtanks and Piscataways, whom Wyatt blamed for the death of Spelman and his men. By the fall of 1623 the English and Patawomekes were allies once again, and the maize trade resumed.[40]

Benefiting from their experience in the maize trade of the 1620s, individuals like Henry Fleet and William Claiborne saw the profit to be had in pelts. By 1630 as the Second Anglo-Powhatan War was slowly coming to an end on the James and York rivers, the beaver trade was beginning on Chesapeake Bay. With the establishment of the Maryland English at St. Mary's City in 1634, Marylanders competed with Virginians in the ever-increasing search for pelts.[41] Although the Chesapeake beaver trade lasted only until the 1650s, as J. Frederick Fausz writes, it "brought Englishmen and Indians together in the most direct and intense form of cultural contact short of war, and yet it . . . demanded . . . that Indians remain Indians, pursuing the skills they knew best without fear of territorial dispossession, and that Englishmen remain Englishmen, performing the services they understood without the need to become Christian crusaders."[42]

Increased Anglo-Algonquian contact brought about by the profitable fur trade on the Potomac River opened the floodgates for European trade goods to pour into the area. With increased contact, first through trade and later through English settlement, the werowances' authority diminished owing to a variety of factors including population decline, displacement or loss of land, discrediting of the priesthood through its ineffectiveness against European diseases, and perhaps loss of clear matrilineal successors to the chieftainship. By the 1650s and 1660s some werowances were being appointed by the English; other werowances governed with their "great men," and in at least one case, groups of "great men" ruled in lieu of a werowance.[43] As the centralized political power of the werowances weakened, so did their control over the tribute and exchange systems, opening up opportunities for greater individual trade and acquisition of goods.

Unfortunately, after the Powhatan Uprising of 1622, English accounts of Virginia Algonquian lifeways are sparse, especially information needed to document the effects of acculturation on the power and authority of the werowances.[44] If the Algonquian werowances' control over European goods, particularly prestige items, waned over time as their authority diminished, then such a change should be reflected archaeologically as an increase in both the number and the diversity of European trade goods found in common burial sites, and in the presence of items formerly reserved for individuals of high status. Assuming a person's status in life is manifested in death by the manner of burial, it is possible to document changes over time in the control, distribution, and acquisition of certain classes of material goods that are preserved in the archaeological record.

To investigate this possibility, an examination was made of archaeological collections from the Potomac Creek area of Stafford County, Virginia. Here, according to Thomas Jefferson, was the location of the "chief town" of the Patawomeke Indians, where the werowance resided.[45] These collections of artifacts and archival materials, now in the Smithsonian Institution, were made between 1869 and 1937, mainly by antiquarians and avocational archaeologists. Consequently there is great variation in the degree of control exercised in the collection and recording of the archaeological materials. Additional research in the same locale by late nineteenth-century professional archaeologists and twentieth-century physical anthropologists has helped offset some inadequacies of the data.[46] Taken together, all of this information can be used to reconstruct and interpret a remarkable series of late prehistoric/protohistoric and historic burial sites of the Patawomeke Indians.

At the Potomac Creek site, a palisaded protohistoric and possibly early historic village, four protohistoric ossuaries were discovered. Ossuaries are large, saucer-shaped pits, usually elliptical in outline, containing mass human reburials. The four ossuaries held at least 41, 67, 77, and 287 individuals of all ages and both sexes. Only items of native manufacture were found in association with the skeletal material in the ossuaries—a few bone awls and clay smoking pipes; a variety of disk, columella, and marginella shell beads (most found with children's skeletons); and "three small pieces" of native copper in one ossuary and "small amounts of native copper" at the western end of another.[47] The communal nature of the reburials, the relative paucity of grave goods per individual, the preponderance of shell beads associated mainly with children, and the limited number and small size of copper objects (ostensibly of native origin) fit the expected pattern of precontact Algonquian society, when the werowances and their successors controlled the distribution of tribute and prestige items.

On another part of Potomac Neck, near a historic Patawomeke occupation at Indian Point, a single flexed burial was reported in 1891. Archival records indicate the skeleton had been placed in a small pit, three feet deep. Associated objects included a large crescent-shaped copper breastplate, tubular copper beads, and "numerous needles 4 or 5 inches" long. Other objects possibly included with the burial were "rough" glass beads and "pipes of clay."[48] Depending upon whether glass beads were in association and whether the copper was of native or European origin, the isolated burial could date from late prehistoric times (about fifteenth century A.D.) to the mid-seventeenth century. With no way of confirming the presence of glass beads or the origin of the copper and no data on the skeleton, further interpretation of this isolated burial is problematic.

In 1869 a most remarkable multiple burial site was discovered by a party of four antiquarians near Indian Point. Their finds were reported by Elmer R. Reynolds in 1880, and it is upon his account, published descriptions of some of the artifacts, and an examination of the Smithsonian Institution collection that the following reconstruction is based (fig. 2).[49] The burial consisted of the extended skeletons of twelve adults, all but one in association with native-made shell beads. Associated with the twelfth skeleton was a diverse array of artifacts—five *Busycon* shell maskettes with stylized human faces in bas-relief (fig. 3); five circular shell gorgets; four small whelk shells; two flushloop "copper" bells; six circular copper gorgets; six quadrangular copper gorgets (fig. 4); a native-made earthenware bowl; approximately four quarts of beads made of rolled sheet copper, bone, clay, and shell; and fifteen drawn round beads of monochrome blue glass. "A cross of white metal of rude construction," wrote Elmer Reynolds, "was found in an erect position, sustained by the earth, between the thumb and forefinger of the skeleton."[50]

The twelfth individual in this multiple grave probably represents a high-status burial dating from about 1608 to 1630, based on the presence of the drawn round blue beads that were most prevalent in the Susquehanna River/Chesapeake Bay region during this period—a time when the English periodically traded with the Patawomekes for Indian souls and maize.[51] Ethnohistorical documentation indicates that the larger objects of sheet copper, such as those described above, were limited to the werowances and others of high status.[52] The *Busycon* maskettes suggest a persistence of native symbolism,

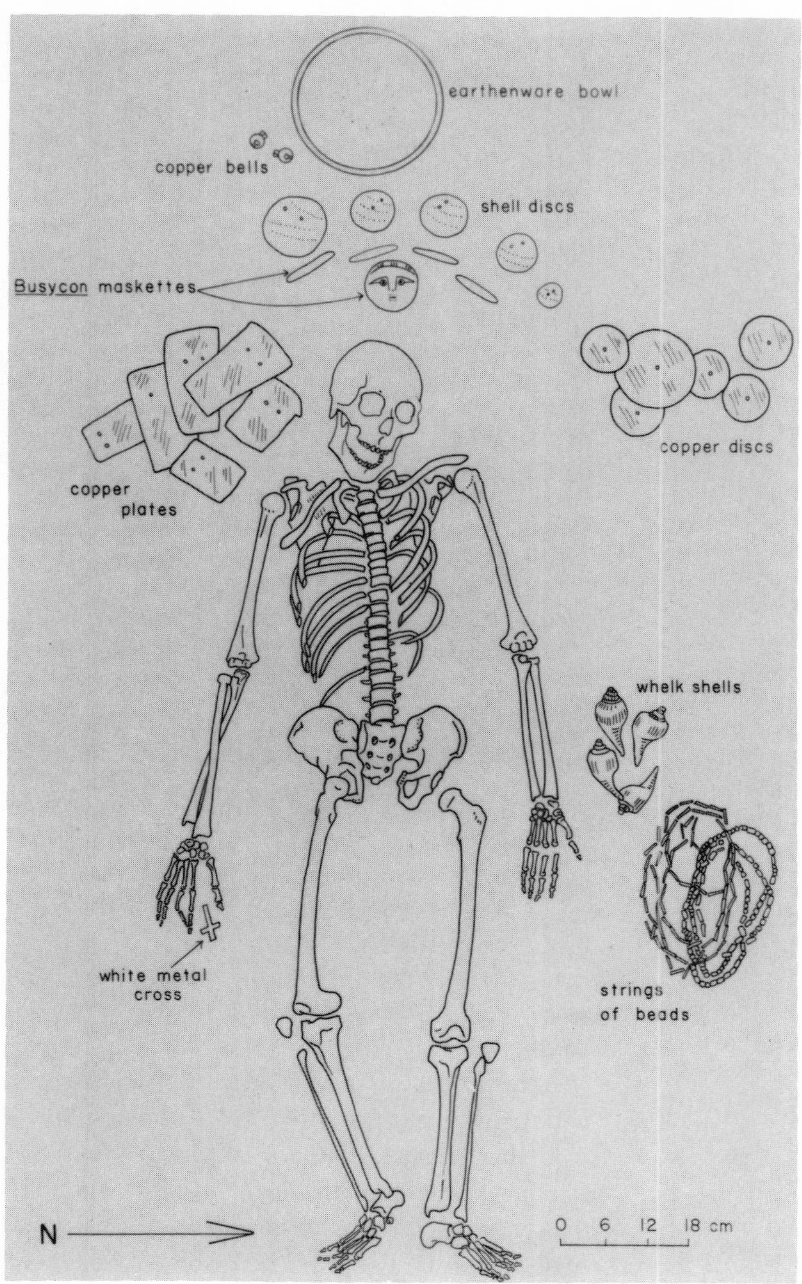

Figure 2 Artist's reconstruction of the twelfth skeleton and associated objects from the high-status multiple burial (circa 1608 to 1630) at Potomac Neck, Virginia.

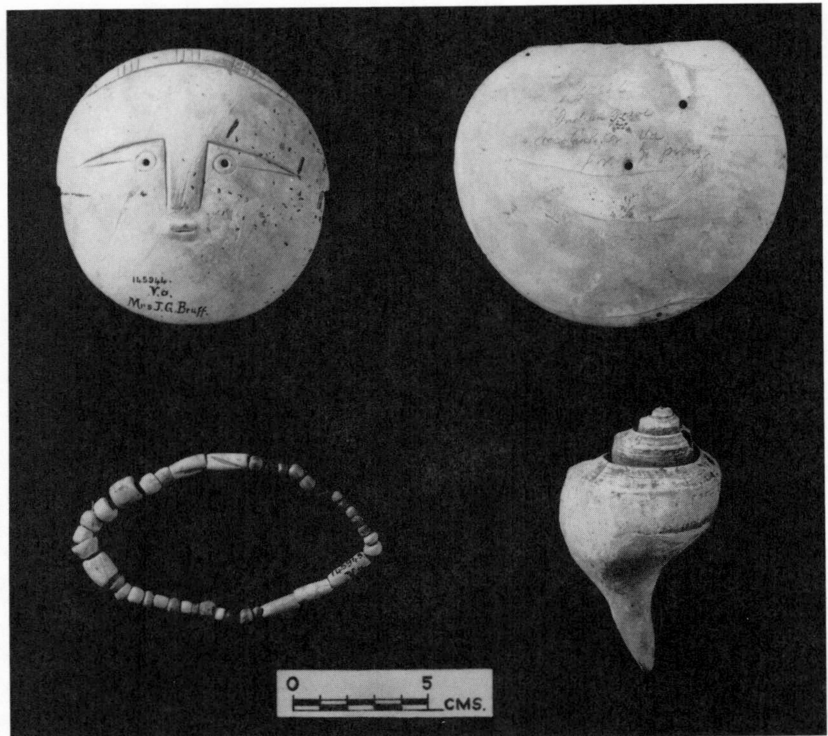

Figure 3 Artifacts from the high-status multiple burial at Potomac Neck, Virginia. *Upper left to lower right: Busycon* maskette with stylized human face; plain *Busycon* pendant; native-made shell beads and European drawn round glass beads; and a small whelk shell (courtesy of the Smithsonian Institution).

and the white cross is perhaps evidence for the inroads of Christian proselytizers.

Another ossuary excavated at the Potomac Creek site was found about seventy feet outside the palisade lines. This ossuary was an oval-shaped pit 37.5 feet long, 15 feet wide, and 5 feet deep, containing the skeletal remains of 181 individuals of all ages and both sexes. Objects associated with burials in the ossuary included thousands of shell columella and disk beads "often associated with children's skeletons," shell gorgets, aboriginal clay smoking pipes, a pair of scissors, and two small flushloop brass bells.[53] Copper was found with twenty-eight skeletons, "usually in the form of tubular beads"—more than sixty tubular copper beads were recovered,

Figure 4 Four quadrangular gorgets or plates made from sheet copper, found with the twelfth skeleton in the high-status multiple burial at Potomac Neck, Virginia (courtesy of the Smithsonian Institution).

along with a few cone-shaped tinklers, a small copper band fitted to a pipestem, and four small square copper plates, at least one of which was associated with an adult male. Glass beads were found with six skeletons, and all were drawn round beads, described by T. Dale Stewart as "small, crudely spherical beads. The majority of these (19) were dark blue in color and ranged up to 4.5 mm in diameter. Other plain colored beads about the same size were violet-blue (3), light blue (2) and green [greenish-blue] (45). Also, there were 8 red beads with black centers and 1 striped bead" (white with alternate red and blue stripes).[54]

This ossuary probably dates from the period of earliest English contact in the Potomac valley, between about 1608 and 1630. Copper objects are mainly small tubular beads, and the relatively few European glass beads are all drawn round beads typical of this period. During this time the authority of the werowance and his immediate supporters was still implicit in the relatively restricted flow of European trade material and status goods to society at large, before the inception of the Chesapeake beaver trade about 1630.

The latest aboriginal burial feature from the vicinity of the Potomac Creek site was a shallow pit, about six to eight feet in diameter, containing at least ten individual burials of children and adults. Some of the objects associated with this group burial include large quantities of disk and columella shell beads; one-half of a shell gorget with a drilled-dot star pattern on the inside; a small whelk shell; a stone pipe; a fragment of a bone comb; two bone awls; a small silver English dram cup dating to about 1640; a brass spur rowel dating to the second half of the seventeenth century; a section of copper chain; six copper buttons; forty flushloop brass bells; and European glass beads. The beads consisted of both drawn tube beads (also known as straw or cane beads) and drawn round beads. The tube beads were small (about 17 mm long and 4 mm in diameter), and most were monochrome red or blue (nine black and one white were also found). The remaining drawn round beads were made of monochrome blue, red, or green glass.[55]

In the lower Susquehanna River red tube beads and some blue, black, and white ones occur most frequently at sites dating 1630 to 1670.[56] Since evidence from the historical documents suggests that sometime between 1655 and 1666 the Patawomekes had abandoned their ancestral lands at Potomac Neck, owing to encroachment by English settlers, the presence of monochrome tube beads, the spur rowel, and the English dram cup help date this group burial to about 1650–66.[57] The change from mass ossuary burials to small group burials of primary interments and the presence of greater quantities of European objects per number of individuals interred is probably a reflection of the changes in aboriginal social and political organization indicative of the weakening power of the werowances.

During late prehistoric and protohistoric times, the difficulties associated with the acquisition of copper helped limit its possession to those with control over other scarce commodities—the werowances and their advisers. Since possession was controlled by the elite, it was associated with the status of the owners and in turn conferred prestige on them, serving to validate and sanctify their rank in society. The four protohistoric ossuaries discovered at Potomac Neck, Virginia, reflect the werowances' control of the distribution of luxury and status goods to the general populace.

Within two years of the establishment of Jamestown, the availability of formerly scarce items such as copper created a temporary crisis within the social and political hierarchy of the James River chiefdoms. Powhatan tried to control the trade and maintain his monopoly. Those werowances farthest from the core of Powhatan's chiefdom and only nominally under his control (e.g., the Patawomekes) could most successfully circumvent this effort. Until other factors (e.g., depopulation, defeats in war, and discrediting of the priesthood) weakened the werowances' authority, they were apparently able to limit the devaluation of copper and its widespread acquisition by the majority of society. At Potomac Neck, the multiple-status burial and an ossuary probably date to the time of earliest English contact in the Potomac valley, about 1608 to 1630. Continued control by the elites of certain luxury and status goods is evidenced by the dozen large copper gorgets and other prestige items associated with the twelfth skeleton in the high-status burial. On the other hand, the ossuary burial of at least 181 individuals contained few status or European items.

The beaver trade in the Potomac-Chesapeake tidewater, about 1630 to 1660, created new possibilities for ownership of copper and other European items. As the fur trade grew and the werowances' authority diminished, the economically restrictive practices formerly enforced by the werowances and their advisers also diminished. This set of circumstances brought about increased opportunities for individual Algonquians to engage in trade and acquire European goods, as exemplified by the greater number of European objects interred per person in the 1650–66 group burial from Potomac Neck.

Moreover, successful Indian trapper/traders could conceivably acquire and keep prestige items, such as copper, thereby flouting the ebbing authority of the werowances. Status achievement was now open to more people who could compete for elite positions by acquiring wealth and employing symbols previously reserved to the werowances and others of high status. Perhaps such a process allowed individuals formerly unable to become advisers or "great men" to rise to such positions, subtly contributing to the decline in power and authority of the werowances.

Acknowledgments

I would like to thank Paul Cissna, Gregory Waselkov, Henry Miller, Jay Custer, R. Michael Stewart, and my wife, Diane Gelburd, for their comments on various drafts of this chapter. Also, I am indebted to T. Dale Stewart for his generosity in allowing me to read and refer to his unpublished manuscripts on the Potomac Creek site. Finally, this chapter has been enhanced by the work of Ellen M. Paige, who produced the artist's reconstruction of the high-status burial shown in figure 2.

Notes

1. J. Frederick Fausz, "The Powhatan Uprising of 1622: A Historical Study of Ethnocentrism and Cultural Conflict" (Ph.D. diss., College of William and Mary, 1977), 224, 229–32.

2. Christian F. Feest, "Nanticoke and Neighboring Tribes," in *Handbook of North American Indians*, vol. 15, *Northeast*, ed. Bruce G. Trigger (Washington, D.C.: Smithsonian Institution, 1978), 240–52; Feest, "Virginia Algonquians," in ibid., 253–70; Feest, "North Carolina Algonquians," in ibid., 271–81.

3. E. Randolph Turner, "An Archaeological and Ethnohistorical Study on the Evolution of Rank Societies in the Virginia Coastal Plain" (Ph.D. diss., Pennsylvania State University, 1976), 92–126; Stephen R. Potter, "An Analysis of Chicacoan Settlement Patterns" (Ph.D. diss., University of North Carolina, 1982), 35–46, 52–83; Lewis R. Binford, "Archaeological and Ethnohistorical Investigation of Cultural Diversity and Progressive Development among Aboriginal Cultures of Coastal Virginia and North Carolina" (Ph.D. diss., University of Michigan, 1964), 74–118; Paul B. Cissna, "The Piscataway Indians of Southern Maryland: An Ethnohistory from Pre-European Contact to the Present" (Ph.D. diss., American University, 1986), 53–99.

4. Marshall D. Sahlins, *Tribesmen* (Englewood Cliffs, N.J.: Prentice-Hall, 1968), 26. This is an anthropological definition of the word "chiefdom," which denotes a society with a greater degree of political centralization than was found among most aboriginal groups in the eastern United States during the colonial period.

5. Potter, "Chicacoan Settlement Patterns," 35–36; Turner, "Rank Societies," 123–24; Binford, "Coastal Virginia," 91–93.

6. Turner, "Rank Societies," 96–100, 105–7; Binford, "Coastal Virginia," 90–91, 93–96. For a different interpretation of the position of werowance see John H. Haynes, Jr., "The Seasons of Tsenacommacoh and the Rise of Wahunsenacawh: Structure and Ecology in Social Evolution" (M.A. thesis, University of Virginia, 1984), 170–72.

7. William R. Gerard, "Some Virginia Indian Words," *American Anthropologist* 7, no. 2 (1905): 229–30; Philip L. Barbour, "The Earliest Reconnaissance of Chesapeake Bay Area: Captain John Smith's Map and Indian Vocabulary, Part II," *Virginia Magazine of History and Biography* 80, no. 1(1972): 46–47; William M. Tooker, "Some More about Virginia Names," *American Anthropologist* 7, no. 3(1905): 525.

8. John Smith, "A Map of Virginia with a Description of the Countrey, the Commodities, People, Government and Religion, 1612," in *Travels and Works of Captain John Smith*, ed. Edward Arber and A. G. Bradley, 2 vols. (Edinburgh: John Grant, 1910), 1:81.

9. William Strachey, *The Historie of Travell into Virginia Britania (1612)*, ed. Louis B. Wright and Virginia Freund, Hakluyt Society, 2d ser., no. 103 (London: University Press for the Society, 1953), 87.

10. Haynes, "Seasons of Tsenacommacoh," 100.

11. Feest, "Virginia Algonquians," 261; Binford, "Coastal Virginia," 94; Turner, "Rank Societies," 108.

12. Strachey, *Historie of Travell*, 107; Smith, "Map of Virginia," 75; Philip L. Barbour,

ed., *The Jamestown Voyages under the First Charter, 1606–1609*, Hakluyt Society, 2d ser., no. 136, vol. 1 (Cambridge: University Press for the Society, 1969), 92; David B. Quinn, ed., *The Roanoke Voyages, 1584–1590*, Hakluyt Society, 2d ser., no. 109, vol. 1 (London: University Press for the Society, 1955), 101–2; George Percy, *Observations Gathered out of "A Discourse of the Plantation of the Southern Colony in Virginia by the English, 1606,"* ed. David B. Quinn (Charlottesville: University of Virginia Press, 1967), 13.

13. Strachey, *Historie of Travell*, 43–44, 57, 104; Smith, "Map of Virginia," 79. Following Smith, the original six groups of Powhatan's inheritance were the Pamunkeys, Mattaponis, Powhatans, Arrohatecks, Appamatucks, and Youghtanunds. Strachey mentions all the groups listed by Smith and adds three more: Orapaks, Kiskiacks, and Werowocomocos.

14. Smith, "Map of Virginia," 51, 82; John Smith, "The Generall Historie of Virginia, New England, and the Summer Isles," in *Travels and Works of Captain John Smith*, ed. Edward Arber and A. G. Bradley, 2 vols. (Edinburgh: John Grant, 1910), 2:514–15; Strachey, *Historie of Travell*, 44, 58–59, 105–6.

15. Strachey, *Historie of Travell*, 58–59; John Smith, "A True Relation of Occurrences and Accidents in Virginia, 1608," in *Travels and Works of Captain John Smith*, ed. Edward Arber and A. G. Bradley, 2 vols. (Edinburgh: John Grant, 1910), 1:11–13; Smith, "Generall Historie of Virginia," 514–15; Potter, "Chicacoan Settlement Patterns," 35–36, 40.

16. Smith, "True Relation," 11.

17. The limits of the Powhatan chiefdom, about 1608, are difficult to establish, owing in part to its rapid and relatively recent expansion, which caused fluctuating alliances and intergroup relations of varying stability. Depending upon the interpretation of the ethnohistorical sources, estimates of the number of petty chiefdoms controlled by Powhatan range from ten to thirty-six. See Turner, "Rank Societies," 133–35; Binford, "Coastal Virginia," 74; Feest, "Virginia Algonquians," 254–56; Potter, "Chicacoan Settlement Patterns," 40–45; Stephen R. Potter, "An Ethnohistorical Examination of Indian Groups in Northumberland County, Virginia: 1608–1719" (M.A. thesis, University of North Carolina, 1976), 15–24.

18. Strachey, *Historie of Travell*, 75.

19. Smith, "True Relation," 10.

20. William Simmonds, "The Proceedings and Accidents of the English Colony in Virginia," in *Travels and Works of Captain John Smith*, ed. Edward Arber and A. G. Bradley (Edinburgh: John Grant, 1910), 2:406.

21. Strachey, *Historie of Travell*, 107.

22. Smith, "True Relation," 32–33.

23. Quinn, "Roanoke Voyages," 98–100.

24. Fausz, "Powhatan Uprising," 248–50, 270–73.

25. Samuel Bemiss, "The Three Charters of the Virginia Company of London, with Seven Related Documents, 1601–1621," in *Jamestown 350th Anniversary Historical Booklet*, no. 4 (Charlottesville: University Press of Virginia, 1957), 54.

26. Susan Myra Kingsbury, ed., *Records of the Virginia Company of London*, vol. 2 (Washington, D.C.: Government Printing Office, 1906), 672.

27. Fausz, "Powhatan Uprising," 253, 283–85, 322–24, 338–42, 512, 582–83; E. Randolph Turner, "Socio-political Organization within the Powhatan Chiefdom and the Effects of European Contact, A.D. 1607–1646," in *Cultures in Contact*, ed. William H. Fitzhugh (Washington, D.C.: Smithsonian Institution Press, 1985), 212–16. Trade with the Algonquian Indians on the James and York rivers was suspended in 1624, 1632, and 1643. See William W. Hening, ed., *The Statutes at Large; Being a Collection of All the Laws of Virginia*, vol. 1 (New York, 1823), 126, 177, 255.

28. Bemiss, "Virginia Company," 63.

29. Lyon G. Tyler, ed., *Narratives of Early Virginia, 1606–1625* (New York: Barnes and Noble, 1907), 213; William Stith, *History of the First Discovery and Settlement of Virginia* (1747; reprint Williamsburg: Virginia State Library, 1912), 240.

30. Philip L. Barbour, "The Earliest Reconnaissance of the Chesapeake Bay Area," *Virginia Magazine of History and Biography* 79, no. 3(1971): 296.

31. Potter, "Indian Groups," 25; Potter, "Chicacoan Settlement Patterns," 49–51, 67; Feest, "Virginia Algonquians," 258.

32. Strachey, *Historie of Travell*, 46.

33. Fausz, "Powhatan Uprising," 282.

34. Ralph Hamor, *A True Discourse of the Present Estate of Virginia* (London, 1615), 4.

35. Ibid., 5.

36. Fausz, "Powhatan Uprising," 283–84.

37. J. Frederick Fausz, "'By Warre upon Our Enemies and Kinde Usage of Our Friends': The Beaver Trade and Interest Group Rivalry in the Development of the Chesapeake, 1607–1652" (paper delivered at the Colloquium in Colonial American History, Institute of Early American History and Culture, Williamsburg, Virginia, October 1982), 6–8.

38. Smith, "Generall Historie of Virginia," 592.

39. Ibid., 596–98.

40. Ibid., 606; Fausz, "Powhatan Uprising," 504–6.

41. J. Frederick Fausz, "Profits, Pelts, and Power: The 'Americanization' of English Culture in the Chesapeake, 1620–1652" (paper delivered at the annual meeting of the American Historical Association, Washington, D.C., December 30, 1982), 2–9. The Susquehannocks were receiving trade goods in the lower Susquehanna valley after 1575, but the nature and extent of the trade system and the exact source of the goods are not known. See Barry C. Kent's *Susquehanna's Indians*, Pennsylvania Historical and Museum Commission Anthropological Series 6 (Harrisburg: Pennsylvania Historical and Museum Commission, 1984), 19–21.

42. J. Frederick Fausz, "Patterns of Anglo-Indian Aggression and Accommodation along the Mid-Atlantic Coast, 1584–1634," in *Cultures in Contact*, ed. William H. Fitzhugh (Washington, D.C.: Smithsonian Institution Press, 1985), 252.

43. Potter, "Indian Groups," 46–47; Stephen R. Potter, "Ethnohistory and the Owings

Site: A Reanalysis," *Quarterly Bulletin* (Archeological Society of Virginia), June-September 1977, 172–73; Gregory A. Waselkov, "Indians of Westmoreland County," in *Westmoreland County, Virginia, 1653–1983*, ed. Walter B. Norris, Jr. (Montross, Va.: Westmoreland County Commission for History and Archaeology, 1983), 25. Among the Piscataways of southern Maryland, clear succession to the paramount chieftainship (or *tayac*) was interrupted between 1641 and 1666 because the tayac had no brother or nephew to succeed him. See James H. Merrell, "Cultural Continuity among the Piscataway Indians of Colonial Maryland," *William and Mary Quarterly*, 3d ser., 36(October 1979): 559, 561–62; and Cissna, "Piscataway Indians," 140–44, 149–53.

44. Turner, "Powhatan Chiefdom," 213.

45. Thomas Jefferson, *Notes on the State of Virginia*, ed. William Peden (New York: W. W. Norton, 1972), 95.

46. Potomac Neck is a narrow strip of land in Stafford County, Virginia. The "neck" is bordered on three sides by water—Accakeek Creek, Potomac Creek, and the Potomac River. In some of the early records pertaining to archaeological discoveries at Potomac Neck, Accotink Creek (in nearby Fairfax County) is incorrectly given as one of the geographical reference points, undoubtedly because of its phonetic similarity to Accakeek Creek. Occasionally later researchers perpetuated the error. The earliest archaeological report on the area is Elmer R. Reynolds, "Ossuary at Accotink, Va.," in *Abstract of Transactions of the Anthropological Society of Washington, D.C.*, prepared by J. W. Powell (Washington, D.C.: Smithsonian Institution, 1881), 92–94. Other accounts include William H. Holmes, William Dinwiddie, and Gerard Fowke, "Archeological Survey of the Tidewater Maryland and Virginia Area," 1891, National Anthropological Archives manuscript 2125, Smithsonian Institution, Washington, D.C.; T. Dale Stewart, "Report on the Excavation of an Indian Site on Potomac Creek in Stafford County, Virginia, Possibly the Site of the Town of Patawomeke Visited by Capt. John Smith in 1608," n.d., manuscript on file, Department of Anthropology, Smithsonian Institution, Washington, D.C.; and Karl Schmitt, "Patawomeke: An Historic Algonkian Site," *Quarterly Bulletin* (Archeological Society of Virginia) 20, no. 1(1965): 1–36.

47. Stewart, "Indian Site on Potomac Creek," 44–54, 69–70, 76–78. These were ossuaries 2, 3, 4, and 5 at the Potomac Creek site. Ossuaries 2, 3, and 4, excavated by amateur archaeologists between 1935 and 1937, contained at least 287, 67, and 41 individuals, respectively. Ossuary 5, excavated by T. Dale Stewart (a physical anthropologist with the Smithsonian Institution) in 1939–40, contained the skeletal remains of 77 individuals.

48. Holmes, Dinwiddie, and Fowke, "Archeological Survey."

49. Reynolds, "Ossuary at Accotink, Va.," 92–94; Ben C. McCary, "A Conch Shell Mask Found in Virginia," *Quarterly Bulletin* (Archeological Society of Virginia) 12, no. 4(1958), n.p.; McCary, "Further Notes on the Melton Mask," *Quarterly Bulletin* (Archeological Society of Virginia) 13, no. 2(1958), n.p.; Joseph D. McGuire, "Pipes and Smoking Customs of the American Aborigines, based on Material in the U.S. National Museum," in *Report of the U.S. National Museum under the Direction of the Smithsonian Institution for the Year 1897* (Washington, D.C.: Government Printing Office, 1899), 428.

50. Reynolds, "Ossuary at Accotink, Va.," 93.

51. Kent, *Susquehanna's Indians*, 212–13; Henry Miller, Dennis Pogue, and Michael Smolek, "Beads from the Seventeenth Century Chesapeake," in *Proceedings of the 1982 Glass Trade Bead Conference*, Rochester Museum and Science Center Research Records 16 (Rochester, N.Y.: Research Division, Rochester Museum and Science Center, 1983), 138–39; Fausz, " 'By Warre upon Our Enemies,' " 6. As noted by Kent, the chronology and popularity of particular beads in the Susquehanna River/Chesapeake Bay region may not apply to areas in the southeastern United States.

52. Quinn, "Roanoke Voyages," 101–2; Quinn, *Observations*, 13; Smith, "Map of Virginia," 75; Strachey, *Historie of Travell*, 107; Barbour, *Jamestown Voyages*, 1:92.

53. Stewart, "Indian Site on Potomac Creek," 37–44.

54. Ibid., 42–44.

55. Ibid., 34–37; T. Dale Stewart, "Archeological Exploration of Patawomeke," manuscript submitted in 1986 for publication in *Smithsonian Contributions to Anthropology*, 75–101.

56. Kent, *Susquehanna's Indians*, 213.

57. Stewart, "Indian Site on Potomac Creek," 23–28; Waselkov, "Indians of Westmoreland County," 20–21, 28.

Cockacoeske, Queen of Pamunkey: Diplomat and Suzeraine

Martha W. McCartney

Cockacoeske, queen of the Pamunkey Indians, donned the mantle of Powhatan's chiefdom in 1656 and governed her people for some thirty years. British archival records that have recently come to light suggest that she worked within the context of the Virginia colonial government in an attempt to recapture the power her people had wielded in the early seventeenth century, when Pamunkey leaders politically dominated the Indians of the Virginia coastal plain. Although Cockacoeske was a leader of considerable influence and political acumen, she has been largely overlooked by modern scholars. Yet colonial documents contain more personal detail about Cockacoeske than is perhaps available on any other Native American woman of her day, and her attempts to reverse the long decline of the Powhatan chiefdom warrant recognition.

Cockacoeske was a relative of Powhatan, the Algonquian paramount chief who ruled the Indians of the Virginia coastal plain when English colonists arrived in 1607. Captain John Smith called Powhatan's mode of government monarchical and described Powhatan himself as an emperor who controlled his territory by placing his brothers, progeny, and other close kin in positions of power within the various districts he ruled.[1] According to Smith, Powhatan, a Pamunkey, governed six tribal territories through the right of inheritance and numerous others that he had acquired by conquest. He was said to have been born at a village called Powhatan, on the upper James River, but his principal residence was at Werowocomoco on the York[2]

The Powhatan chiefdom's leadership descended matrilineally among the sons of the eldest sister, then devolved to the progeny of younger sisters.[3] Following Powhatan's death in 1618, his brother Opitchapam assumed his leadership role. The latter, however, was replaced soon after by Opechancanough, another brother, the great war captain who masterminded the March 1622 Indian attack. This uprising, a concerted attempt by the Indians of the coastal plain to drive the English from their soil, led to the loss of nearly one-third of the colony's population.[4]

Opechancanough's influence (if not necessarily his authority) reportedly extended north to the Potomac River and south to the lower side of the James, eastward to include Virginia's Eastern Shore, and westward to the falls of the colony's major rivers. According to at least one early explorer's account, certain tribes in the region considerably south of the James River also were under his sway.[5] Thus, throughout the first half of the seventeenth century, first with Powhatan and then with Opechancanough, the Pamunkey Indians enjoyed dominance over the native groups in eastern Virginia.

In April 1644 Opechancanough, who was then said to be almost one hundred years old, led a second major Indian uprising that claimed nearly four hundred lives. The assault focused upon the upper reaches of the York River but also extended to the south side of the James. The English, who called Opechancanough "that Bloody Monster," captured him during the retaliatory expeditions that followed, and he was slain while imprisoned at Jamestown.[6]

After the death of Opechancanough, another Pamunkey warrior named Necotowance assumed leadership. Documentary evidence suggests, however, that the effects of the colonists' reprisals against the Indians and the loss of their principal leader had exacted a severe toll, precipitating the disintegration of the once-mighty Powhatan chiefdom. One writer, describing the dissolution or scattering of the tribes that had previously been under common leadership, claimed that Virginia officials had made deliberate efforts to liberate the other natives from the control of the "house of Pamunkey," employing the familiar "divide and conquer" approach in dealing with remnants of the once-powerful Powhatan chiefdom.[7]

In October 1646 Necotowance, "King of the Indians," concluded a treaty with the Virginia government whereby the natives ceded much of their territory to the English and acknowledged that their right to the possession of the remaining land was derived from the English monarch. From that moment they formally became tributaries to the English government. The implementation, or imposition, of a tributary system, which can be likened to the way Powhatan and Opechancanough ruled the tribes under their control, was in fact a tangible symbol of the Indian's political subservience to the English.[8]

In 1648 Necotowance, called "emperor," presented his people's first annual tribute to Virginia's governor. Only "five more petty kings attended him," a reflection of the extent to which the ancient Powhatan chiefdom had disintegrated. That the delicate balance of power between the Indians and the colonists had shifted in favor of the latter is evidenced in Necotowance's statement to his countrymen that "the English will kill you if you goe into their bounds." He noted that skeptical Indians called him a liar for making such a blunt observation, but in fact at least three persons already had been killed for entering the ceded territory.[9]

By 1649 Necotowance had been replaced by Totopotomoy, another Pamunkey male. The written record indicates that, unlike his predecessors, Totopotomoy represented only his own tribe when he interacted with English officials. A legislative act dated March 1649 suggests that by then unified leadership of coastal Virginia's Indians had completely deteriorated, for equal amounts of land were allocated to three Indian leaders, whose people formerly had been subordinate to Opechancanough as paramount chief. Thus, the Pamunkeys probably wielded little if any power over other native groups. Totopotomoy, unlike Necotowance, was called king of the Pamunkeys, not king of the Indians.[10] A staunch ally of the English, Totopotomoy was killed in 1656 while fighting at their side against an outlying Indian group, the Rickohockans, in a conflict later known as the Battle of Bloody Run.

After the death of Totopotomoy his widow, Cockacoeske, became the leader or queen of the Pamunkeys, a role she occupied until her death in the 1680s. She was described by one contemporary as a descendant of Opechancanough, Powhatan's brother.[11] If Totopotomoy was also a descendant, she may have been his cousin as well as his wife. During the nearly thirty years Cockacoeske ruled, her people remained tributaries of the colonial government and, to a considerable degree, attempted to act within the framework of its legal system.

Meanwhile the population of Virginia's tributary Indians declined owing to disease and loss of subsistence habitat. Pressure from stronger, outlying hostile tribes at the heads of the colony's rivers confined them within the bounds of the coastal plain, while the relentless inland expansion of the English frontier compressed them into a steadily shrinking space. Attempts by Virginia Indian leaders to cope with this crisis are mentioned only obliquely in the historical record, which, one should recall, is chronicled from the European perspective. Even so, certain seventeenth-century Virginia documents in British repositories yield new insights on the political complexities of Anglo-American/Native American relationships during this era, particularly during the fourth quarter of the seventeenth century. Contemporary correspondence between Virginia and England during this period also reveals that there was some collusion between colonial officials and certain Indian leaders, principal among whom was the queen of Pamunkey.

An able and politically astute leader, Cockacoeske attempted to assert her dominance while acting within the limits of the colony's legal system, perhaps perceiving that her people's principal hope of survival lay in reestablishing the political unity of the Powhatan chiefdom. As will be seen, she was able to effectively turn the English political system to her own people's advantage, at least for a time. Evidence of Cockacoeske's considerable influence and her quasi-political alliances can be found in contemporary correspondence; in the provisions of the 1677 Treaty of Middle Plantation, a monumental document that governed relations between the colonists and Virginia Indians for nearly a hundred years; and in the fact that she was singled out for special recognition by King Charles II.

During 1676, sporadic Indian raids alarmed the colony's frontier, sparking a popular uprising that became known as Bacon's Rebellion. Outlying settlers rallied behind young Nathaniel Bacon and marched upon the nearest Indians rather than confronting the stronger inland tribes, such as the Susquehannocks and Senecas, who were blamed by some high officials for the incursions.[12] Early on Cockacoeske, who by then had led the Pamunkeys for twenty years, was summoned to the statehouse at Jamestown, where she appeared before a committee of the Governor's Council. One contemporary wrote that Cockacoeske, apparently a commanding personage, "entered the chamber with a comportment gracefull to admiration, bringing on her right hand an Englishmen interpreter, and on her left, her son, a stripling twenty years of age," said to be the offspring of an English colonel. Cockacoeske's head was crowned with a braid of black-and-white wampum peake, three inches broad, and she was clothed in a deerskin mantle that reached from shoulders to feet, a garment whose edges had been trimmed to resemble deep, twisted fringe. Flanked by her companions, Cockacoeske, "with grave courtlike gestures and a majestick air in her face," walked to the head of the council table and sat down. She elected to communicate only through her interpreter, though the council believed she understood the English language very well.[13]

Queried by the council committee as to the number of men she would provide to serve as guides in the wilderness and to assist the English in a campaign against hostile Indians, Cockacoeske kept silent. When pressed further, "after a little musing, with an earnest passionate countenance as if tears were ready to gush out and with a fervent sort of expression [she] made a harangue about a quarter of an hour, often interlacing with a high shrill voice and vehement passion these words, 'Tatapatamoi Chepiack,' i.e. Tatapatomoy dead," a reminder to the council that it was in identical circumstances that her husband and a hundred of his bowmen had lost their lives, for which sacrifice there had been no compensation. At length Cockacoeske agreed to provide twelve warriors from her town, though she was said to have 150 men under her command.[14]

As the rift gradually widened between Bacon's followers and the supporters of Governor William Berkeley, finally flaring into overt military conflict, officials in England who viewed the uprising with grave concern persuaded King Charles II to dispatch special commissioners to Virginia to investigate the causes and extent of the unrest. These commissioners, Sir John Berry, Colonel Francis Moryson, and Herbert Jeffreys, arrived in Virginia early in 1677. Their official correspondence sheds much light on how Virginia's tributary Indians were affected by Bacon's Rebellion and also shows how the natives, in turn, responded to the political climate it created.[15]

According to one record, an Indian interpreter named Wilford, who was executed by Governor Berkeley for his participation in the rebellion, had allegedly "frightened the Queen of Pamunkey from the land she had been granted by the Assembly a month after the peace was concluded with her."[16] Despite the fact that a peace agreement evidently had been reached with the Pamunkeys in March 1676, in August Nathaniel Bacon led a march against the Pamunkeys, who lived on the fringe of the English settlement. The attack may have been inspired by recently enacted legislation entitling settlers to claim property that had been abandoned by the Indians.[17] Riding down upon the Indians' encampment at the edge of a swamp, Bacon's men were impeded by the mire and succeeded only in capturing a small child and killing an elderly woman. Cockacoeske, having ordered her people to refrain from firing upon the English, abandoned the encampment and all her personal belongings. In their pursuit, Bacon's followers took prisoner an old Indian woman, Cockacoeske's nurse or attendant, ordering her to guide them to the natives who had fled. Later, when they discovered she had deliberately misled them, she was put to death.[18]

A short time later Bacon came upon the Pamunkeys at another encampment. During the attack that ensued Cockacoeske escaped, but forty-five of her people were captured. Bacon's men reportedly took away three horseloads of plunder, including Indian mats, baskets, parcels of wampum peake, and pieces of linen, broadcloth, and other English goods the queen was said to value highly. According to a report filed by the king's commissioners, Cockacoeske, though fleeing from Bacon's army, decided to come back "with designe to throw herself upon the mercy of the English [but] she happened to meet with a dead Indian woman lying in the way (being one of her own nation) which struck such a terror in the Queene that fearing their cruelty by that ghastly example she went on her first intended way into the wild woods where she was lost and missing from her own People fourteen days," nearly starving.[19]

The king's commissioners, arriving in Virginia early in 1677, addressed the Grand Assembly of Virginia, admonishing its members to act quickly in establishing peace with the colony's natives. Speaking pragmatically, the commissioners reminded the assembly that the neighboring Indians provided the best guards on the frontier against the more hostile tribes of the continent.[20] They also pointed out that it was Governor William Berkeley who had first conquered the Indians and made peace with them, the breach of which was depriving the colony of the benefit of their trade and labors.[21] Berkeley, in turn, reported to the commissioners that the queen of the Pamunkey Indians, having been driven from her village by Nathaniel Bacon's followers, had returned home and that a good foundation for peace had been laid.[22]

On February 20, 1677, Cockacoeske petitioned Virginia's Grand Assembly for the restoration of her belongings and the land she had abandoned "through the feare of the Rebell Bacon and his accomplices."[23] The assembly, however, granted her scant satisfaction, agreeing only to restore those items that she could prove were hers and insisting that she return any horses or goods in her possession that belonged to the English. In contrast, the king's commissioners were much more sympathetic to her plea, for they reported that she had been "driven out into the wildwoods and there almost famished, plundered of all she had, her people taken prisoners and sold, the Queen robbed of her rich watchcoat [matchcoat] for which she had great value." They added the queen of Pamunkey's name to their list of those who had suffered during Bacon's Rebellion, calling her "a faithfull friend to and lover of the English," and they recommended that she be given a gift in recompense for her sufferings and the loss of her belongings.[24]

On March 27, 1677, the commissioners wrote to Secretary of State Henry Coventry that the kings and queens of the Nottoways, Nansemonds, Appomattocks, and Pamunkeys had met with them, signifying their willingness to conclude a treaty.[25] By the end of April Herbert Jeffreys, who was appointed to act as lieutenant governor during Governor Berkeley's recall to England, publicly expressed his firm belief that harmonious relations with the nearby Indians were essential to the colony's well-being.[26] Soon after Berkeley's departure from Virginia on May 5, Jeffreys set about formally concluding a peace treaty with several groups of neighboring Indians.[27] The king's commissioners' report states that they "sent to the Queene of Pamunkey who not only came in herself but brought in severall scattered nations of Indians, *whome we afterwards reduc'd (as she desired) under her subjection, as anciently they had beene*."[28]

As a consequence of the commissioners' efforts, on May 29, 1677, King Charles II's birthday and the anniversary of his restoration to the throne, a major peace agreement was concluded between colonial officials and certain tidewater Indian groups. This landmark document, commonly known as the Treaty of Middle Plantation, ushered in peaceful relations between the colonists and the Indians of Virginia's coastal plain, governing their official interactions for nearly a century. As will be seen, Cockacoeske, queen of Pamunkey, exerted considerable influence over the treaty's architects, for some of the document's terms were greatly to her advantage.

Herbert Jeffreys, as a special commissioner, wrote to the king on June 11, 1677, describing the treaty ceremony and the protocol observed. The new guardhouse at Middle Plantation[29] had been especially fitted out for the occasion. Jeffreys wrote that

> silence being Proclaimed, the Articles were openly read before them and the severall Enterpreters sworn to expound each distinct paragraph to them which they openly read to their general satisfaction. Then the Queen of Pamunkey was invited within the Barr of the Court to sign this Treaty on behalf of herself and Severall Nations now reunited under her Subjection and Government as anciently, who (with the rest) subscribed and delivered up the same with the most humble Reverence (as to his Majestie) on her bended knees, all of them publically acknowledging to hold their Crowns and Lands of the Great King of England.[30]

This latter sentence is especially significant, for it refers to article 12 of the treaty, which committed several smaller, unspecified Indian nations to Cockacoeske's rule, tangible evidence of her success in manipulating the treaty agreement to her own people's advantage.

Jeffreys continued,

> And myself having signed that part (in behalf of his Majestie) to them they all knelt donne and with low obeysance received it, as from his Majestie's Royall hands, at the same tyme (on their onne free accord) kissing the most acceptable paper of peace one after another. Thus being concluded with the day the Field Pieces were discharged several rounds, with volleys of small shot and Fireworks and Loud Acclamations of Joy all over the Camp and so having Quietly Entertained Our Indian ffriends that night, they departed the next day to their several homes, well satisfied with this treaty.[31]

Cockacoeske's son, called "Captain John West,"[32] endorsed the treaty along with the leaders of three other Indian tribes: the queen of the Weyanokes, the king of the Nottoways, and the king of the Nansemonds. Peracuta, the king of the Appomattocks, though present at the ceremony, was not allowed to sign, for some of his people stood accused of murder. Nicholas Spencer, who later became secretary of the colony, reported that a few Nanzattico Indians also had attended the treaty ceremony but departed without signing.[33] Whether they were invited to participate is unknown.

A month after Herbert Jeffreys wrote to England reporting that the treaty had been executed, Sir John Berry and Colonel Francis Moryson, as commissioners, sent word to the Privy Council that "even the remote Indians when they heard of [the treaty's] justice of their own accord came forward and asked to be included."[34] Thus, if the commissioners' report is to be believed, the natives thought the treaty advantageous.

In early August Berry and Moryson set sail for England, leaving Jeffreys behind as lieutenant governor. The commissioners brought to England not only the report of their investigation into Bacon's Rebellion but also the original treaty document, which they delivered to the Lords of Trade and Plantations at Whitehall. Lord Baltimore, who had just presented to that body a treaty the Maryland government had concluded with the northern Indians, took exception to the fact that Virginia's peace agreement did not extend its protection to his own colony, whereas Maryland's treaty applied to Virginia as well.

In October 1677 the Lords of Trade and Plantations recommended to the king that Lieutenant Governor Jeffreys be ordered to expand the coverage of Virginia's treaty to include Maryland and his majesty's other colonies.[35] The King's Privy Council, meanwhile, issued a directive for the document then in hand to be printed and distributed.[36] On January 18, 1678, Secretary Henry Coventry was instructed to order Lieutenant Governor Jeffreys to expand the Treaty of Middle Plantation, a directive that was carried out sometime between April and June 1680.[37]

Meanwhile, in response to the recommendation Berry and Moryson had made to the king when the first treaty was newly in hand, presents were commissioned for the Indian leaders who had signed the original document. As tangible signs of goodwill and symbols of their rank, crowns and royal robes were to be made for the queens of the Pamunkeys and the Weyanokes and the kings of the Nottoways and the Nansemonds, "the Indians accompting guifts a kind of sacred pledge of friendship." But Cockacoeske, the queen of Pamunkey, "who was robbed of her rich matchcoat by the rebells," was singled out for special recognition.[38]

It was recommended that Cockacoeske receive "a crown and robe, together with a stript [striped] Indian gown of gay colours and a Bracelet of falce stones." For her son, "a scarlett coate belayered with gold and silver lace, with breeches, shoes and stockings, hatt, sword and belt suitable, and a pair of good pistoles" were deemed befitting. Bill books of the Lord Chamberlain's Department detail the nature of the gifts that were prepared for the Indian leaders. According to the bills, the tailors and clothmakers used scarlet cloth, lined with purple manto, for Cockacoeske's regal robe, and they also prepared for her a silver and gold brocade Indian gown, lined with cherry-colored sarcenet, a soft silk. They made a scarlet suit for her son, young John West, just as Berry and Moryson had recommended, plus stockings of scarlet worsted, the latter embroidered with black silk thread. A white beaver hat trimmed with a gold and silver band, a finely embroidered belt, and a sword and pistols decorated with gold and silver also were made for him. For the queen of Pamunkey's interpreter, Cornelius Dabney, a suit of gray cloth was tailored, to be worn with scarlet stockings, and her chief counselor, Seosteyn, received a purple robe lined with scarlet shalloon, a twill-woven woolen. Similar purple robes were prepared for the queen of the Weyanokes and the kings of the Nottoways and the Nansemonds, demonstrating that their rank was perceived as equal to that of Cockacoeske's chief counselor.[39]

A cap of crimson velvet trimmed with ermine fur was fashioned for each of the four Indian rulers. Royal Jewel House invoices disclose that English craftsmen made "small crowns or coronets of thinne silver plate, gilt and adorned with false stones of various colours, with the inscription 'A Carolo Secondo Magna Brittaniae Rege'" for the Indian leaders. For the queen of Pamunkey, the Royal Jewel House also created a bracelet of false stones, just as Berry and Moryson had asked, as well as an undescribed necklace, probably the silver "frontlet" that still survives (fig. 1). Twenty small silver badges bearing the king's name and the title of each tributary Indian leader were prepared.[40]

In June 1680 Governor Thomas Culpeper arrived in Virginia, to succeed Herbert Jeffreys, who had died in December 1678. Among Culpeper's instructions were orders to deliver the king's gifts to the Indian rulers who had signed the Treaty of Middle Plantation. The Executive Council, however, tried to persuade him not to do so, particularly objecting to the crowns, for they felt that jealousy and discord would result if some tributary Indian leaders were to receive gifts *and others did not*. This indicates that by the time the gifts had been brought to the colony, the treaty had been expanded, for when the original agreement was amended, to include Maryland within its protection, it was signed by twelve Indian leaders rather than five, who represented seven Indian groups, rather than four. Besides, the

Figure 1 Silver pendant of the queen of Pamunkey, inscribed with the royal arms of King Charles II (courtesy of the Virginia Division of Historic Landmarks, Department of Conservation and Historic Preservation).

council asserted, "such Marks of Dignity as Coronets . . . must not be prostituted to such meane [inconsequential] persons."[41]

Despite the optimism sparked by the consummation of the Treaty of Middle Plantation, colonial officials soon discovered that it was not the panacea for enduring peace and friendship that its proponents had purported it to be. Two of the treaty's articles proved to be particularly troublesome to Indians and colonists alike, at least one of which, article 12, bore the mark of Cockacoeske's influence. Article 12 specified that "each Indian King and Queen have equall power to govern their owne people and none to have greater power than other except the Queen of Pamunkey to whom several scattered Indian Nations doe now againe owne their antient subjection, and are agreed to come in and plant themselves under her power . . . and are to keep and observe the same towards the said Queen in all things as her Subjects, as well as toward the English." Article 18, on the other hand, stated that "upon any discord or breach of peace happening to arise between any of the Indians in amity with the English . . . they shall repaire to his Majesties Governor by whose Justice and wisdome it is concluded such difference shall be made up and decided."[42] Thus several of the tributary Indian groups were to be placed under the rule of the Pamunkeys, and all the tributaries were to resolve their differences through arbitration before the governor.

It should be recalled that before the signing of the treaty, Commissioners Berry and Moryson wrote a letter stating that certain Indian tribes had been placed under the queen of Pamunkey's aegis, "reduced (as she desired) under her Subjection, as anceintly they had beene," clearly revealing that article 12 was Cockacoeske's idea. She may also have had a hand in the formulation of article 18, believing that colonial officials, with whom she was acquainted, might weigh justice in her favor. Moreover, the Virginia government's obligation to protect the tributary Indians, as recipients of English justice, surely would have been perceived as an advantage, given the natives' diminished strength.[43]

There are several reasons why Cockacoeske would have been able to exert some influence on colonial officials and work within their political system. During the approximately thirty years she ruled as queen of Pamunkey, she maintained close ties with the English government, representing her people in an official capacity. Cockacoeske's period of leadership, which began more than twenty years before Bacon's Rebellion, would have spanned Francis Moryson's term as deputy governor, March to December 1661, at which time Governor William Berkeley was in England. Thus she would have had an opportunity to establish rapport with Moryson himself, a distinct advantage when he returned to Virginia as a special commissioner of the king. Moreover, Cockacoeske's romantic liaison with the English colonel, John West, an important Virginia official and supporter of Governor Berkeley, may have furthered her insight into the machinations of colonial politics, and the presence of their son as a future go-between may have given her an added measure of influence. The account of Cockacoeske's appearance before the governor and council reveals that she was a person of imposing dignity and that she understood the English language. Cockacoeske's appreciation of European goods is evidenced by her possession of "pieces of Lynnen, Broad cloth, and divers sorts of English goods wch the Queene had much value for" when Nathaniel Bacon's men raided her encampment. But there are equally strong indications that Cockacoeske remained true to her native cultural traditions.

Correspondence between officials in Virginia and England discloses that after the 1677 treaty was signed, Cockacoeske attempted to enforce the terms of article 12 by exacting tribute and servility from the tribes placed under her subjection, in sum, trying to reestablish the chiefly dominance enjoyed by the Pamunkey leaders before Opechancanough's death.[44] Though the identity of the Indian groups placed under Cockacoeske's charge is not set forth in either version of the 1677 treaty, the omission of the names of certain prominent tidewater Virginia Indian groups from the list of treaty signatories provides a clue to their identity, especially when viewed in light of the relative propinquity of these groups to the Pamunkey homeland.

Contemporary correspondence identifies the Chickahominys and Rappahannocks as two of the groups subjugated to the Pamunkey leadership, and mention is made of a third Indian nation, perhaps the Mattaponys or Totachus, both of whom, at the time of the 1669 census, were residing in New Kent County, where the Pamunkeys also lived. Another tribe, the Chiskiacks, who at the time of the census were few in number and said to be steadily dwindling, also may have been made subservient to Cockacoeske, though in 1677 they were living in Gloucester County, their home at least since 1629.[45] Some or all of these groups likely constituted the "several scattered nations" subjected to the queen of Pamunkey's leadership.[46]

Even before the second version of the 1677 treaty had been signed, Virginia officials realized that some of the Indians placed under Cockacoeske's rule, notably the Chickahominys and Rappahannocks, strongly resented the attempt to force their subservience and stubbornly refused to cooperate with her, claiming that they had not intended such subjection by subscribing to the peace treaty. In a list of grievances presented by the queen of Pamunkey and her son, Captain John West, to the governor and his council on June 5, 1678, Cockacoeske alleged that the Chickahominys were unwilling to pay tribute, obey her orders, or make her village their home. She also accused them of harboring her son's wife, who had run away. Great mutual enmity is apparent in the nine grievances, for the Chickahominys were accused of poisoning one of Cockacoeske's great men and plotting revenge upon eight more, whereas she herself was alleged by the Chickahominys to have "cutt off soe many Chickahominy heads." A prior tradition of close interaction between the two Indian groups is suggested by the fact that Captain West's absconded wife had been "bred and born at Chickahominy though her Parents were Pamunkeys."[47]

At the end of June Cockacoeske described the state of affairs to Colonel Moryson in a letter, which she dictated to her interpreter. In elegant and courtly language, Cockacoeske professed her loyalty to King Charles II but expressed her dissatisfaction with the Rappahannocks and Chickahominys, "who are very disobedient to my commands." In a politically savvy move, however, she qualified her complaint by assuring Moryson that it was "not that they grudge to be under my subjection."[48]

The affection and esteem in which Cockacoeske held Colonel Moryson is evidenced by her addressing him twice as "Netop," an Algonquian word William Strachey's dictionary translates as "my good friend." At the close of the letter, within the words "Cockacoeske Queen of Pamunkey," she affixed her mark, signifying the communication's authenticity, the same W-like symbol with which she had previously endorsed both versions of the 1677 treaty (see fig. 2).

The Pamunkeys' interpreter, Cornelius Dabney, also dispatched a personal letter to Colonel Moryson on the same day, corroborating

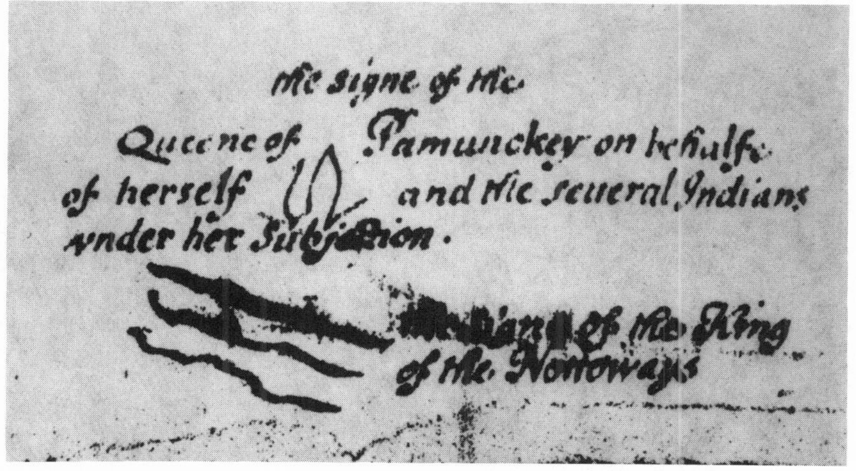

the signe of the Queene of Pamunckey on behalfe of herself and the severall Indians vnder her Subjection.

the marke of the King of the Nottoways

Figure 2 The queen of Pamunkey's mark, endorsing the Treaty of Middle Plantation, May 29, 1677 (courtesy of the Virginia Division of Historic Landmarks, Department of Conservation and Historic Preservation).

Cockacoeske's allegations against the Chickahominys. He alluded to his own misunderstandings with the current governor and other officials, blaming his problems on the malice of the Chickahominy Indians' interpreter, Richard Yarborough, who, Dabney claimed, was attempting to undermine peaceful relations with the tributary Indians by his manipulation of various government officials.[49]

Interestingly, the prose Cornelius Dabney used when writing on Cockacoeske's behalf contrasts markedly with the tone of the letter he sent personally. When acting as the queen of Pamunkey's interpreter, he addressed Moryson as a friend and an equal, whereas when writing on his own behalf he expressed himself with humility and in far simpler language, displaying great deference to Moryson's superior social position. Dabney's letter acknowledges the plight of the tributary Indians who were caught between the colonists' spreading settlement and hostile outlying tribes, for in response to Moryson's request for an elk, he replied that the "Senecas having put our Indians into a feare, dare not go so high to hunt."[50]

The colony's secretary, Thomas Ludwell, writing home to England before the second version of the treaty had been signed, claimed that the peace agreement, by reuniting several Indian groups under the queen of Pamunkey's leadership, had created turmoil. He explained that because "several Indian nations again are united under that family . . . though we are confident the Queen of Pamunkey not mistreats or harms, yet most of the young men of the several townes being dissatisfied, is contemptible at their new subjection to that Queen wch they say was consented to by . . . old men against their [the younger men's] wills." He noted that these young warriors "doe lie off in hiding in the woods and will not come in. . . . To grant them their former liberty, the Queen will take it as a breach of the peace and we cannot force them to her obedience but by hazarding another warr wch would bring on great Disorders if not another Rebellion amongst us."[51]

Ludwell recalled that "upon Governor William Berkeley's conquest of Apechancanough it was by him and the government thought the safest way by setting all the lesser nations at Liberty from that obedience they paid to the house of Pamunkey to keep them divided and indeed the effect may be more advantageous to us for they like to warr with each other and destroy themselves more in a year than we can do it." But, Ludwell said, "since this last war there are severall nations again united under that family which we since find to be troublesome and hazardous." In another letter he declared:

> I could heartily wish those two Articles concerning that subjection and ye making us judges of their differences had been left out, for I never thought it in the interest of this Colony to hinder them from cutting each others throats so we had no hand in it and its plain that upon the conquest of Appechancaenoe and the setting all the tributary nations to that house at Liberty they have weakened themselves more by their Intestine Broyls than ever we could doe by all the Warrs wee have had with them.[52]

The resentment generated by placing under the queen of Pamunkey's dominance certain Indian nations that had been independent since the death of Opechancanough about 1646 was very much apparent during the summer of 1678. Thomas Ludwell wrote on June 8 that "we had at last Court a great contest between the Queen of Pamunkey and a nation which lives neer her whom she takes amongst others to be subjected to her by the last articles of peace . . . upon whom she had imposed a great tax to be paid every Spring and Fall besides great servility in hunting and weeding of corn which they refused to perform." He added that the group claimed "they had never paid it [tribute] since the death of Appechancano, which is about 33 years since and that they intended no such subjection by those articles."[53]

Similarly, Ludwell informed Secretary Coventry on June 28, 1678, that "the Queen [of Pamunkey] lays a great tax to be paid every spring and fall upon a nation who lives near her and are more powerful than she and they not only deny to pay that tax but any such Subjection to her." He added that the queen "was fair to confess they had not paid such tax above these 30 years."[54] In August 1678 Ludwell reiterated that point, stating that the queen of Pamunkey was "imposing a tribute upon them such as they never paid these 33 years since the conquest of Appochankeno [Opechancanough]."[55] Thus, article 12 of the treaty, which bound the Indians subjected to the queen of Pamunkey to pay her tribute comparable to what she herself paid to the colonial government, was an overt attempt by Cockacoeske to reestablish Powhatan's old tributary system.

Though relatively little is known about the immediate fate of the Indian groups that article 12 of the treaty attempted to reunite under the queen of Pamunkey, government records suggest that the Chickahominys and the Rappahannocks retained their independence, though they continued to uphold their groups' commitment to the treaty itself. The Chickahominys continued to reside in a village on the Mattaponi River until at least the first decade of the eighteenth century, an indication that they never did obey the commands of Cockacoeske to seat at the Pamunkey town.[56]

The allocation of separate tracts of land to the Pamunkeys and Chickahominys during this period further implies that they continued to remain separate entities and that the latter never did come under Cockacoeske's subjection. Moreover, on subsequent occasions members of the Chickahominy tribe sought justice on their own behalf through the colony's legal system, a further indication that their group retained its autonomy. The Rappahannocks also appear to have retained their independence, for throughout the last quarter of the seventeenth century they are mentioned separately by name and are documented as residing in the York-Rappahannock peninsula, having removed themselves from the Pamunkeys' territory. Cockacoeske, meanwhile, continued to lead her own people, residing in Pamunkey Neck, the land mass lying between the Pamunkey and Mattaponi rivers that had been the traditional home of her people.

By July 1, 1686, the Pamunkeys' interpreter, George Smith, informed the governor that the Pamunkey queen "was lately dead and that ye Pamunkey Indians did desire that ye late Queen's niece . . . upon [whom] ye right of Government of that Indian nation doe devolve, might succeed."[57] Virginia's governor might have expected to see the succession pass to the queen's own half-English son, but traditional ideas of inheritance still prevailed among the Pamunkeys. In 1702 the name of "Ms. Betty Queen ye Queen" of the Pamunkey Indians was mentioned in a land transaction and by 1708, that of Queen Ann began appearing in official documents. During the first quarter of the eighteenth century, Queen Ann of the Pamunkeys presented a number of petitions to the governor's council and the assembly, continuing Cockacoeske's policy of working within the framework of the colony's laws.[58] But the Pamunkeys never again attempted to reestablish their dominance over the Indians of Virginia's coastal plain.

Notes

1. John Smith, *Travels and Works of Captain John Smith, President of Virginia and Admiral of New England, 1580–1631*, ed. Edward Arber, 2 vols. (Edinburgh: John Grant, 1910), 1:79; E. Randolph Turner, "An Archaeological and Ethnohistorical Study on the Evolution of Rank Societies in the Virginia Coastal Plain" (Ph.D. diss., Pennsylvania State University, 1976), 98–99.

2. Smith, *Travels*, 1:51, 79; William Strachey, *The Historie of Travell into Virginia Britania (1612)*, ed. Louis B. Wright and Virginia Freund, Hakluyt Society, 2d ser., no. 103 (London: University Press for the Society, 1953), 56; John Smith, *Virginia Discovered and Described by Captayne John Smith, 1606* (London, 1612).

3. Smith, *Travels*, 81.

4. Smith, *Travels*, 539.

5. Susan M. Kingsbury, *Records of the Virginia Company of London*, 4 vols. (Washington, D.C.: Government Printing Office, 1906–35), 3:708–10. The account of Abraham Wood, written in 1650, quotes a Nottoway Indian as referring to Opechancanough as his people's old emperor. He is mentioned similarly in connection with the Meherrins. Alexander S. Salley, *Narratives of Early Carolina, 1650–1708* (New York: Charles Scribner's Sons, 1911), 10–15.

6. Robert Beverley, *The History and Present State of Virginia* (1705), ed., Louis B. Wright (Chapel Hill: University of North Carolina Press, 1947), 49–50.

7. Thomas Ludwell, letter to the "Right Honorable," June 30, 1678, in Henry Coventry Papers, vol. 73, Bath 65, fol. 264 (microfilm, Colonial Williamsburg Foundation, Williamsburg, Virginia). The documentary record also reveals that in August 1645 many of the Pamunkey warriors who had been taken prisoner when Governor William Berkeley stormed Opechancanough's stronghold, taking him captive, were trans-

ported by ship from the mainland to Western (now Tangier) Island in Chesapeake Bay, where they were abandoned. H. R. McIlwaine, comp., *Minutes of Council and General Court, 1622–1632, 1670–1676* (Richmond, Va.: Library Board, 1924), 564.

8. William W. Hening, *The Statutes at Large: Being a Collection of All the Laws of Virginia from the First Session of the Legislature in the Year 1619*, 13 vols. (Richmond, Va.: Samuel Pleasants, 1809–23), 1:323–29.

9. Peter Force, *Tracts and Other Papers Relating Principally to the Origin, Settlement, and Progress of the Colonies in North America*, 4 vols. (Gloucester: Peter Smith, 1963), vol. 2, book 8, 25, 35.

10. Warren Billings, "Some Acts Not in Hening's, April 1652, November 1652, November 1652, and July 1653," *Virginia Magazine of History and Biography* 83 (1975): 65–72. Consistent with seventeenth century Anglo-American usage, the terms "king" and "queen" have been applied throughout this chapter to Indian leaders whose titles were likened by Virginia colonists to those of the British monarchy.

11. Force, *Tracts*, vol. 1, book 8, 14–15. T. M., who wrote this account, was an eyewitness; he has been identified by researchers as Thomas Mathew, a Northumberland County planter and burgess to the June 1676 assembly.

12. Wilcomb E. Washburn, *The Governor and the Rebel: A History of Bacon's Rebellion in Virginia* (New York: W. W. Norton, 1972), 20–30; Stephen Saunders Webb, *1676: The End of American Independence* (New York: Alfred A. Knopf, 1984), 21–25. Grievances, presented by county officials to the king's commissioners, who forwarded them to England, reveal that Indian attacks had occurred along the colony's frontier, that is, on the upper reaches of the Rappahannock and Potomac rivers. King's Commissioners, "A Repertory of the General County Grievances of Virginia, October 15, 1677," in Great Britain, Public Record Office, Colonial Office Papers (hereafter cited as PRO, CO) 5/1312, part 1, fols. 318–19 (microfilm at Colonial Williamsburg Foundation, Williamsburg, Virginia).

13. Force, *Tracts*, vol. 1, book 8, 14–15. On identity of the queen's son, see note 32 below.

14. Ibid.

15. Privy Council, letter to Commissioners Inquiring into Grievances in Virginia, November 9, 1676, in Samuel Wiseman's Book of Record, 1676–77, Pepysian Library 2582, Great Britain, Magdalen College, Cambridge (microfilm at Colonial Williamsburg Foundation, Williamsburg, Virginia); Privy Council, Instructions to William Berkeley, October 13, 1676, in PRO, CO 5/1355, fols. 111–14.

16. H. R. McIlwaine and J. P. Kennedy, comps., *Journals of the House of Burgesses*, 13 vols. (Richmond, Va.: Library Board, 1905–15), *1659/60–1693*, 89.

17. Hening, *Statutes*, 2:251.

18. Charles M. Andrews, *Narratives of the Insurrections* (New York: Charles Scribner's Sons, 1915), 125–27.

19. Ibid., 127–28.

20. McIlwaine and Kennedy, *House, 1619–1659/60*, 89; William Berkeley, "Names and

Short Characters of those that have bin executed for Rebellion," in Samuel Wiseman's Book of Record, 1676–77.

21. John Berry, Herbert Jeffreys, and Francis Moryson, "Address of King's Commissioners to Grand Assembly, February 27, 1676/77," in Samuel Wiseman's Book of Record, 1676–77.

22. John Berry, Herbert Jeffreys, and Francis Moryson, letter of Commissioners to Principal Secretary of State, February 27, 1676/77, in Samuel Wiseman's Book of Record, 1676–77.

23. McIlwaine and Kennedy, *House, 1658/59–1693*, 89.

24. Andrews, *Narratives*, 127; Lord Chamberlain's Accounts in Jewel House Warrant Books, ser. 1, 1677–1709, January 18, 1677/78, in PRO, Lord Chamberlain's Papers (LC) 5/108, fol. 8; Lord Chamberlain's Department Wardrobe Accounts, Bill Books, ser. 1, 1675–79, November 1679 entry in PRO, LC 9/275, fols. 264v–265v.

25. John Berry, Herbert Jeffreys, and Francis Moryson, "Commissioners to Mr. Secretary Coventry, March 27, 1677," in Samuel Wiseman's Book of Record, 1676–77.

26. Herbert Jeffreys, Declaration of Colonel Jeffreys, Governor of Virginia, April 27, 1677, in PRO, CO 5/1355 fols. 145–49.

27. John Berry, Herbert Jeffreys, and Francis Moryson, "Commissioners Instructions together with their answers how they have performed the Several Articles," n.d., in Samuel Wiseman's Book of Record, 1676–77; Thomas Notley, lieutenant governor of Maryland, letter to Lord Baltimore, proprietor of Maryland, May 22, 1677, in PRO, CO 1/40, fols. 186–87.

28. Emphasis added. John Berry, Herbert Jeffreys, and Francis Moryson, "Particular Accounts how we yr Majesties Commissioners for the affairs of Virginia have observed and Comply'd with our Instructions" in PRO, CO 5/1371, p. 365.

29. In 1699 Middle Plantation was laid out as the site of Williamsburg, which later became the capital of the colony.

30. Herbert Jeffreys, letter to Right Honorable, June 11, 1677, in Coventry Papers, vol. 73, Bath 65, fols. 64–65.

31. Ibid.

32. Young West, earlier described as the son of an English colonel, was likely the offspring of Captain John West, who by the time of Totopotomoy's death in 1656, owned land in Pamunkey Neck, near Cockacoeske's village. According to one descendant of the elder West, his English wife, Unity, left him because of his liaison with the queen of Pamunkey. George H. S. King, letter to J. P. Hudson, July 14, 1961.

33. Nicholas Spencer, letter to Right Honorable, June 22, 1677, in PRO, CO 1/40, fols. 249–50.

34. Herbert Jeffreys, letter to Right Honorable, June 11, 1677, in Coventry Papers, vol. 73, Bath 65, fols. 64–65; John Berry, Herbert Jeffreys, and Francis Moryson, "Letter of Commissioners to King, July 20, 1677," in Samuel Wiseman's Book of Record, 1676–77.

35. Lords of Trade and Plantations, letter to king, October 19, 1677, in PRO, CO 1/41, fol. 222.

36. Privy Council, Order to Secretary Coventry, October 19, 1677 in PRO, CO 5/1355, fols. 198–200.

37. Privy Council, Order to Secretary Henry Coventry in PRO, CO 5/1355, fols. 243–45. The second treaty agreement, also called the Treaty of Middle Plantation and dated May 29, 1677, contained twenty-two articles, not twenty-one, its extra article extending treaty coverage to Maryland. The second treaty was endorsed not only by the original signatories of the earlier document, but also by Peracuta, the king of the Appomattocks, who previously had not been allowed to sign; Mastegonoe, the king of the Saponis, and Tachapoake, their chief man; Shurenough, the king of the Manakins; Vnuntsquero, the chief man of the Meherrins, and Horehannah, their next chief man; and Pattanochus, who signed as king of the Nanzatticos, Nansemonds, and Portobagos. "Articles of Peace between the Most Serene and Mighty Prince Charles II . . . Concluded the 29th day of May 1677," in Miscellaneous Virginia Records 1606–92, Bland Manuscripts, Papers of Thomas Jefferson, 8th ser. 14:226–33 (microfilm at College of William and Mary, Williamsburg). Note: the Nansemonds mentioned with the Nanzatticos and Portobagos were a Rappahannock River group and should not be confused with the Nansemonds living on the south side of the James River.

38. From Berry and Moryson's letter requesting the presents we learn that she was "of a meane or indifferent stature and somewhat plump of body" and that young John West, whom they called "the Prince, her son and successor," was a "good, brave young man pretty full of stature and slender of body, a great warr captain among the Indians and one that has been very active in the service of the English." Lord Chamberlain's Accounts, Jewel House Warrant Books, ser. 1, 1677–1709, January 18, 1677/78 in PRO, LC 5/108, fol. 8; Wardrobe Accounts, Bill Books, ser. 1, 1675–79, November 1679 entry, PRO, LC 9/275, fols. 264v–265v.

39. Ibid.

40. Ibid.

41. Hening, *Statutes*, 2:275–77; "Treaty," Bland Manuscripts; McIlwaine, *Executive Council*, 1:4. In the more than three hundred years that have elapsed since King Charles II sent gifts to some of Virginia's tributary Indian leaders, confusion has arisen over whether a silver ornament preserved at Jamestown, which is inscribed with the name of King Charles II and the crest of the British monarchy, is Cockacoeske's crown or her necklace. Some nineteenth- and early twentieth-century writers have called it the Pamunkey crown, but the crowns prepared for the queens of Pamunkey and Weyanoke and the kings of Nottoway and Nansemond were, in fact, adorned with false stones. Their maker, according to royal Jewel House account books, submitted a bill "for making new screws and fastening several stones in the crowns," evidence that the coronets were indeed jeweled. Moreover, those crowns were never delivered to the Indian kings and queens but instead were lost at sea. According to a notation made by Governor Thomas Culpeper in the margin of King Charles's instructions to him "to deliver unto them [the Indian rulers] our Royal Presents," Culpeper did "exactly execute all but only the Coronets which by advice of Council there I did not deliver and which were cast away with my goods," a reference to the sinking of the ship trans-

porting his baggage back to England. Thus the silver "frontlet" that has survived three centuries is likely to be the necklace that Jewel House Warrant Books list as being among the items made for Cockacoeske in England. Privy Council, Instructions to Thomas Lord Culpeper, December 6, 1679, in PRO, CO 5/1355, fols. 243–45.

42. "Treaty," Bland Manuscripts; Hening, *Statutes*, 2:275–77.

43. Official records reveal that the tributaries called upon the Virginia government for protection several times during the late seventeenth century.

44. As is seen from the list of grievances about the Chickahominys that Cockacoeske presented to officials on June 5, 1678, and a letter she sent to England on June 29, 1678, her takeover appears not to have been accomplished without bloodshed and resentment.

45. Documentary evidence reveals that the Chiskiacks survived until at least August 1677, at which time they were granted the right to conduct trade in Gloucester County, where they lived. Hening, *Statutes*, 2:411.

46. Hening, *Statutes*, 2:275–77.

47. Queen of Pamunkey (Cockacoeske), The Agrievances of the Queen of Poemunkey and her Sonn Captain John West, June 5, 1678, in PRO, CO 1/42, fol. 177.

48. Cockacoeske, letter to Colonel Francis Moryson, June 29, 1678 in PRO, CO 1/42, fol. 276.

49. Cornelius Dabney, letter to Colonel Francis Moryson, June 29, 1678, in PRO, CO 1/42, fol. 277.

50. Ibid.; Webb, *1676*, 395–96.

51. Thomas Ludwell, letter to Right Honorable, January 30, 1678, in Coventry Papers, vol. 73, Bath 65, fols. 202–3.

52. Ibid. Not only did article 12 of the treaty prove troublesome to colonial officials, but also article 18, which required them to arbitrate disputes among the tributary Indians. That article faced them with a dilemma, for in siding with one tribe they automatically alienated another. Ludwell noted that the Virginia government was obliged not only to settle quarrels among the tributary Indians, but to protect them against warring tribes, something he also found vexing. "Now," Ludwell argued, "we have a warr with those Irachors [Iroquois] but our Indians have not, because the treaty with them at Fort Albany was ordered before our peace was concluded there." Anonymous [Thomas Ludwell], letter to Sir Joseph Williamson, June 8, 1678; Thomas Ludwell, letter to Right Honorable, August 3, 1678, in Coventry Papers, vol. 73, Bath 65, fol. 281.

53. Anonymous [Thomas Ludwell], letter to Sir Joseph Williamson, Secretary of State, in Coventry Papers, vol. 73, Bath 65, unpaginated folio.

54. Thomas Ludwell, letter to "Right Honorable," June 28, 1678, in Coventry Papers, vol. 73, Bath 65, fol. 264.

55. Thomas Ludwell, letter to the "Right Honorable," August 3, 1678, in Coventry Papers, vol. 73, Bath 65, fol. 281.

56. McIlwaine and Kennedy, *House, 1693–1702*, 349; Thomas Story, *A Journal of the Life of Thomas Story* (Newcastle upon Tyne: James and John Wilson, 1747), 162.

57. McIlwaine, *Executive Journals*, 1:79.

58. Louis des Cognets, Jr., *English Duplicates of Lost Virginia Records* (Princeton, N.J.: privately published, 1958), 57; William P. Palmer, ed., *Calendar of Virginia State Papers and Other Manuscripts Preserved in the Capital at Richmond*, 13 vols. (Richmond: Virginia State Library, 1875–93), 1:184–85; Francis Nicholson, letter to his Council, October 22, 1702, in PRO, CO 5/1312, part 1, p. 318.

"Our Bond of Peace": Patterns of Intercultural Exchange in the Carolina Piedmont, 1650–1750

James H. Merrell

In the winter of 1701 the English explorer John Lawson and several companions visited the lands and peoples lying northwest of Charlestown, South Carolina. While traveling among the Santee Indians one hundred miles from the coast, the party stopped overnight at a Santee hunter's empty hut and, Lawson wrote, "made our selves welcome to what his Cabin afforded, (which is a Thing common) the *Indians* allowing it practicable to the *English* Traders, to take out of their Houses what they need in their Absence, in Lieu whereof they most commonly leave some small Gratuity of Tobacco, Paint, Beads, etc." Ten days later a Waxhaw Indian eager to trade intercepted the travelers on their way north to invite them to his town. "We receiv'd the Messenger with a great many Ceremonies," Lawson noted in his journal, "acceptable to those sort of Creatures."[1]

As these episodes indicate, Lawson's party was following a code of conduct governing trade relations between Anglo-American colonists and Indians in the southern upcountry (see fig. 1). The process of drawing up the code's rules and rituals had begun in earnest some fifty years before Lawson passed through, when a handful of trade-minded Virginia colonists turned their sights toward the untapped native populations southwest of the colony.[2] Over the next several decades these men—joined at the end of the century by others from Charlestown—penetrated deeper into the interior. By 1700 contacts with the Indian peoples there had become routine, and piedmont villages from the James River to the Wateree were part of the European trade network, linked to colonial Americans in a relationship that the clergyman and naturalist John Banister in 1679 termed "our Vinculum Pacis"—our bond of peace.[3]

Banister, who was acquainted with the trading community that

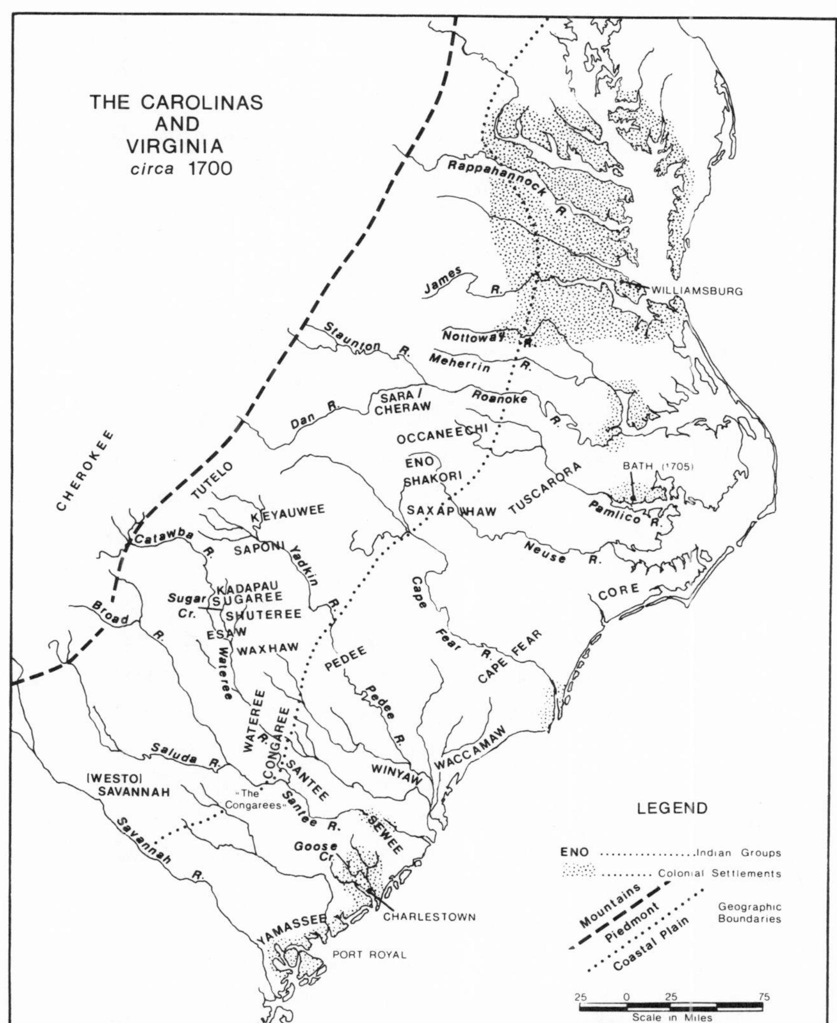

Figure 1 The Carolinas and Virginia, circa 1700.

clustered along the upper James and Appomattox rivers for voyages into the interior, was convinced that the "bond of peace" gave colonists complete control over the Indians. "Since there has been a way layd open for Trade . . . ," he asserted, "many Things which they wanted not before because they never had them are by that means become necessary both for their use and ornament."[4] A generation later John Lawson agreed, claiming that the Carolinians were "absolute Masters over the *Indians* . . . within the Circle of their Trade."

The Santees, for one, had become "very tractable" by virtue of their proximity to South Carolina and their consequent dependence on European technology.[5]

Yet beneath the Anglo-American boasts lay a more complex story. As Lawson's own conduct among the Santees and Waxhaws illustrated, piedmont Indians still shaped the contours of trade, "allowing" an outsider into their domain only if he behaved in "acceptable" ways. Natives entangled in the web of intercultural commerce did not abruptly abandon their own habits or meekly submit to the dictates of a colonist handing out his wares. Rather, upcountry peoples were active participants in the development of exchange across cultural boundaries, and for many years the pattern of trade looked more Indian than European. If with time the balance of economic and cultural power did indeed tip toward the colonists, the trade's effects on piedmont societies remained more evolutionary than revolutionary.[6]

Colonial traders could not change native ways overnight, in large part because the newcomers confronted a deeply rooted system of aboriginal commerce. Few details of the pre-Columbian trade survive, but it was clearly extensive, involving every group and a wide range of products. Although each village could provide itself with the basic necessities of life, peoples occupying different environments had access to certain highly prized commodities. Easily transportable items such as copper, natural dyes, and mica from the interior or shells from the seacoast composed the bulk of the trade, their passage from one hand to the next aided by interpreters, sign language, symbols, or other methods of surmounting linguistic barriers.[7] Beyond distributing these products over a wide area, aboriginal trade probably served as a vital means of maintaining ties among the independent towns scattered through upland river valleys, bringing different peoples together in a formal setting conducive to cementing peaceful relations. Like the exchange of goods, the exchange of people—as "hostages," adoptees, or marriage partners—symbolically confirmed friendship and trust.[8]

The Indians' trade with colonists emerged from these established forms. Some aboriginal exchange even remained untouched by the arrival of Anglo-Americans, for certain native groups still had access to traditional trade goods that were in great demand elsewhere. John Lawson remarked that coastal Indians gathered shells, along with yaupon plants for brewing "*Indian* Tea," "which they carry a great way into the main Land, to trade with the remote *Indians,* where they are of great Value." In return, people near the mountains collected a root to make red powder for paint. "They have this Scarlet Root in great Esteem," Lawson learned, "and sell it for a very great Price, one to another."[9]

At the same time, however, native traders began making subtle adjustments to the European presence without leaving the familiar confines of aboriginal exchange. Those near Anglo-American settlements manufactured wooden bowls, straw baskets, and clay pipes, traded them for raw deerskins at Indian towns to the west "that perhaps," Lawson speculated, "have greater Plenty of Deer," and returned home to finish dressing the skins before selling them to colonists. Both the products and the methods of exchange were wholly traditional; for generations, Indians in the interior customarily traded deerskins to native peoples of the lowcountry. But European demand for pelts, and perhaps also a declining deer population near colonial plantations, gave this traffic larger dimensions and new meaning.[10]

Eventually the cargoes that nearby Indians ferried to distant towns began to include European products as well as native manufactures. In 1670 Cheraw traders already acquainted with the Virginia men were conducting business among Catawba River towns, and it seems safe to surmise that they were peddling glass beads as well as red roots.[11] By the end of the century there was no longer room for doubt. To his surprise, Lawson met headmen in the piedmont who owned horses that had been spirited away from colonial settlements "by some neighbouring *Indian,* and transported farther into the Country, and sold." Liquor proved more popular than livestock, and groups near the sea introduced it to "the Westward *Indians,* who never knew what it was, till within very few Years."[12] Many Carolina natives must have gaped at a horse, tasted rum, or tried on a matchcoat before seeing their first European.

However obtained, most of the new wares were readily absorbed into native life. It was easy enough to come up with words for "gun," "powder horn," or "shot bag" and add them to one's vocabulary, or to substitute glass beads for shells, iron pots for clay vessels, metal bells for tortoise-shell rattles, and cloth for furs.[13] If necessary, Indians could also "fix" a foreign object so it suited their needs. Thus Keyauwee fletchers chipped arrowheads from broken bottles, while hunters, upon acquiring a musket, held it as they would a bow, with the left hand far forward, and then took great pains to "set it streight, sometimes shooting away above 100 Loads of Ammunition, before they bring the Gun to shoot according to their Mind."[14]

When they arrived on the scene, colonial traders were set straight in a similar manner. Men poised at the falls of the James River for a trek into the interior had to learn patience while also mastering the rudiments of the native system of communication, for Indians chose to "let us know . . . by grains of Mayze, or small stones, when they will come in, when they shall have any truck for us to go out, or the like."[15] Once he did enter the upcountry, the colonist found himself playing the trading game by native rules. Relying heavily on local guides, most early adventurers were taken along aboriginal trails.[16] Only John Lederer, who explored the far reaches of the piedmont in 1670, neglected to hire a guide; only Lederer ignored Indian directions—and only Lederer became hopelessly lost, wandering for days over "steep and craggy Cliffs," in "a continued Marish over-grown with Reeds," and across "a barren Sandy desert." After he finally staggered back to Virginia he warned anyone brave (or foolish) enough to try retracing his steps that "the way [is] thorow a vast Forest, where you seldom fall into any Road or Path." Those who did follow in Lederer's footsteps, aware that one did not simply "fall into" a trail, heeded native advice and stuck to established routes.[17]

Upon arriving at a piedmont settlement the colonist became a central player in a social drama directed by the townspeople. His welcome and treatment did not depart from earlier practices, for native hosts made no distinction among visitors, the local headman "always entertaining Travellers, either *English*, or *Indian*."[18] Lederer's description of the etiquette of greeting illustrates the passive stance that the wise colonist adopted in the early years of contact. "Being arrived at a Town," he advised, "enter no house until you are invited; and then seem not afraid to be led in pinion'd like a prisoner: for that is a Ceremony they use to friend and enemies without distinction. You must accept of an invitation from the Seniors, before that of young men," he went on, "and refuse nothing that is offered or set afore you: for they are very jealous, and sensible of the least slighting or neglect from strangers, and mindful of Revenge."[19]

If their guest behaved himself, some piedmont peoples offered him a more permanent place in native society. While Lederer was among the Saponis, for example, they wanted to "oblige me to stay amongst them by a Marriage with the Kings or some of their great Mens Daughters." The bewildered greenhorn managed to escape this fate, but his more experienced successors were less skittish. In Lawson's day traders "have commonly their *Indian* Wives" with whom they lived while among the native inhabitants of the uplands.[20] Here again Indians were treating a colonist like any other visitor, making arrangements designed to place him in the web of kinship that lay at the foundation of native life. Adoption or marriage into this network carried duties and obligations (as well as rights) understood by all in the town. Unfamiliar with relationships based solely on the market, Indians sought to bring colonists to obey the traditional rules governing interpersonal relations. When he took an Indian companion, the trader, to native eyes, accepted local forms of social control.

That Lawson's contemporaries went along with all this is obvious; less clear is just how much they understood of the arrangement's implications. Villagers who welcomed a visiting colonist were acting out behavioral codes that emphasized hospitality to outsiders and the need to establish personal or familial connections to potential trading partners. It appears that their guests continued to consider the economic basis of the relationship paramount. While staying with the Shuterees and other upcountry groups around the turn of the century, for example, the Virginia trader John Evans carefully recorded in his account book payments he made to his "Landlord" and "Landlady" for food and lodging.[21]

Indians who went further and formally accepted a trader into their kinship network invited similar misunderstandings. Colonists leapt at the offer of a mate, but they apparently considered it a shrewd business move more than anything else. "They find these *Indian* girls very serviceable to them," Lawson remarked. "This Correspondence makes them learn the *Indian* Tongue much the sooner," and they enjoy "the Satisfaction of a She-Bed-Fellow" who devoted herself to "dressing their Victuals, and instructing 'em in the Affairs and Customs of the Country. . . . Such a Man gets a great Trade with the Savages."[22] Given the linguistic and economic (not to mention sexual) advantages of these liaisons, a colonial trader would have been a fool to decline the offer.

Thus even men wholeheartedly embracing native hospitality probably knew less than the full story of what they were getting themselves into. Still, outward conformity was better than bumbling ignorance or casual indifference. Whether or not they fully grasped what was going on, colonists heading into the Carolina piedmont at the end of the seventeenth century did so largely on native terms. Just as their journeys were channeled into aboriginal paths, so their encounters with the inhabitants followed cultural pathways set out by their hosts.

An Indian group assimilated people and goods successfully because it was selective in its contacts—both personal and material—with outsiders. Men who failed to respect native customs were given short shrift. "They never frequent a Christian's House that is given to Passion," wrote Lawson, "nor will they ever buy or sell with him, if they can get the same Commodities of any other Person; for they say, such Men are mad Wolves, and no more Men."[23] Similarly, Indian customers chose merchandise most in keeping with established tastes. Many insisted that the colonial trader continue to supply traditional goods like shells.[24] And those willing to consider glass beads instead still wanted them to be a certain size and color. In short, to make a profit a colonist had to mind his manners and work tirelessly to match English goods with Indian preferences.[25]

If efforts to absorb colonists and their wares helped ensure that the early years of intercultural exchange would bring a minimum of disruption to piedmont towns, the products swapped for these goods also promoted adjustment to European intrusion. The principal Indian trade items were baskets, mats, deerskins, and slaves; none marked a radical departure from precontact ways. Piedmont women were accustomed to weaving and dyeing cane baskets or mats, and deer were already a primary source of meat and clothing. Hence the skills for producing these commodities were in place before Europeans arrived.[26]

The colonial demand for Indian slaves entailed equally few dramatic changes in native life, for enslavement of war captives was common in the aboriginal Southeast.[27] Although traders did, as one South Carolina clergyman charged, "excite [Indians] to make War amongst themselves to get Slaves which they give for our European Goods," excitement was in the air already, and it is often difficult to distinguish native from colonial impulses.[28] When Westoes crossed the Santee River to capture people there in 1670, were they after slaves for the colonial trade or victims, as Lederer put it, "to sacrifice to their Idols"? When Santees went off to war against Indians near the mouth of the Winyaw River three decades later, were they bent on settling old scores, acquiring slaves, both, or neither? All that can be known for certain is that the traffic in slaves entailed a large and destructive extension of existing habits, not the creation of an altogether new system for taking and selling human beings.[29]

None of these activities so monopolized the natives' time that the routine subsistence practices that had long sustained Indian Carolina broke down. Hunters still went out after meat to feed their families as well as pelts to sell to colonists. In the spring young men still took time out from the chase and the warpath to plant crops, and women still tended those crops in summer, in winter gathering nuts and other wild plant foods. Moreover, the hunting, planting, and gathering all remained thoroughly grounded in a ceremonial cycle without which, natives believed, life was unthinkable. Elaborate rituals to celebrate the harvest and pray for future bounty continued to occupy the piedmont winter. Hunters supplying food for these ceremonies—and skins for barter—were careful to propitiate the unseen yet powerful forces governing their fortunes. "All the *Indians* hereabouts carefully preserve the Bones of the Flesh they eat," Lawson noted while among the Keyauwees in 1701, "and burn them, as being of Opinion, that if they omitted that Custom, the Game would leave their Country, and they should not be able to maintain themselves by their Hunting."[30]

During the latter half of the seventeenth century, then, inhabitants of the piedmont were able to weave foreigners and their alien wares into the existing cultural fabric without drastically altering its texture or design. Trade was indeed a "bond of peace" that united two cultures in a common enterprise, but only because few colonists dared to challenge native hegemony. Like Lederer, they recognized that they were still guests in a foreign land and therefore had better behave themselves. Lest they forget, news of a friend, relative, or partner killed by Indians somewhere in the interior occasionally reached the coastal settlements to refresh their memory.[31]

Still, the evidence of continuing native control over the trade could not conceal some of the more gradual and more profound effects of participation in the Atlantic economy, effects that existed for a time alongside the signs of control and would eventually replace them.[32] At the most fundamental level, colonists were transforming the very nature of trade in the piedmont. Exchange became more than a means of cementing relations among groups through gifts whose symbolic value outweighed their practical uses. As early as 1670 Lederer, having glimpsed the Indians' education in European methods, was able to capture the transition from one pattern of trade to another. The "remoter Indians," he discovered, were still operating under an older set of rules and therefore "are apt to admire such trinkets . . . as small Looking-glasses, Pictures, Beads and Bracelets of glass, Knives, Sizars, and all manner of gaudy toys and knacks for children." Instead of bartering for these goods, Lederer happily reported, "remoter Indians"—accustomed to considering exchange a form of gift giving—were content to "purchase them at any rate." Those living near the colonists, on the other hand, had learned enough to demand cloth "and all sorts of edg'd tools" as well as "Guns, Powder and Shot, etc." Moreover, these "neighbour-Indians" would "greedily barter for" European merchandise and "spend time in higgling for further abatements" in price.[33]

Before long, despite the efforts of more experienced native traders to screen "remoter Indians" from direct contact with Europeans and their ways, word still spread to distant towns regarding the range of products available from the English and the accepted means of procuring them. By the 1680s the Virginia trader William Byrd was warning his English suppliers that the commodities they shipped to him must be not only the proper size and color but also the right price.[34] The symbolic significance of exchange had by no means disappeared; it was still a form of diplomacy, and Indians never lost their taste for what colonists considered trinkets. But alongside these older forms arose a demand for tools and weapons, an awareness of the value Anglo-Americans attached to the objects involved, and a willingness to hold out for a better deal.

Indians soon enough learned that driving a hard bargain was the best way to procure the fruits of European technology. Yet the taste of some of these fruits proved more bitter than sweet as natives found themselves unable to assimilate every product as readily as they did a string of beads or a new musket. Liquor, for example, disrupted piedmont existence from the first. Though natives sought to treat alcohol as they did other foreign merchandise and make it fit existing cultural and ceremonial forms,[35] its destructive effects were soon painfully obvious. Drunken Indians crippled themselves by falling into campfires or plunging off cliffs; they crippled each other when, inhibitions lowered by drink, neighbors and kinfolk quarreled, shattering the peace of a community. Natives knew too well that rum was a "poisonous Plant" that could "make People sick," yet still they could not resist it. "They have no Power to refrain this Enemy," Lawson observed, nor could they find an antidote for the poison it injected into their lives.[36]

Hidden by the dramatic, even explosive effects of alcohol was a more general, less visible intoxication with foreign technology that grew with each passing year. The first and most obvious dependence was on European firearms. "They think themselves undrest and not fit to walk abroad," remarked one amused Virginian in 1690 of the piedmont Indians living nearby, "unlesse they have their gun on their shoulder, and their shot-bag by their side."[37] By the end of the century it seemed that no self-respecting warrior anywhere in the southern uplands was without a musket.[38]

Picking up a gun did not transform an Indian into a slave of the marketplace, of course. Men still manufactured and used the old weapons, and some limited their reliance on the colonial trader's return by mending a cracked musket stock themselves or fashioning a new ramrod from the same wood used to make arrow shafts.[39] But these were delaying tactics, not declarations of economic independence. The time, effort, and skill invested in crafting the traditional tools fell off precipitously once European substitutes became readily available.[40] Worse still, among those craftsmen copying their European contemporaries rather than their own ancestors, fixing a gunstock or replacing a ramrod was one thing, repairing a broken hammer, a rusted barrel—or an empty shot pouch—quite another. In time Indians were not just accustomed to a steady influx of certain merchandise, they were dependent upon it. And the Europeans who manufactured the guns and distilled the rum were not oblivious to the fact that commercial addictions ensure a steady market.

The transformation of European wares from luxuries to necessities went hand in hand with the metamorphosis of the colonial trader from the passive, timid observer of John Lederer's day to the confident leading player on the piedmont stage he became after 1700. In the course of their many voyages into the interior colonists were bound to pick up the tricks of the trade. From success and failure alike, Anglo-Americans learned the shortest routes, the friendliest Indians, the choicest phrases, the most popular items.[41] The school was a hard one, but graduation had its rewards. One was simply survival; another was profit; a third was a certain assurance that permitted the outsiders to begin placing their own stamp on the patterns of exchange.

The transgressions seemed harmless enough at first. Sometime around the turn of the eighteenth century, for example, traders apparently stopped waiting for a summons from the interior and began setting out from their homes when they pleased. Colonists had once entered the piedmont for a month or two in late winter and early spring to meet Indians recently returned from the winter hunt; the rest of the year, natives had the interior virtually to themselves. After 1700, however, colonial traders came when they liked and stayed as long as they chose, inaugurating an important change in the cadence of the upcountry.[42]

A visitor from the lowlands who stayed longer among his native hosts quite naturally had more opportunities to bend the rules and more confidence—as he detected the Indians' deepening reliance on the merchandise he brought—that he could get away with it. One built a trading hut near but not in the Indian village, which took him out of the headman's dwelling and placed him both figuratively and literally beyond local control.[43] The natives' reaction to this particular innovation is unknown, but other colonial inventions met stiff resistance. The steelyard, a metal contraption for weighing merchandise, proved a particular point of contention between native and newcomer. Any colonial trader venturing to set up this gadget in an Indian town faced "prodigious trouble," according to one Virginia observer, because of the natives' "resolute stupidity and obstinacy in receiving a new custom . . . for they could not apprehend the power and justice of the stilliard." Nowhere was the subtle tug-of-war for control of intercultural exchange more evident. A piedmont resident accustomed to standards of measurement based on the human body—a string of beads by the arm's length, for example, or rum by the mouthful—had no use for this particular foreign import. He could see if the person measuring an arm's length of roanoke was tall or short, he could judge the size of a customer's mouth and detect a surreptitious swallow or two; he could not understand a device designed, manufactured—and often rigged—by strangers. Colonists exaggerated the justice of the steelyard; they did not exaggerate its symbolic power.[44]

As the tug-of-war went on, the intruders mingled careful attention to established custom with callous breaches of etiquette. During that overnight stay in the vacant Santee dwelling, for example, John Lawson left the requisite gift but merely shrugged when he accidentally burned down part of the building while cooking his dinner. Lederer would have departed in haste if not in panic, as he did on more than one occasion when the situation looked ominous; Lawson sauntered away the next morning, unperturbed. Similarly, at a Catawba village farther up the path, Lawson's party headed straight for the headman's house as custom dictated, but the visitors seemed more amused than alarmed when this Indian, his routine offer of a gift flatly refused, "flew into a violent Passion, to be thus slighted, telling the *Englishmen,* they were good for nothing." Once again a comparison with Lederer's probable reaction to such a rebuke is instructive, for it points clearly to the direction trade was taking.[45]

The line between impolite and abusive is blurred, but with time more and more traders clearly stepped across it. In 1715 David Crawley, a Virginia trader, maintained that his South Carolina counterparts had launched a virtual reign of terror in the native Southeast. According to Crawley's indictment, the men from Charlestown robbed their Indian clients, forced burdeners to carry skins vast distances for a pittance, sent the men off on errands and then raped the women, and beat up anyone who dared to protest this sort of behavior.[46] Crawley was a competitor, not an impartial judge of South Carolina's Indian affairs; still, the South Carolina accounts confirm his claims, and worried officials in Charlestown admitted as much when they passed laws to put a stop to the traders' crime spree. But measures that looked stern on paper tended to be feeble hundreds of miles away in Indian country, and the agents sent to bridge the gap between council chamber and council house were as likely to be part of the problem as part of the solution. The traders had run amok, and ultimately many of them paid for their sins with their lives when Yamasee Indians south of Charlestown led a rebellion against the Carolina trading regime in April 1715. The colony's traders were the first casualties, but not the last. In less than a month hundreds more colonists were dead, and Indian warriors seemed bent on driving the rest into the sea.[47]

The connection between that smoldering Santee hut in 1701 and the smoldering lowcountry plantations in 1715 seems clear. Certainly most colonists who gave the Yamasee War's causes much thought blamed the traders, drawing a straight and bloody line from confidence to arrogance through abuses to uprising. For Yamasees and their neighbors south of the provincial capital, it was indeed almost that simple.[48] Not so for the "mixture of Catabaws, Sarraws Waterees etc." from the north who—to the shock and dismay of colonists—joined the fray in late April or early May.[49] For all the evidence that the tides of trade were turning against the piedmont peoples, that dependence was increasing and the traders getting out of hand, the surviving sources yield few hints that the groups there had yet suffered anything like the oppression Yamasees endured; the litany of native complaints issuing from South Carolina's southern flank before 1715 had no counterpart in villages to the north.[50] Given the silence from that direction, it seems unlikely that many of the colonial traders in these "northern" nations had yet stepped over the line from boorish to brutal behavior. Why, then, did piedmont Indians join the rebellion? Once again trade holds the key, but here the causal connection is more difficult to trace than it is farther south. Here it was less the South Carolina trader's assaults on Indians than his assaults on Virginians that brought the "mixture" of Indian warriors from the north down on the colony's head.[51]

The first links in the causal chain were forged late in the seventeenth century when South Carolinians finally woke up to the fact that they had little knowledge of—and less influence over—powerful Indian nations in the colony's own backyard. During its first generation of existence Carolina had directed most of its attention south and west, with the result that the colony's experts could speak with more authority about Indians as far as the Mississippi River than about those much beyond the Santee.[52] To remedy this problem the colony looked to trade, a tried and true means of making friends and influencing peoples. Make an Indian nation dependent on us for weapons, the accepted wisdom went, and it is ours, for "whenever that nation . . . shall misbehave themselves towards us, we shall be able whenever we please by abstaineing from supplying them with Ammunition . . . to ruine them."[53] The only flaw in the plan was that the upcountry Indians being targeted did not need South Carolina's trade; they had goods aplenty from Virginians like David Crawley. The men in Charlestown's corridors of power had an answer to that, too: they declared a trade war against their fellow Anglo-Americans. In October 1698 the South Carolina Commons House of Assembly fired the first shot with a resolution "that the Virginians be Prohibitted from Tradeing in This Province." Over the next fifteen years the war raged, its battlefields as disparate as the piedmont's villages and the Privy Council's chambers. Since neither province could gain the upper hand, the threats and skirmishes, the discriminatory laws and "legal" confiscations, the charges and countercharges went on and on.[54]

For the most part the upcountry Indians remained above the fray, reaping the rewards of neutrals in a war zone. The vicious competition for customers probably meant that goods were plentiful and prices lower. It may also be one reason traders as yet were not guilty of many excesses in the contested region; politeness won points, and Indians with an alternative source of supply—who, as Lawson put it, "can get the same Commodities of any other Person"—had to be handled with kid gloves, not an iron fist. At the same time, however, the intercolonial trade war had pernicious, even lethal, consequences for the neutral natives. Trade was the principal lens through which piedmont Indians viewed the colonial world, and battles between one colony and another presented those Indians with a distorted view of that world. Merely by watching and listening to the squabbling in their midst, natives picked up a great deal. They saw the confrontations and confiscations; they heard the war of words that accompanied this war of nerves, as each colonist tried to persuade natives of his own virtues and his competitors' vices.[55] From experience, then, Indians could conclude that Anglo-Americans looked and acted much alike, they pulled the same wonderful things from their packs, but they were deeply divided, and they quarreled with one another like the "mad Wolves" natives found so distasteful. In the spring of 1715, pressed by Yamasee ambassadors urging war, familiar enough with the traders' penchant for straying from the accepted cultural paths to believe those who predicted that such arrogance would lead only to greater abuse, piedmont nations would act on the information gleaned from years of watching Virginia and Carolina men go at each other. The Carolina traders were killed, their Virginia competitors merely detained so that, to the Indians' way of thinking, the vital connection to Virginia remained unbroken. Then upcountry warriors headed down the Wateree River valley, confident that they could go on killing South Carolinians indefinitely with Virginia's bullets.[56]

They were dead wrong. If, as the beleaguered South Carolinians claimed, Virginia traders had indeed "encouraged our Indians to do what they have done and promised to supply them at a much easier rate than our Indian traders did and that they would give them much better treatment," Virginia officials were not prepared to go along with the scheme.[57] No Crown appointee who valued his career would have knowingly handed Indians the wherewithal to kill fellow subjects of Great Britain. If in April 1715 natives did not know that (because the traders, their only source of information, had not told them), they found out soon enough. Upon learning of South Carolina's desperate plight, Lieutenant Governor Alexander Spotswood rushed the stricken colony precious shiploads of men and supplies, slapped an embargo on Virginia's trade with Indians, and met with South Carolina agents to see what more he could do. When ambassadors from the Cheraws and Catawbas visited Williamsburg in October, they must have been startled to find men from the two provinces, seated amicably side by side, awaiting them as they entered the council chamber.[58]

Piedmont Indians had another surprise in store for them. While learning that the two colonies in fact stood shoulder to shoulder, natives were also discovering that South Carolina's old plan to bring Indians to heel by fostering dependence on European trade had worked after all. Piedmont warriors had all but exhausted their supply of weapons in the initial invasion of the lowcountry; what was left they abandoned as they fled homeward after being defeated by colonial forces on June 13.[59] Any hope of getting more from Virginia was dashed by Spotswood's embargo, and by August colonists holed up in Charlestown began to sense that their native foes "want ammunition and are not able to mend their arms."[60] By then upcountry nations, "their necessity of all manner of goods being very great," were already talking about ending the conflict.[61] The Indians' thirst for European wares was painfully obvious in the negotiations with Virginia, discussions in which headmen invariably spoke of "a Peace and a free Trade" in the same breath. In October the Catawba and Cheraw delegates went even further, bluntly admitting that "they cannot live without the assistance of the English."[62] From a "bond of peace," trade had become a cause of war; now trade's absence promised peace again.

Indians, defeated in war and crushed in the vise of trade, could still hope not only for peace, not only for trade, but even for trade "as formerly," meaning as an arm of diplomacy, with low prices for abundant supplies of goods brought by obedient rather than truculent colonists.[63] Colonial authorities had other ideas. Convinced, as the Commons House put it, that Indians "are no longer to be kept in Subjection [unless] the Necessity or Interest obliges them[,] which may be accomplished by . . . making them Dependent for necessaries of all kinds, and in these keep[in]g them bare and unstored," both South Carolina and Virginia launched reform programs.[64] The various provisions were designed to end unsupervised contacts between colonist and Indian by licensing colonial traders, making them post bond for their good behavior, and—in South Carolina's most ambitious move—requiring native traders to do business at designated posts.

Despite the concerted efforts to direct the flow of trade into different channels, the actual system of exchange that rose from the ashes of the war bore a striking resemblance to the earlier version. By 1717 the Carolina-Virginia trade war had picked up where it left off, with colonists using fair means or foul to gain the advantage. The natives, meanwhile, reaped all the benefits of a buyers' market. After the drought came the deluge, as colonists eager to make up for lost time (and lost profits) flooded the interior with merchandise. This meant that Indians, far from pathetic beggars greedily gobbling any crumbs that the victorious Anglo-Americans happened to throw their way, still had the luxury of being choosy customers. If the quality of the powder, the size of the hoes, the shape of the beads, or the asking price of the item was wrong, colonists would hear about it.[65] And if satisfaction was not forthcoming, an Indian took his business elsewhere. South Carolina's grand plan to entice Catawbas to a trade factory at the Congarees and Cheraws to another along the Winyaw enjoyed only limited success: although Indians did show up at the specified sites, to the policymakers' chagrin the natives also continued to trade at home—"as formerly"—or ventured into the low-country in search of the right price, the right color, the right size.[66]

While Catawbas and their neighbors took the framework of exchange that had been put together in far-off capitals and bent it into something approximating its earlier shape, while goods poured in and prices dropped, one thing did change after the war: the men who helped Indians ignore the official decrees, who brought the goods and haggled over the prices, now seemed somehow tamer. The events of 1715 remained fresh in the minds of those who had escaped death during that fateful spring, and veterans probably passed their memories along to the next generation. Thomas Brown, who would dominate the Catawba trade in the second quarter of the eighteenth century, got his start in the mid-1720s with stock purchased from John Thompson and William Marr, two old hands who may have thrown in some advice at no extra charge.[67] Brown's chief competitor, John Evans, who set up a base along the Santee River at about the same time, may have been related to the Virginia trader of the same name and would have had some stories of his own to tell.[68]

Heading back into the upcountry with eyes open, ears cocked, and minds filled with chilling tales of what had happened there in 1715, few traders were looking for trouble. Where John Lederer's contemporaries had been ignorant and frightened and John Lawson's experienced and arrogant, Thomas Brown's tended to be experienced and frightened. Their very different relations with native women help measure the dimensions of the change that occurred in the aftermath of the Yamasee War. Lederer ran from the prospect of an arranged marriage; the men of Lawson's day jumped at the chance for the wrong reasons; Thomas Brown and John Evans married native women and formed deep attachments to the offspring of these marriages, attachments that suggest an understanding of Indian ways unheard of in Carolina before 1715.[69] As a confirmation of his status Brown became something of an adviser to the Catawbas. Earlier English visitors had scrupulously, then more casually, sought out the native headman before engaging in trade; now Catawba headmen routinely repaired to Brown's trading post "to form their Councils."[70] For his part Evans went even further, taking on the physical risks—and the social rewards—of accompanying Indian war parties, earning himself the title of "our old Freind and Linguister."[71] The contrast with John Lawson's day could hardly have been greater.

In the 1730s William Byrd II charged that the Carolina traders were "petty rulers," "little tyrants" who "pretend to exercise a dictatorial authority over [Catawbas] . . . and use them with all kinds of oppression."[72] Byrd was either a sore loser or out of touch. Men like Brown and Evans knew too well the fate of tyrants in the native Southeast. They achieved influence by behaving correctly—as kinsman, counselor, or warrior—and then exerting that influence through persuasion, not bullying or brute force. Only in this way could they advance their interests—and save their necks. Brown would never have survived two decades trading among the Catawba

River peoples, and Evans twice that, had they been the "petty rulers" their detractors claimed they were.

Indians and colonists so quickly resurrected trade out of the ruins left by the Yamasee War that it is tempting to consider 1715 little more than a bad memory, a brief and unfortunate interruption in the regular rhythms of exchange. Men from Virginia and Carolina—repenting their earlier ignorance and arrogance—rushed back to their piedmont haunts, preached the gospel of commerce with renewed fervor, and converted the Indians once again. It seemed almost too good to be true, and it was. In fact, beneath every peaceful encounter after 1715 lurked the harsh truth that the swift revival of exchange could not hide: although piedmont peoples could still choose where and with whom they would trade, they could no longer choose not to trade at all. Like it or not, Indians were bound to Anglo-America by a chain forged from beads and muskets, kettles and hoes, cloth and powder.

If the chain usually rested fairly lightly on Indian shoulders as the two cultures went about their daily business in the generation following the Yamasee War, it could never be cast off. To remind natives of this, colonists occasionally gave the chain a yank. In a 1727 meeting with the Virginia councillor and trader Nathaniel Harrison, a Sugaree headman reiterated the traditional native understanding of the exchange relationship as a diplomatic tool, a means of confirming friendship. "To shew the kindness we have" for the Virginia people, the Indian said, "we make it our business to kill deer and get skins for their Traders." A set speech, one probably heard by every colonist since Lederer. Once upon a time the response would probably have been a simple nod of assent; not anymore. Harrison scoffed, replying that "we don't look upon that as a particular freindship in you, for . . . I know you are oblig'd to kill deer for the Support of your Women and Children." Underscoring his assessment of their dependent condition, Harrison alluded to the Sugarees' tenuous state of health and reminded their leader of the consequences of being unarmed in a land where slave raids or attacks by roaming Iroquois were a fact of life: "without our freindship in supplying you with Guns, and Amunition you must all starve and what is as bad, become a prey to your Enemies[;] so that the Freindship is from us in trading with and supplying you with these Necessarie Goods, for your support, and Defence."[73]

In time of crisis the insults easily became threats, and the tugs on the chain were harder. When piedmont Indians killed several colonists in the Wateree River valley during the winter of 1737–38, Charlestown rushed to the Catawbas an agent armed with instructions to demand satisfaction. If the headmen proved stubborn, the agent was ordered "to put the Catawba Indians in Mind that when they differed with us and applied to the People of Virginia for a free Trade with them, the People of Virginia knowing in what Manner they had used us, . . . refused to trade with them while they were at Enmity with us; . . . and as the same good Understanding remains between us and Virginia, as at that Time[,] so they may expect in Case they disoblige us to be made sensible of the Resentment of both Provinces."[74] Before 1715 the Indians could have considered this sort of talk mere bluff and bluster; it certainly did not conform to the gist of the traders' whispers in those days. Now they knew better: Virginia and Carolina might squabble, but in time of trouble the differences between them evaporated, leaving Anglo-Americans (who had the manufactures) on one side and Indians (who needed them) on the other.

Even as South Carolina was issuing its threats, the chances of piedmont Indians' playing the Virginia card were increasingly remote, for fewer Virginians were bothering to make the trip. William Byrd II could remember the days when fifteen men leading one hundred packhorses had headed into the piedmont; in the 1730s a good year saw only half that many set out, and by midcentury the number was down to a mere handful.[75] South Carolina had won at last, although by then the prize was hardly worth having: piedmont Indian populations had diminished sharply, and there were no longer enough deer in the area to support very many traders—colonial or Indian. The days of the great piedmont deerskin trade were fast drawing to a close.

Long before that happened, however, the trade had brought Indians to toe the Anglo-American line. From masters of the upcountry they had become, like the Santees Lawson had met, "tractable" peoples unable to inspire much fear in anyone able to calculate the power of the trade. In 1733 Byrd's exploring party came across the remains of a recent Indian encampment in the piedmont, a discovery that was "a little shocking to some of the company." Byrd, who knew the score, was unperturbed. "In case they were Catawbas," he observed drily, "the danger would be . . . little from them, because they are too fond of our trade to lose it for the pleasure of shedding a little English blood."[76] At last, John Banister's words had become more reality than dream: commerce had indeed become the Anglo-American "bond of peace."

Acknowledgments

This chapter is a revised and expanded version of a paper delivered at the annual meeting of the American Historical Association in December 1982, and I would like to thank Robert Mitchell, James Axtell, and particularly Neal Salisbury for their comments on that earlier version. Expanded still further, it appears in my *The Indians' New World: Catawbas and Their Neighbors from European Contact through the Era of Removal* (Chapel Hill: University of North Carolina Press, 1989), published for the Institute of Early American History and Culture; I am grateful to the Institute for permission to publish portions of that work here. Finally, the general thrust of the argument and some of the examples offered here have appeared in "The Indians' New World: The Catawba Experience," *William and Mary Quarterly,* 3d ser., 41(1984): 537–65, and "'This Western World': The Evolution of the Piedmont, 1525–1725," in *The Siouan Project: Seasons I and II,* ed. Roy S. Dickens, Jr., H. Trawick Ward, and R. P. Stephen Davis, Jr., Monograph Series 1 (Chapel Hill: Research Laboratories of Anthropology, University of North Carolina, 1987), 19–27.

Notes

1. John Lawson, *A New Voyage to Carolina,* ed. Hugh T. Lefler (Chapel Hill: University of North Carolina Press, 1967), 24, 39.

2. For the growing interest in this southwestern region, see "A Present Description of Virginia" (London, 1649), in Peter Force, ed., *Tracts and Other Papers, Relating Principally to the Origin, Settlement, and Progress of the Colonies in North America,* 4 vols. (Washington, D.C.: Peter Force, 1836–46), 3:8–10, 13; Edward Williams, *Virginia: More especially the South part thereof, Richly and truly valued . . . ,* 2d ed. (London, 1650), 18, 34–37, I2[A]–I3; "The Discovery of New Brittaine, 1650," and "Francis Yeardley's Narrative of Excursions into Carolina, 1654," all in *Narratives of Early Carolina, 1650–1708,* ed. Alexander S. Salley (New York: Charles Scribner's Sons, 1911), 1–29.

3. John Banister to Dr. Robert Morison, April 6, 1679, in *John Banister and His Natural History of Virginia, 1678–1692*, ed. Joseph Ewan and Nesta Ewan (Urbana: University of Illinois Press, 1970), 42.

4. Ibid. See also John Banister, "Of the Natives," in Ewan and Ewan, *Natural History*, 385.

5. Lawson, *New Voyage*, 10, 23.

6. Students of Indians elsewhere in eastern North America have begun to recognize that natives had an active role in the trade, and some of the themes touched upon here may be pursued in James Axtell, "The English Colonial Impact on Indian Culture," in his *The European and the Indian: Essays in the Ethnohistory of Colonial North America* (New York: Oxford University Press, 1981), 253–65; Francis Jennings, *The Invasion of America: Indians, Colonialism, and the Cant of Conquest* (Chapel Hill: University of North Carolina Press for the Institute of Early American History and Culture, 1975), 85–97; Toby Morantz, "The Fur Trade and the Cree of James Bay," in *Old Trails and New Directions: Papers of the Third North American Fur Trade Conference*, ed. Carol M. Judd and Arthur J. Ray (Toronto: University of Toronto Press, 1980), 39–58; Arthur J. Ray, "Indians as Consumers in the Eighteenth Century," in Judd and Ray, *Old Trails*, 255–71; and Neal Salisbury, *Manitou and Providence: Indians, Europeans, and the Making of New England, 1500–1643* (New York: Oxford University Press, 1982), esp. 47–60, 147–49. Of particular interest for its emphasis on the Indians' understanding of the trade is Christopher L. Miller and George R. Hamell, "A New Perspective on Indian-White Contact: Cultural Symbols and Colonial Trade," *Journal of American History*, 73(1986): 311–28. The Southeast has received less attention, but see John Philip Reid, *A Better Kind of Hatchet: Law, Trade, and Diplomacy in the Cherokee Nation during the Early Years of European Contact* (University Park: Pennsylvania State University Press, 1976), and J. Leitch Wright, Jr., *The Only Land They Knew: The Tragic Story of the American Indians in the Old South* (New York: Free Press, 1981), esp. 93–96, 106–11, 170–74, 221–23, 227.

7. "True Relation of the Vicissitudes That Attended the Governor Don Hernando de Soto . . . Now Just Given by a Fidalgo of Elvas," in *Narratives of the Career of Hernando de Soto*, ed. Edward G. Bourne, 2 vols. (New York: A. S. Barnes, 1904), 1:50–51, 66–67; Garcilaso de la Vega, El Inca, *The Florida of the Inca*, trans. and ed. John G. Varner and Jeanette J. Varner (Austin: University of Texas Press, 1951) 253–54, 285, 310–11, 316, 323; Francisco Fernandez de Ècija, "Testimonio del Viaje . . . ," in Gene Waddell, *Indians of the South Carolina Lowcountry, 1562–1751* (Spartanburg, S.C.: Reprint Company, 1980), 225–27; Joffre Coe, "The Cultural Sequence of the Carolina Piedmont," in *Archeology of Eastern United States*, ed. James B. Griffin (Chicago: University of Chicago Press, 1952), 307, 310–11; James B. Griffin, "Eastern North American Archaeology: A Summary," *Science* 156(1967): 189; George E. Stuart, "Some Archeological Sites in the Middle Wateree Valley, South Carolina" (M.A. thesis, George Washington University, 1970), 115, 128; Sharon I. Goad, "Exchange Networks in the Prehistoric Southeastern United States" (Ph.D. diss., University of Georgia, 1978).

For means of communication, see Elvas, "True Relation," in Bourne, *De Soto Narratives*, 1:50–51, 54–55, 61, 67; "Relation of the Conquest of Florida by Luys Hernandez de Biedma in the Year 1544 . . . ," in Bourne, *De Soto Narratives*, 2:12; Inca, *Florida*, 253–54, 302, 310; "Report of Franciso Fernandez de Ècija," in *The Jamestown Voyages under the First Charter, 1606–1609*, ed. Philip L. Barbour, 2 vols. (Cambridge: University Press for the Hakluyt Society, 1969), 2:295, 298, 299, 302, 314, 317–18; Lawson, *New Voyage*, 48, 49.

8. Lawson, *New Voyage*, 178; William P. Cumming, ed., *The Discoveries of John Lederer* (Charlottesville: University Press of Virginia, 1958), 33. See also Harold Hickerson, "Fur Trade Colonialism and the North American Indians," *Journal of Ethnic Studies* 1(1973): 19–21.

It is difficult to prove that the exchange of people had pre-Columbian origins. But in the early contact period the natives' readiness, even eagerness, to give the Anglo-Americans "hostages" and the occasional reference to individuals living among other peoples suggest that these habits were already in place. See "Yeardley's Narrative," in Salley, *Narratives of Carolina*, 26, 28; "Discovery of New Brittaine," in ibid., 20; Lawson, *New Voyage*, 57, 63–64.

9. Lawson, *New Voyage*, 98, 218, 174. For the Indian tea, see Charles M. Hudson, ed., *Black Drink: A Native American Tea* (Athens: University of Georgia Press, 1979). The root may have been red puccoon, or bloodroot. See Banister, "Of the Natives," 263, 377 n. 35.

10. Lawson, *New Voyage*, 217; see also ibid., 64. For the earlier exchange network, see Ècija, "Testimonio," 226.

11. Cumming, *Discoveries of Lederer*, 31. For the Cheraws' early trade with Virginia, see William Byrd, "A Journey to the Land of Eden, Anno 1733," in *The Prose Works of William Byrd of Westover: Narratives of a Colonial Virginian*, ed. Louis B. Wright (Cambridge: Harvard University Press, 1966), 400; Jack H. Wilson, "Feature Fill, Plant Utilization and Disposal among the Historic Sara Indians" (M.A. thesis, University of North Carolina, 1977), xiv.

12. Lawson, *New Voyage*, 44, 232; see also 48.

13. For trading vocabularies, see ibid., 233–39; Edward P. Alexander, "An Indian Vocabulary from Fort Christanna, 1716," *Virginia Magazine of History and Biography* 79(1971): 303–13. For the substitutions, see Liane Navey, "An Introduction to the Mortuary Practices of the Historic Sara" (M.A. thesis, University of North Carolina, 1982), chap. 4 (beads); Lawson, *New Voyage*, 44–45 (bells), and 46 (iron pot).

14. Lawson, *New Voyage*, 63, 33. William J. Hinke, trans. and ed., "Report of the Journey of Francis Louis Michel from Berne, Switzerland, to Virginia, October 2, 1701–December 1, 1702," *Virginia Magazine of History and Biography* 24(1916): 42. Archaeologists have found glass arrowheads in South Carolina. See Tommy Charles, "Thoughts and Records from the Survey of Private Collections of Artifacts throughout South Carolina: A Second Report" (Institute of Archeology and Anthropology) *Notebook* 15(1983): 31.

15. Banister, "Of the Natives," 384.

16. "Discovery of New Brittaine," in Salley, *Narratives of Carolina*, 8–9, 11, 13, 16–18; "John Clayton's Transcript of the Journal of Robert Fallam," in *The First Explorations of the Trans-Allegheny Region by the Virginians, 1650–1674*, ed. Clarence W.

Alvord and Lee Bidgood (Cleveland: Arthur H. Clark, 1912), 184, 185, 187, 189; Lawson, *New Voyage*, 31, 37, 39, 48, 61.

17. Cumming, *Discoveries of Lederer*, 20, 30, 32, 38–39.

18. Lawson, *New Voyage*, 34.

19. Cumming, *Discoveries of Lederer*, 41.

20. Ibid., 23; Lawson, *New Voyage*, 192, 35.

21. John Evans, "Journal of a Virginia[?] Indian Trader in North and South Carolina [?]," n.p., South Caroliniana Library, Columbia.

22. Lawson, *New Voyage*, 35–36, 192.

23. Ibid., 210.

24. Cadwallader Jones to Lord Baltimore, February 6, 1681/82, Public Record Office, Colonial Office Papers, ser. 1, vol. 48, 115–16 (microfilm copy, reel 327, Virginia Colonial Records Project, Colonial Williamsburg Archives, Williamsburg, Va.); William Byrd to Stephanus Van Cortlandt, August 3, 1691, in *The Correspondence of the Three William Byrds of Westover, Virginia, 1684–1776*, ed. Marion Tinling, 2 vols. (Charlottesville: University Press of Virginia, 1977), 1:163; Inventory of Giles Webb, entered February 1713/14, Henrico County (Va.) Records [Deeds, Wills], 1710–14, part 1, 241 (this and all other Henrico County records cited were consulted on microfilm copies provided by the Virginia State Library, Richmond).

25. Banister, "Of the Natives," 385 (beads). Indians were also particular about the color of cloth and the size of hoes. See Byrd to Perry and Lane, March 29, 1685, 1:30, and Byrd to Arthur North, June 5, 1685, 1:41 (cloth); Byrd to North[?], March 8, 1686, 1:57 (hoes), all in Tinling, *Byrd Correspondence*.

26. "A Narrative of De Soto's Expedition Based on the Diary of Rodrigo Ranjel . . . ," in Bourne, *De Soto Narratives*, 2:102, 104; Inca, *Florida*, 313, 315–16; Banister, "Of the Natives," 384; Lawson, *New Voyage*, 34, 196, 217 (baskets and mats). Ranjel, "Narrative," 2:99; Elvas, "True Relation," 1:66; Lawson, *New Voyage*, 217 (deer).

27. Inca, *Florida*, 329–30. See Theda Perdue, *Slavery and the Evolution of Cherokee Society, 1540–1866* (Knoxville: University of Tennessee Press, 1979), chap. 1.

28. Francis Le Jau to the Secretary, September 15, 1708, in *The Carolina Chronicle of Dr. Francis Le Jau, 1706–1717*, ed. Frank J. Klingberg, University of California Publications in History 53 (Berkeley: University of California Press, 1956), 41.

29. Cumming, *Discoveries of Lederer*, 30; Lawson, *New Voyage*, 30.

30. Lawson, *New Voyage*, 58. For midwinter rituals, see ibid., 34, 39, 42–45, 177. The continuity of subsistence routines is evident throughout Lawson's account.

31. Letter of Abraham Wood to John Richards, August 22, 1674, in Alvord and Bidgood, *First Explorations*, 215–17; Byrd to Thomas Grendon, April 29, 1684, in Tinling, *Byrd Correspondence*, 1:16; Byrd to ?, May 10, 1686, in Tinling, *Byrd Correspondence*, 59; Henrico County Record Book [Deeds and Wills], 1677–92, part 2, 388; Francis Nicholson to the Committee, January 26, 1690/91, CO 5/1306, 43 (Library of Congress transcripts); H. R. McIlwaine et al., eds., *Executive Journals of the Council of Colonial Virginia*, 6 vols. (Richmond: Virginia State Library, 1925–66), 1:254–55.

32. This transition period was even more complex than suggested here. Often the same observers who noted native control of the trade also included in their accounts glimpses of the future, when the tables would be turned. In dividing native from colonial hegemony for analytical purposes, then, to some degree I simplify the shift from one to the other. I am grateful to Neal Salisbury for pointing this out to me.

33. Cumming, *Discoveries of Lederer*, 41–42.

34. Byrd to Perry and Lane, February 2, 1685, in Tinling, *Byrd Correspondence*, 1:29; Byrd to North, June 5, 1685, ibid., 41; Byrd to North[?], March 8, 1686, ibid., 57. For the Indian middlemen, see James H. Merrell, "The Indians' New World: The Catawba Experience," *William and Mary Quarterly*, 3d ser., 41(1984): 551–52.

35. Lawson, *New Voyage*, 18, 210–11; Robert Beverley, *The History and Present State of Virginia* (1705), ed. Louis B. Wright (Chapel Hill: University of North Carolina Press, 1947), 182. I detail these efforts in "The Indians' New World," 550.

36. Lawson, *New Voyage*, 18, 184, 211–12, 240.

37. Banister, "Of the Natives," 382.

38. Lawson, *New Voyage*, 38.

39. Ibid., 107, 175.

40. For the cruder crafts, see Ernest Lewis, "The Sara Indians, 1540–1768: An Ethno-archaeological Study" (M.A. thesis, University of North Carolina, 1951), 310; Joffre L. Coe, *The Formative Cultures of the Carolina Piedmont*, Transactions of the American Philosophical Society, n.s. 54, part 5 (Philadelphia: American Philosophical Society, 1964), 49–50; Michael Trinkley and S. Homes Hogue, "The Wachesaw Landing Site: The Last Gasp of the Coastal Waccamaw Indians," *Southern Indian Studies* 31(1979): 11. In my larger work I also explore the cultural or psychological costs of this loss of craft skills, a loss more difficult to measure from the historical and archaeological record, though one no less important.

41. William Byrd (*Prose Works*) provides the best insight into the culture these men fashioned to survive the rigors of a physical and cultural wilderness. I deal more fully with the traders' acculturation in my study of the Catawbas, *The Indians' New World* (Chapel Hill: University of North Carolina Press, 1989).

42. The evidence for this shift can only be impressionistic. Lederer and some other early explorers did not conform to this timetable (see Alvord and Bidgood, *First Explorations*, passim). But William Byrd's letters from the 1680s suggest that the traders went out in early March and returned home in May. After 1700, on the other hand, traders were reported among the Indians at various times of the year. For pre-1700, see Byrd to Grendon, April 29, 1684, in Tinling, *Byrd Correspondence*, 1:16; Byrd to [Arthur North?], March 3, 1685[/86], ibid., 57; Byrd to Perry and Lane, March 3, 1685 [/86], ibid., 58; Byrd to [Addressee Unknown], May 10, 1686, ibid., 59; Byrd, "Land of Eden," in *Prose Works*, 400; Henrico County Record Book, no. 2, 1678–93 [Deeds, Wills, Settlements of Estates, etc.] (transcript of Henrico County Order Book, 1678–93), 74; Henrico County Record Book [Deeds and Wills], 1677–92, part 2, 487. For the years after 1700, see Lawson, *New Voyage*, 49–50, 60–61; Depositions of Robert Hix and others, enclosed in Edmund Jenings to Board of Trade, October 8, 1709, CO 5/1316, fol. 41 (Library of Congress transcripts, 189–93); Evans Journal, n.p.; "Copy of

Bond required of those authorized to trade with the Western Indians," and "Copy of form of passport given to traders with the Western Indians," in *Calendar of Virginia State Papers and Other Manuscripts, 1652–1781, Preserved in the Capitol at Richmond*, ed. William P. Palmer (Richmond, Va.: R. F. Walker, Superintendent of Public Printing, 1875), 155–56; Louis B. Wright and Marion Tinling, eds., *The Secret Diary of William Byrd of Westover, 1709–1712* (Richmond, Va.: Dietz Press, 1941), 447–48.

43. Lawson, *New Voyage*, 23.

44. Hugh Jones, *The Present State of Virginia, from Whence Is Inferred a Short View of Maryland and North Carolina*, ed. Richard L. Morton (Chapel Hill: University of North Carolina Press for the Virginia Historical Society, 1956), 57. For Indian standards of measurement, see Lawson, *New Voyage*, 203, 232–33; Stanley Pargellis, ed., "An Account of Indians in Virginia," *William and Mary Quarterly*, 3d ser., 16(1959): 231.

45. Lawson, *New Voyage*, 24, 50. For Lederer, see Cumming, *Discoveries of Lederer*, 26, 33.

46. David Crawley to the Lords Commissioners of Trade and Plantations, July 30, 1715, in W. Noel Sainsbury, comp., *Records in the British Public Record Office Relating to South Carolina, 1663–1782*, 36 vols., microfilm ed. (Columbia: South Carolina Archives Department, 1955), 6:110–11.

47. For South Carolina trade and the Yamasee War, see Verner W. Crane, *The Southern Frontier, 1670–1732* (1928; reprint New York: W. W. Norton, 1981), chaps. 5–7; Reid, *Better Kind of Hatchet*, chaps. 4–7; Wright, *Only Land They Knew*, 121–25.

48. Richard Haan has added to the abuses the ecological pressures generated by colonial settlement among the Yamasees. See Richard L. Haan, "The 'Trade Do's Not Flourish as Formerly': The Ecological Origins of the Yamasee War of 1715," *Ethnohistory* 28(1981): 341–58.

49. Le Jau to the Secretary, August 23, 1715, in Klingberg, *Carolina Chronicle*, 163; South Carolina Commons House Journals, May 8, 1715, in William Sumner Jenkins, comp., *The Records of the United States of America*, microfilm ed. (Washington, D.C., 1949), S.C. A.1b, reel 1, unit 4, 398–99.

50. Only one complaint from this region survives, and even it apparently was resolved without bloodshed. See William L. McDowell, Jr., ed., *Journals of the Commissioners of the Indian Trade, September 20, 1710–August 29, 1718* (Columbia, S.C.: State Commercial Printing Company, 1955), 33.

51. In my *Indians' New World* I deal in more depth with the complexities of the causal connections summarized here. Included in that greater complexity are the piedmont Indians' experiences as allies of the colonists during the Tuscarora War of 1711–13, experiences that, I believe, served to confirm the impressions of colonial society that these Indians had already gained from the traders.

52. See Crane, *Southern Frontier*, chaps. 1–3, 109–10, 132–33.

53. Lords Proprietors to the Govern[o]r and Councill att Ashley River in Carolina, March 7, 1680/81, in A. S. Salley, Jr., indexer, *Records in the British Public Record*

Office Relating to South Carolina, 1663–1684 (Atlanta, Ga.: Foote and Davies for the Historical Commission of South Carolina, 1928), 116, 118.

54. A. S. Salley, Jr., ed., *Journals of the Commons House of Assembly of South Carolina for the Two Sessions of 1698* (Columbia: State Company for the Historical Commission of South Carolina, 1914), 22. For the trade war, see Crane, *Southern Frontier*, 153–57.

55. For example, see the aspersions cast by William Byrd II below.

56. McIlwaine et al., *Executive Journals*, 3:405–6. Just who was among the Indians at the time and who was killed is unclear, though the fact that Indians discriminated against South Carolinians and in favor of Virginians seems clear from this reference and from those cited in note 57.

57. "Extracts of several letters from Carolina relating to the Indian Warr . . . ," in William L. Saunders, ed., *The Colonial Records of North Carolina*, 10 vols. (1886–90; reprint New York: AMS Press, 1968), 2:251. See also ibid., 252–53; McIlwaine et al., *Executive Journals*, 3:405–6; Robert Daniell and others to Spotswood, June 22, 1715, in Palmer, *Calendar of Virginia State Papers*, 181–82; "Memorial from Mr. Kettleby and several merchants trading to Carolina . . . ," in Saunders, *Colonial Records of North Carolina*, 2:201–2.

58. McIlwaine et al., *Executive Journals*, 3:411–12. For the shipments, see ibid., 402–4; Spotswood to the Lords Commissioners of Trade and Plantations, July 15, 1715, in R. A. Brock, ed., *The Official Letters of Alexander Spotswood, Lieutenant-Governor of the Colony of Virginia, 1710–1722*, Collections of the Virginia Historical Society, n.s. 1 and 2 (Richmond: Virginia Historical Society, 1882–85), 2:119–20.

59. Rev. William Tredwell Bull to the Secretary, August 16, 1715, in Society for the Propagation of the Gospel in Foreign Parts, manuscript A, XI, 58 (microfilm, Library of Congress). See also Le Jau to the Secretary, August 23, 1715, in Klingberg, *Carolina Chronicle*, 163–64; Boston *News-Letter*, July 11, 1715.

60. Le Jau to John Chamberlain[?], August 22, 1715, in Klingberg, *Carolina Chronicle*, 162. See also Memorial from Kettleby, in Saunders, *Colonial Records of North Carolina*, 2:201; Boston *News-Letter*, October 31, 1715.

61. Spotswood to Secretary Stanhope, October 24, 1715, in Brock, *Spotswood Letters*, 2:131. See also McIlwaine et al., *Executive Journals* 3:406, 412, 422, 447; "Passport to the Southern Indians to come to Virginia to treat for peace and commerce," in Palmer, *Calendar of Virginia State Papers*, 182.

62. McIlwaine et al., *Executive Journals*, 3:406, 412. See also ibid., 3:422.

63. Ibid., 3:422.

64. Commons House Agents to the Lords Commissioners of Trade and Plantations, December 5, 1716, PRO-SC, 6:265. Virginia's law, actually passed in 1714 on the eve of the Yamasee War, was based on the colony's painful experiences with illegal traders during the Tuscarora War. See W. Neil Franklin, ed., "An Act for the Better Regulation of the Indian Trade: Virginia, 1714," *Virginia Magazine of History and Biography* 72(1964): 141–51; McDowell, *Journals of the Commissioners of the Indian Trade*,

325–29. The best scholarly discussion of South Carolina's postwar reform efforts is in Reid, *Better Kind of Hatchet*, chaps. 8–12.

65. McDowell, *Journals of the Commissioners of the Indian Trade*, 95, 144, 156, 180, 211–12.

66. For the Congarees garrison and the northern trade factory, see ibid., passim. For the lowcountry trade, see South Carolina Upper House Journals, January 5, 1722, and November 28, 1733, Records of the States, S.C. A.1a, 1/1, 150, and 2/1, 668–69; Thomas Cooper and D. J. McCord, eds., *The Statutes at Large of South Carolina*, vol. 3 (Columbia, S.C.: A. S. Johnston, 1838), 332, 371–72; South Carolina Commons House Journals, September 14–15, 1733, Records of the States, S.C. A.1b, 4/1, 1127, 1129–30; *South-Carolina Gazette*, December 19, 1743.

67. South Carolina Commons House Journals, May 24, 1734, Records of the States, S.C. A.1b, 4/3, 186.

68. Public Treasurer's Accounts, December 9, 1725, Ledger A, 1726, fol. 57, South Carolina Department of Archives and History, Columbia; Evans to Governor James Glen, December 16, 1755, in *Documents Relating to Indian Affairs, 1754–1765*, ed. William L. McDowell, Jr. (Columbia: University of South Carolina Press for the South Carolina Department of Archives and History, 1970), 89; Evans to Governor William Henry Lyttelton, September 7, 1759, William Henry Lyttelton Papers, William L. Clements Library, Ann Arbor, Michigan. A John Evans also served in the Congarees trade factory. See McDowell, *Journals of the Commissioners of the Indian Trade*, 202, 320.

69. Samuel Cole Williams, ed., *Adair's History of the American Indians* (1930; reprint New York: Promontory Press, 1974), 369; South Carolina Council Journals, April 27, 1748, Records of the States, S.C. E.1p, 3/4, 233.

70. South Carolina Council Journals, July 25, 1744, ibid., 2/3, 427.

71. South Carolina Council Journals, May 6, 1760, ibid., 8/3, 120; Catawbas to Glen, October 15, 1754, *Indian Affairs Documents*, 14.

72. William Byrd, "History of the Dividing Line betwixt Virginia and North Carolina Run in the Year of Our Lord 1728," in Wright, *Prose Works*, 311.

73. "An Acco[un]t of Nathaniel Harrison's proceedings when he went out . . . to meet with the Cautaubau Indians . . . ," enclosed in Lieutenant Governor William Gooch to Board of Trade, September 21, 1727, CO 5/1321, 11 (Library of Congress transcripts, 13–14).

74. J. H. Easterby, ed., *The Journal of the Commons House of Assembly, November 10, 1736–June 7, 1739* (Columbia: Historical Commission of South Carolina, 1951), 488.

75. Byrd, "History," 308.

76. Byrd, "Land of Eden," 393.

The Three Lives of Keowee: Loss and Recovery in Eighteenth-Century Cherokee Villages

M. Thomas Hatley

The Cherokee farming town of Keowee was abandoned three times in the thirty years between 1750 and 1780. The earliest Keowee was emptied in the late 1740s at the climax of war between the Cherokees and the Creeks.[1] Soon again a thriving place, Keowee was abandoned a second time amid smallpox outbreaks, famine, and warfare with the colonies.[2] After the peace, the houses were rebuilt and fields replanted with borrowed seed corn.[3] The third reformation of the town was to be the last on the old site. Its inhabitants, fatigued and pressured by the rapidly moving white farmers' frontier to the east, slowly moved away.

On the eve of the Revolutionary War William Bartram turned away from the slow, muddy Savannah and rode north along the clearer river that shared the town's name. But upon arriving at Keowee he was disappointed to find only "several dwellings inhabited by white people concerned in the Indian trade." In the surrounding valley bottom the naturalist observed an emptiness made more disturbing by evidence of recent abandonment, a vacant mountain valley where "the vestiges of the ancient Indian dwellings are yet visible on the feet of the hills bordering and fronting on the vale, such as the posts or pillars of their habitations."[4]

The short history of Keowee tells more than the story of a single unlucky place. The residents of Keowee were not alone in either their suffering or in their determined will to survive the hardships of the eighteenth century. Other Cherokee towns also faced destruction and accomplished reconstructions of their own, and though some towns resisted final abandonment more successfully than Keowee, no Cherokee hamlet could offer its people sanctuary against hard times. Towns like Keowee survived through most of the eighteenth century as the homeplaces of Cherokee life, but by the middle years of the century village economies, settlement patterns, and demography were all undergoing rapid change. The experience of collective change, and the vital tribal resistance that shaped its course, was not confined to the villagers of Keowee, or even to the Cherokees as a whole, but was a historical experience to which indigenous folk across the southeastern region could also lay claim (see fig. 1).

'They Are Not Now Half": Village Population Decline

The central influence on the eighteenth-century Cherokee villages was a painful and prolonged population decline. The histories of towns such as Keowee encapsulate this demographic and economic theme. The places families walked away from in the depression of the 1930s—the piedmont of Georgia, the Texas panhandle or the sandhills of Nebraska—offered no scenes of rural decay more striking than Cherokee settlements hard hit by warfare or famine. William Bartram recognized the characteristic landscape of depression and out-migration around the Keowee ghost town. Other white contemporaries of the tribespeople were even better positioned than Bartram to understand the demographic riptide that had caught Keowee. Four traders, forty-year veterans of the mountain villages, testified in 1751 to the population disaster they had witnessed during their long residence in the towns. "The nation," they reported, "in our time has been greater than at present. We remember since there were six thousand stout men in it. They are not now half."[5]

The "true and exact account" of the Cherokee population submitted by missionary Francis Varnod to his English home office provides an early and exceptionally valuable corroboration of this impression.[6] Varnod's "account" reveals a damaged tribal population in 1721, with at least two significant symptoms of ill health. First of all, the Cherokee sex ratio was slightly skewed, with women outnumbering men in the towns by a small margin.[7]

Another, much more significant population feature was indicated by the Varnod figures: the proportion of children in the villages was much lower than would be expected in a normal population. If Varnod's Cherokee data are compared with contemporary figures for other major tribes of the same period and region, the mountain towns rank at the bottom in percentage of children.[8] The youthful population cohort of the 1720s matured into a proportionally small adult generation by the middle years of the century. Thus the dimin-

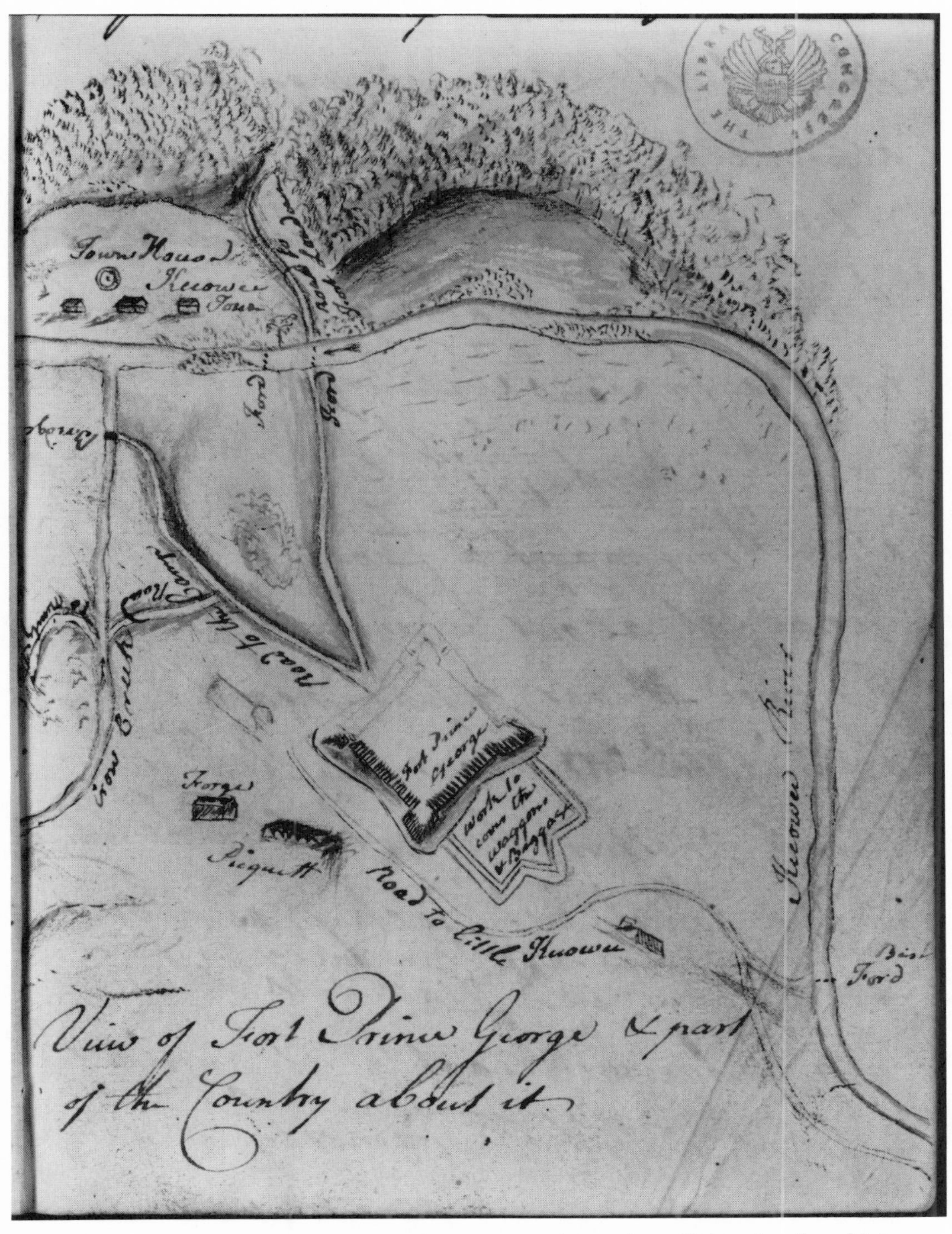

Figure 1 Keowee and Fort Prince George, from Christopher French's journal, 1761 (courtesy of the Library of Congress).

ished number of children lowered the resilience of the Cherokee population, and whatever upward rebound may have occurred from time to time was all too easily erased by war and disease. For this reason the Cherokee population showed few intervals of recovery and either declined or simply failed to grow through most of the century.[9]

Slow population recovery from seventeenth-century losses, compounded by mortality suffered during invasion by eighteenth-century colonial armies and pathogens, further undermined the Cherokee towns from within. Epidemics are remembered almost as clearly as war in the historical record. The smallpox epidemic among the tribe in 1738 may have killed half of the tribespeople; the disease recurred a generation later in 1759–60 during the so-called Cherokee War with the English colonists, and again in the early 1780s.[10] These outbreaks drew some of their intensity from a background of chronic sickness in the towns, which set the stage for damaging synergies of "infection with infection."[11] Precisely this kind of epidemiologic double-threat occurred in 1760 when a handful of western towns already suffering from smallpox were hard hit by "a violent disorder in their stomach and a flux." This outbreak changed the map of the western Cherokee settlements at one stroke; an informant reported "that in Eyoree they had lost about sixty men, women and children, and in Settiquoh, thirty-five, and Nottehh was almost depopulated by it, most that escaped the disorder there having removed from thence."[12]

The well-being of towns' economies was inseparable from the health of their residents. For example, malnutrition (prompted by warfare or crop failure) would have increased the severity and duration of cases of measles, a disease that did killing work among southeastern tribespeople.[13] Warfare affected many villages and in its wake left survivors and noncombatants weakened and susceptible to disease. The scorched-earth campaigns waged by the colonial whites during the Cherokee and Revolutionary wars killed far more people by creating starvation in the towns than by battlefield combat. A colonial officer remembered the scene near the Keowee garrison in 1761: "These creatures had been reduced to live for a considerable time upon old-Acorns, a food that we know will barely keep Hogs alive and their hunger was so pinching that some of them were detected in grabbling up the grains of Corn and beans after they were planted around the Fort."[14]

Though natural causes—drought or insect pests—are readily identifiable and have traditionally been blamed for famine, hunger, like sickness, has not only an environmental but also a social pathology. Damage to community safety nets, whether stored food supplies or medical care, could trigger starvation in the villages.[15] During the war with the colonies in 1759–61, basic town-based social services were taxed far beyond their limits. Dwellings and storehouses were burned. Even the promise of new crops in the field was destroyed without much effort. "It may not be amiss to observe," as a colonial military campaigner noted, "that ten acres of Indian corn are much sooner and easier pulled up and effectually destroyed than one of wheat or any British grain; as 'tis supposed, there are at least 1000 stalks of wheat for one of Indian corn in an acre of ground, and a stalke of this may be pulled up with very little trouble or stooping."[16]

The late-colonial military campaigns against the Cherokees cost much more than a "little trouble" for the colonists. Yet the overwhelming hardships were suffered by the tribespeople. Invasions, famine, and disease outbreaks, especially when they occurred in combination to create "crisis times" of short but immensely damaging duration (and of which the three years of the Cherokee War are the best example), disrupted the older round of village activities and crippled the effectiveness of the basic life support provided in the towns. By the end of the century, the obstacles of the time were remembered in the stories of town elders, but they were also revealed in a silent, but just as compelling, record of economic change.

"Little Farms": Depopulation and Mountain Farming

Farming constituted the fundamental underpinning of the "social services" on which the health of the villagers depended. In threatened villages such as Keowee, tribespeople improved their odds of survival not only by rebuilding houses but also by replanting fields in new ways. Cherokee towns, like farm communities the world over, were not only habitations but also designs for agricultural production. This double-sidedness meant that changes in the appearance or geography of the towns themselves also reflected underlying economic adjustments. The traditional shape of the Cherokee town was linear, snaking alongside rivers where moist and nitrogen-rich alluvial soils could be found. In 1761 the 120 houses of Nukassee were, to the appraising eye of an English captain, "straggling" in a thin line as they followed the bends of the Little Tennessee River, the houses themselves placed far enough apart that they could not be "commanded by a single muskett shott."[17]

When towns with a diffuse and extensive settlement pattern like that of Nukassee lost population, the cultivation of faraway fields became more difficult. Effective communal work in land clearing and tending (which was originally carried out mostly on larger fields away from the towns) required time, which was growing scarcer in the towns. Distant outfields were easy targets during war, and military engagements with colonial forces encouraged the abandonment of outfields as temporary measures. And this shift often became permanent. James Adair observed the change in planting locations, writing that "planting a great many fields of beans and pease, in distant places after the summer crops were over" had "contracted since the general peace."[18] As a result of these factors, the microgeography of Cherokee farming changed; fields moved nearer the villages and, consequently, closer to the household domains of Cherokee women.[19]

Nearly all of the new crops acquired by the Cherokees during the colonial period fit into the gardens tended by women. William Bartram labeled these gardens "little plantations" and only with great effort avoided trampling the "lots" as he rode into Cowee town in 1775.[20] James Adair stressed the household tie of "small farms" by noting that "every dwelling-house has a small field pretty close to it."[21] Annual crops new to the Appalachians, such as the sweet potato, were planted in these spots by the middle decades of the century. Domestic animals accepted by the Cherokees, notably hogs and chickens, were fed from garden sites. While confined to "convenient penns" during the growing season, hogs were fattened on the surplus of culled wild garden plants such as "long pursly and other wholesome weeds" gathered in the course of tending.[22] Thus selective crop and animal introductions, along with parallel changes in cultivation style, increased the productivity of indigenous Appalachian farming at a time of great need. The recasting of agroecology and field patterns partially bridged the farm labor gap and allowed the villages to better resist famine, disease, and warfare.

The progressive impact of population stress within the Cherokee farming economy could also be seen in the decline in the actual number of Cherokee towns. The Varnod list contained the names of fifty-two towns, but forty years later the number had dwindled to fewer than thirty-five.[23] However, the pace of this decline, 10 percent per decade over this interval, may well have been slower than the overall drop in Cherokee population. If this was in fact the case, not only did the number of towns fall, but the average size of the villages also decreased. Furthermore, because villages were the productive center of tribal agriculture, the diminished number of towns can be understood as a proxy agricultural statistic—and a negative one. The loss of each town entailed the loss of the prior investment made over many years in clearing fields and building storehouses. Less concrete but just as important was the alienation of environmental information, hard won on some sites through generations of experiment, of individual fields, microclimates, and soils, knowledge crucial to farming success.

The Cherokees had an affection for individual places and townsites that cannot be evoked by statistics and that was based on just such close observation. The repeated recolonization of the Keowee townsite reflected this continuing identification and understanding of local landscapes. The meanings of many Cherokee town names recall landscape familiarity that was threatened in the eighteenth century. Kunstutsiyi meant "sassafras place," Kulsetsiyi identified "honey-locust place," and Itseyi meant "new green place."[24] Rebuilding towns like Keowee or the neighboring village of Seneca after forced abandonment seems in retrospect to have been a poor piece of strategy, since other pullbacks often followed.[25] However, there was an economic wisdom in returning to the favorable locations and easily reopened fields of the old towns. For towns suffering severe casualties, the labor saved by not creating a new town from scratch was a persuasive reason to risk staying with old sites.

While the option of rebuilding was favored at certain towns, it was clearly not always possible. Although there seems to have been an abundance of room in a depopulated countryside, the dynamics of mid-eighteenth century settlement patterns sometimes meant that just the opposite was true. For example, during the 1760s some towns had begun to occupy distinctly unproductive sites, not accommodating to farming, along higher-elevation river valleys. For instance, a soldier-diarist of the Cherokee War judged one such settlement, the town of Allijoy, "but a poor place standing upon a narrow strip of Land under high hills" where fields were restricted to "deep narrow bottom, surrounded by very high mountains."[26] Towns such as Allijoy may have offered refuge from the brunt of conflict in more exposed parts of Cherokee territory, but such safety was bought at an economic cost.

The dark shading of the picture presented of Allijoy and other eighteenth-century Cherokee townscapes foreshadowed hard times to come. The occupation of marginal village sites was a first step toward the eventual breakup of tribal towns late in the century and the transformation of the Cherokee territory into a land of more or less isolated farmsteads, somewhat like those of white farmers.[27] Yet until the 1780s the Cherokees seem to have determinedly remained villagers. Against the corrosive population stress that taxed Cherokee farming in various ways and the recurrent persecution by the colonists that took a toll in the lives of Keowee and Allijoy, the Cherokees survived by adapting their farming to the hard circumstances of the century. However, the Cherokee economy was too complex for a complete solution to be found solely in the reform of farming.

"Buying as We Do": Crops as Commodities in Two Marketplaces

During the late colonial period, village subsistence crops were at times also commodities for exchange. Commerce between the Cherokees and the colonists involved far more than buying and selling such "consumer goods" as cloth. The most basic elements of village nutrition, such as corn, also emerged as trade items. The role of crops as both village foods and commodities revealed some of the stresses affecting production and exchange in the villages, as well as an accommodation made by villagers to their changing subsistence situation.

During the worst years for the Cherokees, entire regions failed to achieve a proper harvest, and these oscillations were made more erratic by the tribe's decline in population—and hence in available labor. Natural enemies of crops—insect outbreaks and frosts—worked along with social disruptions to exaggerate the normal swing of corn supplies between plenty and scarcity.[28] On the one hand, abundance was liberally documented by colonial invaders in the villages, who paused with torch in hand to comment on the sophistication of the tribe's farming: "The neatness of these towns and their knowledge of agriculture would surprize you," wrote one correspondent, "they abounded in every comfort of life, and may curse the day we came among them."[29]

Further causes of stress lay outside the village boundaries and were related to regional trends affecting other tribal economies in the Southeast. The declining circulation of tribal foods in a damaged network of intertribal trade also affected the subsistence base of the tribe. Corn, along with other commodities, had been an element in a precontact, intertribal trading system that had helped compensate for local insufficiencies.[30] The breakdown of this trade owing to the political disruptions of the period progressively heightened the problems the villages faced in continuing to achieve a reliable food supply.

The midcentury scarcity of salt—another vital element of nutrition and one for which the tribespeople had been largely dependent upon trade—suggests the former importance of indigenous commerce and the consequences of its disruption, already in full swing at the beginning of the eighteenth century. Highly valued by the tribe and unavailable in the Cherokee mountains, salt had been acquired by the tribe through indigenous supply lines stretching from the limestone country to the west and north.[31] The widespread use by the middle of the eighteenth century of an ersatz salt, made from the ashes of plants and consequently poor in sodium, suggests the disruption of the salt trade. As a consequence of the virtual interdiction of salt trading, the health of the villagers was unavoidably affected for the worse.[32] And the villages became more and more tied to bargaining with colonists for salt.

The changing pattern of corn exchange is better documented than the trade involving salt and is no less suggestive of basic changes in subsistence possibilities for the tribe. With good harvests the Cherokees supplied corn to their neighbors, whether Native American or white. The reply of Connecortee of Chota, a principal Overhill liaison with the English, to a request for corn to feed South Carolina's military construction crews in 1756 throws light on the traditional conduct of transactions for a critical food:

> 'Tis true it is very hungry times here but what little we have we will share it with them and when there is a Want we will all want together, 'tis true it is very hungry Times and believe we shall be all very poor but in the Fall of the Year we shall recover our Flesh and grow fatt again. We get nothing here but what we

buy from one another and what Cloaths we buy from Mr. Elliott. It is as if it was lent us for we are obliged to give it away again for corn. We have but little amongst us and your people may also have a part of what there is for buying as we do, one from another.[33]

Connecortee's message contains the phrases of reciprocity—"we will all want together"—that were essential to the traditional conduct of Cherokee trade. This obligation, stated several times in the passage, translates roughly into the following: because we share corn as a matter of courtesy and necessity among ourselves, we shall do the same for you. The willingness to participate in formalized sharing, perhaps derived from past scarcities of vital foods, provided an ethical motivation for the cycling and redistribution of corn and other elements essential to the stability of traditional Cherokee subsistence. However, hard and even hostile bargaining over price had, at least by the middle of the century, become part of Cherokee negotiations concerning the sale of corn. In a letter to Charlestown, the commander of the English garrison at Fort Loudoun apologized for the high price he was forced to pay to the Cherokees for "ten Cannoes" of corn and laid the blame squarely on the villagers: "I perceive that they begin to grow very saving of their corn on account of the great Famine that was amongst them last year. Indeed I must say that there was a very wrong method to purchase their corn, too much salt was given to the Indians for it, by which means they were soon supplied with salt and immediately ceased to bring any more corn."[34] During the siege of the Overhills fort, the Cherokees were still selling corn to their near-hostages, but for a price so high that the garrison managed to meet the asking price only by "almost stripping themselves (both men and women), to make one joint public stock."[35]

"The Wenches, as Usual, Brought Corn": Cultural Restraints in Trading

Women played a dominant role not only in growing corn but also in selling it. The role of indigenous women in supplying colonial military garrisons was well documented because it was a cause of unease on the colonial Cherokee War home front, since sexual and commercial traffic were presumed to go together as partners in subversion. "The wenches, as usual, brought corn," and other sentences to the same effect regularly inspired alarm among readers of the Charlestown newspaper.[36] However, Cherokee women, in spite of their often ambiguous role in political crises, clearly managed to avoid the market dependency into which "settlement tribes" and other crossroad-peoples were falling at midcentury. Among the Catawbas, the marketplace had usurped traditional tribal farming in providing food for the villages. "King Haigler," the tribe's spokesman to South Carolina, acknowledged this reliance on white farmstead-produced foods and accepted it as a benefit of peace with Charlestown: "So long shall we live in peace with all the Indians and Brothers with the white People, we can go where we will to purchase corn or hunt for there is nothing to hurt us but sickness."[37]

Traditional village products such as herbs for medicines and dyes were collected mainly by Cherokee women and traded even more extensively than corn. Sales of medicinal herbs, like corn trading, must be understood in the context of trading and gift giving within the village as well as colonial marketplace economies. Gathering plants remained largely women's (and perhaps children's) work, as it traditionally had been, but Cherokee women also embraced the economic opportunities extended by an enthusiastic colonial demand for materia medica.

By the 1760s the Cherokees were major southeastern suppliers of three plants, each adapted to Appalachian hill habitats: Indian pink, ginseng, and Virginia snakeroot.[38] The dried roots of these plants had become high-value commodities in part because of the changing disease environment of the colonies. Parasites newly imported to the Southeast created a new demand for Indian pinkroot in ports like Charlestown, where during the 1760s the "worm fevers" remedied by the herb were rife among children.[39] Not only was the herb consumption of the "lowcountry" of South Carolina and Georgia substantial, but merchants shipped a large volume of the dried plants from Charlestown to England. Fourteen barrels of dried Virginia snakeroot left the dock in 1764 alone.[40]

Such a large quantity of herb export provides a crude index to the considerable time required in the mountain villages of the Cherokees to gather and dry the plants. Collecting had to take place at many kinds of sites, and at only certain seasons. As a result, some villagers may have been tempted to neglect the farming tasks that overlapped with the collection seasons of the herbs. This situation had occurred earlier around Montreal, where the local tribespeople were "so taken up with the trade that they could not be engaged for any other business."[41] However, the Cherokees seem to have managed to avoid this problem, even while they fully participated in the new enterprise.

The limits enforced by the villagers themselves to avoid labor conflict were reinforced by the biological response of the plants themselves. As John Drayton reported from South Carolina late in the century: "Ginseng has been so much sought after by the Cherokee Indians that it is by no means so plentiful as it used to be in this state."[42] Though the villagers could scarcely be blamed for the declining statewide ginseng population late in the century, local scarcities obviously did occur and limited profitable collection. Such scarcity may partially explain the high prices (at least relative to the colonial market price) paid for ginseng by neighboring tribal trade partners of the Cherokees. For instance, one ginseng root was bringing three buckskins (20 or 30 percent of the price of a gun in the colonial trade) in the Lower Creek towns by 1770.[43]

However, the commercial logic of intercolonial or intertribal trade did not completely govern the exchange of corn or herb stocks. In both cases, cultural restraints implicit in Cherokee patterns of governance and gender relationships also dampened the scale of participation. For instance, a certain degree of control over gathering ginseng was exercised by priestly authorities and through the less formal almanac wisdom of the townspeople. By collecting for commercial purposes herbs that had ritual uses among the tribe, village women likely found themselves in conflict with the priestly elders, with whom they also clashed in other domains (for instance, in farming activities when male "rainmakers" accused the female farmers of conspiring to rob them of their "fee" for a good summer's rainfall). However much the village women may have chafed at restrictions and admonitions from the "old cunning prophets" about herb collecting, they listened with at least some measure of respect.[44] Perhaps a kind of village compromise was made, as was often the case in consensual Cherokee politics.

Whatever the exact terms of this compromise, the collection of ginseng for sale to white merchants continued long after the colonial period and coexisted with a noncommercial, ritual collection practiced by Cherokee shamans. Working in the 1880s, James Mooney recorded the persistence of sacred formulas employed in digging the "little man" (as ginseng was called). The ceremony began with the shaman asking forgiveness from the mountainside where he was about to dig the root of the plant. Only after this invocation could the shaman put his hoe into the "flesh" of the mountain, the "great man."[45] Market collectors, if they bothered with this formality at all, must have dramatically shortened it in order to quickly fill the barrels on the Charlestown docks; however, at least a few and perhaps many Cherokees long preserved a degree of restraint in the commercial pursuit of the "little man."

The Deerskin Trade as a Damaging Village Cottage Industry

Another trading endeavor affected the village economy in a more extensive and less controlled fashion. Killing deer and preparing deerskins for trade are usually depicted as activities carried out on the hunting grounds and, consequently, the nearly exclusive handiwork of Native American men helped by female companions. While this may have been accurate in the earlier years of the trade, by the middle years of the century, many skin-preparation tasks—scraping, tanning or smoking the hides, and transporting the finished leather—had grown into cottage industries operating out of the villages. Both the diminished resident labor pool of the towns and the contraction (forced by competition with settlers for white-tailed deer) of hunting territories toward settled areas contributed to the intensification of trade-connected work in the towns. The large volume of deerskin leather shipped from Charlestown and other ports, of which a large fraction was of Cherokee origin, suggests the scale of village work required in producing the skins.[46]

Each of the tens of thousands of tanned skins sent to Charlestown represented an accumulation of village labor. The traditional brain-tanning process could take a week or more, and this, as well as many other tasks, was undertaken by "poor hunters and women."[47] The early years of the trade, when human "burdening" was still the rule, may have been the harshest for villagers, with women carrying more of the load even than "poor hunters." In his trip up the Savannah River, Mark Catesby witnessed the manner in which tribal "women serve instead of packhorses carrying the skins of deer which they kill, which by much practice they perform with incredible labor and patience. I have often travelled with them fifteen or twenty miles a day for many days successively, each woman carrying at least sixty and sometimes eighty weight at their back."[48] Horses offered a way of transforming this hard task, so they were quickly adopted by the tribe. Leather rapidly moved from human to horseback, and the Cherokees even became providers of packhorses to white traders for a time.

Cherokees continued to participate heavily in the deerskin trade up until the Revolutionary War. But as early as the 1760s there were periodic problems in this commerce that reflected the diminished labor resources of the villages. Maintaining a proper quality of skins shipped from the mountains had by then become a chronic concern for colonial merchants. The Directors of the Indian Trade, empowered in the wake of the Cherokee War to oversee the operation of the newly regulated trade, complained in 1763 of "the enormous foul Dressing of Deer Skins by the Indians, and their still leaving the same incumbered with Hoofs and Snouts, so detrimental to the Leather."[49]

Processing large quantities of skins grew increasingly difficult with fewer persons, and tribal control of the carrying trade had ended before midcentury. Given these facts and the escalating strain of processing skins, it was not surprising that the Cherokees, especially village women, never (as far as records show) protested the proposal of a former trader who had planned in the late 1750s to build a "tanyard and shoe and harness factory" near one of their towns.[50] What became of this trader and his entrepreneurial ambitions apparently went unreported. However, within two decades the demand for deerskins had started to decline, along with the incentive of tribespeople and white merchants alike to trade. Many Cherokees, especially the female farmers of the diminished towns, must have welcomed the slipping away of the deerskin trade and the intensive labor obligations it had created for them.

Rum, Red Stroudwater, Guns, and Eagles: The Impact of Gender-Related Trading

The deerskin trade absorbed the efforts of many Cherokee men and overshadowed the effects of other commercial entanglements with the colonies. However, there was also a less well known form of deerskin trading within the villages, where deerskins and leather were used as a kind of currency. The purchases made in the villages were different from the items bought at trading houses. Five hundred dressed skins, paid to the family of a murder victim, was the prevailing cost of absolution from the crime; two pounds of leather in one case excused the killer of a village dog.[51] James Adair remembered a village's pooling contributions amounting to two hundred pounds of leather to pay for killing a "large eagle" to be used in village rituals.[52] Headmen quoted Josiah Wedgwood's agent a very steep price of "five-hundred weight of leather for every ton" of "ayoree white earth" from a pit near Cowee.[53] John Stuart described the way such prices were reckoned. "If one man kills another's horse, breaks his gun, or destroys anything belonging to him, by accident or intentionally when in liquor; the value in deerskins is ascertained before the Beloved Man; and if the aggressor has not the quantity of leather ready he either collects it amongst his relations or goes into the woods to hunt for it."[54]

The cost of village-purchased goods and of services such as crime-related compensation set by headmen was high relative to the usual cost of items in the colonial trade. For instance, a gun listed for only fourteen pounds of leather just after the Cherokee War.[55] The cost of the trade gun (though often presumed to be ultimate in high-technology trade items most valuable to the tribe) seems modest and even undervalued next to prices paid for eagles, ginseng roots, or buying off revenge in the villages.

In the village-centered commerce, as well as in the better-known trade with whites, men were the primary sellers and purchasers of goods. Consequently the various goods and services obtained in these transactions for the most part reflected the values and preferences of Cherokee men. For Cherokee warriors, rifles, eagle wings, horses, red cloth, and eventually even rum were essential to the proper conduct of Cherokee manhood. Of course women also benefited from the colonial trade by acquiring iron hoes, fabric scraps for dying, dresses, and even sidesaddles. But it is arguable that the male-to-male conduct of most transactions made it impossible for indigenous women to benefit as much as did Cherokee and white men.[56]

While women did not share equally from the acquisition of trade goods, they also paid a disproportionate price by laboring to produce the finished deer leather, and in this way they subsidized a male-dominated commerce. Because deerskin work absorbed the efforts of towns already taxed by depopulation, the volume of the trade represented a direct and increasing expenditure of the village labor and a distraction from basic subsistence tasks. Another, less direct cost was also entailed in the long absences of men from the villages while hunting. The work of women was therefore increased in several ways by both intra- and extravillage trading by men.

The tension between the economic activities of Cherokee men and women is highlighted in the different trading modes utilized by Cherokee women selling corn and by Cherokee men selling deerskins. Whether sold inside or outside the village boundaries, deerskins were less raw trade material than, in a sense, indigenous commercial paper freely traded at whatever price the market would bear. On the other hand, corn was bought and sold much more conservatively. In fact, corn was often given away in the villages in accordance with traditional subsistence ways. When corn was traded to whites, however, the price asked was often very high. High prices for Cherokee corn sold to village outsiders and respect for reciprocal trading inside the towns were consistent elements of domestic economic adaptation. Corn prices were used defensively, to shield essential foods from being drawn into the colonial marketplace. In this way important routines of cooperation in the distribution of these essential commodities within the village agricultural economy were preserved.

The apparent distinction in trading strategy between the Cherokee sexes may also reflect lessons women learned from their first hand observations of the problems in the villages induced by the deerskin trade. Even though there were more limited trading opportunities for corn than for deerskins outside the villages, Cherokee women seem to have also been more reticent than men about selling their harvest. As the principal sellers (or givers) of corn, Cherokee women played a significant role in avoiding the close and damaging market link forged by Cherokee men in their involvement with the colonial deerskin trade. When they chose to do so they traded corn, but on their own terms and in accordance with their own interest in maintaining the female dominance of the Cherokee domestic subsistence economy. Significantly, Cherokee women were willing to become active participants in colonial commerce in other arenas than core farming activities, for example, in collecting and selling herbs. But the trading conducted by Cherokee men was more overtly commercial, much more extensive, and more closely attuned to the pattern of personal political leadership that increasingly marked the public arena of intercultural relations. An unmistakably Cherokee and distinctly male pattern of consumption, funded by deerskin production and trade, increasingly became a route to personal prestige and power for some Cherokee men. In this light the existence of two gender-related trading patterns among the tribe seems to reflect both the distinctive experiences and the collective ambitions of the Cherokee sexes.

"Across the Open Plain": Brittleness in the Village Forest Economy

Other economic conflicts developed as a result of the separate evolution of apparently unconnected village-based economic pursuits. The advent of the horse in the mountain towns early in the century, for example, immediately conflicted with the farming activities of women. Those who had acquired European animals, mainly men but sometimes women, were forced to "tether the horses with tough young bark-ropes, and confine the swine to a convenient penn, from the time the provisions are planted, till they are gathered in." Owners who balked at these restraints were likely to find the women "as good as their word, by striking a tomohawk into the horse."[57] Yet men seem to have won out, and horses became a fixture of villages. By the 1760s, James Adair could write that "almost everyone hath horses, from two to a dozen."[58]

Other land-based activities combined with widespread horse husbandry to profoundly change the outlying village landscape. For example, conflict with white settlers over access to good land and village labor scarcity had by the 1760s caused the Cherokee hunters to pull back their hunting activities into the hills of the tribal heartland. Since fire was the traditional tool the Cherokees used to enhance hunting success, the pullback translated into more frequent low-intensity burning by deer hunters. As a result of the effects of increased fire and grazing, which overrode the natural tendency of the Appalachians toward forest, the Cherokee country progressively took on a more open and pastoral look.[59]

The changed landscape surrounding the Cherokee villages presented a problem for continuing ancient and important subsistence activities of female villagers. The progressive disappearance of easily accessible forests near villages meant new difficulties in collecting the nuts, fruits, and herbs that were a familiar part of Cherokee subsistence. The quality and reliability of forest gathering, in many respects a kind of quasi-agriculture, had been enhanced over generations by selecting and protecting valuable shrubs and trees.[60] During the early eighteenth century, collecting nuts and processing them into oil still complemented village diets of corn, beans, and sweet potatoes. William Bartram was impressed during his visit to the tribe by the "incredible amount" of hickory nuts he saw gathered and converted to oil by village women.[61]

Over centuries village gathering had evolved a flexible and opportunistic style designed to take advantage of temperate-forest phenomena even less predictable than annual nut crops. For example, passenger-pigeon flocks arrived in the Tennessee River valley at irregular intervals. Returning to habitual roosts, the flocks hovered like a "biological storm" in the forest while taking advantage of the same surplus nutfall the tribespeople sought.[62] The sudden advent of the flocks caused the Cherokees to switch quickly from nut to pigeon collection, after which the birds themselves were processed into storable fat. "The pigeons," Mark Catesby wrote, "afford them some years great plenty of oyl which they preserve for winter use . . . with it they also supply the want of fat in wild Turkeys; which in some Winters become very lean of being deprived of their food by the numerous flights of the migratory pigeons devouring the acorns and other mast."[63]

Though gathering was not as labor-intensive as farming, its success was also affected by population decline. The ability to be in the right place at the right time to take advantage of a fleeting appearance of nuts, pigeons, or herbs depended upon a latitude of time for work. Maintaining this flexibility—whether in fields or in forests—was increasingly difficult as both labor and time became scarcer in the villages. With the transformation of the semicultivated Cherokee countryside into a quite different land in the last quarter of the eighteenth century, the villages found themselves to a degree cut off from an old and formerly dependable source of sustenance.[64]

The new appearance of the "Cherokee country" was due largely to tensions stemming from activities—hunting and horse keeping—dominated by Cherokee men. William Bartram observed that while men were hunting away from the villages, "the whole care of the house falls on the women, who are then obliged to undergo a good deal of labor, such as cutting and bringing home the winter's wood, which they toat on their back or head a great distance, especially those of the ancient large towns, where the commons or old fields extend some miles to the woodland."[65] For the farmer/villager (who was in all likelihood a woman) changes in the heartland often meant longer and less profitable workdays.

One legacy of the intercultural conflicts of the previous century and a half was the vegetational instability of the grassy parklands, where European plants, assisted by fire and other disturbances, had colonized the habitats of native species. This botanical invasion mirrored the social realities in the villages; young forests and "old fields" no longer effectively concealed approaches to the towns. Revolutionary-era militia, mimicking the invasion of the plants, seized upon the new open surroundings of some Cherokee villages as easy avenues for horseback attack. South Carolinian Andrew Pickens led such a raid in 1781; armed with specially smithed short swords, his men hacked to death the unarmed occupants of a village as they fled defenseless and on foot "across the open plain" newly fringing their town.[66]

Bittersweet Survival: "Greatest Prosperity in Their Way"

The name of the persistently resettled town of Keowee meant "mulberry grove place." Like many other Cherokee town names, the meaning of Keowee evoked more than local scenery; it concealed an oblique economic reference. Mulberry trees had been one of the forest species encouraged near the villages by the tribespeople as a source of food and fiber. In 1724 Mark Catesby returned to Charlestown from his trip up the Savannah River with "an Indian apron made of the bark of wild mulberry," quite possibly made by Cherokee women.[67] Their mastery of this traditional material and others was so admired by Edmond Atkin that he described the Cherokees as "the most ingenious Indians."[68] The Cherokee women of one town were themselves confident enough of their craft, and of the political and economic status it implied, to ask an early Carolina colonist to send to "that good Woman," Queen Anne, "a present from them viz a large carpet made of mulberry bark for herself to sit on and twelve small ones for her Counsellours."[69]

The possibility of profitably rechanneling the products of the useful mulberry tree did not escape diligent colonial development experts. The earl of Egmont, searching for a livelihood for the settlers in newly established Georgia, jotted this bit of intelligence in his journal: "The Chickasaws report they have a multitude of mulberry trees in their country, and if instructed to make silk, will bring great quantities."[70] In spite of the ambitions of the colonists, however, neither the Chickasaws nor their neighbors to the east, the Cherokees, proved to be easily "instructed." The inhabitants of "mulberry grove place" and other villages continued to carry on with adaptations of the old ways, making baskets of bark instead of silk cloth.

A kind of cultural self-instruction took place in the survival of this and other elements of village work. The most successful and visible economic adaptation to population loss, the "little farms," appeared in the villages themselves. Based on garden cultivation and the acquisition of crops and domestic animals new to the Appalachians, the improved manner of village farming added a crucial measure of crop productivity while overcoming the labor problems that stemmed from depopulation. In this way the Cherokees removed themselves from the breakdown encountered in the farming of neighboring groups such as the Catawbas. Even after the crisis time of the Cherokee War, the tribe was reported to have soon rebounded and to have temporarily seized the "greatest prosperity in their way" before the fighting of the Revolution took it away again. The "fowl houses," hog pens, potato storage pits, and corn houses destroyed during the Revolution were reconstructed and continued to contribute in large measure to the survival of the towns.[71]

In contrast to farming evolution, Cherokee hunting underwent an unprofitable involution. The tools of the hunter—especially fire—were forced back on the villages by diminished numbers of hunters, land cessions, and other factors. By the last quarter of the century, the Cherokee country and the opportunities it offered had been altered. Older subsistence pathways, particularly those related to the gathering carried out by women, were foreshortened. Even the mulberries probably disappeared with frequent burning, so that the village residents either walked farther to find them or did without. The herb and skin trade also added to the work of the increasingly shorthanded villages. These pressures were added to by the gender-based split in the conduct of trade inside and outside the towns. The skins of deer initially hunted by men were sold less cautiously than were the corn crops cultivated by women. By late in the century, the underlying distinction between successful agriculture and a troubled hunting economy had grown more definite; a deeper wedge had been driven into the gender-related economic pursuits of the villagers.

But villagers, male or female, remained Cherokees first of all. The casualties of this struggle in places like Keowee were not forgotten, and the history of this and other more successful Cherokee towns suggests the hardship overcome throughout the century. The Cherokees continued to rebuild their towns in the face of the military aggression and economic power of colonial society. Equally impressive was the way the Cherokees resisted threats from the outside while addressing critical problems within their towns. However, these conflicts did not subdue the voice of village consensus among the Cherokees. During the long eighteenth-century struggle, the Cherokees fought to avoid either political or economic colonization, an intention reflected in the famous words of Utsidsata, Corn Tassel, "We are a separate people!"[72]

Notes

1. Wilbur R. Jacobs, *Indians of the Southern Colonial Frontier: The Edmond Atkin Report and Plan of 1755* (Columbia: University of South Carolina Press, 1954), 53; James Mooney, "Myths of the Cherokees," in *Nineteenth Annual Report of the Bureau of American Ethnology for the Years 1897–98*, part 1 (Washington, D.C.: Government Printing Office, 1900), 525.

2. Lud. Grant to James Glen, August 20, 1755, in *Documents Relating to Indian Affairs, Colonial Records of South Carolina, 1754–1765*, ed. William L. McDowell, Jr., ser. 2, vol. 3 (Columbia: University of South Carolina Press, 1958), 74; Alex Miln to Governor Lyttelton, February 24, 1760, in *Documents Relating to Indian Affairs*, 3:498.

3. As the winter of 1761 came on, the Keowee town leader Tistoe returned with "200 Indians to resettle there"; *South Carolina Gazette*, June 20–27, November 7–14, 1761. In 1767 the settlement on the west side of the Keowee River was already called "Old Keowee." After the Revolution the former town residents may have regrouped north of the former Fort Prince George. See Betty A. Smith, "Distribution of Eighteenth-Century Cherokee Settlements," in *The Cherokee Indian Nation: A Troubled History*, ed. Duane H. King (Knoxville: University of Tennessee Press, 1979), 46–60.

4. William Bartram, *Travels of William Bartram*, ed. Mark Van Doren (1791; reprint, New York: Dover Publications, 1955), 270–71.

5. Memorial of Robert Bunning and Others, November 22, 1751, *Documents Relating to Indian Affairs, May 21, 1750–August 7, 1754*, ed. William L. McDowell, Jr., ser. 2, vol. 2 (Columbia: University of South Carolina Press, 1970), 148.

6. The original population estimate was included in a letter from Francis Varnod to the secretary, Society for the Propagation of the Gospel in Foreign Parts, 1 April 1723,

Letters from the Carolinas, Letter Book 18, doc. 173 (microfilm copy in Western Carolina University Library). This document was reprinted in Berthold Fernow, *The Ohio Valley in Colonial Days* (Albany: J. Munsell's Sons, 1890), 273–74.

7. The sex ratio for the Varnod figures is 97 men per 100 women; compare with modern Amerindian populations, which are reported to have an average sex ratio of 108 men to 100 women among all censused groups of Panama and the United States. F. Salzano writes further that the "excess of males is expected in populations with a low average age"; this observation suggests that the sex ratio reported by Varnod, dominated by women, may have been consistent with a relatively "old" early eighteenth-century Cherokee population. See Francisco M. Salzano, "Genetic Aspects of the Demography of American Indians and Eskimos," in *The Structure of Human Populations*, ed. G. A. Harrison and A. J. Boyce (Oxford: Clarendon Press, 1972), 238–39; Ludwik Krzywicki, *Primitive Society and Its Vital Statistics* (London: Macmillan, 1934), 232–34. Eighteenth-century observers commented on the longevity of Cherokee women as opposed to tribal men. See Samuel Cole Williams, ed., *Adair's History of the American Indians* (1930; reprint, New York: Promontory Press, 1974), 241; Samuel Cole Williams, ed., *Lieut. Henry Timberlake's Memoirs* (Johnson City, Tenn.: Watauga Press, 1927), 81.

8. Compare Krzywicki, *Primitive Society*, 253; Salzano, "Genetic Aspects," 238.

9. John Stuart to Board of Trade, April 19, 1764, in Great Britain, Public Record Office, Colonial Office Papers (hereafter cited as PRO, CO) 323/17/170 (microfilm copy in the Western Carolina University Library).

10. Peter H. Wood, "The Impact of Smallpox on the Native Population of the Eighteenth-Century South," *New York State Journal of Medicine* 87(January 1987): 30–36; Williams, *Adair's History*, 244; Alex. Miln to Governor Lyttelton, 24 February 1760, in *Documents Relating to Indian Affairs*, 3:498.

11. Ann G. Carmichael, "Infection and Hidden Hunger," in *Hunger and History: The Impact of Changing Food Production and Consumption Patterns on Society*, ed. R. I. Rotberg and T. K. Rabb (Cambridge: Cambridge University Press, 1983), 59.

12. *South Carolina Gazette*, September 6–13, October 18–26, 1760.

13. Carmichael, "Infection," 59.

14. Henry Laurens, "A Letter Signed Philolethes," March 2, 1763, in *The Papers of Henry Laurens*, vol. 3, ed. Philip M. Hamer and George C. Rogers, Jr. (Columbia: University of South Carolina Press, 1972), 286.

15. The connection between famine and disease has been reported by Western historians since Thucydides but is still highly controversial. See Carmichael, "Infection," 50–66; Carl E. Taylor, "Synergy among Mass Infections, Famines and Poverty," in Rotberg and Rabb, *Hunger and History*, 285–303; Roland Mousnier, *Peasant Uprisings in Seventeenth-Century France, Russia and China* (New York: Harper and Row, 1970), 305–19; Amartya K. Sen, *Poverty and Famines: An Essay on Entitlement and Deprivation* (New York: Oxford University Press 1981), 1–217.

16. Christopher Gadsden, *Some Observations of the Two Campaigns against the Cherokee Indians in 1760 and 1761 in a Second Letter from Philopatrios* (Charlestown:

Peter Timothy, 1761), 53 (Readex microprint edition in the Vanderbilt University Library).

17. Captain Christopher French, "An Account of the Towns in the Cherokee Country with Their Strengths and Distance," *Journal of Cherokee Studies* 2(Summer 1977): 297.

18. Williams, *Adair's History*, 94. Adair's explanation hinged more on village politics than on economics, though both factors were related.

19. Thomas Hatley, "Holding Their Ground: Cherokee Women and Their Agriculture" (paper delivered at Conference on the Appalachian Frontier, George Mason University, Harrisonburg, Virginia, March 1985); Diane Rothenberg, "Mothers of the Nation: Seneca Resistance to Quaker Intervention," in *Women and Colonization: Anthropological Perspectives*, ed. Mona Etienne and Eleanor Leacock (New York: Praeger, 1980), 78.

20. Bartram, *Travels*, 284.

21. Williams, *Adair's History*, 435.

22. Williams, *Adair's History*, 242.

23. Varnod, "True and Exact Account"; Ensign John Boggs, "A List of Towns in the Cherokee Nation," February 21, 1757, in *Documents Relating to Indian Affairs*, 3:412–13; French, "Account," 297–99. French lists twenty-five towns, Boggs thirty-four.

24. Mooney, "Myths," 517, 525.

25. Bartram, *Travels*, 269.

26. French, "Account," 297–98; The distinction made by traders between rich and poor towns may have related to agricultural production and population as well as to political or commercial standing. Anthony Dean to Governor Glen, April 13, 1752, in *Documents Relating to Indian Affairs*, 2:259–60.

27. Compare Richard Pillsbury, "The Europeanization of the Cherokee Settlement Landscape prior to Removal: A Georgia Case Study," *Geoscience and Man* 22(1983): 56–69.

28. During his visit Henry Timberlake was told of the recent "badness of crops." Williams, *Timberlake's Memoirs*, 67; also see Raven of Hiawassie to Glen, June 5, 1748, South Carolina Council Journal, book 15, 364 (microfilm in South Carolina Department of Archives and History); Reply of James Beamer to Governor Glen in "Proceedings of the Council concerning Indian Affairs," July 6, 1753, in *Documents Relating to Indian Affairs*, 1:447; Raymond Demere to Governor Lyttelton, July 28, 1756, in *Documents Relating to Indian Affairs*, 3:150; John Chevillette to Governor Lyttelton, March 1, 1757, in *Documents Relating to Indian Affairs*, 3:344; Captain Rayd. Demere to Governor Lyttelton, January 12, 1757, in *Documents Relating to Indian Affairs*, 3:313.

29. *South Carolina Gazette*, October 26, 1760.

30. Compare Neal Salisbury, *Manitou and Providence* (New York: Oxford University Press, 1982), 30, 145; William Cronon, *Changes in the Land* (New York: Hill and Wang, 1983), 92–97.

31. Isham Clayton to Captain Rayd. Demere, 7 July 1756, in *Documents Relating to Indian Affairs*, 3:140. Saline and sodic soil licks as well as mineral springs are widely distributed through areas underlain by sedimentary rock and are largely missing from the Appalachian and Piedmont geologic provinces. Robert L. Jones and Harold L. Hanson, *Mineral Licks, Geophagy and the Biogeochemistry of North American Ungulates* (Ames: Iowa State University Press, 1985), 134–35. For a superb account of precontact salt manufacture and trade, see Ian W. Brown, *Salt and the Eastern North American Indian* (Cambridge: Peabody Museum, Harvard University, 1980).

32. Williams, *Adair's History*, 122; The physiology of higher plants works to exclude rather than to accumulate sodium, and except for certain salt-marsh grasses and herbs, these plants would have been poor sources of this particular human nutrient.

33. Connecortee to Governor Glen, March 20, 1756, in *Documents Relating to Indian Affairs*, 3:108–9.

34. Captain Rayd. Demere to Governor Lyttelton, October 28, 1756, in *Documents Relating to Indian Affairs*, 3:232; John Chevillette to Governor Lyttelton, March 1, 1757, 3:344.

35. *South Carolina Gazette*, August 9–13, 1760.

36. *South Carolina Gazette*, September 6–13, 1760.

37. The Catawba King to Governor Glen, March 11, 1753, in *Documents Relating to Indian Affairs*, 1:370–71; Williams, *Adair's History*, 234.

38. In the colonial materia medica Virginia snakeroot (*Aristolochia serpentaria* L.) was a diaphoretic (and was tried as a plague cure in London), ginseng (*Panax quinquefolium* L.) was a tonic, and Indian pink (*Spigelia marlandica* L.) was a vermifuge. See Benjamin Barton, *Collections for an Essay towards a Materia Medica of the United States* (Philadelphia: Edward Earle, 1810), 1:51–52; and Jacob Bigelow, *American Medical Botany* (Boston: Cummings and Hilliard, 1818), 1:6–7. The Cherokees used ginseng in their villages on "religious occasions." Williams, *Adair's History*, 388–89. For plague reference, see *London Magazine* 14(1745):568.

39. Early Carolina physician John Milligan speculated on the origin of these parasite infections: "Worm fevers are very frequent and common to all ages, though children of all ages suffer most . . . the sweet potato, Indian corn or maize and pompion, all much used in diet, seem to have a larger share of the eggs of these mischievous insects than the rest of the farinaceous or leguminous kind." John Milligan, "Description of South Carolina," in *Historical Collections of South Carolina*, ed. B. R. Carroll (New York: Harper, 1838), 2:498.

40. Joseph Gayle, "The Nature and Volume of Exports from Charlestown, 1724–1774," *Proceedings of the South Carolina Historical Association* 4(1937): 32.

41. Quoted in Bigelow, *American Medical Botany*, 2:89–90.

42. John Drayton, *The Carolinian Florist of Governor John Drayton*, ed. Margaret B. Meriwether (manuscript, 1807; Columbia: South Caroliniana Library, 1943), 109.

43. William Bartram, "Observations on the Creek and Cherokee Indians," *Transactions of the American Ethnological Society* 3(1853): 47; Williams, *Adair's History*, 388.

44. Williams, *Adair's History,* 89–91; Alexander Longue, "A Small Postscript on the Ways and Manners of the Indians Called Cherokees," ed. David H. Corkran, *Southern Indian Studies* 21(October 1969): 1–16.

45. Mooney, "Myths," 339; Jack F. Kilpatrick and Anna G. Kilpatrick, "Cherokee Rituals Pertaining to Medicinal Roots," *Southern Indian Studies* 16(October 1964): 24–25.

46. When the Cherokee War closed the trade paths to the Cherokees, deerskin export volumes also fell substantially. See John Stuart to Board of Trade, April 19, 1764, PRO, CO 323/17/240 (microfilm copy in the Western Carolina University Library); Verner Crane, *The Southern Frontier, 1670–1732* (1928; reprint New York: Norton, 1981), 327–31; R. Nicholas Olsberg and Helen Craig Canon, *Duties on Trade at Charleston, 1784–89,* South Carolina Microcopy 6 (Columbia: South Carolina Department of Archives and History, 1972). For an approximation of intravillage demand for shoes and other items, see Richard M. Gramley, "Deerskins and Hunting Territories: Competition for a Scarce Resource of the Northeastern Woodlands," *American Antiquity* 42(1977): 601–5.

47. Mark Catesby, *The Natural History of Carolina, Florida and the Bahama Islands* (London: Printed at the expense of the author, 1731–43), 1:ix.

48. Mark Catesby, "Of the Indians of Carolina and Florida," Royal Society, Decade I (no date, ca. 1730), no. 186 (microfilm copy in the Library of Congress).

49. The Directors to Edward Wilkinson, June 21, 1763, in *Documents Relating to Indian Affairs,* 3:586–87.

50. Fort Loudoun Association, "Contemporary Newspaper Accounts of the Massacre of the Fort Loudoun Garrison and the Plight of the Captive Survivors" (microfilm copy in Tennessee State Library and Archives), 16 (10) 58.

51. Stuart to Board of Trade, April 19, 1764, 257–58.

52. Williams, *Adair's History,* 32.

53. William L. Anderson, ed., "Cherokee Clay, from Duche to Wedgwood: The Journal of Thomas Griffiths, 1767–1768," *North Carolina Historical Review* 63(October 1986): 503, 507.

54. Stuart to Board of Trade, April 19, 1764, 257.

55. For example, "Table of Goods and Prices," July 9, 1762, in *Documents Relating to Indian Affairs,* 3:567.

56. Theda Perdue, "Southern Indians and the Cult of True Womanhood," in *Web of Southern Social Relations: Woman, Family and Education,* ed. Walter J. Fraser, Jr., R. Frank Saunders, Jr., and Jon L. Wakelyn (Athens: University of Georgia Press, 1985), 35–52.

57. Williams, *Adair's History,* 436.

58. Williams, *Adair's History,* 242.

59. See the discussion of fire in various southeastern habitats in E. V. Komarek, "Effects of Fire on Temperate Forests and Related Ecosystems," in *Fire and Ecosystems,* ed. T. T. Kozlowski and Nelson Ahlgren (New York: Academic Press, 1974), 261–65;

John G. W. DeBrahm, *Report of the General Survey in the Southern District of North America*, ed. Louis DeVorsey, Jr. (Columbia: University of South Carolina Press, 1971), 181. Compare Emily W. B. Russell, "Indian-Set Fires in the Forests of the Northeastern United States," *Ecology* 64 (January 1983): 78–88.

60. Hatley, "Holding Their Ground."

61. Bartram, "Observations," 32.

62. "Biological storm" was Aldo Leopold's phrase for the passage of pigeon flocks through deciduous forest.

63. Mark Catesby, "Of the Aborigines of North America," Royal Society, Decade I (no date, ca. 1730), no. 19, 8 (microfilm copy in the Library of Congress).

64. "Report of Brethren Steiner and von Schweinitz," in *Early Travels in the Tennessee Country: 1540–1800*, ed. Samuel Cole Williams (Johnson City, Tenn,: Watauga Press, 1928), 477–78, 490–91; French, "Account," 83, 98.

65. William Bartram, "Observations," 31.

66. Andrew Pickens to Lyman Draper, Draper Collection, 3XX, 141–49; F. W. Pickens to Charles H. Allen, 26 March 1848, in "Transcripts of Dr. John H. Logan," *Historical Collections of the Joseph Habersham Chapter of the Daughters of the American Revolution* 3(1910): 94–97.

67. Mark Catesby to Sir Hans Sloane, November 27, 1724, British Museum, Sloane Manuscripts 4047/290 (microfilm in Western Carolina University Library).

68. Jacobs, *Indians of the Southern Colonial Frontier*, 49.

69. Price Hughes to Duchess of Ormonde, October 13, 1715, quoted in Crane, *Southern Frontier*, 103 n. 101.

70. "Journal of the Earl of Egmont," in *Colonial Records of Georgia*, ed. Allen D. Candler (Atlanta: Franklin Printing and Publishing, 1904–16), 5:10.

71. Martin Schneider, "Report of His Journey to the Upper Cherokee Towns," in Williams, *Early Travels*, 257; Williams, *Adair's History*, 443.

72. Corn Tassel, "Cherokee Reply to the Commissioners of North Carolina and Virginia, 1777," trans. William Tatum, *Journal of Cherokee Studies* 1(Fall 1976): 129.

Part Three Symbols and Society

Introduction by M. Thomas Hatley

In his foreword to the 1873 edition of *Antiquities of the Southern Indians*, author Charles Colcock Jones thanked the friends who had helped him assemble a "cabinet" of the "arts and manufactures" of the southern tribespeople. Jones used the contents of this cabinet—"relics" and assorted old papers—to construct his history of Native Americans in the South.[1] In the following three chapters, many of the same objects that found their way into Jones's "cabinet"—plats and surveys of mounds, maps, honorific titles of address inscribed on treaty documents or recorded in council books—have again been taken down from the felt-lined shelf and, one by one, carefully reexamined. Understood not only as artifacts but also as evidence of perishable historical events, they provide a new perspective on interaction between people and peoples during a specific time in the colonial Southeast. Each reminds us of the complicated psychological scalings, from personal meetings to public rituals, that general labels such as "culture contact" can often conceal. The maps drawn in the clear hand of Chickasaw graphic style; the "earth-dwelling" mounds; and the gender-based grammar of formal diplomatic greeting between the French and the southern tribes all provide new glimpses of the elusive connection between symbol and life in the colonial Southeast.

What was understood between natives and colonists through exchanged information—whether for mutual gain or for the darker, one-sided goals of commercial or political advantage—was just as easily misunderstood or even manipulated. Patricia Galloway suggests that the French learned just enough about Choctaw kinship to be counterproductive in the very negotiations they had hoped to sway through alternating expressions of familiarity and power. Choosing to present themselves metaphorically as the fathers of the tribe, the French were received as such by the Choctaws, who "proceeded to treat them as their matrilineal society taught them they should: as kind, indulgent nonrelatives who had no authority over them." In Choctaw society the French would have commanded more real respect—or at least engendered less damaging confusion—by taking on the identity of true Choctaw authority figures, such as uncles on the mother's side.[2] Galloway's chapter suggests the importance of understanding not only what was said at councils, but also the unintended "non-verbal leakage"—the gestures and glances that accompany all human communication.[3] Further, Galloway reminds us that kinship and gender must be seen not only as structures of social organization, but also as critical variables in negotiation and other political affairs usually regarded as the domain of Euro-American-style male authority.

The French did not have a monopoly on asking bad questions or stopping short of the answers. However, questions were sometimes not asked or not answered for a reason. For instance, no evidence of the long residence of the southeastern tribes was more substantial than the "mounds" scattered across the region. It was convenient for whites interested in undermining native claims of ancient residence in the land to ask tribespeople two questions about them: Did you build them? Do you know who did? The answer was usually negative on both counts, and possibly for reasons of privacy, politeness, or hostility, the conversations seem to have been stopped by tribespeople at this point.

The conclusion for the first gentlemen-archaeologists of the nineteenth century was that the original mound-builders—and with them the secrets of the mounds themselves—were long dead and gone, and that the mound-builders had no genetic connection to the tribes that populated the young United States. This interpretation was truer to ideology than to archaeology. If the props could be knocked from under contemporary Native Americans' claims to ancient ancestry, their rights to an inheritance of land encompassing the southeastern interior could be weakened and their territories opened to legal "taking." The argument for an extinct American mound-building civilization also conveniently gave scholars, self-conscious about the supposed immaturity of North American culture, something to use in countering the claims to priority of European writers (who were beginning to brag on the great age and importance of Old World creations such as the pyramids). For the most part, the mound-builder hypothesis persisted in the popular mind until recently. Archaeologists have now decided that the mound-builders did not vanish but were the real ancestors of the indigenous southeastern peoples the colonists encountered.[4]

Just as the mound-builders live on in this sense, Vernon J. Knight suggests that mounds have survived into this century as vital metaphors of Amerindian culture. The reality was in the image—not in the piled dirt—and the image was with the people, a way of seeing that could be protected like a mental "ark of the covenant" and deployed wherever tribal people found themselves. Knight's contention that mound-making represents an unbroken southeastern cultural tradition enduring over at least one thousand years will be startling, especially for readers accustomed to thinking of eastern Amerindian cultures as scattered and cut off from their roots. Inquiring into the survival of the mound image in the Southeast suggests that these roots remain both strong and deep and provides a clue to the lasting cultural identity of the modern tribal minority. Knight's discussion of mound metaphors allows us to begin to bridge the ten thousand year gap separating "prehistoric" transcontinental movements of peoples, ideas, and artistic designs and the life of the colonial—and perhaps even the present-day—indigenous Southeast.[5]

The indigenous maps made in the colonial Southeast represent a vast summation of meetings and exchanges of information, both intertribal and intercolonial, between far-flung villages and the coastal enclaves of European power. Though some of the maps Gregory Waselkov discusses have a distinctive personal content or style (notably the sad disorientation in the autobiographical map drawn by the refugee called Lamhatty), most reflect sharply delineated lines of diplomacy, trade, and alliance. A few are drawn in a "realistic" style as charts of rivers and roads and must have been immediately understandable to the colonial authorities who requested them. Another more stylized group of maps, employing the indigenous circle-mapping style, must have seemed very foreign to the colonials, who augmented them with explanatory legends and notes. In fact, these maps were shipped home to England not only in diplomatic pouches but also in boxes of "curiosities" designed to strike royal patrons' fancy for American exotica.

More than simply cartographic illustrations of the political protocol of the indigenous Southeast, these diverse maps have an energy, an elegance of design, and a language of their own. The coexistence of both "realistic" and "metaphorical" maps produced during the same period suggests that their makers were fluent in two mapping languages and testifies to the diverse regional pathways of communication. The double mapping styles of the colonial-period tribespeople corresponded to the multilingual abilities of native southeasterners, many of whom included in their linguistic repertory Mobilian, the commercial lingua franca of the lower South. Learning to read maps like these brings home the necessity of becoming literate in the vibrant verbal and nonverbal languages of the Southeast, with their rich symbols and intercultural inflections.[6]

Though these various subjects—mounds, maps, and treaties, "artifacts" in the broadest sense—have too long been stored in infrequently opened cabinets, at the hands of these authors they raise fresh issues. Each will inspire questions for which there is increasing enthusiasm among writers on the indigenous past of the Americas. After all, some of the oldest and seemingly best-known questions can once again become the most interesting when reexamined in fresh ways. This point is forcefully made throughout the following chapters, where the authors help us see familiar archaeological artifacts and historical documents in an unexpected light. With these new perspectives on the symbolic life of the southeastern tribes, we can understand the impatience of James Adair when he scorned the European council translators of the eighteenth century, for whom the "golden trophes and figures" of the tribal "talks" were more than "illiterate interpreters can well comprehend, or explain."[7] In the following chapters we are fortunate to be led by able guides and interpreters farther down the path of knowledge that some among each generation have followed since the first encounter between colonists and tribespeople in the Southeast.

Notes

1. Charles Colcock Jones, Jr., *Antiquities of the Southern Indians, Particularly of the Georgia Tribes* (New York: Appleton, 1873), iv.

2. For case studies of kinship and gender issues in colonization outside the South, see Mona Etienne and Eleanor Leacock, *Women and Colonization: Anthropological Perspectives* (New York: Praeger, 1980).

3. For suggestive approaches to the conduct of councils and meetings, see Ashley Montagu, *Manwatching: A Field Guide to Human Behavior* (London: Chatto, Bodley

Head and Johnathan Cape, 1978), 106–12. The phrase "non-verbal leakage" is from this book, which also contains a fine bibliography of works on nonverbal communication.

4. An early study is Cyrus Thomas, "Report on the Mound Explorations of the Bureau of Ethnology," in *Twelfth Annual Report of the Bureau of Ethnology* (Washington, D.C.: Government Printing Office, 1894), 17–742. Also see two companion volumes by Robert Silverberg, *The Mound Builders of Ancient America: The Archaeology of a Myth* and *The Mound Builders* (New York: New York Graphic Society, 1968; reprint, Athens: Ohio University Press, 1986).

5. For a controversial discussion of ancient Amerindian artistic origins and affinities see Terence Grieder, *Origins of Pre-Columbian Art* (Austin: University of Texas Press, 1982).

6. For comparison with the Euro-American cartographic tradition and suggestions of indigenous sources of colonial geographic knowledge, see William P. Cumming, *The Southeast in Early Maps* (Princeton: Princeton University Press, 1958). On language, see James M. Crawford, *The Mobilian Trade Language* (Knoxville: University of Tennessee Press, 1978); Emanuel J. Drechsel, "Towards an Ethnohistory of Speaking: The Case of Mobilian Jargon, an American Indian Pidgin of the Lower Mississippi Valley," *Ethnohistory* 30(1983): 165–76.

7. Samuel Cole Williams, ed., *Adair's History of the American Indians* (1930; reprint, New York: Promontory Press, 1974), 55.

"The Chief Who Is Your Father": Choctaw and French Views of the Diplomatic Relation

Patricia Galloway

When anthropologists set out to study a culture-contact situation, the first thing they look for is evidence of acculturation. When the object of historical study is the contact of Europeans with Native Americans, this is also the case, but all too seldom do scholars make any effort to treat both sides equally in the analysis: they apply the methods of anthropology to the Native Americans, the methods of history to the Europeans. As a result, the original inhabitants of the continent are seen as victims rather than as active agents in this drama,[1] and the extended European state becomes the fixed formal stage upon which the natives writhe in the throes of their tribal passions.

For the colonial period, reconstructing the meaning and function of Indian social institutions will always remain more difficult than describing comparable institutions among the Europeans who dealt with the Indians. It is fortunate that at least we can understand the European institutions, for the Indians were certainly acting upon their own view of them, and to understand how Indian institutions responded to contact with Europeans it is indispensable that we discover what the Indians sought to achieve through their response. If the French were clearly attempting to manipulate Choctaw power brokers, the Choctaws were certainly trying to return the favor.

I shall propose a thesis that explores both sides of the diplomatic interface in the same way: Indian as seen by European and European as seen by Indian. I shall argue that in the diplomatic relations between the Choctaws and the French in the eighteenth century, the French colonial governors, conditioned by their own patrilineally biased society and ignoring a Choctaw institution that would have offered them more authority, adopted the metaphorical position of "father" to the Choctaws, and the Choctaws then proceeded to treat them as their matrilineal society taught them they should: as kind, indulgent nonrelatives who had no authority over them. The governors, well aware that the Choctaws could represent a formidable enemy at their gates, were forced to play this role until the end of their regime.

This is a very simple thesis, so simple that at first glance it may seem frivolous. Inevitably, too, less than perfect evidence and a confusion in levels of discourse hamper any effort to document its validity. To make sense of the thesis it will be necessary to reconstruct what each group thought of the other's institutions and, behind that, the reality of the institutions themselves.

Before arguing that the Indians used a certain kinship mechanism for diplomacy, I must show that it is valid to see the external diplomacy of certain ethnic groups having matrilineal descent and tribal social organization as a metaphor for how lineages dealt with one another within that group. Since the example here is a major southern tribe, I shall draw mainly upon what is known of the southeastern Indians to establish this point.

Like most of the southeastern tribes, the Choctaws at contact reckoned kinship matrilineally. John R. Swanton established in his 1931 study that matrilineal descent groups and exogamous moieties made up Choctaw social structure.[2] Fred Eggan then proposed that the Choctaw system of matrilineal descent had reflected the pure Crow pattern before European contact,[3] and Alexander Spoehr carried out work that demonstrated Eggan's thesis.[4]

Within a matriliny the roles of the men must be clearly defined if the group is to maintain stability.[5] The brothers of the women of the lineage hold authority over household and lineage activities and children. They are charged with managing the property of the householders, their sisters, and with assuring the continuity of lineage holdings by approving and arranging marriages for its women. They also maintain the traditions and customs of the tribe as a whole by taking charge of the education of their sisters' sons. And the role of primary authority in the lineage, held by the oldest male, passes regularly to his eldest sister's eldest son rather than to his own, who belongs to a different lineage. This whole complex of patterns granting certain kinds of authority to the maternal uncles of a matriliny is designated by the anthropological term "avunculate," and it constitutes one of the distinctive features of matrilineal societies.

The in-marrying men in this picture, the husbands of the women of the lineage, cannot develop relationships of authority within the lineage without creating unacceptable tensions; besides, as their own sisters' brothers, they enjoy an opportunity to exercise authority within their own lineage. Their role in the conjugal family, then, gives them the opportunity to display affection without authority toward their own children, and they are looked upon by those children as the indulgent parent. Because they also have no important educational responsibilities, the children are not obliged to pay any particular attention to them when it comes to advice about proper conduct within their society. That this role remained extremely well established among the Choctaws was forcefully demonstrated during the nineteenth century when, in an effort to conform to white conventions, the Choctaws enacted legal sanctions against fathers for not supporting their families or serving as the authority figures in them.[6]

Spoehr has noted that an elder male of a lineage might have the same authority over the activities of the lineage as the mother's brother does over her children.[7] This idea can be very fruitful, especially when examined more closely in terms of the structural pose of a sociopolitical system for diplomacy.[8] Gearing has described how the Cherokees arranged themselves for the four main functions of their lives: food procurement, dealing with death and other serious events of life, making corporate political decisions, and making war; the Choctaws ordered their society in much the same ways.[9] Although the structural pose for war sometimes arrogated to itself de facto the conduct of extratribal relations, generally speaking the appropriate mechanism for dealing with such matters throughout the Southeast was the council structure, where mature deliberation was the governing principle in making corporate decisions.

Demonstrating that the heads of the council served as a sort of corporate avunculate for the group they led is not easy, nor would Gearing consider the concept of a council exercising authority at all as valid for the Cherokees, but I believe it can be argued for the post-contact Muskogean groups. In Creek society, for example, the senior male of each matrilineal clan was known as the "clan uncle," and he represented the clan in council and enjoyed great authority in the lineage itself.[10] We can test the validity of an extension of this concept by simply comparing the functions served by the council for the whole group and by the senior male for the lineage. The council was entrusted with weighty matters like the food supply, justice, and negotiation or war with external entities. The senior male of a lineage was supposed to organize the lineage for farming and procuring game, to ensure the defense of a member of the lineage who had behaved unlawfully, and to lead the lineage in pursuing revenge when a member had been killed. At both levels the bearer of responsibility had to display conduct that was wise, deliberative, and authoritative.

It is a bit easier to establish that an extratribal entity was treated by the tribe or tribal subgroup as the lineage treated another lineage. Much has been written about one of the major tools of southeastern Indian diplomacy, the calumet ceremony. Whatever its origin, Donald Blakeslee has argued effectively that it was in use in the Southeast well before the coming of any Europeans;[11] hence it was a working instrument for intertribal diplomacy that the Europeans encountered and were forced to act as though they accepted—thus accepting by implication the connotations of the ceremony. Apparently the most frequent aboriginal use of the calumet ceremony was cementing trade alliances,[12] but newly uncovered evidence shows that among the Chickasaws and the Choctaws the ceremony had been further elaborated to encompass diplomatic alliances through the adoption of a leading man among the potential allies. I want to suggest that this institution was the vehicle through which intertribal diplomatic alliances operated in terms of social structure: the ally nation was "adopted" as a fictive lineage within the tribe. This phenomenon will be discussed in more detail after the development of additional evidence.

The foregoing description of social institutions for diplomacy applies to a society that had already altered considerably from its precontact state. By the early eighteenth century the Muskogean Indians of the Southeast had been adjusting for two hundred years to the new reality of European presence. All over the Southeast the late prehistoric hierarchical chiefdoms that had built towns and ceremonial centers on the bounty of floodplain agriculture had been severely shaken and almost universally shattered by the impact of European diseases during the sixteenth century.[13] In the course of the seventeenth century they mostly reorganized as the "tribes" we know: shifting and resilient groupings of locally autonomous villages, any one of which could stand on its own for subsistence and social requirements, each possessing its local "big man" or chief. In this restructured Indian world, authoritarian institutions had been smashed and abandoned. Instead, kinship and hospitality were the operative forces, blood vengeance the negative sanction.

The French came into contact with the Choctaws for the first time in 1699/1700, when Pierre Le Moyne d'Iberville led the first expeditions to establish a colonial beachhead on the Gulf coast. From the start, as had been the case in all their dealings with Native American tribes, the French presented themselves as "father" to the Choctaws, expecting to play a role toward them analogous to their own notion of a *père de famille*. This notion was of course rooted in the patrilineal traditions of the French, and it is obvious that they expected the analogy to be played out in just this way—they extended it by referring to the Indians as their children.[14] French cultural arrogance precluded any astonishment that the Choctaws should apparently accept this role without objection, and that they did so probably reinforced the French conviction of its suitability. The Choctaws and other Native Americans, of course, were not offended by such an approach, since they were accustomed to conduct diplomacy in terms of fictive kinship. But they must have wondered why the French leaders chose to present themselves as in-marrying affine rather than as mother's brother.

How then must French institutions have looked to the Choctaws? Historians have made a profession of contrasting the authoritarian French regime and its transplanted institutions with the more egalitarian behavior of the English shopkeepers,[15] but they have overlooked the fact that inevitably the perfect scheme of administration planned in France would be altered by local conditions. In isolated Louisiana, which France treated as a stepchild anyway, circumstances reduced the colony's official policies to little more than the strengths and inclinations of its leading personalities, much as the ubiquitous insects and fungus reduced government buildings to the most durable of their constituent materials.

The organization of the Louisiana colony was meant to be the basically authoritarian one of the French military. The general scheme, even under the monopolies of Crozat, Law, and the Company of the Indies, consisted of a governor with authority over the military personnel and in charge of implementing the colony's Indian policy, assisted by a commissary or finance officer who administered funds and supplies of matériel and merchandise. Between them, the governor and commissary were to share in the "general police" of the colony—to see that order was kept and justice done. After 1712 the governor and commissary were assisted in legal administration by the Superior Council, which became the colony's highest court.[16]

What the Indians saw, however, was not this ideal administrative structure, which was incomplete at the colony's earliest shaky beginnings and which in any case was vitiated by quarrels between the governor and commissary. Instead, they observed something more familiar and understandable: that the real armature of the Louisiana colony for most of its history was a family: the Le Moynes. The personal self-interest of this band of brothers generally appeared to coincide with the needs of the colony in its early years, and they controlled it through de facto domination of the governorship even when someone else actually held the position. Le Moyne tenure of this leading role was so constant over the first twenty years of the colony's history that it must have been influential in shaping the Choctaw concept of the function of the governor in the French colony. And fate had it that the most important of those brothers, Bienville, not only took the trouble to learn Choctaw, but had no children of his own and exercised influence through his sisters' sons.[17]

The Choctaws thus saw a small tribe, numbering in the hundreds at first and never larger than several thousand, a fraction of Choctaw numbers. This tribe claimed to owe allegiance to a "great chief" in the Big Village across the water, but in Louisiana itself it was led by a war chief, the governor who controlled the troops, and a peace chief, the commissary general who controlled the goods in the warehouses. These two chiefs often quarreled instead of alternating their authority according to consensus, and although they eventually acquired a council to help them, they even quarreled with this council on occasion. The war chief exercised an astonishing life-and-death authority over his warriors, and since he generally held the balance of power, this small tribe seemed always to be on a war footing. Yet neither he nor the peace chief seemed to have great influence over the councils of the great chief and his supplies of merchandise. Impressive as the prestige goods offered by the French might seem, they were nearly always in short supply, and the fine quality of the most desirable of them—guns and ammunition—emphasized the warlike nature of the French tribe.

Just as the Europeans failed to notice the systemic implications of what they perceived as the anomalous institution of matriliny, so too the Choctaws apparently failed to grasp fully the patricentric bias of the French social fabric. How were they to realize that the meaning of "father" to the French might differ from their own concept? They met in their villages only the missionary, who was strangely wedded to his gods; the trader and interpreter, who were more interested in complying with Indian ways than in imposing their own; the officer and soldier, who had a strong interest in Choctaw women and proved appallingly reckless in battle. So far as is known, no Choctaw lived permanently among the French, so no Choctaw saw much of commercial or domestic life in the settlements; what they knew of French villages was learned through participation in the annual celebration of alliance at the present giving, with its fine speeches, ceremonies, feasts, and opportunities for trading. The vivid presence of Bienville and his brothers and their sisters' sons, which so powerfully dominated these annual events, must have scotched any Indian suspicion that Frenchmen behaved strangely toward their sons.

These two sets of attitudes and social conventions interacted in diplomacy. Swanton quotes a French description of the Choctaw structural pose for council that gives a basic sketch of the sort of corporate entity the French thought they had to deal with:

> In each village, besides the chief and the war chief, there are two Tascamingoutchy ["made a war chief"] who are like lieutenants of the war chief, and a Tichou-mingo ["assistant chief"] who is like a major. It is he who arranges for all of the ceremonies, the feasts, and the dances. He acts as speaker for the chief, and oversees the warriors and strangers when they smoke. The Tichou-mingo usually become village chiefs. They (the people) are divided into four orders, as follows. [The first are] the head chiefs, village chief, and war chief; the second are the Atacoulitoupa [Hatak-holitopa] or beloved men (hommes de valleur); the third is composed of those whom they call simply tasca or warriors; the fourth and last is atac emittla [hatak imatahali?]. They are those who have not struck blows or who have killed only a woman or a child.[18]

This account mixes several levels of analysis from our point of view. The first part of it deals with the structure of the top levels of village council, biased toward the structural pose for war, while the second describes somewhat incompletely a sorting of the entire population of the group in full council, omitting the women. There seems to be no sense of the several levels of organization, which were lineage, village, and division, and how these levels might have been related through kinship mechanisms. By examining this question we can attempt to establish how the metaphorical avunculate of the Choctaw council functioned in external diplomacy.

Within the lineage, as has been seen, the senior man or men bore the responsibility of authority. We do not know how village headmen or chiefs were chosen, but from accounts of village government we may assume that one of the requirements was the "moral virtuosity" that Gearing describes for the Cherokees.[19] The witness cited above suggests there was some sort of established succession in the village; perhaps the chief chose his *tichou-mingo* as a potential successor, and if so there is some evidence that he chose him from his own lineage.[20] It is also clear that the chief and his council were most often older men—the French regularly describe village chiefs as such; many are shown as almost feeble.[21]

The three divisions in the Choctaw nation as encountered by the French—Eastern, Western, and Sixtowns—were very real. Swanton has brought forward evidence that the Sixtowns or Southern division was a different ethnic group; even a century later they spoke a different dialect and wore their ornaments in a distinctively different way.[22] Archaeological evidence suggests that the Eastern and Western divisions may also have represented different ethnic backgrounds.[23] In any case, as *political* divisions they not only were present in 1700, but were still present and exerting political influence after Removal a century and a half later.[24]

The divisions had already become truly political entities by the time of contact. Although village membership in a division might shift over time, the divisions held steadily to certain territorial loci, based as they were on landholding of a kind by kinship groups.[25] How they were governed is also described in the first part of the passage quoted above; they had a chief who had his functionaries and a council of older men, just as the villages did. The division chief was usually, if not always, a village chief also, and it seems that his functionaries remained the same at both levels.[26] On the division level of the council, however, it is likely that other village chiefs and older men representing lineages filled the places. Full council, as it met for annual ceremonies and other events of moment, such as the conduct of diplomacy, would consist of the entire population of the division, classed as described in the second part of the description above but including women. The office of chief of the whole nation was a late introduction fostered by the French, and the division remained the operative unit of Choctaw "national" politics.[27]

The French records give little information about Choctaw councils, because except for the traders, whose voices are only rarely heard in the documents, the French were apparently never in the villages (or welcome in the villages, or in the right village) when such gatherings took place. Possibly, in their vain search for something like a national council, the senior French leaders simply overlooked village or divisional ones. There is thus no direct documented observation of a Choctaw council, although there are accounts by Frenchmen who were kept at a distance and given reports of the progress of a council.[28] From this limited evidence we can say with some assurance that the council strove for consensus and that those who disrupted it were disapproved of; that everyone present at the council had a chance to speak; and that the division council made decisions of peace and war, which were then supposed to be carried out by the chosen war chief.[29] The practice with regard to embassies is less clear, but although we have only second hand information about embassies to other tribes, there is ample opportunity to observe the embassies sent to treat with the French.

The Choctaws seem to have employed something very like an abbreviated council structure for the direct conduct of diplomatic relations with the French at the beginning. When Henri de Tonti traveled among the Choctaws and Chickasaws to request their participation in an alliance in 1702, the Choctaws, after having had several days to consider the matter, sent to Mobile not one man, but a party consisting of three men and two women. Tonti's letters suggest strongly that the three men represented the three divisions of the Choctaw nation.[30] As the relationship between the French and the Choctaws developed, it became the practice for the Choctaws to travel to Mobile every year to give and collect presents and to trade deerskins. In this activity the Choctaws seemed to attend by division, sending at a minimum chiefs, officials, and honored men, so that the meetings often took a month or more, a fact the French governors bitterly lamented.[31] Thus the Choctaws conducted external diplomacy using in some way all of the persons who made up the council or corporate avunculate. To further investigate the actual conduct of this diplomacy, we must now turn to the details of diplomatic interaction.

In testing the hypothesis that the Choctaws actually did take the French at their word and treat them as fathers, the overt use of kinship terminology is highly relevant, since, as has been shown, the Choctaws did consciously use the kinship metaphor in diplomacy. There are five terms that appear consistently in the reports of French and Indian speeches: father, child, brother, elder brother, younger brother; and these terms fall into two groups, father-child and brother. I shall examine usages by both of the interacting groups to attempt to determine two things: how the Choctaws applied kinship terms to the French, since we think we understand what the Choctaws meant by them; and how the Choctaws perceived the French as applying kinship terms to them.

French usages are most frequently represented in the written record; the men who wrote the documents were fond of recording their own eloquence. There is no guarantee that what we read is precisely what the Indians heard, but for present purposes we will assume it is. For the Choctaw usages, we are at the mercy of the interpreters, but again we will assume that what we read is what was stated and simply hope in both cases that the aggregate of examples in the sample will correct for error. It will also be necessary to quote examples at some length, since we need to look not only at the use of the words themselves but also at the implications attached to that use.

"Father" and "child," of course, were used by both sides in their transactions to refer to the relationship the French had specified from the beginning, with the "father" term referring to the governor of the colony and the "child" being the Indians. French usages strongly stressed love and kindliness between father and child—precisely what the Choctaws would expect. A speech on behalf of Governor Périer, regarding a promised redress of Choctaw grievances about poor treatment from French traders and delivered by Régis du Roullet in 1729, exemplifies this theme: "You know that the Great Chief is your father and that he carries you all in his heart, that he seeks nothing else than to enrich you and to make you happy and content. . . . Ah! the heart of the Great Chief is deeply grieved. He is greatly pained to think that the French of whom he is the master treat you so ill, you who are his children and his friends."[32] In 1744 Governor Vaudreuil reported a speech of a similar tenor that he gave to the Choctaws at the time of the presents in nominally asking their consent to conclude a Chickasaw peace: "As the Choctaws in these latest wars had acted in concert with us and had always conducted themselves not only as faithful allies but even as children who were extremely attached and perfectly devoted to the Great Chief of the French, their father, I was unwilling to conclude anything without their consent."[33]

More generally, however, the French use of the term was in a context in which the father-child relationship implied the child's obligation to perform requested actions. In presenting the conditions of peace to the Chickasaws in 1744, the interpreter/trader Renochon, representing Vaudreuil, told them "that the great chief of the French, their father, was granting them gladly the peace . . . if they would carry out the conditions . . . that then he would regard them as his children."[34] When Beauchamp went among the Choctaw villages in 1746 to demand retribution for the murder of three Frenchmen, he constantly stressed that he was bringing "the word of M. de Vaudreuil their father"; in reproving the Choctaws for failing to go to war with the Chickasaws as they had promised, he said, "Instead of keeping the word that they had given their father, most of them fell asleep in their cabins."[35] Finally, Governor Kerlérec combined the tenderness theme with that of obligation when he told the Choctaws: "as long as they behaved well, they would always find a father's heart in the Great Chief of all the French."[36]

By contrast, the Choctaws referred to the French "father" exclusively in terms of love and kindness; there is rarely even mention of obligation on the part of the "children." In complaining to their missionary, Father Baudouin, of the haughtiness and cruelty of Governor Périer's minion Régis du Roullet as keeper of the Yowani post warehouse, they expressed their hope of the return of a governor like Bienville: "Frenchmen will come at once who will have the pity of a father for them and whose experience and courage will obtain for them a peace like the one that they enjoyed several years ago."[37] Upon Bienville's return in 1732, he wrote to Maurepas of one of many expressions of confidence from the Choctaws referring to his having armed them in the early days of the colony: "they must regard me as their father since I had set them free of slavery to the English."[38] When Vaudreuil met with Choctaw chiefs to discuss ways of ending the Choctaw civil war in 1749, "Alibamon Mingo addressed all the Choctaws and told them that I had just spoken to them like a father touched by the misfortunes of their nation."[39]

When Kerlérec arrived in the colony to take up the governorship in 1754, the Choctaws made a great thing of adopting him: "Before their departure from the different villages they held general assemblies where it was agreed they would give me the Choctaw names Youlakty Mataha Tchito, anké achoukema, which in our language means King of the Choctaws and greatest of the race of the Youlakta, which is the finest and the oldest; all this ends with anké achoukema, which means a very good father."[40] After this ceremony, Kerlérec proceeded with his plans to weld a southern alliance by trying to persuade the Choctaws to keep peace with the Alabamas, Tallapoosas, and Abihkas, French allies among the Upper Creeks:

> Since they had adopted me as their father, they ought to listen to my word and my will, which was to see the roads white between the Alabamas and them; that the former having been for a long time our allies and our friends, I ought to regard them likewise as my children, and do everything I could to reestablish tranquillity among them for that reason. . . . The oldest medal chief began to speak, and said to me: "We see clearly, my father, that you love your children, that you are a good father who ought to be listened to . . . henceforth we place our vengeance beneath your feet that you may trample it deeply into the sand."[41]

There is a rather strange incident in the record that illustrates quite clearly a French failure to understand Choctaw kinship obligation concepts and Choctaw rejection of French assumptions, which I cite here because it makes an idiosyncratic use of the "father" terminology. In 1734 Diron d'Artaguette, commandant at Mobile, went among the Choctaws to dissuade them from trading with the English. In what he apparently thought was a stroke of cleverness, he claimed to have been compelled to see them by a dream: "As I was at home sleeping very soundly I felt a hand pulling me by the foot. I awoke with a start. It was the spirit of your fathers who spoke to me as follows: 'As you are the father of the Choctaws, as you have a good heart for them, and as we see them on the point of falling over a precipice . . . we . . . tell you to go and dissuade them.' "[42] This obviously did not cut much ice with his interlocutors; according to Bienville's report one of the important chiefs remarked drily: "I have neither dreamed nor seen the spirits."[43]

In contrast to "father-child" references, the French made very little use of the "brother" terminology. When they did so, it seemed to be modeled upon the Indian usage, as when Régis du Roullet reproved the Choctaw Red Shoe: "If he wished that hereafter I should regard him as my brother, he ought to tell his warriors to have no dealings with the Chickasaws."[44] The Choctaws, on the other hand, used this terminology often to refer to their relationship with Frenchmen other than the governor. For example, Régis also reported the speech of the man recognized by the French as great chief of the Choctaw nation, who referred to Diron d'Artaguette as "my brother, Mr. Diron, chief of Mobile, who gave me a medal and a big letter of consideration."[45]

After the Natchez massacre of their French garrison in 1729, a Choctaw told Périer, "I am very sorry about the death of our brothers." When told that it was suspected that the Choctaws were part of the conspiracy, the man said he could not believe that, "because of the friendship that we have for our brothers the French."[46] In one instance the "brother" term was further specified. The chief of the Cushtushas, in supporting arguments of Lusser in a Choctaw council in 1730, said "he considered the Frenchman whom he had with him as his elder brother."[47] This term was not unknown in intertribal diplomacy; the Choctaws and the Chickasaws considered the Alabamas a kindred senior to their own, and the Alabamas in one instance referred to their relationship with the Chickasaws as one to younger brothers.[48] Taken in aggregate, these references display a degree of consistency that suggests that the referents of the terms being used were sufficiently similar in the minds of both parties to have been viable and communicative terms for their relationship. But what did these terms mean to the communicating parties? The most revealing contexts for investigating their meaning are those in which the terms are juxtaposed.

The first example, a speech delivered in the presence of Bienville and Diron d'Artaguette by the Choctaw great chief after the present giving in 1736 made a distinction between father and brother on the basis of relative authority: " 'Bad messages have often been brought us in which I have placed no faith, and I shall listen only to those that come from you [Bienville], my father. And you, my brother,' he added, speaking to M. Diron, 'I exhort to be more circumspect in the future than you have been, because since you are a chief your words and your actions have more weight than those of a private person.' "[49] The chief speaking obviously considered himself a peer of his "brother," whatever his standing vis-à-vis his "father" may have been.

The Indians of Louisiana were quite aware of the career of Vaudreuil and his father in Canada before he arrived as governor of Louisiana, and they were especially impressed with his influence on the ferocious northern Indians. The Chickasaws, proposing to exchange French hostages for peace, greeted him with a notice of that fact: "All the red men of the North are your children," they reminded Vaudreuil. "If you wish to regard us as your children, listen to our word. . . . We love your Frenchmen. We regard them as our brothers."[50]

Finally, there is a very clear indication of how the kinship terms so far examined fit into the model of adoption of allies as a fictive tribal lineage. Indian allies of the French, asked to capture French deserters from the wilderness posts and return them to the French, invariably did so on condition they not be punished. One such instance in the 1750s involved the Choctaws. Alibamon Mingo's plea for pardon for deserters combines all the kinship terms I have discussed:

> I know well . . . that these Frenchmen have done wrong, but that will show the red men so much the more clearly that M. de Vaudreuil, their father, has consideration for their requests. He can easily imagine the infinite pain that it would give the Choctaws to see shed the blood of people who every day bring them the things they need, and that with great difficulty. Furthermore are not these Frenchmen, so to speak, our brothers; do we not dwell, as it were, in the same cabin? I hope therefore that the great chief of the French will not refuse his children the favor that they ask of him.[51]

Not only did the chiefs lately allied with the French in the Choctaw civil war ask for this pardon, but they accompanied their request with a present of five deerskins, which another chief described as "a white sign for us, which shows that the blood of these Frenchmen must not be shed inasmuch as it would be the Choctaw nation that would be the cause of their death."[52] Thus it seems clear that the Choctaws took this fictive kinship of alliance seriously. But there may be something even more interesting here. In this example the Choctaws seem to be trying to avoid the blood guilt of responsibility for a death. Such blood guilt was a problem, however, only when a member of *another* lineage was killed; it would not be incurred by the death of a sibling;[53] hence it is just possible that this example indicates that the French "brothers" of the Choctaws were classificatory brothers rather than sons of the same father.

How do these usages correspond with kinship terminology among the Choctaws? First there is the caveat that in trying to examine kinship terminology of the Choctaws in the eighteenth century we are trying to hit a moving target: as Eggan proposed[54] and Spoehr tried to prove,[55] the Choctaws were on their way from a prehistoric/early historic Crow pattern to another form under acculturative pressure, and all the variations in this trajectory could be seen in the different Muskogean tribes of the Southeast. Yet the kinship data gathered by

Figure 1 Choctaw terms of relationship, self male, after John R. Swanton, *Source Material for the Social and Ceremonial Life of the Choctaw Indians*, Bureau of American Ethnology Bulletin 103 (Washington, D.C.: Government Printing Office, 1931), 85.

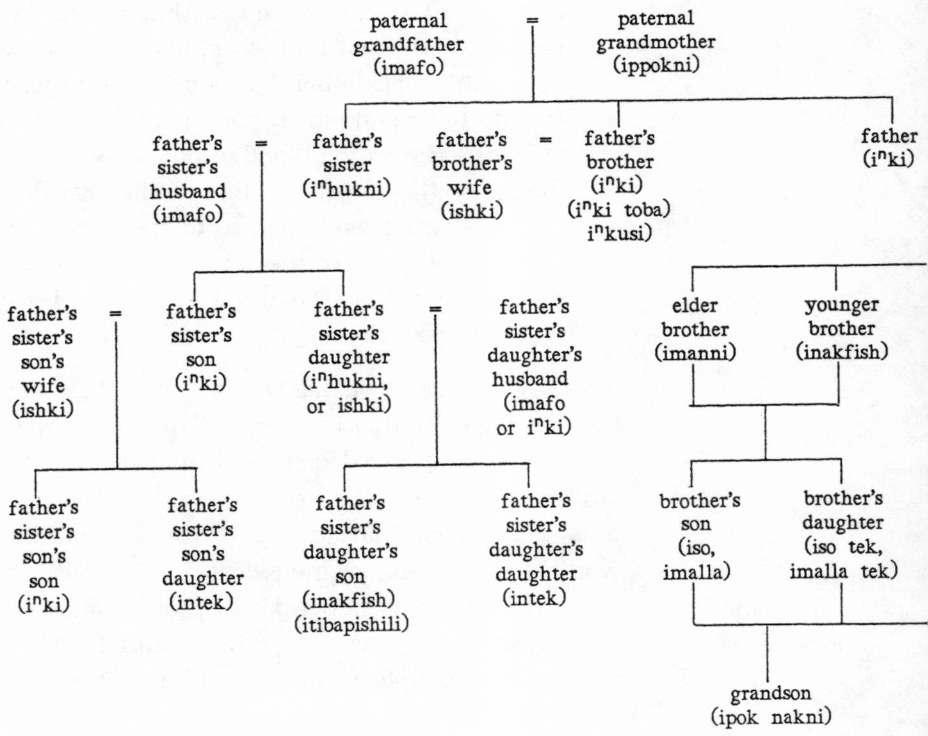

researchers, from whatever period, agree very clearly that the only people a man might term his brothers were the sons of his father and those of his father's sister's daughter (see fig. 1).[56] This is the key to the proof of the thesis I am arguing. In no case were any of the descendants of the maternal uncle referred to as "brother," even in "aberrant" schedules. In other words, kin and nonkin were separated terminologically, and a "brother" could fall on the side of the father, as nonkin. Hence the Choctaws, in referring to the governor as their father and his men as their brothers, *did* intend that these kinship terms be taken to mean what they meant in Choctaw culture.

If this is true, then it is necessary to examine Choctaw-French diplomatic relations in a new light. With the foregoing evidence in mind, it is now time to return to the institution the Choctaws used to establish external alliances. As we have said, the calumet ceremony was the primary instrument of alliance in the native societies of the Southeast and indeed of much of North America. Among the Chickasaws and apparently the Choctaws, however, it had been uniquely institutionalized. The evidence for this comes from a newly discovered letter from Thomas Nairne written about the

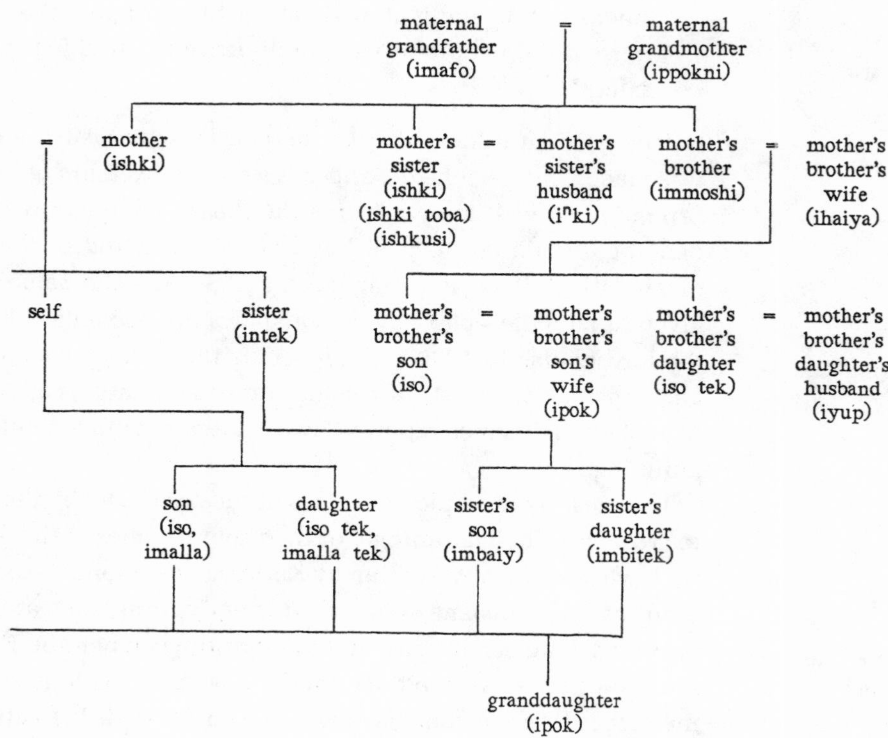

Chickasaws in 1708, a letter that emphasizes the analogy between external diplomacy and the conduct of interlineage relations. Nairne explains the function of the calumet ceremony and of the official known as *fanimingo* ("squirrel chief"):

> The Chicasaws Yassaws and other people of these parts have one pretty rationable Esteablishment that is that any fameily of a nation who pleases usually chuse a protector or freind out of another fameily. He thus chose is generally some growing man of Esteem in the Warrs, they who chuse & owne him for the head or Chief of their Fameily, pay him severall little devoirs as visiting him with a present upon their returnes from hunting saluting him by the name of Chief. Then he is to protect that Fameily and take care of it's concerns equally with those of his own. Thus likewise Two nations at peace, each chuse these protectors in the other, usually send them presents. His bussiness is to make up all Breaches between the 2 nations, to keep the pipes of peace by which at first they contracted Freindship, to devert the Warriors from any designe against the people they protect, and Pacifie them by carrying them the Eagle pipe to smoak out of, and if after all, ar unable to oppose the stream, are to send the people private intelligence to provide for their own safety.[57]

Nairne goes on to describe the method by which such a fanimingo was made, and what he describes is a detailed version of the calumet ceremony so well known in the Southeast, complete with singing, dancing, "striking the post," and ritual cleansing of the anointed chief—all of it lasting four days.[58] This was the same treatment given to La Salle's party by the Quapaws in 1682 and to Iberville by the Bayogoulas in 1700.[59] Evidence that the Choctaws knew of and participated in such a practice in intertribal relations appears in the lists of chiefs' names reported by the French, which contain several fanimingos.[60]

The clearest example of the use of the ceremony by the Choctaws to create a French fanimingo for themselves comes in the description we have already seen written by Kerlérec, last French executive governor of the Louisiana colony. But every year at least, at the Mobile present-giving ceremonies and at other times when the French sent important emissaries to the Choctaws, we hear the long-suffering remark that three or four days were taken up with the calumet ceremony. If it can be assumed that at least part of the time the Choctaws were honoring fanimingos, then clearly they were concerned to adopt in this way people they perceived as important French officials and to reiterate the commitment by renewal of the ceremony.

This notion of a revered person who could intercede with his own group for the group that so honored him explains a lot in the practice of diplomacy among the Choctaws. For one thing, the description of the duties of the fanimingo toward those who made him suggests that the ceremony establishes a fictive kinship relation obliging the fanimingo to perform many of the duties within his own group that he would perform if he were the senior male in a lineage that was a subgroup of it—that he would act, in short, as a clan uncle for the adopting group in the councils of his own people.

Since the French had little understanding of the Choctaw practice or its meaning and therefore did not intentionally choose to "make" a fanimingo, it would be hard to establish the existence of a Choctaw fanimingo in Nairne's sense who represented the French.[61] There were instances in which the French presented pipes to southeastern groups—Iberville's presentation of a pipe in the form of a ship comes to mind[62]—but no clear evidence that any French ceremony was ever construed by the Choctaws as honoring one of them as the French fanimingo. It is possible to think that perhaps the Choctaws understood the institution of systematic present giving by the French—which was designed to influence in their favor those chiefs they considered the most important—as creating some sort of obligation similar to the fanimingo institution. Over time the present-giving ceremonies became more and more elaborate, as a special building was erected for the purpose and the French governors banqueted the Choctaw chiefs for days on end, singling out a very few for special recognition with medals and parchment citations.[63] And chiefs especially honored by the French through the presentation of medals, when they ceased to support the French, apparently felt some kind of moral crisis themselves, since in at least two cases such chiefs cast their medals into running water and destroyed or gave away other French presents.[64]

There are tantalizing hints in the literature that the French might have made more use of the fanimingo institution. In 1732 the officer Lusser was invited to extend his stay in the pro-French Concha village by a fanimingo who had given him intelligence about dangerous events in the nation at a crucial time and had agreed to mediate a disturbing quarrel over justice given to the French for a murdered man; a few days later Lusser lectured what must have been another fanimingo at Bouctoucoulou about the faithfulness due to the French.[65] Although it does not show French use of the fanimingo, this incident casts further light upon the role in that the fanimingo of Bouctoucoulou asserted that peace with the Chickasaws, then being blamed by the French for the Natchez revolt, was a desirable end—and Lusser then says: "He was taking the thing very much to heart, being calumet chief of this nation."[66] Thus the fanimingo probably was a calumet chief, a sort of "secretary of state" of his village or division in that he was the designated fanimingo for all external diplomatic relations with other Indian groups. But it seems that the French never made effective use of this official, perhaps because their patrilineal bias made them incapable of understanding the institution. Instead they chose to adopt via the distribution of medals such division and village chiefs as were useful to them.

Yet the Choctaws for their part did their best to create French fanimingos. How strange it must have seemed to them to so adopt the leading men of the French and to find them insisting upon being considered fathers! It should have been disappointing as well, since as uncles they would have been of the same lineage as the Choctaws, which in this metaphorical context meant of the same tribe. Since only the notion of the fanimingo as "clan uncle of the Choctaws in the councils of the French" would have a clearly institutionalized meaning for the Choctaws, they would have had to fall back on the concept of the father's role in the family and then to graft that onto the fanimingo concept. Yet Kerlérec's adoptive name, "support of the Inholahta [the senior moiety] and a very good father," indicates that the Choctaws were able to assimilate the French obsession to their own institution and profit by it at the same time. In fact the reason the governors attended the meetings in Mobile so assiduously, in spite of seasickness and fever, was that they received considerable presents from the Choctaws.[67] In return the Choctaws hoped that the French governor would send good reports of them and enable them to obtain trade goods from the French king. If the governor insisted upon being considered their father, then they were so much the better off—there was no necessity to obey him where it was inconvenient or dangerous to do so, and among their father's kin they would always be received fondly. Experience with these "father" fanimingos over time must have reinforced the Choctaw belief that this mongrel concept was correct, since the continual shortages of French trade goods argued strongly that their fanimingo's influence in his own group's councils was meager at best, and he continued to flatter and cajole them almost no matter what they did.

Thus there was an ironic truth in the way the fanimingo concept was modified, since in fact the Louisiana governors' influence at the French court was inconsiderable. And the Choctaws behaved with essential impunity, as they would toward a father. The French attempt to manipulate Choctaw government and war making through a hierarchical system of presents had guaranteed that nothing would be more expensive or less reliable than assuring the constancy of the Choctaws as allies.[68] Part of this, of course, was due to misunderstanding of the Choctaw notion of war. But some of the problem must be attributed to the French failure to understand what they had gotten themselves into and their insistence that the Choctaws see things as they did. The French never understood that they had become a fictive Choctaw lineage, separate from other Choctaw lineages but included within the same tribe, in spite of the fact that the records are full of Choctaw use of kinship terms with reference to them. Even when the Choctaw divisions fought a civil war over the French failure to take up their lineage duties and avenge themselves on some Choctaw murderers of Frenchmen, the French remained in this instance too afraid of Choctaw numbers to trust the assertion that kin-group vengeance was required.[69] Because they needed the Choctaws more than the Choctaws needed them, the French tried to fulfill Choctaw demands for trade goods and presents even at times when they had not enjoyed adequate reciprocity. Small wonder the Choctaws then assumed that the French governor meant what he said when he insisted upon being accepted as a father: fathers were kind and generous, but they had no authority.

Notes

1. James Axtell, *The Indian Peoples of Eastern America* (New York: Oxford University Press, 1981), xv.

2. John R. Swanton, *Source Material for the Social and Ceremonial Life of the Choctaw Indians*, Bureau of American Ethnology Bulletin 103 (Washington, D.C.: Government Printing Office, 1931), 76–90.

3. Fred Eggan, *The American Indian: Perspectives for the Study of Social Change* (New York: Cambridge University Press, 1980), 27–37.

4. Alexander Spoehr, *Changing Kinship Systems*, Field Museum of Natural History Anthropological Series 33, no. 4 (Chicago: Field Museum Press, 1947).

5. David M. Schneider, "The Distinctive Features of Matrilineal Descent Groups," in *Matrilineal Kinship*, ed. David M. Schneider and Kathleen Gough (Berkeley: University of California Press, 1966), 1–29.

6. Eggan, *American Indian*, 29.

7. Spoehr, *Kinship Systems*, 201.

8. Fred Gearing, *Priests and Warriors: Social Structures for Cherokee Politics in the Eighteenth Century*, Memoir 93 (Washington, D.C.: American Anthropological Association, 1962).

9. Swanton, *Source Material*, 55–102; Charles Hudson, *The Southeastern Indians* (Knoxville: University of Tennessee Press, 1976), 184–257.

10. John R. Swanton, "Social Organization and Social Usages of the Indians of the Creek Confederacy," in *Forty-Second Annual Report of the Bureau of American Ethnology* (Washington, D.C.: Government Printing Office, 1928), 55–102.

11. Donald J. Blakeslee, "The Origin and Spread of the Calumet Ceremony," *American Antiquity* 46, no. 4(1981): 759–68.

12. Ibid., 765–66. The widespread trade and culture contacts that crisscrossed the Southeast during the Mississippian period had to be supported by some sort of mechanism to make contact possible; whether or not the mechanism was the full-blown calumet ceremony of the eighteenth century is really immaterial. The early date of the Nairne description of the *fanimingo* institution (see below) suggests that the mechanism *was* fictive kinship.

13. Henry Dobyns, *Their Number Become Thinned: Native American Population Dynamics in Eastern North America* (Knoxville: University of Tennessee Press, 1983), 298–334.

14. A typical example (a speech from Governor Périer to the Choctaw chiefs, delivered by Régis du Roullet in 1729): "You know that the Great Chief [i.e., Périer] is your father and that he carries you all in his heart . . . you who are his children and his friends" (Archives des Colonies, ser. C13A [henceforth AC, C13A], vol. 12: fols. 74–74v, Journal of Régis du Roullet).

15. Wilbur Jacobs, *Wilderness Politics and Indian Gifts: The Northern Colonial Frontier, 1748–1763* (1950; reprint Lincoln: University of Nebraska Press, 1966), 29–45.

16. James D. Hardy, Jr., "The Superior Council in Colonial Louisiana," in *Frenchmen and French Ways in the Mississippi Valley*, ed. John Francis McDermott (Urbana: University of Illinois Press, 1969), 87–101.

17. Bienville had several nephews who served as officers in Louisiana military posts, and several of them were involved in Indian diplomacy. Perhaps the most notable was a son of his sister Jeanne Le Moyne, Gilles Augustin Payen de Chavoy de Noyan (known as "Noyan"), who served as acting governor for Bienville during the Chickasaw campaign of 1736, undertook an important diplomatic mission to the Choctaws for Bienville in 1738, and commanded as king's lieutenant in New Orleans after 1741;

Patricia Kay Galloway, ed., *Mississippi Provincial Archives: French Dominion*, vol. 4 (Baton Rouge: Louisiana State University Press, 1984), 96n.

18. Swanton, *Source Material*, 91, quoting from the so-called Anonymous Memoir (Ayer Collection, Newberry Library); Swanton's parenthetical comments.

19. Gearing, *Priests and Warriors*, 44–46, 66–67.

20. A particularly clear example of this practice seems to emerge in the career of Toupa Oumastabé of Concha. Identified as a "brother" of the important chief Alibamon Mingo of Concha, in 1731 he was an honored man of his village; but by 1746 he was "captain" of Concha; in 1731, when Alibamon Mingo became chief of the eastern division, he asked that Toupa Oumastabé be given the office of second chief of Concha; Galloway, *Mississippi Provincial Archives*, 4:66, 279.

21. At the beginning of the troubles leading to the Choctaw civil war, the great chief of the nation told Beauchamp that he was "old and no longer in a position to be able to undertake anything" (AC, C13A, 30:231v, Beauchamp's Journal, 1746).

22. Swanton, *Source Material*, 56–57.

23. John Blitz, *An Archaeological Study of the Mississippi Choctaw Indians*, Archaeological Report 16 (Jackson: Mississippi Department of Archives and History, 1985). Blitz's reanalysis of all known collections of Choctaw pottery from archaeological sites shows that there are at least two pottery traditions combined into the Choctaw assemblage.

24. Angie Debo, *The Rise and Fall of the Choctaw Republic* (Norman: University of Oklahoma Press, 1961), 151; Swanton, *Source Material*, 96–97; Arthur H. DeRosier, Jr., *The Removal of the Choctaw Indians* (Knoxville: University of Tennessee Press, 1970), 166.

25. The Eastern, Western, and Sixtowns divisions were on the watersheds of the Tombigbee, Pearl, and Pascagoula rivers, respectively.

26. This was apparently the case; in the documents we never hear of a different set of officials for the district chiefs.

27. Dunbar Rowland and Albert Sanders, trans. and ed., *Mississippi Provincial Archives: French Dominion*, 3 vols. (Jackson: Mississippi Department of Archives and History, 1929–32), 1:156; AC, C13A, 14:184, Baudouin to Salmon, November 23, 1732.

28. Such a situation seems to be reflected in the report of the 1745 Concha assembly (AC, C13A, 29:191–92v, Louboey to Maurepas, October 6, 1745). There are many other such examples, but perhaps the most striking is found in Beauchamp's 1746 journal, which reports at length the view of a Frenchman on the outside looking in—with great difficulty—as the Choctaws made the decisions that would eventuate in a civil war (AC, C13A, 30:222–40v).

29. This was true until the ascendency of Red Shoe in the 1730s. His influence grew beyond that of war chief until he no longer followed the inclinations of the council. Cf. AC, C13A, 14:189v-190, Baudouin to Salmon, November 23, 1732.

30. Patricia Galloway, "Henry de Tonti du village des Chactas, 1702: The Beginning of the French Alliance," in *La Salle and His Legacy*, ed. P. Galloway (Jackson: University Press of Mississippi, 1982), 146–75.

31. Kerlérec's complaint in 1754 is typical (AC, C13A, 38:129, Kerlérec to De Machault d'Arnouville, December 18, 1754).

32. AC, C13A, 12:74–74v, Régis du Roullet's Journal, 1729.

33. AC, C13A, 28:204–204v, Vaudreuil to Maurepas, February 2, 1744.

34. AC, C13A, 29:197, Louboey to Maurepas, October 6, 1745.

35. AC, C13A, 30:235v, Beauchamp Journal, 1746.

36. AC, C13A, 40:148v, Kerlérec's Memoir on the Indians, December 12, 1758.

37. AC, C13A, 14:192–192v, Baudouin to Salmon, November 23, 1732.

38. AC, C13A, 18:158v, Bienville to Maurepas, April 23, 1734.

39. AC, C13A, 33:20, Vaudreuil to Rouillé, March 3, 1749. Alibamon Mingo was the senior chief of both the eastern division and the senior moiety, the I^{n}holahta.

40. AC, C13A, 38:123, Kerlérec to De Machault d'Arnouville, December 18, 1754. The translation Kerlérec offers here is quite correct: *i^{n}ki* means "father," and *achukma* means "excellent, benevolent"; Cyrus Byington, *A Dictionary of the Choctaw Language*, Bureau of American Ethnology Bulletin 46 (Washington, D.C.: Government Printing Office, 1915).

41. AC, C13A, 38:125v–126.

42. AC, C13A, 18:194v, Bienville to Maurepas, September 30, 1734. Lest the reader imagine that Bienville invented this ludicrous story to discredit Diron, one can refer to Diron's own much briefer version in AC, C13A, 19:129–129v, Diron to Maurepas, September 1, 1734.

43. AC, C13A, 18:195v, Bienville to Maurepas, September 30, 1734.

44. AC, C13A, 15:206v, Régis du Roullet to Maurepas, 1729–33.

45. AC, C13A, 12:78v, Régis du Roullet Journal, 1729.

46. AC, C13A, 12:39v–40, Périer to Maurepas, March 8, 1730.

47. AC, C13A, 12:127v, Lusser's Journal, 1730.

48. AC, C13A, 22:226, Diron d'Artaguette to Maurepas, May 8, 1737.

49. AC, C13A, 21:141v–142, Bienville to Maurepas, February 10, 1736.

50. AC, C13A, 28:92–92v, Chickasaw Chiefs to Vaudreuil, August 1743.

51. AC, C13A, 35:357, Dupumeux to Beauchamp, June 18, 1751.

52. AC, C13A, 35:358, Dupumeux to Beauchamp, June 18, 1751.

53. Compare the example of the French attempt to have Red Shoe killed during the Choctaw civil war. They found that the only way this could be done without initiating a string of blood revenge killings was to have a kinsman of his own lineage do the deed: AC, C13A, 30:237v.

54. Fred Eggan, "Historical Changes in the Choctaw Kinship System," *American Anthropologist* 39(1937): 34–52.

55. Spoehr, *Kinship Systems.*

56. Swanton, *Source Material*, 85, gives a kinship schedule that includes the appropriate Choctaw words.

57. Alexander Moore, ed., *Nairne's Muskhogean Journals: The 1708 Expedition to the Mississippi River* (Jackson: University of Mississippi, 1988) text is quoted from the second letter, dated April 12, 1708.

58. Ibid.

59. For the Quapaw version of the ceremony see Pierre Margry, *Découvertes et établissements des Français dans l'ouest et dans le sud de l'Amérique Septentrionale (1614–1754)* (Paris: Maisonneuve, 1879), 1:553–54, from the narrative of Nicolas de La Salle. For Iberville, see Richebourg Gaillard McWilliams, ed., *Iberville's Gulf Journals* (University: University of Alabama Press, 1980), 46; in this case the Bayogoulas explicitly told Iberville that he was being made the ally of several mostly Choctaw-related tribes.

60. AC, C13A, 12:89–90v, Régis du Roullet to Maurepas, 1729.

61. Note that in the "Anonymous Relation" account of Choctaw social organization quoted above, the fanimingo is not even mentioned.

62. McWilliams, *Gulf Journals*, 46.

63. Presents were first given, of course, as soon as Iberville met a new group of Indians, but they were systematized by Bienville and his other brother Châteaugué in the 1720s to create a hierarchical redistributional system in which the great chief received all the presents and was to divide them among lesser chiefs, and so on (for a list, see AC, C13A, 12:90v, Régis du Roullet, Journal, 1729). The first medals were given before 1732, as chiefs with them appear on lists of names by that time (Archives du Service Hydrographique, vol. LXCII2, no. 14–1, portefeuille 135, document 21, Journal of Régis du Roullet). Kerlérec, who was only the last of the governors to recognize their value for the style of diplomacy developed by the French (AC, C13A, 40:150v–152v, Kerlérec's Memoir on the Indians, 1758), had a large building erected in Mobile to accommodate the present-giving ceremonies (AC, C13A, 37:202v, Bobé Descloseaux to Rouillé, November 27, 1753).

64. In 1729 the so-called great chief of the Choctaws was insulted by Diron d'Artaguette, commander at Mobile, as a result of which "I threw my medal and my big letter into the water" (AC, C13A, 12:79, Régis du Roullet Journal, 1729). That this was a ceremonial act is suggested by what followed, in that the next day "the Great Chief sent his son to look for his medal and his big letter that he had fished for when he learned of my [Régis's] arrival, but which he had not yet worn. He took it in his hand and holding his fan in the other he came with ceremony to say these words to me: . . . If I threw away my medal it was because my brother, Mr. Diron, sent me word that I was a woman; that he did not wish to see me any more, and because, since I did not get any coat last year, I was ashamed to wear it" (ibid., 83v–74). The identical procedure occurred for a similar reason in 1746, when Mongoulacha Mingo of Chickasawhay, hearing "that the authority of the medal chiefs was being taken away to be given to the red chiefs . . . made him decide to cut off his medal and throw it into a stream" (AC, C13A, 30:225v, Beauchamp's Journal, 1746). In the sequel, this chief sided with Red Shoe against the French and was put to death by pro-French warriors of his village "for having cut off and thrown away the medal with which he had been decorated for supporting the mission of the Reverend Father Baudouin" (AC, C13A,

32:216, Beauchamp to Maurepas, October 24, 1748). Being the French god's fanimingo was clearly no joke.

65. AC, C13A, 12:108–108v, Lusser to Maurepas, 1730.

66. AC, C13A, 12:109v, Lusser to Maurepas, 1730.

67. The French documents, most of them either written or vetted by the governors, have little to say about this, but there is plenty of evidence in the form of letters from discontented officers complaining of the profitability of the governorship to show that such presents were given and that they were ample. One of the accusations against Bienville in the 1707–8 investigation of his administration was that he had sold meat brought him by the Indians "in exchange for the presents that the King gives them" (AC, C13A, 2:256, Abstract of Testimony). Bienville himself remarked rather drily with reference to the new governor, de l'Epinay: "The governors are ordinarily jealous about giving the presents themselves" (AC, C13A, 5:63, Bienville to Regency Council). This was not unusual or new; it may be recalled that La Salle had nearly been buried by the pelts and other gifts piled on him by the Quapaws in 1682.

68. Richard White, *The Roots of Dependency* (Lincoln: University of Nebraska Press, 1983), 50–51.

69. See Patricia Galloway, "Choctaw Factionalism and Civil War, 1746–1750," *Journal of Mississippi History* 44(1982): 289–327.

Symbolism of Mississippian Mounds

Vernon James Knight, Jr.

At least three centuries separate the prehistoric Mississippian cultures from the best ethnographic descriptions of their descendants, the historic southeastern Indians. The transformation that took place across this span seems so thoroughgoing that students of Mississippian culture often hesitate to use analogies based on southeastern ethnographic and ethnohistorical materials. Though dramatic changes occurred over this interim, spotty documentary and archaeological records make it hard to determine the precise nature of these changes. But much of the result can be summed up by the term "deculturation"—a loss of cultural elements, including, it is assumed, much of the richness and detail of Mississippian mythology, beliefs, and ceremonialism. The obscurity of historical processes leading to this deculturation has lent Mississippian culture a mystique that is not shared by other very late prehistoric cultures of the New World.

One of the cultural elements long assumed to have been lost during this transformation was the platform mound, a hallmark of Mississippian culture. When questioned about the origin of the mounds that dotted the region, historic southeastern Indians sometimes claimed these monuments were built by long-vanished people of whom they had no knowledge. Much was made of this, of course, by proponents of various "lost tribe" theories who imagined a superior race of mound-builders preceding that of the "red Indians." Even once it was established as fact that the southeastern Indians' ancestors had indeed built the mounds—and in the not too distant past—the nature and symbolism of Mississippian platform mounds still remained largely a mystery.

A few ethnologists, however, have noticed certain features in southeastern Indian ritual that seem relevant to the problem of Mississippian platform mounds. It appears, in fact, that although Indians of the historic era were no longer building large mounds, the beliefs underlying the practice survived. When viewed at the level of symbolism the problem dissolves, and the "loss" of platform mound ceremonialism can be seen as merely a change of emphasis within an unbroken ritual tradition. The primary aim of this chapter is to demonstrate briefly the extent of mound-related symbolism in historic southeastern Indian language, folklore, and ritual practice. These elements do not directly explain all the observed archaeological details concerning Mississippian platform mounds, as no one would expect them to, but they do give us a foothold in beginning to understand one element of the Mississippian belief system. We can begin with some lexical data.

An eighteenth-century Muskogee-language term for the large prehistoric Mississippi period mounds scattered throughout the Creek country of Alabama and Georgia was *ekvn-like,*[1] a compound that translates literally as "earth placed" or "earth sitting." Since *liketv* also denotes placement in the sense of "dwelling" or "residence," a freer translation might be "earth dwelling." *Ekvnv,* meaning "earth" or "world," provides the root of the first part of the compound. This root word also appears in Muskogee terms for cave, mountain, hill, earthquake, and other features and properties of the physical world.[2]

A Yuchi term for mound has parallel associations. This is *sʔaet-shine(ha),* literally "land sitting," from a root connoting "earth" or "mountain."[3] Here, though, the reference is not to large Mississippi period earthworks. Instead, it is apparently the term applied to the small ceremonial mounds still used in Yuchi square grounds.

In both of these southeastern languages, artificial mounds are conceived metaphorically as "earth sitting." This is more than just a descriptive phrase. The "earth" invoked here is the cosmological world concept, the earth island, an idea highly charged with symbolic associations in native southeastern belief systems. As this suggests, mound constructions may be understood in one sense as icons. It can be shown that artificial mounds among the historic southeastern Indians operated as conventional world symbols.

Artificial mounds occasionally figure in Muskogee origin myths, in contexts that illuminate their symbolic significance. This body of folklore shows that traditional knowledge concerning large earthworks persisted well into the modern era.[4] Mounds appear primarily in Muskogee myths associated with the towns of the Kasihta and Coweta. In one version, Kasihta warriors encounter and subsequently kill certain survivors of a vanquished enemy town. The survivors are found to be in mourning for their dead kinsmen, and they are engaged in building earthen mounds. From the context, the mounds are apparently intended, at least partly, for the burial of the dead.[5] The Kasihtas themselves also construct large mounds in the texts of at least two myths. The mounds are built to invoke supernatural assistance and protection and to provide a locus for purification ritual before battle. Black drink, the ritual emetic tea, is taken on the summit. The mounds are described as being hollow or as having a central chamber, in which people assemble to fast and purify themselves.[6] During a mythical attack by Cherokees, Coweta warriors hidden within a ceremonial mound surprise their assailants as they "pour up from the bowels of the earth" to defeat the Cherokees.[7]

This imagery of people emerging from a hollow in a mound is analogous to several Muskogee texts in which ancestors issue from underground. A Tukabatchee example compares this emergence to ants pouring out of the earth, presumably from an anthill, which substitutes for the mound in the Kasihta example.[8] In some cases this ancestral point of origin has an association with mountains, but in a text recorded by Benjamin Hawkins the mountains are replaced by two artificial mounds, supposed to be in the forks of the Red River.[9]

Several of John Swanton's Muskogee informants identified the place where the ancestors came up out of the ground as "the navel of the earth," a metaphor invoking the connection between the navel and birth or fertility.[10] There is a further connection between the "navel of the earth" and death. According to some Muskogee sources, the eventual fate of the Indians is judged to be a return into the earth at this place, just as each individual human body returns to the ground at death.[11] Additional light on this metaphor is gained from a nineteenth-century Chickasaw source. One of Henry Schoolcraft's informants noted that the Chickasaw term current for the old Mississippian mounds in their country signified "navels." "They thought that the Mississippi was the center of the earth, and those mounds were as the navel of a man in the center of his body."[12]

The motif of a great mound with a hollow chamber in its center appears again in Choctaw origin and migration mythology. In accounts collected by Henry Halbert, the large platform mound at Nanih Waiya in Winston County, Mississippi, was considered the *ishki chito*, the "great mother," of the Choctaw tribe. "In the very center of the mound, they say, ages ago, the Great Spirit created the first Choctaws, and through a hole or cave, they crawled forth into the light of day."[13] David Bushnell collected a southern Choctaw version that adds that men emerged out of the mound together with grasshoppers and that certain men remaining inside were transformed into ants.[14] This parallels the Tukabatchee myth in respect to ants as underground dwellers that emerge to colonize the earth.

A much different account is the Choctaw migration myth recorded by Gideon Lincecum, in which the Nanih Waiya mound appears as a cultural construction erected by the Choctaws at the end of their wanderings. In the Lincecum myth the term applied to the large platform mound is *yokni chishinto*, literally "earth elevated in the shape of a mound," where again *yokni* expresses the native earth concept with a variety of connotations. One of the most remarkable accounts in southeastern Indian traditional lore is the detailed description (see Appendix) of the building of a large quadrilateral, multistage platform mound. The Lincecum myth also discusses the building of the smaller conical mound at the Nanih Waiya site, supposed to be erected as a foundation for the sacred pole. The larger platform mound is again represented as possessing a central chamber, as in the Choctaw creation myths collected by Halbert and Bushnell. But here, since this is a mortuary mound, the chamber harbors not living progenitors but the ancestral dead. The mound has been erected by the Choctaws for the placating of ancestral spirits and, at the same time, for the spiritual renewal of the living. As a symbolic manifestation of world renewal, the mound surfaces are replanted with trees after the mound is completed.[15]

Cherokee tradition repeats some of these images. The Cherokees conceived the Nikwasi Mound at Franklin, North Carolina, as having a central chamber inhabited by powerful spirits called the Immortals, who could pour forth by the hundreds to assist humans in battle. The symbolic equivalence of mound and sacred mountain is implicit in the belief that the Immortals possessed another lodge beneath Pilot Knob. Collapsed Cherokee townhouses of the historic era were ritually buried beneath a mantle of earth and clay, and the

Cherokees believed that the large Mississippian mound in the town of Toqua, in east Tennessee, had been built in this manner.[16]

Large earth mounds, then, of recognizable Mississippian-like form and structure, were far from ignored or forgotten among the historic southeastern Indians. Linguistic and traditional material from Muskogee, Yuchi, Chickasaw, Choctaw, and Cherokee sources yields a reasonably coherent picture of mounds as symbols. Mounds possess symbolic associations with autochthony, the underworld, birth, fertility, death, burial, the placation of spirits, emergence, purification, and supernatural protection. They are metaphorical mountains, anthills, navels, or womblike "earth mother" representations. All are related ideas of native southeastern belief, and they find objective expression in the artificial mound as an earth or world icon.

The constructions invoked in each of the sources cited so far are all large earthworks. Some appear to be purely mythological images, whereas others have real referents, some of which can be identified today as Mississippi period platform mounds. They differ greatly in scale from the smaller ceremonial earth mounds constructed in modern times within the square grounds of the Muskogees, Oklahoma Seminoles, and Yuchis. These small ceremonial mounds nevertheless are connected historically and developmentally to earlier, much larger earthworks. This connection will be shown presently, but first it is worth considering the nature and significance of small earthworks as observed ethnographically.

This brings us to the concept of *tadjo*, the Muskogee and Oklahoma Seminole name for ceremonial square ground mounds. These mounds, including the Yuchi equivalents, are rebuilt each year in connection with a purification rite, the sweeping of the square ground. Yuchi examples, and perhaps Muskogee and Seminole versions as well, appear to be made up partly of dirt from square ground sweepings and partly of fresh dirt dug up nearby. In each case the new mound covers the remnant of the mound built the previous year. The mounds serve as a focal point in certain dances performed during the green corn ceremony. These are the buffalo dance and war dances among the Muskogees and Seminoles, in which the dance leader or singer may stand on the mound. Among the Yuchis the mound figures mainly in the dance-related ceremony called "jumping the mound." These mounds are distinct from other small mounds formed by successive ash piles from the annually renewed sacred fires.[17]

Other uses of the term *tadjo* show the significance of the connection between mounds and purification by sweeping. The low ridge formed around the square ground from repeated sweepings is also called *tadjo* in Muskogee and Seminole contexts.[18] The term may also refer to the circular area surrounding the ball pole at some Muskogee square grounds. This again is an area purified each year by sweeping, resulting in a low circular ridge around the margin, and sometimes a low central mound on which stands the ball pole, a "world tree" symbol.[19]

Some of these uses of the term *tadjo* appear to refer to a place [20] or to structural components of the square ground, but the term may also refer to the substance "swept dirt." This connotation of substance appears in the phrase "mound of *tadjo*," referring to the ceremonial mound.[21] In all cases, however, the emphasis is clearly on the symbolically polluted earth removed from an area to be purified and subsequently deposited in an accretional earth construction.

No other information is available concerning the detailed symbolic meanings of *tadjos* and their Yuchi equivalents. Nevertheless, some essential features are apparent that have definite counterparts in the large constructions appearing in southeastern traditional sources and potential counterparts in Mississippian constructions. *Tadjos* are accretional objects, ritually constructed and ritually employed. They involve the symbolic manipulation of earth in the creation of an objective focus for purification. This occurs within the broader context of communal ceremonies directed to world renewal and agriculture.

Evidence can now be summarized in support of the contention that *tadjo*-type constructions of the modern era are lineal descendants of large platform mounds. First, not all reported *tadjo* constructions are as small as the ones seen at modern square grounds in Oklahoma. Swanton described and illustrated a *tadjo* at an abandoned nineteenth-century Tukabatchee square ground in Oklahoma that is comparable in size to some Mississippian mound stages. This was a platform four feet high and, estimating from Swanton's photograph, perhaps thirty feet in diameter. According to Swanton, the mound was the site of the Tukabatchee buffalo dance and war dances.[22] There are no apparent *tadjo*-like constructions mentioned in the earlier eighteenth-century source materials on the Muskogees, but they definitely used substructure mounds, as did the Cherokees.

In the Chattahoochee valley town of Apalachicola, abandoned by approximately 1755, Bartram observed that both the square ground and the rotunda had been elevated on low substructure mounds (fig.1).[23]

The account of John Howard Payne, describing the Tukabatchee green corn ceremony in Alabama in 1835, provides a documentary bridge between the addition of earth mantles to large pyramidal mounds and the more recent *tadjos*. Payne describes two mounds at Tukabatchee. One, perhaps both, still exists at the site, and the larger mound of the two is a typical truncated pyramid begun probably in Late Mississippi (Shine II phase) times. Payne observed the uses of these mounds during the ceremonies, but more important, he noticed that both were renewed before the observances. The large mound, used as a dance platform during the "gun dance," had been given a new coat of earth scraped from the adjacent square ground. Here then is rather stunning testimony documenting Creek mound construction in the nineteenth century, involving the addition of an earth mantle (albeit a thin one) to a genuine Mississippian platform mound. The ritual context, moreover, is unambiguous. The symbolism is that of world renewal and purification within the framework of communal green corn ceremonialism. The mantle was composed of *tadjo* in the sense of that term as a substance.[24]

What, then, is the significance in this context of timber buildings on Mississippian mound summits? Two observations may help clarify this issue. First, numerous well-documented Mississippian mound stage surfaces never supported a structure of any type. At the Mississippi-period Cemochechobee site in Georgia, for example, only four (or possibly five) of ten mantle surfaces in Mound B supported structures, and none of the five mantle surfaces in Mound A yielded any evidence of a structure.[25] Second, the high degree of diversity seen in summit structure types and inferred activities (contrasted with the homogeneity of mound structure) suggests the involvement of several kinds of social groups, or Mississippian institutional domains, in summit use.

This suggests that the symbolism of mound-building ritual and of the mound as an icon may be viewed as analytically independent of the wide variety of summit uses, whether sacred or secular, potentially sponsored by a corresponding variety of social domains in Mississippian culture. The platform mound and its fundamental

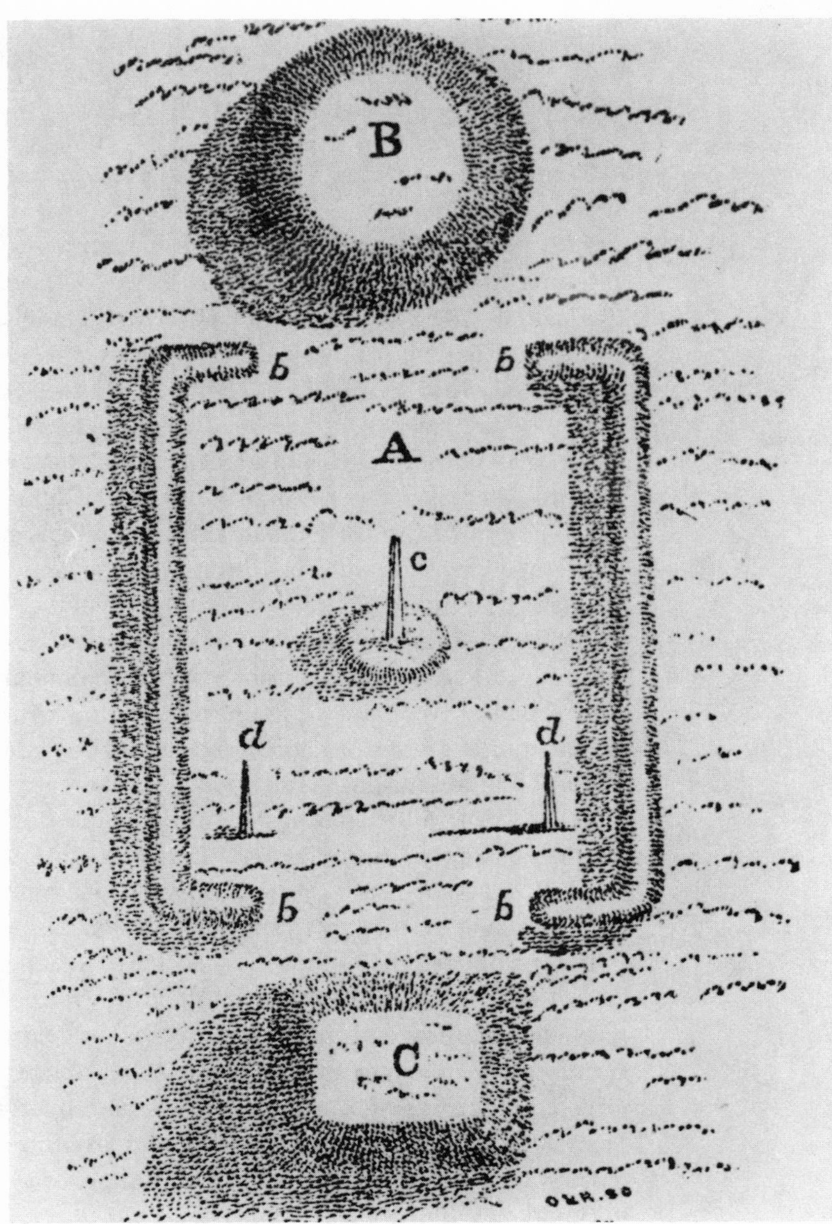

Figure 1 Diagram of a Muskogee ceremonial center, 1789 (from William Bartram, "Observations on the Creek and Cherokee Indians," *Transactions of the American Ethnological Society* 3, part 1 [1853]: 52).

symbolic associations may be interpreted as an expression of a broad-based communal cult type, oriented to earth, fertility, and purification, whereas summit use seems clearly the product of several more restricted orders of social organization and ritual.[26]

As Antonio Waring surmised in the 1940s, purification by the addition of blanket mantles is a dominant theme in the ritual of platform mound construction.[27] The complete sealing of earlier constructions by mantle addition appears to be a kind of burial symbolism, sometimes complete with summit offerings resembling grave goods. It is no contradiction to say that it is also a kind of world renewal symbolism, since the burial of old surfaces effects renewal.[28]

These are the most conspicuous images identifiable in Mississippian platform mound ceremonialism. Other formal characteristics of Mississippian mounds may also be appropriate to their interpretation as manipulable earth symbols. The "earth island" as a cosmological entity among the southeastern Indians was normally conceived as flat-surfaced and as manifesting four world directions. A Muskogee source conceives of the earth as both flat and square, dropping off on four sides.[29] The quadrilaterality and flat-topped configuration of most Mississippian mounds may express this image concretely in an appropriate medium, earth. Even earthen ramps, a common feature of Mississippian platform mounds, may have symbolic significance, with possible affinities to the symbolism of "rain roads" and related pathways to the middle of world center icons in the Plains and the Southwest. Such world centers are called "mother earth navels" in the Rio Grande pueblo area, and they are replanted in renewal rituals.[30] These features recall Muskogee and Chickasaw sources connecting mounds with navels, and the traditional Choctaw replanting of Nanih Waiya mound.

Several of the objective characteristics of Mississippi-period platform mounds thus are also seen to be consistent with the image of the mound as an earth icon in later southeastern Indian belief. It seems justifiable, in light of the evidence for continuity, to claim that these are manifestations of an unbroken southeastern ritual tradition. This tradition employs earth mounds, either figuratively or actually, as earth icons in communal world renewal ceremonialism. Such a ritual tradition evidently predates Mississippian culture, and it survives in the green corn ceremonialism of the displaced southeastern tribes of Oklahoma.

Appendix

Extracts from Gideon Lincecum, "Choctaw Traditions about Their Settlement in Mississippi and the Origin of Their Mounds," *Publications of the Mississippi Historical Society* 8(1904): 521–42.

[After wandering for forty-three years in search of a homeland, the Choctaws reached central Mississippi, burdened with the bones of their deceased relatives. The Choctaw *minko*, or headman, called his people together and addressed them as follows:]

"Let us call this place; this, Nunih Waya encampment, our home; and it shall be so, that when a man, at his hunting camp, in the distant forests, shall be asked for his home place, his answer will be, 'Nunih Waya.' And to establish Nunih Waya more especially as our permanent home, the place to which when we are far away, our thoughts may return with feelings of delight and respectful pleasure, I propose that we shall by general consent and mutual good feelings select an eligible location within the limits of the encampment and there, in the most respectful manner, bring together and pile up in beautiful and tasteful style the vast amount of bones we have packed so far and with which many of the people have been so grievously oppressed. Let each set of bones remain in its sack, and after the sacks are closely and neatly piled up, let them be thickly covered over with cypress bark. After this, to appease and satisfy the spirits of our deceased relatives, our blood kin, let all persons, old and young, great and small, manifest their respect for the dead, by their energy and industry in carrying dirt to cover them up, and let the work of carrying and piling earth upon them be continued until every heart is satisfied. These bones, as we all know, are of the same *iska*, the same kindred. They were all the same flesh and blood; and for us to pile their bones all in the same heap and securely cover them up will be more pleasing to the spirits, than it will be to let them remain amongst the people, to be scattered over the plains, when the sacks wear out in the hands of another generation who will know but little and care less about them. . . ."

Men were then appointed to select an appropriate place for the mound to be erected on, and to direct the work while in progress. They selected a level piece of sandy land, not far from the middle creek; laid it off in an oblong square and raised the foundation, by piling up earth which they dug up some distance to the north of the foundation. It was raised and made level as high as a man's head and beat down very hard. It was then floored with cypress bark before the work of placing the sacks of bones commenced. The people gladly brought forward and deposited their bones until there were none left. The bones, of themselves, had built up an immense mound. They brought the cypress bark, which was neatly placed on, till the bone sacks were all closely covered in, as dry as a tent. While the tool carriers were working with the bark, women and children and all the men, except the hunters, carried earth continually, until the bark was all covered from sight constituting a mound half as high as the tallest forest tree. . . .

At the Nunih Waya encampment, everything went well and there were no complaints. Their hunters made wide excursions, acquainted themselves with the geography of the country to the extent of many days' journey around. But, as yet, they had discovered no signs of the enemy, or of any other people. In this happy condition of health and plenty—for they had enlarged their fields and were harvesting abundant crops of corn—years rolled round; the work on the mound was regularly prosecuted; and at the eighth green corn dance celebrated at Nunih Waya, the committee who had been appointed at the commencement, reported to the assembled multitude that the work was completed and the mound planted with the seeds of the forest trees, in accordance with the plan and direction of the *minko*, at the beginning of the work.

The *minko* then instructed the good old Lopina, who had carried it so many years, to take the golden sun to the top of the great mound and plant it in the center of the level top.

When the people beheld the golden emblem of the sun glittering on the top of the great work which, by the united labor of their own hands, had just been accomplished, they were filled with joy and much gladness. And in their songs at the feast, which was then going on, they would sing:

> "Behold the wonderful work of our hands; and let us be glad. Look upon the great mound; its top is above the trees, and its black shadow lies on the ground, a bowshot. It is surmounted by the golden emblem of the sun; its glitter (tohpakali) dazzles the eyes of the multitude. It inhumes the bones of fathers and relatives; they died on our sojourn in the wilderness. They died in a far off wild country; they rest at Nunih Waya. Our journey lasted many winters; it ends at Nunih Waya."

Notes

1. A different Muskogee term glossed as "mound," *ekvn-hvlwuce*, is given in R. M. Loughridge and David M. Hodge, *English and Muskogee Dictionary* (1890; reprint Ocmulgee: Baptist Home Mission Board, 1964), 120. There is no evidence, however, that this term was applied to artificial constructions. It seems properly to mean "hillock" or, literally, "little mountain." (The symbol *v* is pronounced in English as *u* in "but." The symbol *c* is pronounced as *ch*.)

2. Benjamin Hawkins, "A Sketch of the Creek Country in the Years 1798 and 1799," *Georgia Historical Collections* 3, no. 1(1848): 39; Loughridge and Hodge, *Dictionary*, 120, 157.

3. W. L. Ballard, "English-Yuchi Lexicon," undated typescript, Columbus Museum of Arts and Sciences, Columbus, Georgia. The symbol ˀ is a glottal stop.

4. Early authorities such as Bartram, Swan, and Hawkins state or imply a degree of ignorance on the part of Muskogee informants concerning the origin of particular mounds or mound groups. The specific mounds in question were perhaps centuries old at the time of these inquiries and seem to have possessed no immediate ritual importance to the local inhabitants, hence these statements. This should not be interpreted, however, as indicating that the Muskogees of the period were not acquainted with the ritual significance of mound construction. In fact, there is substantial evidence of such knowledge.

5. John R. Swanton, "Social Organization and Social Usages of the Indians of the Creek Confederacy," in *Forty-second Annual Report of the Bureau of American Ethnology* (Washington, D.C.: Government Printing Office, 1928), 57.

6. These are activities normally appropriate for the structures of Creek ceremonial grounds.

7. Swanton, "Social Organization," 54–57.

8. Ibid., 65.

9. Ibid., 52, 53; Hawkins, "Sketch," 81–83.

10. Swanton, "Social Organization," 52, 63–64.

11. Ibid., 77.

12. Henry Rowe Schoolcraft, *Historical and Statistical Information Respecting the History, Condition, and Prospects of the Indian Tribes of the United States*, 6 vols. (Philadelphia: Lippincott, 1851–57), 1:311.

13. Henry S. Halbert, "The Choctaw Creation Legend," *Publications of the Mississippi Historical Society* 4(1901): 293. A description of the Nanih Waiya site is provided by Calvin S. Brown, *The Archaeology of Mississippi* (University: Mississippi Geological Survey, 1926), 24–28.

14. David I. Bushnell, Jr., "Myths of the Louisiana Choctaw," *American Anthropologist*, n.s., 12(1910): 527. Robert L. Hall, "The Cultural Background of Mississippian Symbolism" (unpublished typescript in possession of the author, 1984), 44, sees a distant connection between this and Aztec origin accounts featuring a "grasshopper hill" (Chapultapec, in modern Mexico City) possessing an opening leading to underground caverns.

15. Gideon Lincecum, "Choctaw Traditions about Their Settlement in Mississippi and the Origin of Their Mounds," *Publications of the Mississippi Historical Society* 8(1904): 521–42. Cf. the shorter Cherokee account of mound construction and consecration in James Mooney, "Myths of the Cherokee," in *Nineteenth Annual Report of the Bureau of American Ethnology*, pt. 1 (Washington, D.C.: Government Printing Office, 1900), 395–96, 501–2; Cyrus Byington, *A Dictionary of the Choctaw Language*, Bureau of American Ethnology Bulletin 46 (Washington, D.C.: Government Printing Office, 1915), 107, 367.

16. Mooney, "Myths of the Cherokee," 330, 336–37, 477; William C. Sturtevant, "Louis-Philippe on Cherokee Architecture and Clothing in 1797," *Journal of Cherokee Studies* 3(1978): 200.

17. James H. Howard, *Shawnee! The Ceremonialism of a Native American Tribe and Its Cultural Background* (Athens: Ohio University Press, 1981), 113, 141, 146; Swanton, "Social Organization," 219.

18. Swanton, "Social Organization," 190; Howard, *Shawnee!* 111.

19. Albert S. Gatschet, *A Migration Legend of the Creek Indians*, Brinton's Library of Aboriginal American Literature, 1, no. 4 (Philadelphia, 1884), 176; Swanton, "Social Organization," 60, 266.

20. See Loughridge and Hodge, *Dictionary*, 199.

21. Swanton, "Social Organization," figs. 35, 54.

22. John R. Swanton, "The Interpretation of Aboriginal Mounds by Means of Creek

Indian Customs." in *Smithsonian Institution, Annual Report for 1927*, 498; Swanton, "Social Organization," 219, pl. 5a.

23. Frances Harper, ed., *The Travels of William Bartram*, naturalist's edition (New Haven: Yale University Press, 1958); William Bartram, "Observations on the Creek and Cherokee Indians," *American Ethnological Society Transactions* 3, no. 1(1853): 52.

24. John R. Swanton, "The Green Corn Dance," *Chronicles of Oklahoma* 10(1932): 170–95; Vernon James Knight, Jr., *Tukabatchee: Archaeological Investigations at an Historic Creek Town, 1984*, Report of Investigations 45 (Moundville: University of Alabama, Office of Archaeological Research, 1985).

25. Frank T. Schnell, Vernon James Knight, Jr., and Gail S. Schnell, *Cemochechobee: Archaeology of a Mississippian Ceremonial Center on the Chattahoochee River* (Gainesville: University of Florida Press, 1981).

26. Vernon James Knight, Jr., "The Institutional Organization of Mississippian Religion," *American Antiquity* 51(1986): 675–87.

27. Antonio J. Waring, Jr., "The Southern Cult and Muskhogean Ceremonial," in *Waring Papers*, ed. Stephen Williams, Peabody Museum Papers 58 (Cambridge, Mass.: Peabody Museum, Harvard University, 1968), 58. Citing Lewis and Kneberg's account of Hiwassee Island mound construction, Waring concluded that "the sealing off of the old structure was more important than the purely architectural consideration of creating an imposing temple foundation."

28. Vernon James Knight, Jr., "Mississippian Ritual" (Ph.D. diss., University of Florida, 1981); Knight, "Institutional Organization."

29. John R. Swanton, "Religious Beliefs and Medicinal Practices of the Creek Indians," in *Forty-second Annual Report of the Bureau of American Ethnology* (Washington, D.C.: Government Printing Office, 1928), 477.

30. Robert L. Hall, "Medicine Wheels, Sun Circles, and the Magic of World Center Shrines," *Plains Anthropologist* 30(1985): 181–93.

Indian Maps of the Colonial Southeast

Gregory A. Waselkov

Drawing maps was within the competence of every adult southeastern Indian of the colonial period. Early colonizers, such as Captain John Smith, John Lawson, Pierre Le Moyne d'Iberville, and René-Robert Cavelier, Sieur de La Salle, found native North Americans to be proficient cartographers whose geographical knowledge greatly expedited the first European explorations of the region. For a century and a half, information imparted by means of ephemeral maps scratched in the sand or in the cold ashes of an abandoned campfire, sketched with charcoal on bark, or painted on deerskin was incorporated directly into French and English maps, usually enhancing their accuracy. Once this fact is appreciated, one can no longer share the astonishment of Governor James Glen of South Carolina, who in 1754 wrote, "I have not rested satisfied with a verbal Discription of the Country from the Indians but have often made them trace the Rivers on the Floor with Chalk, and also on Paper, and it is surprizing how near they approach to our best Maps."[1] Though the governor might not have conceded or even realized the fact, the information contained in Glen's best maps of the interior Southeast was originally derived in large part from Indians.

Christopher Columbus first discovered the existence of an indigenous mapmaking tradition among the American Indians when, on his fourth voyage in 1502, he waylaid a Mayan trading canoe carrying an old man who drew charts of the Honduran coast.[2] From the English colony at Jamestown, established in 1607, came the earliest records of southeastern Indian maps. The Powhatan Algonquians spontaneously produced maps on at least three occasions, ranging in scope from a simple one showing the course of the James River to an ambitious map depicting their place at the center of a flat world, with England represented by a pile of sticks near the edge.[3] Only rarely, however, did European explorers express any interest in Indian cosmography; their curiosity generally was limited to the locations of rivers, paths, and settlements. When traveling through totally unfamiliar terrain, this sort of geographical information proved invaluable to numerous Englishmen and Frenchmen seeking new lands to exploit. As a consequence, Indians sometimes withheld such information, according to John Lawson: "I have put a Pen and Ink into a Savage's Hand, and he has drawn me the Rivers, Bays, and other Parts of a Country, which afterwards I have found to agree with a great deal of Nicety: But you must be very much in their Favour, otherwise they will never make these Discoveries to you; especially, if it be in their own Quarters."[4] Lawson evidently lost their favor because of his encroachments on Indian lands while serving as surveyor-general of the North Carolina colony, for he was the first Englishman killed in the Tuscarora War of 1711.

But on the whole, geographically uninformed Europeans seldom were disappointed in their hundreds of requests for Indian maps.[5] Unfortunately, few of these maps now are extant, even as transcripts. G. Malcolm Lewis has suggested that Europeans were primarily interested in the information content, which could be incorporated directly into their own printed maps, and had little regard for the ethnographic value of original Indian maps as artifacts.[6] Of the six southeastern maps discussed in this essay, five survive in the form of contemporary transcripts and the sixth is an English manuscript map with a considerable Indian contribution. The Powhatan mantle, a large decorated deerskin cloak, while not a geographical map in the strict sense, does share several important features with Indian maps and so is included here. The discussion below is limited to a comparison of these few remaining examples of southeastern Indian cartography, followed by a brief historical commentary and detailed place-name analysis for each of these maps.

Given the present-day rarity of colonial-period Indian maps, the very existence of these six suggests that they may be in some way atypical or at least not necessarily representative of the entire range of maps produced by Indians of the Southeast. Such an inference seems justified when one considers the origins of the maps and the intentions of the mapmakers, insofar as they are known or can be deduced.

Francis Nicholson, who served as governor in Maryland, Virginia, and South Carolina, seems to have been responsible—either directly or indirectly—for collecting and preserving four of the surviving maps. The earliest map in this group was drawn by Lawrence van den Bosh in 1694, incorporating information "on the left Side of Messacippi River, which discription I lately reced. of the French Indian" (fig. 1). Soon after his arrival in Maryland, Nicholson, the newly appointed royal governor, requested a copy from van den Bosh, who seems to have obtained his information from either an Illinois or a Shawnee Indian, perhaps a member of the Shawnee band that had settled near van den Bosh's home the previous year. In 1698 Nicholson interviewed a different band of Shawnees from a village on the Savannah River and persuaded one of the Indians (with the assistance of a Frenchman who lived with them) to draw

Figure 1 Van den Bosh/French Indian map, 1694 (courtesy of the Edward E. Ayer Collection, Newberry Library, Chicago).

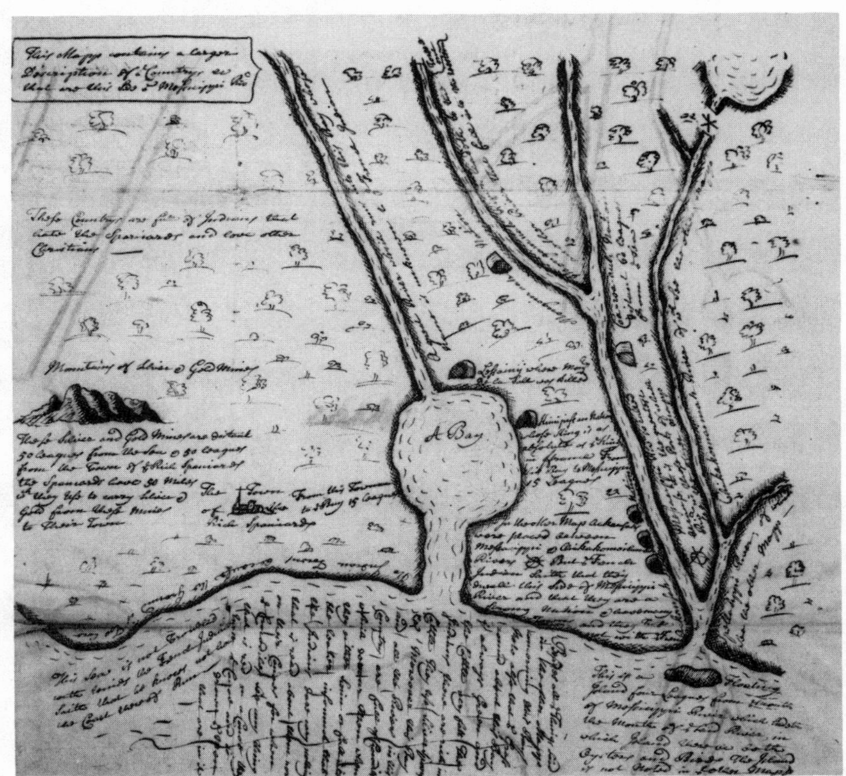

"a rude draught of the route to the nearest French settlements, and by the Mississippi to the gulf."[7] That map no longer exists, so we cannot assess its accuracy, but Nicholson was impressed by its general agreement with Father Louis Hennepin's map of the region.[8] This is of particular interest in light of Nicholson's 1699 letter to Governor Black of South Carolina, whom he urged to interrogate "Indians which you can rely upon, and lett them draw out the Country as Hennepin says one of the Shauanee Indians did for him for I think at least 400 leagues wch he found to be true."[9] The expansion of French trade and settlements in the Mississippi valley during the late seventeenth and early eighteenth centuries worried Nicholson, and he took every opportunity to learn more about the inhabitants and routes through what he termed "the Western inland frontier."[10]

The second surviving map, drawn early in 1708 by the Towasa Indian Lamhatty, depicts his travels in captivity from the Florida Gulf coast to Virginia (fig. 2). Colonel John Walker, who kept the Indian in servitude for a few months, sent Lamhatty's original map to Governor Jennings of Virginia. In so doing perhaps Walker was continuing a practice endorsed by Francis Nicholson, who had actively solicited Indian maps while governor from 1698 to 1705. However that may be, colonial officials preserved a contemporary copy of the map, a brief Towasa vocabulary, and two accompanying letters.

The next two maps, in chronological sequence, are copies of painted deerskin originals presented to Nicholson after he was appointed governor of South Carolina in 1720. One details the distribution of the predominantly Siouan-speaking tribes of the South Carolina piedmont, some of which were probably loosely confederated by this time and collectively known to the English as Catawbas (fig. 3). Headmen of the Catawbas were among those Indian leaders summoned to meet the new colonial governor upon his arrival in Charlestown in 1721, so Nicholson probably received the original deerskin map sometime in that year. A second deerskin map, with extensive notations in Chickasaw, probably came into Nicholson's possession during a meeting and exchange of presents in 1723 at a Chickasaw camp near the Savannah River (fig. 4). Two years later, this most diligent collector and solicitor of southeastern Indian maps returned to England for the last time.

The final set of surviving maps exists in the form of two copies

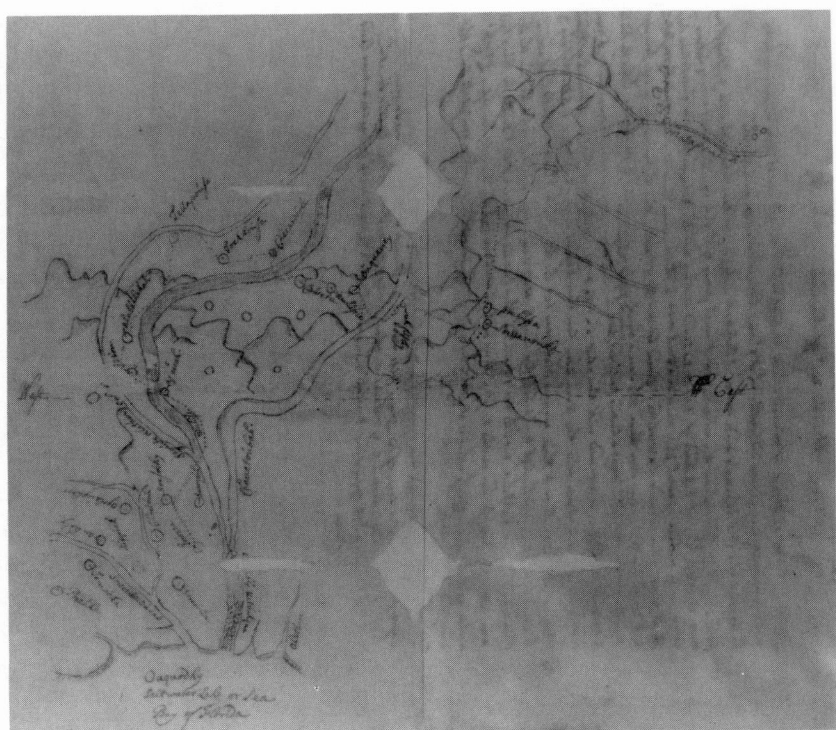

Figure 2 Lamhatty map, 1708 (courtesy of the Virginia Historical Society).

drafted by Alexandre de Batz at New Orleans in 1737, during a lull in the long war between the French and the Chickasaws. Like the two maps just described, these originally had been painted on skins. One, referred to here as the Chickasaw/Alabama map, portrays the geographical disposition of Chickasaw allies and enemies as explained to an Alabama Indian emissary sent to the Chickasaws by the French (fig. 5). The other map is a plan of the Chickasaw villages, drawn by the same Alabama headman acting as a spy in anticipation of a renewed French attack (fig. 6).

Our sample of six maps can be divided, for discussion, into two groups reflecting the different intentions of their makers. In the van den Bosh/French Indian, Lamhatty, and Alabama maps, the primary concern was to convey information about the landscape by attempt-

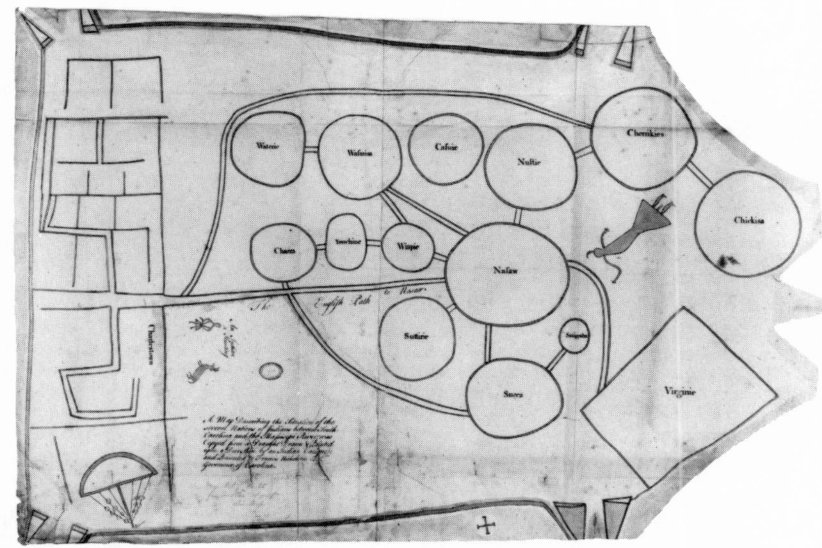

Figure 3 English copy of a Catawba deerskin map, circa 1721 (courtesy of the British Public Record Office).

Figure 4 English copy of a Chickasaw deerskin map, circa 1723 (courtesy of the British Public Record Office).

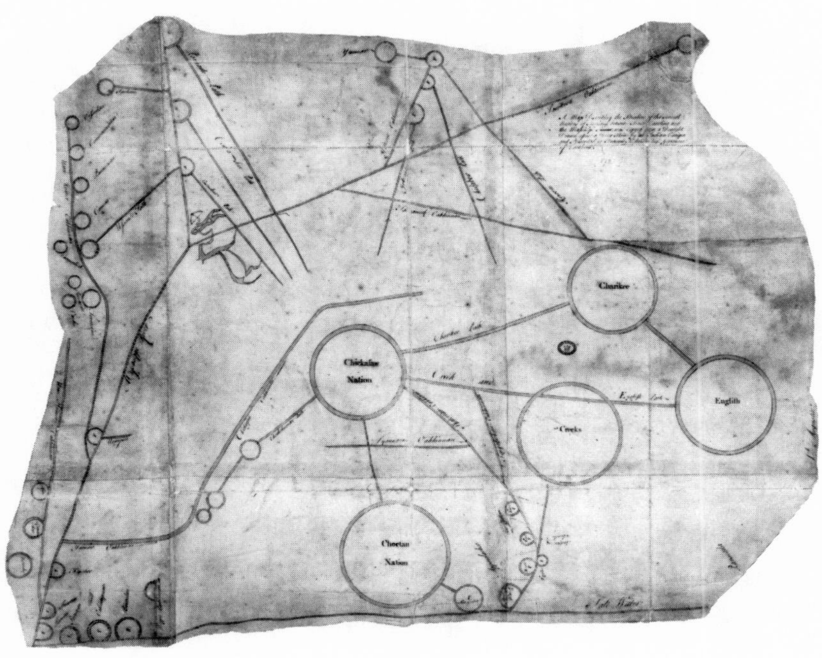

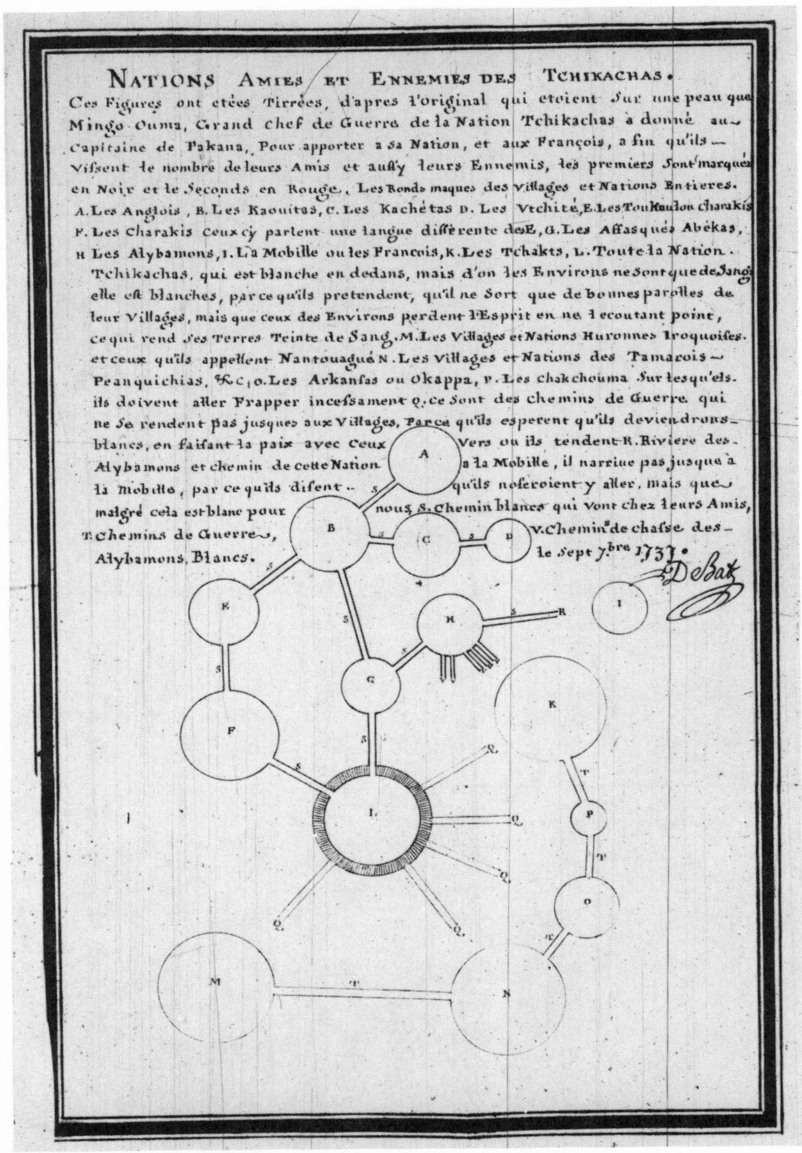

Figure 5 French copy of a Chickasaw/Alabama map, 1737 (courtesy of the Archives Nationales, Paris).

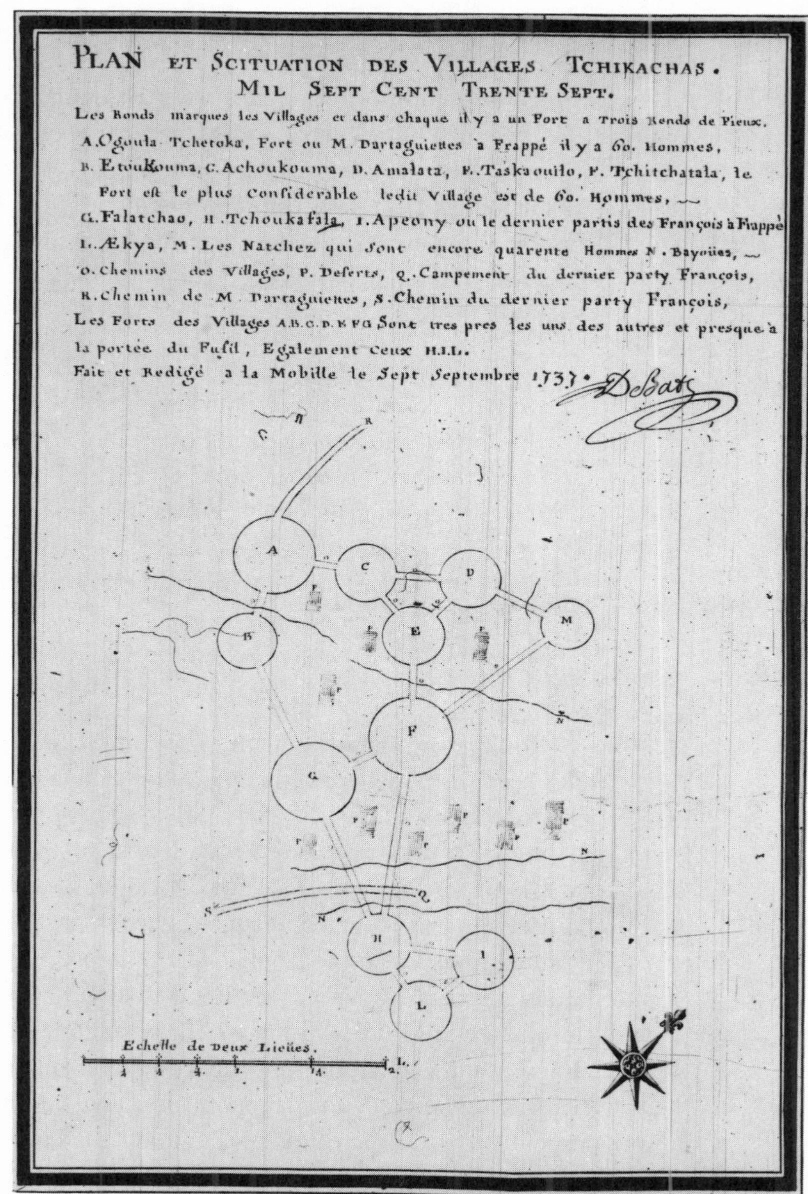

Figure 6 French copy of an Alabama Indian map, 1737 (courtesy of the Archives Nationales, Paris).

ing to delineate river courses, networks of paths, locations of mountain ranges, and placement of villages, all in proper spatial relationship to one another. European colonists most frequently requested this type of Indian map, which could be directly transferred to printed form, occasionally with attributions to Indian sources.[11] This also was the commonest sort drawn by the native southeasterners for their own use. Undoubtedly Baron de Lahontan's 1703 description of the northeastern Indians is applicable to the Southeast as well:

> They draw the most exact Maps imaginable of the Countries they're acquainted with, for there's nothing wanting in them but the Longitude and Latitude of Places: They set down the True North according to the Pole Star; the Ports, Harbours, Rivers, Creeks and Coasts of the Lakes; the Roads, Mountains, Wood, Marshes, Meadows, etc. counting the distances by Journeys and Half-Journeys of the Warriors and allowing to every Journey Five Leagues. The sechorographical Maps are drawn upon the Rind of your Birch Tree; and when the Old Men hold a Council about War or Hunting, they're always sure to consult them.[12]

Although the Catawba, Chickasaw, and Chickasaw/Alabama maps also contain considerable geographical detail, their main function was to portray social and political relationships. Such a shift in the mapmakers' perspective required a new set of conventions to represent their social world, a set that differed from the more familiar conventions used to represent the southeastern landscape. Social distance (based, for example, on the degree of kin relatedness between social groups) and political distance (the degree of cooperation between groups, or the extent of control over groups) could be effectively mapped, but only by replacing absolute measures of Euclidean distance with a flexible, topological view of space. Topological distortion is especially evident in the Catawba and Chickasaw/Alabama examples, where distance scale and orientation to cardinal points vary continuously as one moves from place to place within each map.

Actually, topological distortion of physical space occurs in all the maps (and for that matter in contemporary European maps of the region). Although the evidence to support such an assertion is sparse, we may suppose that most southeastern Indians in the early eighteenth century were intimately familiar with a fairly small region. Lamhatty, for example, drew the Towasa homeland, the area best known to him, more accurately, in greater detail, and to a larger scale than the rest of his map. He also made numerous errors in locating river courses and confluences once he was carried beyond his own territory. De Soto found an equally limited range of geographical knowledge among the Indians during his traverse of the Southeast in the mid-sixteenth century. Presumably the "catchment area" or home territory, the region of daily subsistence activities and closest kin ties, was as closely circumscribed for most native southeasterners as it was for Lamhatty, who unfortunately was the only one to leave us a visual depiction of his small world. Thus the distortion found in this individual type of map is attributable largely to cumulative errors by those who attempted to accurately portray the physical landscape of areas about which they had only superficial knowledge.[13]

In contrast to the apparent geographical parochialism of Lamhatty's personal depiction is the Chickasaw deerskin map, an extraordinarily comprehensive view of what could be termed the "Greater Southeast." This map was drafted by a Chickasaw headman who probably had access to information accumulated by other tribe members. In other words, the great breadth of geographical knowledge indicated by this map, ranging as it does from Texas and Kansas in the west to New York and Florida in the east, may represent the *collective* knowledge of the Chickasaws in 1723, even if no individual Chickasaw had ever traveled so widely. This possibility also applies to the similar Catawba and Chickasaw/Alabama maps, which likewise were drawn by headmen.

These three maps have a number of important features in common, the interpretation of which can provide insights concerning the southeastern Indians' organization of their social environment and how they perceived their world. One obviously significant characteristic is the maze of paths and rivers carefully detailed on each map and connecting many of the other map elements. Rivers and trails, distinguished only in the captions, merge to form communication networks that define the limits of mapped space, which is otherwise unbounded. Rivers arise and flow to their outlets within the confines of the maps, and paths end at the most distant villages or tribal domains. These are self-contained worlds.

They are also ethnocentric worlds. In each case the cartographer has placed his native group near the map center with paths radiating outward from the focus of attention. This results in a concentric, hierarchical organization of social space; the mapmaker's village or tribe occupies the exclusive innermost position, and all others are relegated to an outlying ring. On the Catawba map, small Siouan groups occupy the inner ring surrounding the centrally located Nasaws, who dominated the Catawba confederacy, while the English colonies and non-Siouan Cherokees and Chickasaws compose the outer ring. In this manner the Catawba headman expressed social and psychological reality schematically by his manipulation of topological space.

The use of circles to represent human social groups, from the level of villages to entire tribes, is the single most widely shared symbolic feature of southeastern Indian maps (the exception being the Europeanized van den Bosh/French Indian map). In this context the circle, one of the basic symbolic forms in the Southeast since prehistoric times,[14] probably represents the social cohesion of the group, mirroring the village plan common to many southeastern native societies of the period. An early example of the same symbolic use of circles can be seen on the deerskin mantle attributed to Powhatan and dating to about 1608 (frontispiece). Here thirty-four solid circles or roundlets, apparently representing all the separate chiefdoms at least nominally under Powhatan's control, are arranged in the familiar concentric pattern around three central figures, one of which presumably is Powhatan himself (placed in an egocentric rather than an ethnocentric position). The distribution of roundlets is essentially symmetrical, suggesting that there was no attempt to show the actual geographical distribution of the tributary chiefdoms. In its symbolic content and organization, this decorated cloak differs little from the later Catawba, Chickasaw, and Chickasaw/Alabama maps. The Catawba mapmaker expanded the metaphor of the social circle when he drew a rectangular grid plan of Charlestown and a square representing Virginia. This dichotomy carries the clear message that Indians were alike in being circular people; the English were square. Other symbolic oppositions, either implied or explicit, occur throughout these documents. In the concentric structure of some maps we see an inherent opposition between us and them, the center and the fringes of the world. In other cases color draws the contrast, as in the use of black paint to indicate allies and red to identify enemies on the Chickasaw/Alabama map. Here too trails appear to end before reaching a circle, signifying a "broken" path traveled only by war parties and distinguished from the continuous roads of peace.

By recognizing and attempting to interpret the symbolic content of the maps, we begin to understand that they are indeed political documents, graphic depictions of the balance of power among the southeastern Indians. Consider the Chickasaw map of 1723 and the Chickasaw/Alabama map of 1737. Despite the fourteen years that separate the two maps and the different audiences they were intended for (the first Governor Nicholson of English South Carolina and the other Governor Bienville of French Louisiana), the message remained essentially the same. The long war against the French and their numerous Indian allies left the Chickasaws nearly surrounded by enemies and increasingly dependent upon the distant English. But whether one's viewpoint was friendly Charlestown or hostile Nouvelle-Orléans, the Chickasaws remained a significant political entity in the region. They knew, as their maps clearly illustrated, that they still occupied a critical position at the center of the southeastern trading network. Paths interrupted by war translated to paths unusable for trade or hunting, a fact the Chickasaws found equally useful whether in requesting continued aid from the English or in peace negotiations with the French.

The Catawba headman, in his map, made a similar plea that the English recognize the Catawbas as a significant political and economic force, despite their small numbers, by virtue of their strategic location astride the crossroads of the principal trading paths from Virginia to South Carolina and from there to the numerically and economically more important Cherokees and Chickasaws. The Spanish, French, and English had long manipulated their own maps of the Southeast to propound comparable political statements, such as when each laid claim to the other's colony by extending the titles "Florida," "Louisiane," and "South Carolina" across the entire region. So they should have had little difficulty grasping the central messages carried by Indian maps and achieved through the deliberate selection and studied arrangement of symbols.

Other sorts of information included in symbolic form in these maps may not have been so readily understood by the Europeans. Both the French and the English tended to view the southeastern Indians as comprising a discrete number of autonomous tribal societies with fixed membership and relatively stable territorial boundaries, thus imposing a conformity to European notions of social and political order. Anthropologists have long understood that Native American societies held shifting views of social boundaries and inclusiveness, some evidence of which can be seen in the Indian maps. James Merrell has pointed out with regard to the Catawba map, for example, "Though colonial records had virtually ceased to mention them, Nassaws, Sugarees, Waterees, Cheraws, Saxapahaws and others still populated the mapmaker's world. Independent groups bounded by circles and linked to each other—and to Virginia and Charles Town—by paths, these entities represented the reality of Indian life as the natives saw it. 'Catawba' was nowhere to be found."[15] Other instances abound. On the earlier of the two Chickasaw maps, the rubric "Creeks" subsumed a wide range of ethnic diversity. On the later map that term was elaborated, apparently by the Alabama Indian collaborator, who separately depicted the component polities of the Creek confederacy. Lamhatty, whether by design or because of his confusion, seems to have employed the same circular map symbol for individual villages (in Towasa country) and related clusters of villages (in the Creek country). Perhaps the visual similarity between the Alabama map of the Chickasaw villages and the other maps of larger social and political groups presents the clearest evidence that the circles on these maps represent polities of significance to Indians in the particular context in which each map was drawn. They do not necessarily correspond to the "tribes" conceptualized by European colonists.

Another notable feature of the three social/political maps, and one whose meaning may have been obscure to the European recipients, is the scaling evident in the sizes of the numerous circles. Since this seems unlikely to have been selected at random, what relationships *were* specified on the basis of relative circle size? G. Malcolm Lewis has suggested that the Indians employed a range of different-sized circles as a proportional technique for showing differences in tribal populations.[16] Because we are fortunate enough to have population estimates nearly contemporaneous with the Catawba and Chickasaw maps, Lewis's idea can be explored.

First consider the 1723 Chickasaw deerskin map with its forty-three circles. Governor Bienville wrote a report a few years after the map was drawn listing the number of gunmen (a frequently used term indicating those men and boys capable of acting as warriors or hunters—about a quarter of the population) for twenty-two of the groups mentioned on the map.[17] In addition, a comparable Cherokee gunmen estimate is available from a 1721 census.[18] When the population data for the twenty-three societies are compared with circle diameters on the map (fig. 7), two distinct clusters can be observed. Nineteen groups, each with fewer than 1,000 gunmen, are represented by a series of smaller circles, but within this cluster circle size does not correlate accurately with population size. A cluster of larger circles representing the more populous groups—the Creeks (2,500), Cherokees (3,510), and Choctaws (8,000)—also includes, somewhat incongruously at first glance, the Chickasaws, with only 800 gunmen. And among these four, the Chickasaw circle is proportionally the largest in relation to population. Evidently population alone does not adequately explain the Chickasaw mapmaker's intentions. Perhaps these are more clearly understood when we recall the ethnocentric perspective common to all of these maps. In the social environment of the Chickasaws in 1723 there were at least two types of societies: an exclusive group of numerically, militarily, politically, or economically dominant societies (which naturally included the Chickasaws and the English) and another including the rest of the southeastern tribes, relatively insignificant by comparison.

Similar concerns shaped the Catawba mapmaker's world. According-

Figure 7 Comparison of map circle size and population size for twenty-three groups shown on the Chickasaw deerskin map of circa 1723.

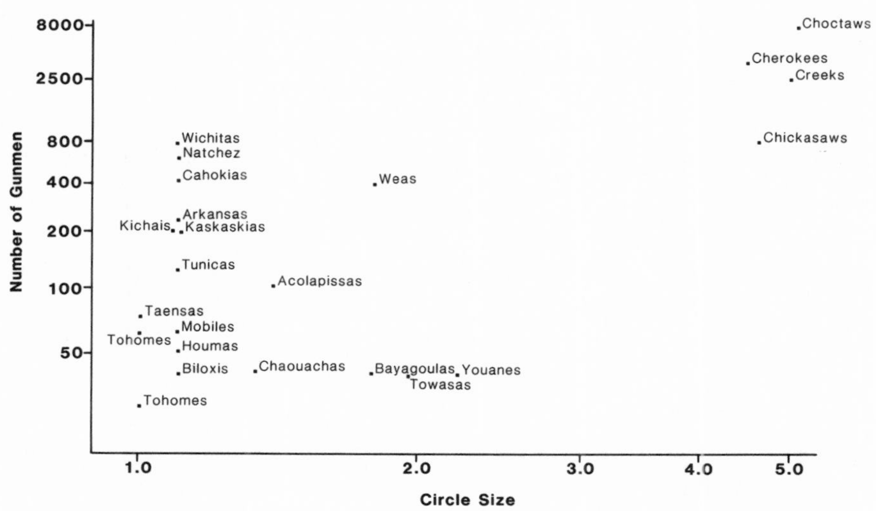

ing to a 1720 census, the seven Catawba villages (probably corresponding to the circles labeled Nasaw, Nustie, Casuie, Wiapie, Suttirie, Succa, and Saxippaha) contained 1,470 persons.[19] When circle size is again correlated with population, this time there does seem to be a proportional relationship, at least when comparing the Catawbas with other Siouan tribes, the smaller Wasmissas and the even less populous Charras. However, the correlation breaks down in the case of the Chickasaws and particularly the Cherokees, who had almost eight times the population of the Catawbas but were represented by only one-quarter of the encircled area. Catawba ethnocentrism has led to the exaggeration of those map features most significant to the mapmaker and the reduction of peripheral elements, a distortion commonplace in the cartographic views of most cultures.

This consideration of the half-dozen surviving southeastern Indian maps brings us to the inescapable conclusion that, though every one of these documents is a representation of geographical reality, reality is perceived from culturally determined points of view. The messages encoded in visual form on these maps are only partially decipherable because our ignorance of this lost world is so great. But we can appreciate, through an imperfect understanding of these unusual and remarkable maps, the multidimensional complexity of the Southeast in the colonial era.

Powhatan's Mantle, circa 1608

Title: [Deerskin Mantle Ornamented with Shell Beads, Reported to Have Belonged to the Virginia Algonquian Chief, Powhatan]

Size: 233 cm x 150 cm

Original: Tradescant Collection, Ashmolean Museum, Oxford.

Reproductions:[20]

Description: This ethnographic artifact consists of four tanned deerskins pieced together with sinew to form a cloak or mantle and decorated with thirty-seven figures made from numerous small marine shell beads sewn onto the garment.[21] The figures include a centrally placed human in front view flanked by two animals shown in profile. The animal on the right, which probably represents a white-tailed deer, has cloven hooves, a short, thin tail, and large ears, while the other animal has claws, a long tail, and relatively small ears—perhaps it is a wolf or mountain lion. The remaining thirty-four design elements are spirally formed roundlets placed in approximate symmetry on either side of the midline. Many of the shell beads have fallen away, leaving only thread holes to mark the original locations of two roundlets and the hind legs and tails of the two animals.

An entry in a 1656 catalog of curiosities collected by John Tradescant describes an item, which is probably this same mantle, as "Pohatan, King of Virginia's habit all embroidered with shells, or Roanoke." Portions of this collection were purchased by Elias Ashmole in 1659 and composed part of the Ashmolean collection donated to Oxford University in 1679.[22] The Tradescants, elder and younger, had visited Virginia and may have procured the cloak there.[23]

Figure 8 Drawing of Powhatan's mantle.

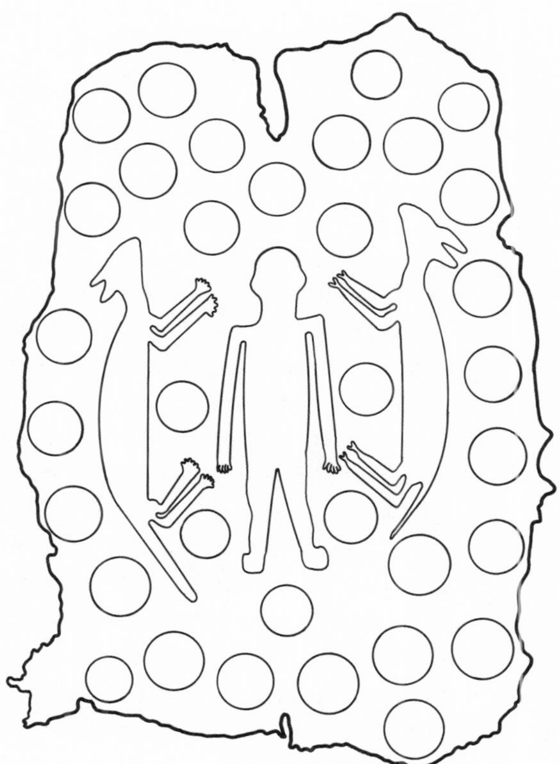

Another perhaps more plausible, but equally circumstantial, argument for derivation can be traced through the earliest Virginia colonial documents. Late in 1608 Captain Christopher Newport, at the behest of the Virginia Company of London, staged a farcical "coronation" ceremony for Powhatan. Since Powhatan apparently viewed the bestowal of a scarlet robe and copper crown as a gift from King James I deserving of reciprocity, "he gave his old shoes and his mantle to Captain Newport." Newport sailed for England in December and arrived in England by mid-January 1609. On March 5 of that year the Spanish ambassador, Don Pedro de Zúñiga, wrote to King Philip III that Powhatan "has sent a gift to this king," meaning James I of England.[24] This unspecified gift could have included the mantle presented to Newport, which might then have found its way to the Tradescants.

Whatever the ultimate origin of this mantle, it is undoubtedly a southern Algonquian artifact of the type described by John Smith. "The better sort use large mantels of Deare skins, not much differing in fashion from the Irish mantels. Some imbrodered with white beads, some with Copper, other painted after their manner."[25]

In addition to their aesthetic function, the decorative shell bead patterns may carry considerable symbolic import, particularly if the mantle is attributable to Powhatan. Randolph Turner has suggested that the thirty-four roundlets perhaps represented the districts under Powhatan's control.[26] He based his supposition on a 1612 reference by William Strachey, who noted that Powhatan's "petty Weroances in all, may be in nomber, about three or fower and thirty, all which have their precincts, and bowndes, proper."[27] Strachey went on to enumerate thirty-two werowances from the area of the James and York rivers. This list, however, includes both greater and lesser werowances, corresponding to about twenty-four districts.[28] This limited area seems to have been the core of the chiefdom, the extent of Powhatan's absolute control.[29] But there is considerable evidence that as many as thirty-six districts were claimed by Powhatan and were subject, in some degree, to his influence.[30] Considered in this light, Smith's map of 1612 and Strachey's descriptions of the geographic limits of Powhatan's power closely coincide, and the mantle attributed to that chief can be interpreted not as a statement of absolute control over a circumscribed region, but as a claim to broader hegemony over a core area plus an incompletely consolidated periphery.

Van den Bosh/French Indian Map, 1694

Title: Discription of ye Countryes that are this side ye Messacippi River

Size: 33 cm x 31 cm

Original: Ayer Collection no. 59, the Newberry Library, Chicago.

Reproductions:[31]

Description: This manuscript map is accompanied by a letter (both are copies of lost originals) from Lawrence van den Bosh to Governor Francis Nicholson of Maryland, dated "From North Sassifrix, ye 19th Day of October 1694." Van den Bosh has been identified as Laurent van den Bosck, an ordained Anglican priest from the Carolinas, who later resided in North Sassafras Parish, Cecil County, Maryland, near the falls of the Susquehanna River.[32] The letter states that he

Figure 9 Keyed drawing of the van den Bosh/French Indian map.

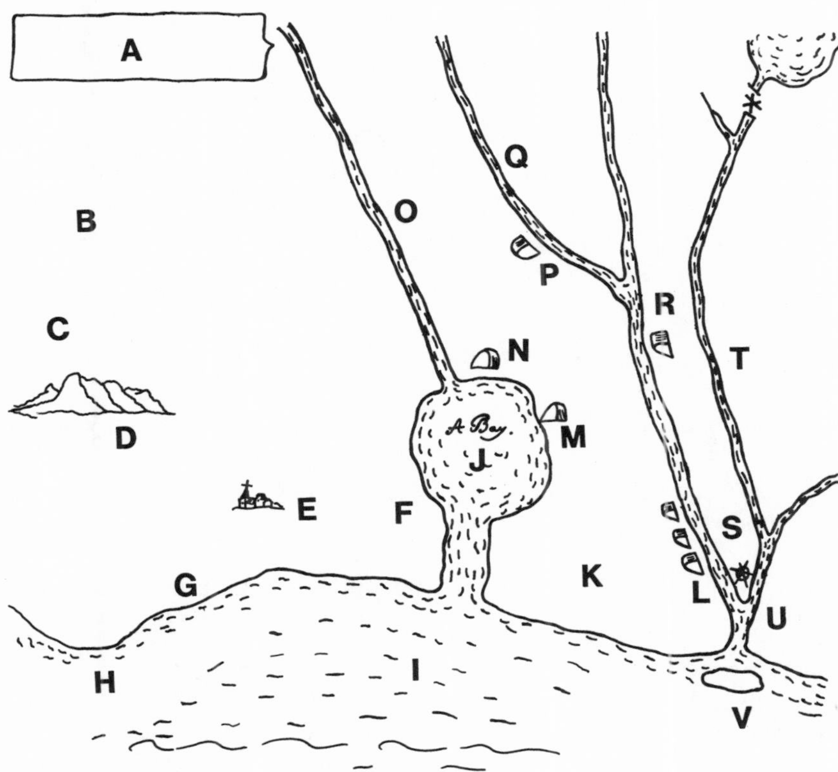

obtained his information "on the left Side of Messacippi River, which discription I lately reced. of the French Indian." The identity of this Indian remains unknown, but it is interesting to note that "Wittowees, Twistwees and naked Indians" (i.e., Miamis and other western Indians) encouraged by the French, raided the Maryland colony at the falls of the Susquehanna and Potomac rivers during the 1690s.[33] Perhaps more relevant is the appearance of the Frenchman Martin Chartier and a band of Shawnees in Maryland in 1692. By the following year these Indians were settled on the south bank of the lower Elk River in Cecil County, not far from van den Bosh's residence. Before 1690 they had lived near the French outpost at Starved Rock (Fort St. Louis on the Illinois River), which was La Salle and Tonti's base for western and southern exploration.[34] The accompanying letter reads as follows:

> Copy of a Letter to Collo Nicholson Govr of Maryland
> Sr
>
> I intended at first to Send this Map to yor Excy by Collo Hermans, but in that Regard being Disapointed of my purpose I gave it to Mr Hensbys [?], who forgott to carry it to yor Excy, in fine Mr Robinson was pleased to take it and to promise that he would deliver it unto yor Excy wch if he hath done 'tis well if not I send now again to yor Excy (by Mr Tarkington) a copy of the Same Mapp and a larger description of the Countrys River ec that are on the left Side of Messacippi River, which discription I lately reced of the French Indian. If this Labour of Mine hath the happiness to please yor Excy I will rejoice for it and I shall think my Pains not to have been Spent in vain In ye mean while I am & will Remain
>
> Yor Excy ec
>
> Lawrence Vanden Bosh
>
> From North Sassifrix
> ye 19th Day of Octobr
> 1694

Legend A. This Mapp contains a larger Discription of ye Countrys ec that are this side ye Messicippi Rivr

B. These Countrys are full of Indians that hate the Spaniards and love other Christians

C. Mountains of Silver & Gold Mines

D. These Silver and Gold Mines are distant 50 leagues from

the Sea & 50 leagues from the Town of ye Rich Spaniards the Spaniards have 50 Miles [Mules?] wch they use to carry Silver & Gold from these Mines to their Town

E. The Town of the Rich Spaniards

F. From this Town to ye Bay 15 leagues

G. No Indian Towns because the Ground is Too low

H. This Sea is not Troubled with winds the French Indian Saith that he knows not how the Coast thereof Runs

I. Besides all ye Things Said in the other Mapp concerning this Bay Note also that ye Grass round about this Bay is always Green and the Cattle very fatt The Indians there are rich in Cattle They use Silver Spoons &c Moreover this Bay and all the Rivers in this Country are full of Crocodiles which devour Men when they either Swim or fall into the Water insomuch that the Indians dare cary nothing that is read about them nor on their Canoes for when ye Crocodiles See any thing that is red on a Canoe they turn ye Canoe and so drown ye Men that are in it

J. A Bay

K. In the other Map Ackansahs were placed between Messacippi & Chikakomaimah Rivers But ye French Indian Saith that they dwell this Side of Messicippi River and that they are a Strong Nation & have many Towns and they Trade not with ye French

L. Ackansah Nation

M. Kinipiseau Nation whose King is as absolute as ye King in France From this Bay to Messicippi 15 leagues

N. Lessainy where Monsr De la Sale was killed

O. A great River which runs into this Bay whose name is unknown to ye French Indian

P. Mongoin nah Nation

Q. Mongoin nah River leadeth to the Towne [?] another River that fall in to the western one

R. Coa-roa-auh Nation distant 60 leagues from ye Sea

S. Messacippi Rivr so called because it is the greatest Rivr in those Parts of islands see the other Mapp

T. Chikakomaimah River of wch See the other Mapp

U. Ipellasippi River; of which See the other Mapp

V. This is a Floating Island four leagues from ye mouth of Messicippi River which hideth the Mouth of ye Said

River, in which Island there be both Oysters and Birds
The Island is not Noted in ye other Mapp

Compared with other seventeenth-century French and Spanish maps, this map is the most accurate rendering of the lower Mississippi valley, superseded only by the 1703 Delisle map, which incorporated the discoveries of Iberville and Bienville. According to van den Bosh's map legend, this enhanced accuracy is largely attributable to the "French Indian" who contributed, apparently to a significant extent, to the drafting and captions. There are a few parallels to Louis Hennepin's 1683 map and other derivations of the La Salle era explorations,[35] such as the "Silver and Gold Mines" (A) that are usually referred to as the "Mines St. Barbe" in the Spanish province of New Biscay. But Hennepin misplaced most of the Indian groups and had a muddled notion of the river systems of the lower valley. Van den Bosh, with his Indian collaborator, accurately portrayed Galveston Bay (J), the Trinity River (O), and the villages of the Cenis ("Lessainy," N) near where La Salle was murdered in 1687. The Cenis were the Hasinais, a confederacy of Caddoan speakers.[36] The map legends indicate some confusion over the correct location of the Ackansah (L), the Illinois Algonquian name for the Quapaws, whose villages were situated near the mouth of the Arkansas River.[37] Kinipiseau (M) was La Salle's name for the Mugulashas, who occupied the west bank of the Mississippi River above the present site of New Orleans.[38]

The schematic description of the Mississippi River (S) includes what appears to be one fanciful detail: the "Floating Islands" (V) at the mouth. In fact, this not only alludes to the driftwood and other debris that collected around the channel's unique "mud lumps," obscuring the entrance for early navigators,[39] but also refers directly to the amazing floating islands of swamp vegetation that are sometimes dislodged by spring flooding and drift back and forth for weeks on the tides at the edge of the Gulf. The Chikakomaimah River (T) has been depicted in correct relationship to the main river if it is in fact the Yazoo, but is name and position suggest it may be related to de Soto's "Chucagua," which La Salle thought "is different from the Mississippi and . . . goes along side by side with it."[40] The Ipellasippi River (U), shown as a tributary of the Yazoo, is presumably the Big Black River, which actually flows into the Mississippi separately.

Farther upstream (R) are found the Coa-roa-auh (Koroas).[41] One puzzling feature of this map is the presence of the Mongoin nah Nation (P) and Mongoin nah River (Q) branching westward from the Mississippi. This name probably refers to the Moingwena band of the Illinois, who lived on the Des Moines River in eastern Iowa from at least as early as 1673 to about 1700.[42] The inclusion of an upper Mississippi River valley tribe and river in this schematic map of the lower valley suggests that the Moingwenas were of particular significance to the mapmakers. Perhaps van den Bosh's "French Indian" collaborator was a Moingwena Illinois; some Illinois had accompanied La Salle on his explorations of the Mississippi River valley, and one could have joined (by marriage, for instance) the Shawnee band at Starved Rock before their move to Maryland.

Note that if (Q) does refer to the Des Moines River, then the mention of another river nearby "that fall in to the western one" would be a logical reference to the neighboring Nebraska River, which descends into the Missouri. Alternatively, if (Q) represents a rough approximation of the Missouri or the Arkansas, then "the western one" might refer to the much more distant Colorado, already known vaguely by rumor among the English colonists to flow toward the Pacific. The entire map can be seen as an early English attempt to make sense of a century's accumulation of imperfect, and often misleading, geographical accounts concerning the midcontinent, with the help of an Indian informant who had some direct experience with the region.

Lamhatty Map, 1708

Title: Mr. Robert Beverley's Acct. of Lamhatty

Size: 30 cm x 27 cm

Original: Lee Family Papers (MS 1, L51, fol. 677), Virginia Historical Society, Richmond.

Reproductions:[43]

Description: This manuscript map is evidently a contemporary copy of an original drawn by Lamhatty, a Towasa Indian, for Colonel John Walker of King and Queen County, Virginia, in 1708. According to a letter written by Walker,

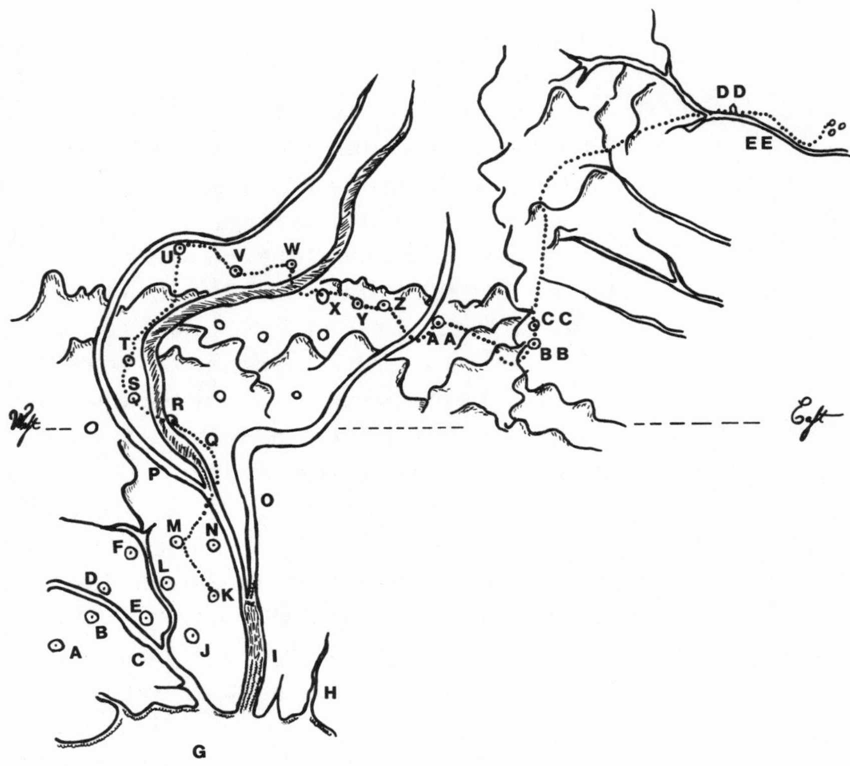

Figure 10 Keyed drawing of Lamhatty's map.

On Saturday, ye 3d of Janr Instant an Indian came naked of armes into one of ye houses of the upper Inhabitants in this County, upon which the people there tied him by ye arm & brought him to me, they got to my house with him on ye day following, at first I put him in Irons and would have brought him to yor: Honr, but the extremity of ye weather prevented any passage over Yorke River. After three days finding him of a seeming good humour, I let him at liberty about the house where he still continues; I got ye Interpreter and a tuscarora Indian to talk with him, he at all times seemd verey inclinable to be understood, and was verey forward to talk, but neither of them could understand him.

What I have learnt from him in this long acquintance is thus he calls his name Lamhátty, and his town Towása near which there were nine other nations of Indians confederates with his Town, under distinct names for ye particular, but all under the common name of Towása's, which are described by those O's on

> ye North side the East and West line; those O's on ye South side ye sd. line with severall others which he sayes are there, have also their particular names, but all under the common name of Tuscaróras he says, that not far from their Town is great falls, and a little below that a great salt water [lak]e, whose waves he describes to tumble and roar like a sea he sayes He was taken prisoner 9 months agoe; that he was 3 months in carrying to Telapoúsa where they made him work in ye groun That there they use canoes that he was 2 mo. in carrying through ye 6 next Towns, and one month in passing from ye 6th from Telapoúsa to ye 7th, where he was sold, vizt. Sowanóuka They in a short time took him out a hunting, vizt. 6 men 2 women & 3 children, along ye ledge of Lower mountains, (as he at first described to us by heaps of dirt tho' his geography has not made him hit it right in this draught) Whence he run away from them and in 9 dayes time came to ye house by Robert Powells where he was taken and brought to me He sayes that ye first time ye Tuscaróras made warr, they swept off 3 of their nations clear and ye next time 4 more, and ye other three run away The map is all his own drawing which I thought might be satisfaction to your honr to send, ye red line denotes his march, ye black lines, ye Rivers, & ye shaded lines ye mountains, which he describes to be vastly big among some of those Indian Towns, for ye rest I must referr yor Honr: to ye map; he seems very desirous to stay, if I might have yor: Honrs: leave to keep him.[44]

On the reverse of the surviving manuscript map is an account of Lamhatty's experiences written by Robert Beverley, which essentially corroborates Walker's relation and adds some significant details.

> Lamhatty an Indian of Towása of 26 years of age comeing naked & unarmed into the upper inhabitants on the north side of Mattapany in very bad weather in ye Xt. mass hollidays anno 1707 gives this accot.
>
> The foregoeing year ye Tusckaróras made war on ye Towasas & destroyed 3 of theyr nations (the whole consisting of ten) haveing disposed of theyr prisoners they returned again, & in ye Spring of ye year 1707: they swept away 4 nations more, the other 3 fled, not to be heard of. 'twas at this second comeing that they took Lamhatty & in 6 weeks time they caryed him to

Apeikah from thence in a week more to Jäbon, from thence in 5 days to tellapoúsa (where they use canoes) where they made him worke in ye Ground between 3 & 4 months. then they carryed him by easy Journeys in 6 weeks time to Oppónys from thence they were a month crossing ye mountains to Souanoúka: where they sold him A party of ye Souanoúka's comeing a hunting Northward under the foot of ye mountains took him with them, there were of ye Souanoúkas, 6 men 2 women & 3 children, he continewed with them about 6 weeks, & they pitched theyr Camp on ye branches of Rapahan: River where they pierce ye mountains, then he ran away from them keeping his course E b S & E S E. Crossing 3 branches of Rapahan: River & thrice crossing Mattapany till he fell in upon Andrew Clarks house which he went up to & Surendered himselfe to ye people they being frightned Seized upon him violently & tyed him tho he made no manner of Resistence but Shed tears & Shewed them how his hands were galled and Swelled by being tyed before; whereupon they used him gentler & tyed ye string onely by one arme till they brought him before Lt. Collo. Walker of King & Queen County where is at Liberty & Stays verry Contentedly but noe body can yet be found that understands his language.

Postscript [*torn*] after some of his Country folks were found servants [*torn*] he was Sometimes ill used by Walker, became verry melancholly often fasting & crying Several days together Sometimes useing little Conjurations & when Warme weather came he went away & was never more heard of.[45]

The map notations are as follows:

A. Poúhka
B. Tomoóka
C. Sowoólla·Oubab·
D. Asilédly [or Aulédly or Anlédly]
E. Ephíppick
F. Ogolaúghoos
G. Ouquodky, Saltwater Lake or Sea, Bay of Florida
H. Alatám
I. [*torn*]hbly Netúckqua [or Uetúckqua]
J. Sowoólla
K. Towása
L. Choctóuh
M. Socsoóky
N. Susenpáh
O. Chauctoúbab·
P. Sayénte Alatám Oúbab
Q. Wichise
R. Apéicah·

S. Jäbou· [or Jäbon·]
T. Alabáchehah
U. Tellapoúsa
V. Tockhoúsa
W. Cheeawoóle
X. Caweta
Y. Awhíssie
Z. Oŭquáney
AA. Oukfúsky
BB. Sowanoúka
CC. Poehússa
DD. R. Powels
EE. Matapani R.

The following discussion agrees generally, but not in every respect, with the interpretations of David Bushnell and John Swanton concerning these accounts, the map notations, and a sixty-word Towasa vocabulary found with Walker's letter.[46] As Swanton discovered, there are a number of errors in Walker's and Beverley's accounts. For instance, the Towasa villages are represented on the map by circles on the south (not north) side of the east-west line. Second, the English were apparently misled by the Tuscarora interpreter, who, although he could not understand the Towasa language, claimed that his people had made war on the Towasas and that they occupied the numerous towns Lamhatty visited during his captivity. Most of these towns actually were inhabited by Upper and Lower Creeks, but recent writers occasionally have accepted the self-serving interpreter's story.[47]

Lamhatty's homeland lay along the Florida Gulf coast (G, Ouquodky), apparently around the Chipola (C) and west of the Apalachicola (I) and Ochlockonee (H) rivers. This region was originally occupied by the Chatots (or Chacatos). Two Spanish missions were established there in 1674, and soon afterward the missionaries built Sabacola Mission, at the confluence of the Chattahoochee (P) and Flint (O) rivers. Other Christianized Chatots moved to the Apalachee missions farther east. Beginning in 1685, the Spanish missions increasingly became targets of English-inspired slave raids by Creeks, Yamasees, and Yuchis from the north. Three raids by the Creeks in 1702–4 (including one led by Colonel James Moore of South Carolina), effectively destroyed the Timucuan and Apalachee missions in northern Florida, resulting in the killing, dispersal, or enslavement of most of the resident Indian population. The Creek attacks on Towasa villages in 1706 and 1707 were a continuation of the protracted slaving wars instigated by the Carolinians.

In fact, the Towasa confederation seems to have consisted primarily of refugees from the attacks on Apalachee and Timucua a few years before. In support of this contention, parallels can be drawn between several of the town names and the Indian names of earlier Spanish missions. For instance, Choctóuh (L) is certainly a Chatot village, probably consisting of a remnant of San Carlos de Chacatos in Apalachee. Sowoólla (J) probably was a group of refugees from Sabacola, later known as the Sawokli village of the Lower Creeks,[48] and Tomoóka (B) may be a Timucua village. The name of a fourth town, Asilédly (D), is reminiscent of San Miguel de Asile, the westernmost of the Yustega Timucuan missions disrupted by the 1704 raids.[49] Ephíppick (E) may be a settlement of missionized inhabitants from Santa Cathalina de Afuica, destroyed in 1685. Ogolaúghoos (F) could refer to San Joseph de Ocuia, an Apalachee mission destroyed in 1703.[50] According to Swanton's analysis of the Towasa vocabulary accompanying Walker's 1708 letter, Lamhatty spoke a Timucuan dialect,[51] and as will be explained below, his village (K) seems to have been associated with the Chatots. Finally, several river names, Alatám (H), and Sayénte Alatám Oúbab (P) may reflect the name of the Apalachee mission of Nuestra Señora de la Candelaria de la Tama (cf. Santa la Tama). One might disagree with some of the proffered identifications, but the number of similarities is impressive and consistently suggests that the Towasa towns formed a short-lived confederation of refugee Timucuans, Apalachees, and Chatots who had sought mutual protection but were soon attacked and again dispersed by the Creeks. Between July and September of 1706, after the first raid mentioned by Lamhatty, bands of surviving Chatots and Towasas made their way to Mobile, where they received French protection.[52]

During his captivity, Lamhatty was taken to a number of Creek towns indicated on his map. Bushnell and Swanton both assumed that the map notations refer to specific towns, but some of them actually seem to be names of more inclusive social groupings (just as Lamhatty alternatively applied the name "Towása" to his village and to the ten-town confederacy). During the late seventeenth and early eighteenth centuries, the English, Spanish, and French consistently referred to groups such as the Apalachicolas, Coosas, Alabamas, Tallapoosas, Abekas, and Ocheses; only later did the terms Upper Creek and Lower Creek come into vogue, perhaps as a reflection of increasing political centralization in the course of the eighteenth century.[53] Considered in this light, Lamhatty's Creek "town" names can be correlated with the following intermediate-sized polities: Apéicah·(R) and Jäbou·(S) (Abekas and Jiape, or Hillabees, on the Coosa River),[54] Alabáchehah (T, Alabamas [?] on the upper Alabama River), Tellapoúsa (U, Tallapoosas on the lower Tallapoosa River), Tockhoúsa (V, Coosas on the Coosa River), Caweta (X, Cowetas on the Ocmulgee River), Awhíssie (Y) and Oŭquáney (Z) (Ochisis and Oconees on the Oconee River). A list of Creek "nations" or villages dating from 1700 also includes a number of comparable names (i.e., Apicales, Alebamons, Ouacoussas, Choualles, and Couitas).[55]

The identity of Lamhatty's Towasas has puzzled ethnohistorians ever since Bushnell discovered the map in 1908. In the post–de Soto era, the name first appears in 1675 as the name of a village and "province" situated at the confluence of the Coosa and Alabama rivers in central Alabama. In the aftermath of the Chatot rebellion that same year, many Chatots found refuge with the Towasas, far from Spanish retribution. Numerous Christian Chatots remained among the Towasas eleven years later when Marcos Delgado visited the region.[56] Still in the same location in 1700, the "Touachee nation" was included on a village list elicited from native informants by the French explorer Charles Levasseur.[57] From this point the Towasas disappear from central Alabama, next appearing in northwest Florida. Perhaps there had been a falling-out among the various refugee villages composing the Alabamas, of which the Towasas had apparently been preeminent. If so, the Towasas could have joined their old acquaintances, the Chatots, who could finally have had an opportunity to repay a thirty-year-old debt of hospitality. Since Lamhatty is thought to have spoken a Timucuan dialect, even stronger ties may have drawn the Towasas to Florida.

Lamhatty's detailed geographical knowledge seems to have been limited to the immediate vicinity of the Towasa towns and adjacent Gulf coast. This is apparent from his river locations and names, which seem accurate in the southern reaches but become progressively distorted north of the east-west line. Based on our knowledge of Creek town locations at that period, it seems that Lamhatty inaccurately connected the Tallapoosa (west of U) and the Ocmulgee (Q) rivers with the Chattahoochee (P), and the Oconee (east of Z) with the Flint (O). Thus Lamhatty's map consists of two reasonably accurate halves that have been crudely meshed along the "east-west" line. These errors are easily attributable to Lamhatty's understandable disorientation in unfamiliar country, where he frequently crossed rivers that he mistakenly equated with those flowing through Towasa territory. Swanton failed to grasp this point, even going so far as to claim that the Wichise River (Q) was the Chattahoochee,[58] although the name Ochese Creek is known to have referred to the Ocmulgee River, the location of the Cowetas (X) in 1707.[59]

Lamhatty was traded by his Creek captors to one of the bands of Shawnees (BB) living on the upper Savannah River.[60] He soon escaped and made his way to the English settlements on the Mattaponi River (EE), but others of his tribe may have been among the Indian slaves brought into Charlestown by the Savannahs in 1707.[61] As noted by Beverley, Lamhatty endured the cruelty of his English master for a time, finally wandering off into the forest, "& was never more heard of."

Catawba Deerskin Map, circa 1721 (English Copies)

Titles: (Copy 1) This Map describing the Scituation of the Several Nations of Indians to the N.W. of South Carolina was coppyed from a Draught drawn & painted on a Deerskin by an Indian Cacique and presented to Francis Nicholson Esqr. Governour of South Carolina by whom it is most humbly Dedicated To His Royal Highness George Prince of Wales [above a crown and a banner]
(Copy 2) A Map Describing the Situation of the several Nations of Indians between South Carolina and the Massisipi River; was copyed from a Draught Drawn & Painted upon a Deer Skin by an Indian Cacique; and Presented to Francis Nicholson Esqr. Governour of Carolina.

Size: (1 and 2) 112 cm x 81 cm

Originals: (1) Additional MS 4723 (formerly Sloane MS 4723), British Museum, London. (2) Colonial Office Library 700, North American Colonies, General no. 6(1), Map Room, Public Record Office (PRO), Kew, London.

Reproductions: (1)[62] (2)[63]

Description: Two copies exist of a lost original, which, as the titles indicate, was painted on a deerskin. Both copies were redrawn in red ink on paper cut in the shape of deerskins; they are quite similar, so a single description will serve, with discrepancies noted as necessary.

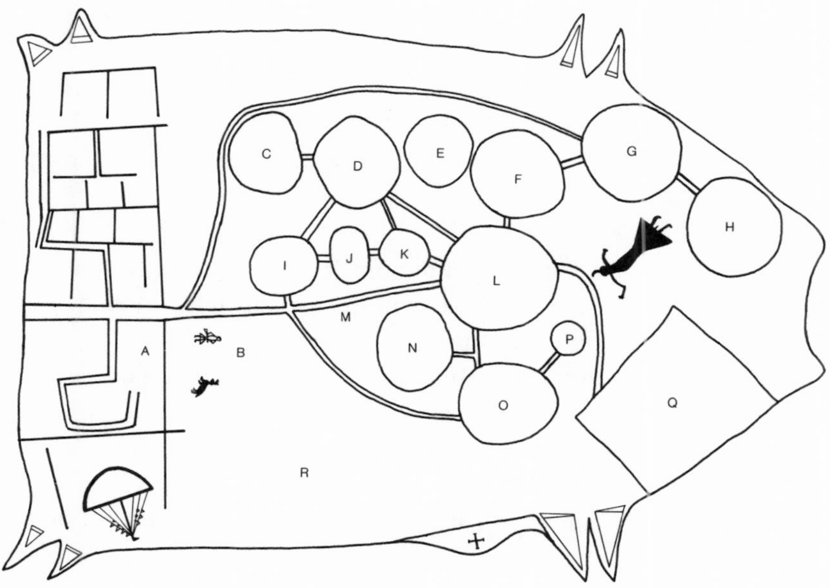

Figure 11 Keyed drawing of the Catawba deerskin map.

The central features are thirteen circles labeled with Indian names and connected by an intricate network of double lines representing paths. Along the left side of the map is "Charlestown," with its rectangular street grid and a ship in harbor with pennants flying. In the lower right corner is a large rectangle labeled "Virginie." The deerskin is bounded on the top, left, and bottom by a solid red line. Below the bottom line, set apart from the other map elements, is a Greek cross. At the corners are pairs of isosceles triangles (partly colored red on the PRO copy), presumably representing deer hooves. In addition to the titles (which differ between the copies, as already noted), there are two other interesting features. One is a large female (?) figure shaded entirely in red, with a feather (?) in her hair, arms outstretched, wearing a skirt and having what appears to be a tail. The other consists of a pair of figures, a male carrying a musket facing a buck, and the caption "An Indian a Hunting."

The map notations are as follows:

A. Charlestown
B. An Indian a Hunting
C. Waterie
D. Wasmisa
E. Casuie
F. Nustie
G. Cherrikies
H. Chickisa

I. Charra
J. Youchine
K. Wiapie
L. Nasaw
M. The English Path to Nasaw
N. Suttirie
O. Succa
P. Saxippaha
Q. Virginie
R. [*titles; see above*]

Governor Francis Nicholson obtained the original deerskin map sometime between his arrival in Charlestown on May 29, 1721, and his departure for London on May 17, 1725. As was customary upon the appointment of a new colonial governor, Indian leaders from each of the major tribes were summoned in 1721 to meet Nicholson. Among these were Creeks and Cherokees, "as also the Catawba: A Head man out of each Town of each Nation to come down."[64] Nicholson probably took this opportunity to solicit a map from "an Indian Cacique," who is generally thought to have been from one of the South Carolina piedmont tribes that were clearly of principal interest to the mapmaker. The British Museum copy (1) may have been among the "several curiosities" from South Carolina that Nicholson presented to the Prince of Wales soon after his return to England.[65]

Several of the names on the map are readily recognizable: Charlestown (A), Virginia (Q), Cherokees (G), and Chickasaws (H). The others refer to the numerous small tribes situated in the South Carolina piedmont in the 1720s. Collectively known to the English as Catawbas, these predominantly Siouan-speaking peoples settled near one another for mutual protection and may have been loosely confederated by this time. A 1715 census, taken just before the Yamasee War, lists seven villages of "Catapaws," one "Sarow" village, and four "Waccomassus" villages in this region.[66] William Byrd noted in his diary in 1728 that "about three-score Miles more [from Crane Creek, North Carolina] bring you to the first Town of the Catawbas, call'd Nauvasa, situated on the banks of Santee river. Besides this Town there are five Others belonging to the same Nation, lying all on the same Stream, within a Distance of 20 miles."[67]

Byrd's "Nauvasa" corresponds to Nasaw (L), the largest circle and evidently the mapmaker's focus of interest. From this point paths radiate to the neighboring piedmont Indians and to the English colonies. According to James Merrell, "Prior to the Yamassee War colonists . . . [labeled] Indians in the Catawba/Wateree River valley

Esaws, Catawbas, and Usherees, using none of these terms in a consistent manner. . . . By 1715 even Esaw/Usheree disappeared, to emerge later as 'Nassaw,' a principal town of the 'Catawba' Nation. Catawba itself had become the common term, though it remained unclear exactly what peoples this word included."[68]

Nustie (F) is equivalent to "Neustee," one of six Catawba towns mentioned in 1754.[69] Succa (O) and Suttirie (N) represent two tribal groups whose similar names caused much confusion among the English. The Succas (also known as the Shoccories, Sughas or Tansequas)[70] and the Suttiries (Sugerees, Sutarees, Satarees, Shuterees)[71] established villages near the Nasaws in the early eighteenth century, and together they formed the nucleus of the Catawbas.

Most of the other groups portrayed on the map eventually were assimilated by the Catawbas, but precisely when is not known. The Charras (I) (or Saras, Saraws, Charraws, Cheraws)[72] maintained a distinct identity and separate landholdings until at least 1738, but before that they cooperated with the Catawbas in negotiations with the English. Likewise, the Saxippahas (P) (Sasapahaes, Saxabahaws, Sissipahaws)[73] formed a separate political entity at least as late as 1717, though they too eventually sought refuge by coalescing with the Catawbas.

The Wateries (C) (or Waterees)[74] occupied a single large town and, according to James Adair, spoke a "Dialect" different from the "Katahba."[75] Another linguistically distinct group was the Casuies (E) (Coosoes, Kussoes, Coosahs),[76] who originally lived in coastal South Carolina before moving westward to join the Catawbas.

Wasmisa (D) probably refers to the Waccamaws (Wassamassaws, Washamsaws, Wackamaws).[77] This group was closely associated with the Pedees from 1716 to 1755; of the two, the Waccamaws were more populous. In 1727 they inhabited a village one-half mile from the Catawbas.[78] The remnant of a third tribe, the Wawees, apparently was affiliated with the Waccamaws and Pedees in 1716.[79] This group might conceivably be the Wiapies (K) shown on the map near Wasmisa. "Weaipee Town" is referred to in a 1741 list of headmen receiving commissions from the English, but by 1756 the "Weyappees" seem to have merged with the Nasaws.[80]

The final group, identified on the map as Youchine (J), may be a band of Yuchis who temporarily joined the Catawbas. James Mooney pointed out that the Catawba word "nieya" (meaning "people" or "Indians") was often abbreviated to "nie" or "ye" (as in "Kataba nie" or "Yuchi nie").[81] However, I know of no independent historical reference to Yuchis living near or with the Catawbas in the 1720s.

Although this map may appear to be rather schematic, the placement of Indian groups and paths was actually precise, reflecting the mapmaker's detailed geographical knowledge of the South Carolina piedmont. (Incidentally, the British Museum copy [1] has an additional path connecting Wasmisa [D] and Charra [I] that is lacking in the PRO version [2]. Another difference is the placement of the path from Suttirie [N], which leads directly to Nasaw [L] in the PRO version but intersects the Nasaw [L]–Succa [O] path on the other copy.) If the map is turned so that Charlestown (A) is to the lower right and Virginie (Q) is at the top (i.e., to the north), the viewer can more easily compare the deerskin map with two approximately contemporary English maps, the War Map of 1715[82] and Colonel Bull's map of 1738.[83] All three show the English Path to Nasaw (M) or the Catawba Path (running from Charlestown up the east side of the Wateree River to Nasaw, by way of the Charras), the Occaneechi Path (from Virginia to Nasaw), and the Cherokee Path (from Charlestown to the Cherokees, following the Savannah River, and on to the Chickasaws). An important difference between the Indian and English maps is the Indian's use of a variable scale, which allowed him to include such distant groups as the Cherokees, Chickasaws, and Virginians while simultaneously depicting the relative locations of the piedmont societies. Nine of these Indian groups (D, E, F, J, K, L, N, O, and P) probably occupied a tightly circumscribed area around the Catawba River, the Wateries (C) being situated farther south and the Charras (I) to the southeast. Thus the mapmaker accurately conveyed the proper spatial ordering of map elements by manipulating distance, which permitted him to provide a great deal of information regarding the Siouan groups as well as providing a regional perspective, all within the irregular confines of a deerskin.

Chickasaw Deerskin Map, circa 1723 (English Copy)

Title: A Map Describing the Situation of the several Nations of Indians between South Carolina and the Massisipi.; was Copyed from a Draught Drawn upon a Deer Skin by an Indian Cacique and Presented to Francis Nicholson Esqr. Governour of Carolina.

Size: 145 cm × 114 cm

Original: Colonial Office Library 700, North American Colonies, General no. 6(2), Map Room, Public Record Office, Kew, London.

Reproductions:[84]

Description: The history of this map is similar to that of the Catawba map. Sometime during his tenure as governor of South Carolina, Francis Nicholson obtained the deerskin original, now lost. This document is a copy on deerskin-shaped paper with figures outlined in black ink and filled in with red paint. As with the Catawba map, the ethnicity of the mapmaker is not specified in Nicholson's map title, but it can be inferred with reasonable certainty from the map's content.

Several of the map notations include words that are western Muskogean in origin (i.e., *Oakhinnau,* "river"; *Ucau,* "water"; *Humer,* "red"; *Benelee,* "settlement").[85] This language group consists of several dialects of the Choctaw language and Chickasaw, which is considered either another dialect of Choctaw or a distinct, but very similar, language.[86] In addition, a trade jargon known as Mobilian

Figure 12 Keyed drawing of the Chickasaw deerskin map.

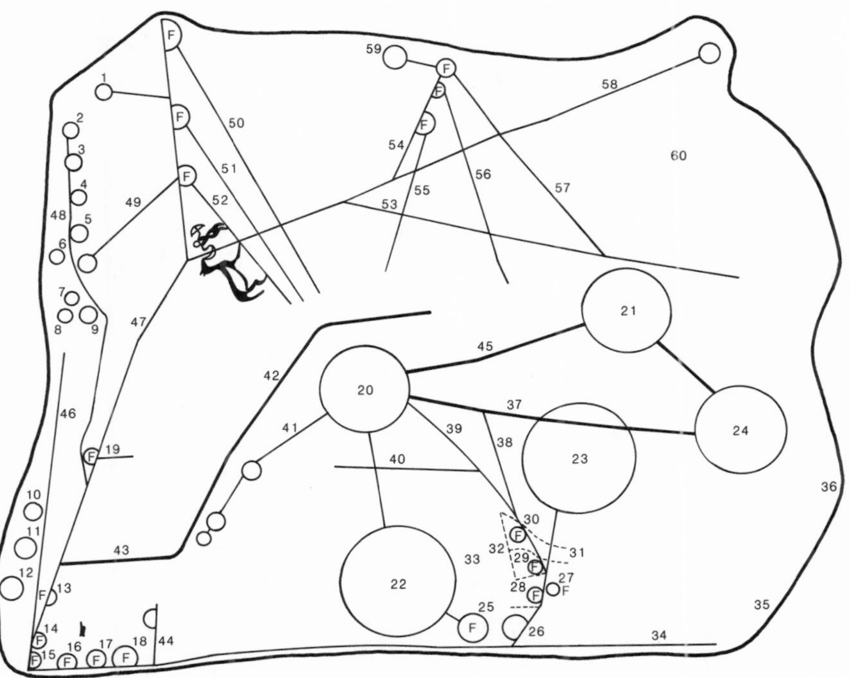

developed during the historic period in the Southeast to facilitate intercultural contact, and the basis of this pidgin language was Chickasaw.[87] Unfortunately the western Muskogean word list on the map is too brief to permit a positive identification of the language spoken by the mapmaker.

Chickasaw is the most likely of the three, however. During Nicholson's residency in Charlestown, the Chickasaws were at war with the French until early in 1725 and maintained close trade ties with the English. The Choctaws, on the other hand, seem to have had no direct contact with the South Carolina government from before the 1715 Yamasee War until late in 1725, after Nicholson's departure for England. In 1723 a small band of Chickasaws settled near Savannah Town at the invitation of the English and in September met with Nicholson, with whom "presents were exchanged."[88] A reasonable surmise is that this map was among the Chickasaw presents to the governor. The map organization also suggests a Chickasaw perspective. That group is placed at the center of the map (20) with paths and river routes radiating from the "Chickasaw Nation." Also, numerous tribes with the letter "F" next to their names (denoting alliance with the French) encircle the Chickasaws, a fact they probably would have wanted to emphasize to the English.

This map presents many interpretive challenges, primarily because the orthography is so unusual. Some of the tribal names seem to be unique to this map and remain unidentified. The keyed notations are as follows:

1. Sauhau
2. Vossulau
3. Commaucerilau
4. Pauneasau
5. Causau
6. Carenahish
7. Sovuasau
8. Vauhu
9. Tovocolau
10. Kejos
11. Katutaucheu
12. Notauku
13. Nauchee (F)
14. Tunecau (F)
15. Humau (F)
16. Sovuasau (F)
17. Oakculapesar (F)
18. Biuculau (F)
19. Ucaupau (F)
20. Chickasaw Nation
21. Charikee
22. Choctau Nation
23. Creeks
24. English
25. Noe India (F)
26. Came in the Indian War
27. Tausau (F)
28. Movele (F)
29. Tume (F)
30. Tume (F)
31. Chocktau Benelee
32. Elav Chickasau au abbe
33. Appaulachee
34. Salt Water
35. Pensacola
36. St. Augustine

37. Creek and English Path
38. Tongolickau Oakhinnau
39. Shaterrau Oakhinnau
40. Tyannacau Oakhinnau
41. Chockchumau Path
42. Chickasau Oakhinnau
43. Yausau Oakhinnau
44. Hoppe Oakhinnau
45. Charikee Path
46. Ucau Humer Oakhinnau
47. Massasippe River
48. Ucau Humer Oakhinnau
49. Ussaule Path
50. Pavuaule Path
51. Cow' a-keer Path
52. Cuscuskeer Path
53. Ta[ ]canuck Oakhinnau
54. Yoltenno Oakhinnau
55. Yoltenno Path
56. Chickabou Path
57. Kenocolu Path
58. Senottova Oakhinnau
59. Yaumeer
60. [*title; see above*]

Beginning with the large circles in the center, the locations of the Chickasaws (20), Cherokees (21), Choctaws (22), and Creeks (23) are clearly marked. To the south and southeast are the Gulf of Mexico (34), Spanish Pensacola (35), St. Augustine (36), and the English colony of South Carolina (24). The Savannah River Path to the Cherokees, also shown on the Catawba map, is unlabeled here (between 21 and 24), but the Upper Trading Path (37)[89] and the Cherokee-Chickasaw Path (45) are both indicated. The rivers in this area are recognizable from their relative locations, although the meanings of the names given them are obscure (Tyannacau [40] = Noxubee, Shaterrau [39] = Tombigbee). "Tongolickau" (38) is probably a garbled Chickasaw variant of Tuscaloosa, the colonial period designation of the Black Warrior River.[90] The area near Mobile, where several refugee tribes were relocated by Governor Bienville, is shown in considerable detail. Included are the Mobile village (28), the two Tohome villages (29, 30), the general location of four Apalachee villages (33), and the position of three Choctaw villages (31) that is otherwise unspecified in period maps and documents.[91]

Across the river from the Mobile Indians were the Taensas (27), who arrived in 1715. Those who "came in the Indian War" (26) may refer to the Chatots and Towasas, refugees from Creek slaving raids of 1706 and 1707, but this is not certain. The identity of "Noe India" (25) is not known, although the Choctaw town of Youane occupies this spot, far to the southeast of the other Choctaw towns, on the de Crenay map.[92] Four dotted lines crisscross the area, perhaps indicating trails or tribal territory boundaries. Finally, paralleling the upper Mobile River is a phrase (32) that seems to translate as "Elaw, the Chickasaw, kills [or 'was killed'] here." The small refugee tribes situated here were frequent targets of Chickasaw attacks during this period.

Leading southwest from the Chickasaws was the Natchez Trace (41),[93] which passed through Chakchiuma, Koroa, Ofogoula, and Yazoo lands. The adjacent river is the Yazoo (43), known as the Chickasaw River (42) in its upper reaches.[94] The lower Mississippi River (47) tribes include the Natchez (13), Tunicas (14), Houmas (15), Chawashas (16, placed too far upstream),[95] Acolapissas (17), and Bayagoulas (18). A small red pointing hand was drawn just above 16 and 17. "Hoppe Oakhinnau" (44) probably refers to the Pearl River,[96] where the Biloxis were situated.

Along the left edge of the deerskin, the Chickasaw headman portrayed three Caddoan tribes identifiable as the Nadacos or Anadarkos (12, part of the Hasinai Confederacy, with villages on the Neches River),[97] the Kadohadachos (11), and the Kichais (10), both on the Red River (46).[98] Farther up the Mississippi River were the Quapaws or Arkansas (19) at the mouth of the Arkansas River (48), which is shown with numerous tribes in its upper reaches. These include the Touacaras or Tawakonis (9),[99] the Tawehash or Taovayas (6, 7, and 8), the Cancy or Lipan Apaches (5),[100] the Paniassas or Wichitas (4),[101] and probably the Comanches (3), usually called Paducas by the French.[102] The meaning of "Vossulau" (2) remains a mystery. That the Chickasaws were personally acquainted with at least some of these tribes was discovered by Jean-Baptiste Bénard de La Harpe during his visit to a Tawakoni village in 1719. A week after his arrival, a lone Chickasaw appeared with trade goods, apparently acting as a middleman for either French or English traders.[103]

To the east are shown three paths leading to French-allied tribes. From north to south, these are the Peoria (cf. Peoualen) Path (50) to the upper Illinois River, the Cahokia Path (51), and the Kaskaskia Path (52).[104] An armed warrior leading a horse appears on the Kaskaskia Path, perhaps symbolizing an attack by the Chickasaws on that tribe. The "Ussaule Path" (49) probably corresponds to the path followed by Dutisné in 1719 when he traveled overland from Kaskaskia to the Osages.[105] "Sauhau" (1) may be the Missouris, judging from their location northwest of the Cahokias. Unfortunately, these last two names are otherwise unknown.

The Ohio River (58) is named for the Senecas, situated in western New York.[106] Branching to the southeast is the Tennessee River (53; the name is only partly legible because of a crease in the manuscript). On the Wabash River (54) are three more French allies, with paths leading to each tribe from the southeast. "Yoltenno"(55) is probably equivalent to Ouyatenon or Wea.[107] Chickabou (56) may derive from Kickapoo.[108] I do not recognize "Kenocolu" (57). The Miamis may be represented by the term "Yaumeer" (59).[109]

Thomas Hatley described this map as the "first unified cartographic depiction of the now familiar southeastern 'region.' "[110] Actually, it covers an even larger area encompassing approximately 700,000 square miles, from southeastern Texas (12) to southwestern Kansas (3) on the west and northeastern Florida (36) to western New York (the circle at the end of 58) on the east. The range and depth of this unnamed Chickasaw headman's cartographic knowledge was extraordinary; undoubtedly much of the map's significance was beyond the grasp of Nicholson or any of his European contemporaries.

Chickasaw/Alabama Map, 1737 (French Copy)

Title: Nations Amies et Ennemies des Tchikachas. [Nations Friendly and Hostile to the Chickasaws.]

Size: Not determined

Original: Archives des Colonies, ser. C13A, vol. 22, fol. 67, Archives Nationales, Paris

Reproductions:[111]

Description: In 1730 the Chickasaws offered protection to about 200 Natchez Indians who were the object of a French war of extermination, thereby involving themselves in a protracted war against the French and their Choctaw allies. After receiving repeated rebuffs to French demands for surrender of the Natchez refugees, Governor Bienville launched a two-pronged attack on the Chickasaws. Owing to poor communication, the northern force of 400 men (consisting of Illinois regular troops and militia and Miami, Iroquois, and Kaskaskia warriors) led by Major Pierre d'Artaguette arrived at the Chickasaw towns before the main army. D'Artaguette's small force was totally defeated on March 25, 1736, and most of the captured

Frenchmen were subsequently burned alive. Bienville's army of 600 French troops and 600 Choctaws did not reach the Chickasaw villages until May 26. This second attack also failed, and they were compelled to retreat.[112] It was to gain the release of two French captives and to produce a map of the Chickasaw villages that the Captain of Pakana, an Alabama war leader, was dispatched as a French emissary to Chickasaw country in June 1737. While there he met with Mingo Ouma, a war leader from the village of Ogoula Chitoka, who professed respect for the French and a desire for peace. To the Captain of Pakana, Mingo Ouma proposed that the Alabamas and Chickasaws join forces to kill the remaining Natchez and then destroy the Chakchiumas.[113] He also, according to the map legend, presented the Alabamas and the French with this map painted on a skin.

The surviving copy, redrawn and transcribed by the engineer and draftsman Alexandre de Batz, was sent to France.[114] The captions translate as follows:

> These figures were taken from the original which were on a skin that Mingo Ouma, great war chief of the Chickasaw Nation, gave to the Captain of Pakana to take to his Nation and to the French, in order that they might see the number of their friends and also their enemies; the former are indicated in black and the second in red. The circles denote villages and entire nations.

A. The English
B. The Cowetas ["Kaouitas"]
C. The Kasihtas ["Kachetas"]
D. The Yuchis ["Utchite"]
E. The Tugaloo Cherokees ["Toukouloo Charakis"]
F. The Cherokees ["Charakis"] who speak a different language than E
G. The Okfuskees ["Affasques"] Abekas ["Abekas"]
H. The Alabamas ["Alybamons"]
I. Mobile or the French
K. The Choctaws ["Tchakts"]
L. The whole Chickasaw ["Tchikachas"] Nation, which is white within, but the space surrounding it is of nothing but blood. It is white because they claim that only good words come from their villages, but those of the surrounding coun-

try lose their minds by not listening to them at all, and this stains their lands with blood.

M. The Huron ["Huronnes"] and Iroquois ["Iroquoises"] villages and nations and those they call Nantouague

N. The villages and nations of the Tamaroas ["Tamarois"], Piankashaws ["Peanquichias"], etc.

O. The Arkansas or Quapaws ["Okappa"]

P. The Chakchiumas ["Chakkchouma"], whom they are going to attack at once

Q. These are warpaths that do not go as far as the villages, because they hope that they will become white when they make peace with those toward whom they lead.

R. River of the Alabamas ["Alybamons"] and the path from that nation to Mobile. It does not go as far as Mobile because they say they would not dare to go there, but in spite of that it is white for us

S. White paths that lead to their friends

T. War paths

V. Hunting paths of the Alabamas ["Alybamons"], white. 7th of September, 1737, De Batz.

In the original, the bend around L and "broken paths" were drawn in red. Only a few names on this map present any interpretive difficulties. The English (A), Lower Creeks (B, C) and Yuchis (D), Cherokees (F), the French (I), Choctaws (K), Chickasaws (L), Arkansas (O), and Chakchiumas (P) are all clearly recognizable. "Toukoulou Charakis" (E) refers to Tugaloo, an important Lower Cherokee town. Three regional subdivisions of the Upper Creeks (G, H) are mentioned, "Affasques Abekas" (G) being the run-on names of the Okfuskees or Tallapoosas situated on the Tallapoosa River and the Abekas on the middle Coosa River.

Among their northern enemies were the Hurons (M), more commonly known to the English as Wyandots in the eighteenth century, and the "Nantouague" (M), which was a southern synonym for Iroquois (cf. "Nottawagees").[115] "Tamarois" (N) apparently signified not simply the Tamaroas but all of the Illinois tribes, just as the Piankashaws (N) represented the Miami tribes.[116]

Patricia Galloway has suggested that both of the maps copied by de Batz were originally drawn by the Captain of Pakana, in support of which she cites a letter from Diron d'Artaguette to Maurepas dated October 24, 1737, which mentions "the explanations that the Captain of Pakana has made himself and from which he has drawn the two maps enclosed herewith which I take liberty of sending you with an albino deerskin, which was sent to me for a present as an unexampled rarity."[117] There is little doubt that these are the same two maps to which d'Artaguette refers, and Galloway is almost certainly correct regarding the origin of the Chickasaw villages map, as is discussed below. But her case is much weaker that an Alabama Indian drew the original of this map. In addition to the explicit statement found in the de Batz legend that the map was given to the Captain of Pakana by Mingo Ouma, the document contains some internal evidence of having been drawn by a Chickasaw. For instance, the central figure and focus of the map is the circle representing the Chickasaws, following a structural convention found repeatedly in Indian maps, whereby each mapmaker placed his own tribe in a position of importance near or at the middle. And like the 1724 Chickasaw deerskin map presented to the English, this map emphasizes the plight of the Chickasaws, nearly surrounded by their French-inspired enemies. The theme is similar, although the informational content of the map is much less than that of the earlier one. The Chickasaw original may have been altered somewhat by the Alabama headman (possibly by the addition of the Alabama Hunting Paths [V]), but the map appears to have been drawn predominantly from a Chickasaw perspective.

Although Mingo Ouma's peace overture was rejected by Bienville, his imagery was not lost on the French. At a conference with the southern tribes in 1754, Governor Kerlérec echoed Mingo Ouma's words with his proclamation that "the French desire nothing so much as to see *all the roads white* forever and a firm peace between the red men."[118]

Alabama Map, 1737 (French Copy)

Title: Plan et Scituation des Villages Tchikachas. Mil Sept Cent Trente Sept. [Plan and Situation of the Chickasaw Villages, 1737.]

Size: Not determined

Original: Archives des Colonies, ser. C13A, vol. 22, fol. 68, Archives Nationales, Paris.

Reproductions:[119]

Description: Like the previous map, this one was redrafted from an Indian original by Alexandre de Batz and sent to France in 1737 as plans were being made for a second major offensive against the Chickasaws. Patricia Galloway has determined that the original of this map was undoubtedly produced by the Captain of Pakana, an Alabama headman who visited the Chickasaws during July 1737.[120]

At the end of his report on his spying mission, the Captain of Pakana told the French, "There is nothing left for me to do but to tell you about what their situation and their forces are, according to what I saw myself. I was in ten villages and I saw the one of the Natchez, which made the eleventh. The Chickasaws told me that there were two other forts. I do not know if they were lying but I did not see them. In each village there is a fort with three rows of posts and no earth between."[121] This closely accords with the map legend translated here:

> The circles indicate the villages and in each one there is a fort with three rows of posts.
> A. Ogoula Tchetoka, fort where M. d'Artaguette attacked; there are 60 men.
> B. Etoukouma
> C. Achoukouma
> D. Amalata
> E. Taskaouilo
> F. Tchitchatala; the fort is the most important, the said village is of 60 men.
> G. Falatchao
> H. Tchoukafala
> I. Apeony, where the last party of Frenchmen attacked
> L. Aekya
> M. The Natchez, who still have forty men
> N. Bayous
> O. Paths between the villages
> P. Fields ["Deserts"][122]
> Q. Encampment of the last French party
> R. M. d'Artaguette's Road
> S. Road of the last French party
>
> The forts of the villages A, B, C, D, E, F, G are very near each other and almost within musket range. Likewise those desig-

nated H, I, L. Prepared and drawn up at Mobile, September 7, 1737. De Batz[123]

Most of these village names are found on de Crenay's Map of 1733[124] and in the English trader James Adair's description of his life with the Chickasaws.[125]

Captain of Pakana	*DeCrenay*	*Adair*
A. Ogoula Tchetoka	Ongoulastoga	
B. Etoukouma		
C. Achoukouma	Chochouma	
D. Amalata		Amalahta
E. Taskaouilo	Tascaolou	Tuskawillao
F. Tchitchatala	Tchichatala	Shatara
G. Falatchao	Falatchao	Phalacheho
H. Tchoukafala	Tchoukaffala	Chookka Pharaah
I. Apeony	Apeony	
L. Aekya	Aekeia	Hykehah
	Tchikoulechasto	
		Yaneka
		Chookheereso

Adair also gave the name of the Natchez village (M) as Nanne Hamgeh.[126]

This map is unique in its identification of field locations in relation to village sites, data that should be of considerable value to archaeologists studying Chickasaw settlement patterns. De Batz presumably added the scale and north arrow, neither of which may be very reliable. But there is a general agreement between topographical descriptions of the 1736 battlefields and the Captain of Pakana's village and stream placements. According to Governor Bienville, their Choctaw guides marched the French army "here and there in the woods as if to lead us to the large prairie where is the main part of the Chickasaw and Natchez villages led us at last to a prairie which is possibly a league in circumference in the middle of which we saw three small villages situated in a triangle on the crest of a hill at the foot of which an almost dry stream was flowing. This small prairie is only a league distant from the large one and is separated from it by a wood,"[127] all of which coincides closely in detail with the Alabama map.

Acknowledgments

David Dye helped translate a Chickasaw phrase. Patricia Galloway, John H. Hann, Thomas Hatley, G. Malcolm Lewis, James Merrell, and Peter H. Wood read and commented extensively on all or part of this chapter. To all I am most grateful. Any faults that remain are entirely my responsibility.

Notes

1. William L. McDowell, Jr., ed., *Documents Relating to Indian Affairs, May 21, 1750–August 7, 1754* (Columbia: South Carolina Archives Department, 1958), 536.

2. Justin Winsor, *Christopher Columbus* (Boston: Houghton Mifflin, 1891), 442; cited by Louis DeVorsey, "Amerindian Contributions to the Mapping of North America: A Preliminary View," *Imago Mundi* 30(1978): 71.

3. Edward Arber, ed., *Capt. John Smith, Works (1608–1631)* (Birmingham: English Scholar's Library, 1884), 55, 124, 339; Philip L. Barbour, ed., *The Jamestown Voyages under the First Charter, 1606–1609,* Hakluyt Society, 2d ser. 136–37 (Cambridge: University Press for the Society, 1969), 82, 84; G. Malcolm Lewis, "The Indigenous Maps and Mapping of North American Indians," *Map Collector* 9(1979): 25–26.

4. John Lawson, *A New Voyage to Carolina,* ed. Hugh T. Lefler (Chapel Hill: University of North Carolina Press, 1967), 214.

5. For excellent general reviews of native North American mapmaking, see DeVorsey, "Amerindian Contributions," 71–78; G. Malcolm Lewis, "Indian Maps," in *Old Trails and New Directions,* ed. Carol M. Judd and Arthur J. Ray (Toronto: University of Toronto Press, 1980), 9–23; G. Malcolm Lewis, "Indian Maps: Their Place in the History of Plains Cartography," *Great Plains Quarterly* 4(1984): 91–108; cf. Catherine Delano Smith, "Cartography in the Prehistoric Period in the Old World," in *The History of Cartography,* vol. 1, ed. J. B. Harley and David Woodward (Chicago: University of Chicago Press, 1987), 54–101.

6. Lewis, "Indigenous Maps," 25, 32; idem, "Indian Maps," 12.

7. Verner W. Crane, "The Tennessee River as the Road to Carolina: The Beginnings of Exploration and Trade," *Mississippi Valley Historical Review* 3(1916): 11.

8. Verner W. Crane, *The Southern Frontier, 1670–1732,* ed. Peter H. Wood (New York: W. W. Norton, 1981), 60–61.

9. Lewis, "Indian Maps," 14.

10. Great Britain, *Public Record Office, Calendar of State Papers Colonial Series, America and West Indies* (hereafter cited as *PRO, Calendar*), vol. 14, *January, 1693–14 May, 1696* (London: Her Majesty's Stationery Office, 1903), 518.

11. Usually the attributions are anonymous. For example, Thomas Kitchin's 1760 map of the Cherokee country mentioned by William P. Cumming, *The Southeast in Early Maps* (Princeton: Princeton University Press, 1958), 231, carries the legend, "Engrav'd

from an Indian Draught." Knowledge of the most distant Indian villages shown on John Smith's 1612 map of Virginia was obtained "by relation," as were the captions shown in blue on the Velasco map of 1611. See Barbour, *Jamestown Voyages*, following 374; C. A. Weslager, *The English on the Delaware: 1610–1682* (New Brunswick, N.J.: Rutgers University Press, 1967), 11–13. For a consideration of unattributed uses of Indian maps, see G. Malcolm Lewis, "Indicators of Unacknowledged Assimilation from Amerindian Maps on Euro-American Maps of North America," *Imago Mundi* 38(1986): 9–34.

12. Cited by DeVorsey, "Amerindian Contributions," 76.

13. G. Malcolm Lewis has made the point that, in the absence of reasonably precise surveys, the content of Euro-American as well as native maps was topological, with outlines, dimensions, and directions inserted almost independent of the superimposed map graticules. See his "Changing National Perspectives and the Mapping of the Great Lakes between 1755 and 1795," *Cartographica* 17(1980), fig. 9. See also James H. Merrell, "Natives in a New World: The Catawba Indians of Carolina, 1650–1800" (Ph.D. diss., Johns Hopkins University, 1982), 20.

14. Charles M. Hudson, *The Southeastern Indians* (Knoxville: University of Tennessee Press, 1976), 155–56; Jon Muller, "Serpents and Dancers: Art of the Mud Glyph Cave," in *The Prehistoric Native American Art of Mud Glyph Cave*, ed. Charles H. Faulkner (Knoxville: University of Tennessee Press, 1986), 36–80.

15. Merrell, "Natives in a New World," 190.

16. Lewis, "Indian Maps," 14–15.

17. Dunbar Rowland and A. G. Sanders, trans. and ed., *Mississippi Provincial Archives: French Dominion*, 3 vols. (Jackson: Mississippi Department of Archives and History, 1927–32), 3:526–39.

18. Gary C. Goodwin, *Cherokees in Transition: A Study of Changing Culture and Environment prior to 1775*, Research Paper 181 (Chicago: University of Chicago, Department of Geography, 1977), 109.

19. *PRO, Calendar*, vol. 31, *January, 1719 to February, 1720* (London: His Majesty's Stationery Office, 1933), 302.

20. Edward B. Tylor, "Notes on Powhatan's Mantle, Preserved in the Ashmolean Museum, Oxford," *Internationales Archiv für Ethnographie* 1(1888), pl. XX (colored engraving); David I. Bushnell, Jr., "Virginia—from Early Records," *American Anthropologist* 9(1907), pl. V (photograph); Christian F. Feest, "Virginia Algonquians," in *Handbook of North American Indians*, vol. 15, *Northeast*, ed. Bruce G. Trigger (Washington, D.C.: Smithsonian Institution Press, 1978), 261 (photograph).

21. The shells were identified as *Marginella nivosa* by Tylor, "Notes," 217. They are probably *Prunum apicinum*.

22. John Tradescant, *Musaeum Tradescantium* (London: John Grismond and Nathanael Brooke, 1656), 47; Bushnell, "Virginia," 38.

23. Christian F. Feest, "Virginia Indian Miscellany II," *Archiv für Volkerkunde* 21(1967): 10.

24. Barbour, *Jamestown Voyages*, 414, 257.

25. Arber, *Capt. John Smith*, 361. The Jesuit missionaries in Maryland wrote in their annual letter of 1639, "The only peculiarity by which you can distinguish a chief from the common people is some badge; either a collar made of a rude jewel, or a belt, or a cloak, oftentimes ornamented with shells in circular rows." Anonymous, "Extracts from the Annual Letters of the English Province of the Society of Jesus," in Clayton C. Hall, ed., *Narratives of Early Maryland, 1633–1684* (New York: Charles Scribner's Sons, 1910), 125.

26. E. Randolph Turner III, "An Archaeological and Ethnohistorical Study on the Evolution of Rank Societies in the Virginia Coastal Plain" (Ph.D. diss., Pennsylvania State University, 1976), 133.

27. William Strachey, *The Historie of Travell into Virginia Britania*, ed. Louis B. Wright and Virginia Freund (London: Hakluyt Society, 1953), 63.

28. Strachey, *Virginia Britania*, 63–69; Turner, "Virginia Coastal Plain," 134.

29. Stephen R. Potter, "An Ethnohistorical Examination of Indian Groups in Northumberland County, Virginia: 1608–1719" (M.A. thesis, University of North Carolina, 1976), 18–24.

30. Barbour, *Jamestown Voyages*, 374; Susan M. Kingsbury, ed., *The Records of the Virginia Company of London*, vol. 3 (Washington, D.C.: Government Printing Office, 1933), 708; Bushnell, "Virginia," 32.

31. William P. Cumming et al., eds., *The Exploration of North America, 1630–1776* (New York: G. P. Putnam's Sons, 1974), 151, fig. 226 (photograph). Note that parts of the legend are incorrectly transcribed in the editors' caption.

32. Lewis, "Indian Maps," 14.

33. *PRO, Calendar*, vol. 15, *1696–1697* (London: Her Majesty's Stationery Office, 1904), 420; William A. Hunter, "The Historic Role of the Susquehannocks," in *Susquehannock Miscellany*, ed. John Witthoft and W. Fred Kinsey (Harrisburg: Pennsylvania Historical and Museum Commission, 1959), 17; a letter to Governor Nicholson from Lawrence van den Bosh accompanying Ayer MS map 59, quoted courtesy of the Edward E. Ayer Collection, Newberry Library, Chicago.

34. Barry C. Kent, *Susquehanna's Indians*, Anthropological Series 6 (Harrisburg: Pennsylvania Historical and Museum Commission, 1984), 79; Charles Callender, "Shawnee," in Trigger, *Handbook*, 630.

35. Sara J. Tucker, *Indian Villages of the Illinois Country, Part I (Atlas)*, Scientific Papers 2 (Springfield: Illinois State Museum, 1942).

36. John R. Swanton, *The Indian Tribes of North America*, Bureau of American Ethnology Bulletin 145 (Washington, D.C.: Government Printing Office, 1952), 316.

37. Henri Joutel, *A Journal of the Last Voyage Perform'd by Monsr. de la Sale* (London: A. Bell, 1714), 155; Swanton, *Indian Tribes*, 213–14.

38. Richebourg G. McWilliams, ed., *Iberville's Gulf Journals* (Tuscaloosa: University of Alabama Press, 1981), 87–89; Swanton, *Indian Tribes*, 208–9.

39. Richebourg G. McWilliams, "Iberville at the Birdfoot Subdelta: Final Discovery of the Mississippi River," in *Frenchmen and French Ways in the Mississippi Valley*, ed. John F. McDermott (Urbana: University of Illinois Press, 1969); Peter H. Wood, "La

Salle: Discovery of a Lost Explorer," *American Historical Review* 89(1984): 305; Edwin Way Teale, *North with the Spring* (New York: Dodd, Mead, 1951), 76–82.

40. F. LeMaire, *Carte Nouvelle de la Louisiane* (Paris, 1714); Swanton, *Indian Tribes*, 188; La Salle quoted in Wood, "La Salle," 309.

41. McWilliams, *Gulf Journals*, 72–75; Swanton, *Indian Tribes*, 188.

42. Charles Callender, "Illinois," in Trigger, *Handbook*, 673; J. Joseph Bauxar, "History of the Illinois Area," in Trigger, *Handbook*, 595; also see Guillaume Delisle's maps of 1703 and 1718 illustrated by Cumming, *Early Maps*, pls. 43, 47.

43. David I. Bushnell, "The Account of Lamhatty," *American Anthropologist* 10(1908), pl. XXXV (facsimile drawing); John R. Swanton, "The Tawasa Language," *American Anthropologist* 31(1929): 441, map 1 (facsimile drawing); Rainer Vollmar, *Indianische Karten Nordamerikas* (Berlin: Dietrich Reimer Verlag, 1981), 48 (facsimile drawing).

44. Swanton, "Tawasa Language," 437.

45. Bushnell, "Account of Lamhatty," 568–69. Reprinted with permission from the collections of the Virginia Historical Society, MS 1, L 51, fol. 677).

46. Ibid., 568–74; Swanton, "Tawasa Language," 435–53.

47. Cumming, *Early Maps*, 176; J. Leitch Wright, Jr., *The Only Land They Knew* (New York: Free Press), 143, 146; Thomas C. Parramore, "The Tuscarora Ascendancy," *North Carolina Historical Review* 59(1982): 307–26.

48. John R. Swanton, *Early History of the Creek Indians and Their Neighbors*, Bureau of American Ethnology Bulletin 73 (Washington, D.C.: Government Printing Office, 1922), 141.

49. Jerald T. Milanich, "The Western Timucua: Patterns of Acculturation and Change," in *Tacachale*, ed. Jerald Milanich and Samuel Procter (Gainesville: University Presses of Florida, 1978), 64, 66.

50. Mark F. Boyd, Hale G. Smith, and John W. Griffin, *Here They Once Stood: The Tragic End of the Apalachee Missions* (Gainesville: University of Florida Press, 1951), 11; B. Calvin Jones, "Colonel James Moore and the Destruction of the Apalachee Missions in 1704," *Florida Division of Archives, History and Records Management, Bureau of Historic Sites and Properties Bulletin* 2(1972): 25.

51. Swanton, "Tawasa Language," 451–53; Mary R. Haas, "Southeastern Languages," in *The Languages of Native America*, ed. Lyle Campbell and Marianne Mithun (Austin: University of Texas Press, 1979), 319; James M. Crawford, "Timucua and Yuchi: Two Language Isolates of the Southeast," in Campbell and Mithun, *Languages of Native America*, 333.

52. Swanton, *Early History*, 134–38; Rowland and Sanders, *Mississippi Provincial Archives*, 2:25; Jay Higginbotham, *Old Mobile: Fort Louis de la Louisiane, 1702–1711* (Mobile: Museum of the City of Mobile, 1977), 288 n. 1; George E. Lankford, "Ethnohistory: A Documentary Study of Native American Life in the Lower Tombigbee Valley," in *Cultural Resources Reconnaissance Study of the Black Warrior Tombigbee System Corridor, Alabama*, ed. Eugene Wilson (Mobile: University of South Alabama, 1983), 50, 60.

53. Gregory A. Waselkov and John W. Cottier, "European Perceptions of Eastern Muskogean Ethnicity," in *Proceedings of the Tenth Annual Meeting of the French Colonial Historical Society*, ed. Philip Boucher (Lanham, Md.: University Press of America, 1985), 23–45.

54. Christian F. Feest, "Creek Towns in 1725," *Ethnologische Zeitschrift* (Zurich) 1(1974): 173.

55. Vernon J. Knight and Sherrée L. Adams, "A Voyage to the Mobile and Tomeh in 1700, with Notes on the Interior of Alabama," *Ethnohistory* 28(1981): 181.

56. Lucy L. Wenhold, *A Seventeenth Century Letter of Gabriel Diaz Vara Calderón, Bishop of Cuba, Describing the Indians and Indian Missions of Florida*, Smithsonian Miscellaneous Collections 95, no. 16 (Washington, D.C.: Government Printing Office, 1936), 10; John H. Hann, "Florida's Terra Incognita," *Florida Anthropologist* 41(1988): 61–107; Mark F. Boyd, "The Expedition of Marcos Delgado from Apalache to the Upper Creek Country in 1686," *Florida Historical Quarterly* 16(1937): 14; Irving A. Leonard, ed., *Spanish Approach to Pensacola, 1689–1693* (Albuquerque: Quivira Society, 1939), 221; Swanton, *Early History*, 137–39.

57. Cf. Knight and Adams, "Voyage," 190; Lankford, "Lower Tombigbee Valley," 51.

58. Swanton, "Tawasa Language," 443.

59. Verner W. Crane, "The Origin of the Name of the Creek Indians," *Mississippi Valley Historical Review* 5(1918): 340; Swanton, *Early History*, 215; Carol A. I. Mason, "The Archaeology of Ocmulgee Old Fields, Macon, Georgia" (Ph.D. diss., University of Michigan, 1963), 231.

60. See Edward Crisp's map of 1711, illustrated by Cumming, *Early Maps*, pl. 44; Swanton, "Tawasa Language," 446; John R. Swanton, *The Indians of the Southeastern United States*, Bureau of American Ethnology Bulletin 145 (Washington, D.C.: Government Printing Office, 1946), 184–86.

61. William R. Snell, "Indian Slavery in Colonial South Carolina, 1671–1795" (Ph.D. diss., University of Alabama, 1972), 126.

62. Justin Winsor, ed., *Narrative and Critical History of America* (New York: Houghton Mifflin, 1887), 349 (crude facsimile drawing); R. H. Gabriel, ed., *The Pageant of America*, vol. 2 (New Haven: Yale University Press, 1929), 22 (facsimile drawing); Douglas S. Brown, *The Catawba Indians: The People of the River* (Columbia: University of South Carolina Press, 1966), following p. 32 (facsimile drawing); J. Ralph Randolph, *British Travelers among the Southern Indians, 1660–1763* (Norman: University of Oklahoma Press, 1973), following p. 112 (photograph); Hudson, *Southeastern Indians*, 271 (photograph); Vollmar, *Indianische Karten*, 51 (photograph); Merrell, "Natives in a New World," fig. 2 (facsimile drawing).

63. M. Thomas Hatley III, "The Dividing Path: The Direction of Cherokee Life in the Eighteenth Century" (M.A. thesis, University of North Carolina, 1977), map 4 (photocopy).

64. A. S. Salley, ed., *Journal of His Majesty's Council for South Carolina: May 29, 1721–June 10, 1721* (Atlanta: Foote and Davies, 1930), 18; *PRO, Calendar*, vol. 32, *March, 1720 to December, 1721* (London: His Majesty's Stationery Office, 1933), 336.

65. Bruce T. McCully, "Governor Francis Nicholson, Patron *par Excellence* of Religion and Learning in Colonial America," *William and Mary Quarterly* 39(1982): 330–31. G. Malcolm Lewis has argued for a 1720 date for this and the following map on the grounds that the governor is referred to in the map legends as "Francis Nicholson Esqr." and he was purportedly knighted in that year. In this Lewis is mistaken, since Nicholson was never rewarded with knighthood as has commonly been supposed. See Lewis, "Indian Maps," 21 n. 18; Leonard W. Labaree, "Francis Nicholson," *Dictionary of American Biography* (New York: Scribner's, 1934), 7:501.

66. Chapman J. Milling, *Red Carolinians* (Columbia: University of South Carolina Press, 1969), 222; *PRO, Calendar,* 32:302.

67. William Byrd, *Histories of the Dividing Line betwixt Virginia and North Carolina* (New York: Dover, 1967), 300.

68. Merrell, "Natives in a New World," 189; also see James Mooney, *The Siouan Tribes of the East,* Bureau of Ethnology Bulletin 22 (Washington, D.C.: Government Printing Office, 1894), 68–69.

69. Milling, *Red Carolinians,* 247.

70. Mooney, *Siouan Tribes,* 62; Lawson, *New Voyage,* 61; Merrell, "Natives in a New World," 251; Verne E. Chatelain, *The Defenses of Spanish Florida, 1565–1763,* Publication 511 (Washington, D.C.: Carnegie Institute of Washington, 1941), map 8.

71. Lawson, *New Voyage,* 49; Frank G. Speck, "Siouan Tribes of the Carolinas as Known from Catawba, Tutelo, and Documentary Sources," *American Anthropologist* 37(1935): 218; Merrell, "Natives in a New World," 85, 251; Wayne C. Temple, *Indian Villages of the Illinois Country, Part II (Atlas Supplement),* Scientific Papers 2(1) (Springfield: Illinois State Museum, 1975): pl. LXVII.

72. Mooney, *Siouan Tribes,* 60; *PRO, Calendar,* vol. 34, *1724–1725* (London: His Majesty's Stationery Office, 1936), 281; William L. McDowell, Jr., ed., *Journals of the Commissioners of the Indian Trade, September 30, 1710–August 29, 1718* (Columbia: South Carolina Archives Department, 1955), 163; Merrell, "Natives in a New World," 14, 115, 215, 309.

73. Swanton, *Indian Tribes,* 84; McDowell, *Journals,* 163; Merrell, "Natives in a New World," 251.

74. Mooney, *Siouan Tribes,* 81; Speck, "Documentary Sources," 221; Milling, *Red Carolinians,* 225.

75. James Adair, *The History of the American Indians* (New York: Johnson Reprint, 1968), 235–36.

76. Adair, *History,* 235–68; McDowell, *Journals,* 112, 114; Gene Waddell, *Indians of the South Carolina Low Country, 1562–1751* (Spartanburg, S.C.: Reprint Company, 1980), 267.

77. Mooney, *Siouan Tribes,* 77; McDowell, *Journals,* 80, 96, 111, 218; Milling, *Red Carolinians,* 226; Waddell, *Indians,* 341.

78. Merrell, "Natives in a New World," 312.

79. McDowell, *Journals,* 96.

80. The Public Accounts of John Hammerton, Esqr., Secretary of the Province, Inventories LL, 1744–46, I-57. South Carolina Department of Archives and History, Columbia; John (?) Evans, "Cuttahbaws Nation. men fit for war 204 In ye year 1756," Dalhousie Muniments, General John Forbes Papers, Document 2/104. Microfilm copy in the South Carolina Department of Archives and History, Columbia.

81. Mooney, *Siouan Tribes*, 69.

82. Winsor, *Critical History*, 346.

83. Chatelain, *Defenses*, map 8.

84. Hatley, "Dividing Path," map 3 (facsimile drawing).

85. See Albert Gallatin, *A Synopsis of the Indian Tribes of North America*, Transactions and Collections 2 (Philadelphia: American Antiquarian Society, 1836), 307–67; Cyrus Byington, *A Dictionary of the Choctaw Language*, Bureau of American Ethnology Bulletin 46 (Washington, D.C.: Government Printing Office, 1915).

86. James M. Crawford, "Southeastern Indian Languages," in *Studies in Southeastern Indian Languages*, ed. James M. Crawford (Athens: University of Georgia Press, 1975), 26; Mary R. Haas, "The Classification of the Muskogean Languages," in *Language, Culture and Personality*, ed. Leslie Spier et al. (Menasha, Wis.: Sapir Memorial Publishing Fund, 1941), 54–55.

87. James M. Crawford, *The Mobilian Trade Language* (Knoxville: University of Tennessee Press, 1978). The word order of the single complete sentence on the map does not correspond to the standard Mobilian sequence.

88. Crane, *Southern Frontier*, 273–74; *PRO, Calendar*, vol. 33, *1722–1723* (London: His Majesty's Stationery Office, 1934), 352.

89. John H. Goff, "The Path to Oakfuskee," *Georgia Historical Quarterly* 39(1955): 1–36, 152–71.

90. Swanton, *Early History*, pl. 5.

91. Lankford, "Lower Tombigbee Valley," 52–58.

92. Rowland and Sanders, *Mississippi Provincial Archives*, 1:116.

93. William E. Myer, "Indian Trails of the Southeast," in *Forty-second Annual Report of the Bureau of American Ethnology* (Washington, D.C.: Government Printing Office, 1928), pl. 15.

94. Albert S. Gatschet, *A Migration Legend of the Creek Indians*, vol. 1 (Philadelphia: D. G. Brinton, 1884), 91; cf. Swanton, *Early History*, pl. 5.

95. Swanton, *Indians*, 204.

96. Compare the pronunciations of "*Hoppe* Oakhinnau" and "Rivière *aux Perles*"; Swanton, *Early History*, pl. 5. "Hoppe" may, alternatively, be a corruption of "Houspé," used in 1699 to refer to the Ofos; see Jean Delanglez, "Documents: Tonti Letters," *Mid-America* 21(October 1939): 228 n. 30.

97. Swanton, *Indian Tribes*, 315; McWilliams, *Gulf Journals*, 154.

98. Mildred M. Wedel, "J.-B. Bénard, Sieur de La Harpe: Visitor to the Wichitas in 1719," *Great Plains Journal* 10(1971), La Harpe's map of 1725; Mildred M. Wedel, *La*

Harpe's 1719 Post on Red River and Nearby Caddo Settlements, Texas Memorial Museum Bulletin 30 (Austin: University of Texas, 1978).

99. John R. Swanton, *Source Material on the History and Ethnology of the Caddo Indians*, Bureau of American Ethnology Bulletin 132 (Washington, D.C.: Government Printing Office, 1942), 58; Wedel, "Visitor to the Wichitas," 45.

100. Mildred M. Wedel, "Claude-Charles Dutisné: A Review of His 1719 Journeys, Part II," *Great Plains Journal* 12(1973): 157; Charles N. Tyson, *The Red River in Southwestern History* (Norman: University of Oklahoma Press, 1981), 30; W. W. Newcomb and T. N. Campbell, "Southern Plains Ethnohistory," in *Pathways to Plains Prehistory*, ed. D. G. Wyckoff and J. L. Hofman, Memoir 3 (Norman: Oklahoma Anthropological Society, 1982), 36.

101. Mildred M. Wedel, "The Ethnohistoric Approach to Plains Caddoan Origins," *Nebraska History* 60(1979): 186.

102. Tyson, *Red River*, 30.

103. Pierre Margry, *Découvertes et établissements des Français dans l'ouest et dans le sud de l'Amérique Septentrionale (1679–1754)*, vol. 6 (Paris: Maisonneuve et Ch. LeClerc, 1888), 297; also see Tanner's chapter in this volume.

104. Callender, "Illinois," 673, 680.

105. Wedel, "Visitor to the Wichitas," La Harpe's map, ca. 1725.

106. Thomas S. Abler and Elisabeth Tooker, "Seneca," in Trigger, *Handbook*, 516.

107. Charles Callender, "Miami," in Trigger, *Handbook*, 689; Rowland and Sanders, *Mississippi Provincial Archives*, 3:534.

108. Charles Callender, Richard K. Pope, and Susan M. Pope, "Kickapoo," in Trigger, *Handbook*, 662.

109. Compare "Yaumeer" with the traditional name, "Meearmeear"; C. C. Trowbridge, *Meearmeear Traditions*, ed. Vernon Kinietz, Occasional Contributions 7 (Ann Arbor: University of Michigan Museum of Anthropology, 1938); Callender, "Miami," 688.

110. Hatley, "Dividing Path," 52–53.

111. Baron Marc de Villiers, "Note sur deux cartes dessinées par les Chickachas en 1737," *Journal de la Société des Américanistes* 13(1921), pl. 1; Patricia D. Woods, *French-Indian Relations on the Southern Frontier, 1699–1762* (Ann Arbor, Mich.: UMI Research Press, 1980), illus. 4, p. 133 (facsimile drawing); Vollmar, *Indianische Karten*, 56 (photograph); Patricia Kay Galloway, ed., *Mississippi Provincial Archives: French Dominion*, vols. 4–5 (Baton Rouge: Louisiana State University Press, 1984), vol. 4, facing p. 142 (photograph).

112. Arrell M. Gibson, *The Chickasaws* (Norman: University of Oklahoma Press, 1971), 48–53; Joseph L. Peyser, "The Chickasaw Wars of 1736 and 1740: French Military Drawings and Plans Document the Struggle for the Lower Mississippi," *Journal of Mississippi History* 44(1982): 5–6.

113. Rowland and Sanders, *Mississippi Provincial Archives*, 3:703; Galloway, *Mississippi Provincial Archives*, 4:149–51.

114. David I. Bushnell, Jr., *Drawings by A. DeBatz in Louisiana, 1732–1735*, Smithso-

nian Miscellaneous Collections 80, no. 5 (Washington, D.C.: Government Printing Office, 1927): 1–2; Samuel Wilson Jr., "Ignace François Broutin," in *Frenchmen and French Ways in the Mississippi Valley*, ed. John F. McDermott (Urbana: University of Illinois Press, 1969), 250, 279.

115. William N. Fenton, "Northern Iroquoian Culture Patterns," in Trigger, *Handbook*, 320.

116. Callender, "Illinois," 673–80; Callender, "Miami," 681–89.

117. Galloway, *Mississippi Provincial Archives*, 4:150, caption facing p. 142; Rowland and Sanders, *Mississippi Provincial Archives*, 1:308; Galloway has recently suggested (pers. comm., 1986) that the maps were copied by de Batz at a distribution of presents to Alabama and other Indian allies held about September 7, 1737, in Mobile and attended by the Captain of Pakana. Diron d'Artaguette probably then sent the copies to France, followed or accompanied by a letter critical of Bienville's inefficiency in pursuing the Chickasaw War, which had led to the death of Diron's brother Pierre.

118. Italics added; Galloway, *Mississippi Provincial Archives*, 5:146–47. Also see Adair, *History*, 159.

119. Marc de Villiers, "Deux Cartes," pl. II; Woods, *French-Indian Relations*, illus. 3, p. 131 (facsimile drawing); Vollmar, *Indianische Karten*, 55 (photograph); Galloway, *Mississippi Provincial Archives*, vol. 4, facing p. 154 (photograph); James R. Atkinson, "The Ackia and Ogoula Tchetoka Chickasaw Village Locations in 1736 during the French-Chickasaw War," *Mississippi Archaeology* 20(1985), fig. 5 (photograph).

120. Galloway, *Mississippi Provincial Archives*, 4:154 n. 27.

121. Ibid., 4:150.

122. John F. McDermott, *A Glossary of Mississippi Valley French, 1673–1850*, Studies in Language and Literature 12 (St. Louis: Washington University, 1941), 66.

123. This translation is corrected from Rowland and Sanders, *Mississippi Provincial Archives*, 1:357.

124. Swanton, *Early History*, pl. 5.

125. Adair, *History*, 353–54; also see John R. Swanton, "Social and Religious Beliefs and Usages of the Chickasaw Indians," in *Forty-fourth Annual Report of the Bureau of American Ethnology* (Washington, D.C.: Government Printing Office, 1928); Bernard Romans, *A Concise Natural History of East and West Florida*, (New York, 1775); Daniel H. Usner, Jr., "Frontier Exchange in the Lower Mississippi Valley: Race Relations and Economic Life in Colonial Louisiana, 1699–1783" (Ph.D. diss., Duke University, 1981), 77.

126. Adair, *History*, 225.

127. Rowland and Sanders, *Mississippi Provincial Archives*, 1:304; see Atkinson, "Chickasaw Village Locations in 1736," 61–70.

The Contributors

Amy Turner Bushnell is an assistant professor of history at the University of South Alabama in Mobile and the author of *The King's Coffer: Proprietors of the Spanish Florida Treasury, 1565–1702* (1981). She was formerly historian with the Historic St. Augustine Preservation Board.

Patricia Galloway, special projects officer for the Mississippi Department of Archives and History, is an ethnohistorian specializing in the early history of the Muskogean tribes. She is the editor of volumes 4 and 5 of the *Mississippi Provincial Archives: French Dominion* documentary series and of two collections of essays, *La Salle and His Legacy* (1982) and *The Southeastern Ceremonial Complex: Artifacts and Analysis* (1989).

M. Thomas Hatley, a forester and environmental historian, is the author of articles dealing with subjects ranging from gardens to human protohistory. He is coauthor, with Michael Thompson and Michael Warburton, of *Uncertainty on a Himalayan Scale* (1986). His work on this book was supported by an Appalachian Studies Fellowship from Berea College.

Vernon James Knight, Jr., assistant professor of anthropology at the University of Alabama and secretary to the Alabama de Soto Commission, is editor of *Southeastern Archaeology* and coauthor of two books, *McKeithen Weeden Island: The Culture of Northern Florida, A.D. 200–900* (1984) and *Cemochechobee: Archaeology of a Mississippian Ceremonial Center on the Chattahoochee River* (1981).

Martha W. McCartney has conducted historical research on Virginia's archaeological sites for many years. Formerly historian to the Virginia Division of Historical Landmarks Research Center for Archaeology, she is currently a research consultant to the James Madison University Archaeological Research Center and to the Jamestown-Yorktown Foundation.

James H. Merrell teaches history at Vassar College. A former fellow of the Newberry Library's D'Arcy McNickle Center and the Institute of Early American History and Culture in Williamsburg, Virginia, he is the author of *The Indians' New World: Catawbas and Their Neighbors from European Contact through Era of Removal* (1989) and, with Daniel K. Richter, has edited *Beyond the Covenant Chain: The Iroquois and Their Neighbors in Native North America, 1600–1800* (1987).

Stephen R. Potter is regional archaeologist, National Capital Region, for the National

Park Service, and a research associate of the Smithsonian Institution. His research interests include the ethnohistory of eastern North American chiefdoms.

Marvin T. Smith teaches anthropology at the University of Georgia. His publications include several articles on southeastern archaeology and ethnohistory, and a book, *Archaeology of Aboriginal Culture Change in the Interior Southeast: Depopulation during the Early Historic Period* (1987). He is president of the Society for Bead Researchers, an international group interested in glass trade beads.

Helen Hornbeck Tanner, a research associate of the Newberry Library, began her career with the publication in 1963 of *Zéspedes in East Florida, 1784–1790*. Her most recent publication is the *Atlas of Great Lakes Indian History* (1987), the development of which she guided for over ten years as project director and editor. She is a former president of the American Society for Ethnohistory and currently serves on the board of the Society for the History of Discoveries.

Daniel H. Usner, Jr., is an associate professor of history at Cornell University. The recipient of an American Council of Learned Societies Fellowship for 1987–88, he is the author of several articles and a book, *Indians, Settlers, and Slaves in a Frontier Exchange Economy: The Lower Mississippi Valley before 1783*, that will soon be published.

Gregory A. Waselkov is an archaeologist and ethnohistorian at the University of South Alabama where he leads a long-term study of the colonial-period Creek Indians of Alabama. His publications include more than thirty articles and monographs on subjects including historic archaeology, zooarchaeology, shell-midden studies, and a new introduction to Daniel H. Thomas's classic study, *Fort Toulouse: The French Outpost at the Alabamas on the Coosa* (1989).

Peter H. Wood, a former Rhodes scholar, teaches early American history at Duke University, where his research interests center on intercultural relations. He is the author of *Black Majority: Negroes in Colonial South Carolina from 1670 through the Stono Rebellion* (1974); coauthor, with Elizabeth Fenn, of *Natives and Newcomers* (1983), a brief history of early North Carolina; and coauthor, with Karen Dalton, of *Winslow Homer's Images of Blacks* (1988).

INDEX

Other volumes in the Indians of the Southeast series include:

Creeks and Seminoles
The Destruction and Regeneration of the Muscogulge People
By J. Leitch Wright, Jr.

The Southeastern Ceremonial Complex
Artifacts and Analysis
Edited by Patricia Galloway Exhibition Catalog by David H. Dye and Camille Wharey